CUNARD

THE MOST FAMOUS OCEAN LINERS IN THE WORLD™

Library by Ocean Books
www.oceanbooks.com

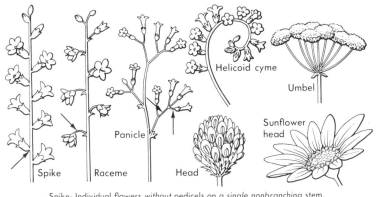

Spike: Individual flowers *without* pedicels on a *single nonbranching* stem.
Raceme: Individual flowers *with* a pedicel on a *single nonbranching* stem.
Panicle: Flowers with a pedicel and on a *branched* raceme.
Helicoid cyme: A coiled branching stem with youngest flowers at tip.
Umbel: All flowers have pedicels attached at same point.
Head: A dense cluster of flowers without pedicels on a single stem.

FLOWER ARRANGEMENTS ON STEM (INFLORESCENCES)

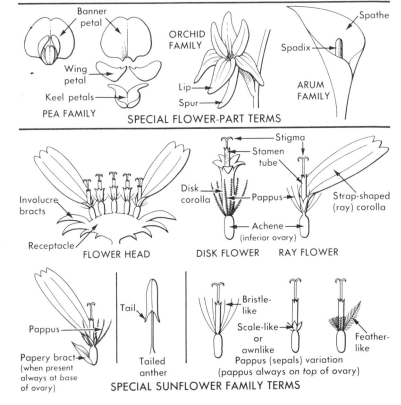

SPECIAL FLOWER-PART TERMS

SPECIAL SUNFLOWER FAMILY TERMS

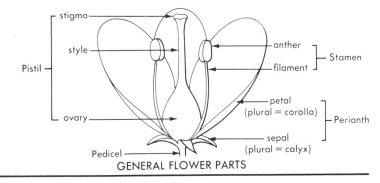

GENERAL FLOWER PARTS

- stigma
- style
- Pistil
- ovary
- anther
- filament
- Stamen
- petal (plural = corolla)
- sepal (plural = calyx)
- Perianth
- Pedicel

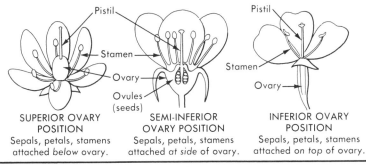

SUPERIOR OVARY POSITION
Sepals, petals, stamens attached *below* ovary.

SEMI-INFERIOR OVARY POSITION
Sepals, petals, stamens attached *at side* of ovary.

INFERIOR OVARY POSITION
Sepals, petals, stamens attached *on top* of ovary.

Pistil
Stamen
Ovary
Ovules (seeds)

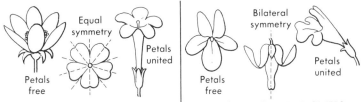

REGULAR-SHAPED FLOWERS
All petals of same size and shape.
Flower can be divided at *many places* to obtain equal mirror halves.

Petals free
Equal symmetry
Petals united

IRREGULAR-SHAPED FLOWERS
Two or more petal sizes and shapes.
Flower can be divided at *only 1 place* to obtain equal mirror halves.

Petals free
Bilateral symmetry
Petals united

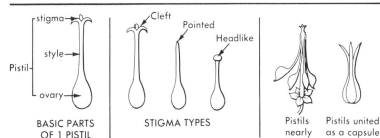

- stigma
- style
- Pistil
- ovary

BASIC PARTS OF 1 PISTIL

Cleft
Pointed
Headlike

STIGMA TYPES

Pistils nearly separate
Pistils united as a capsule

PISTIL-PART VARIATIONS

Pacific States Wildflowers

THE PETERSON FIELD GUIDE SERIES®
Edited by Roger Tory Peterson

Advanced Birding—*Kaufman*
Birds of Britain and Europe—*Peterson, Mountfort, Hollom*
Birds of Eastern and Central North America—*R.T. Peterson*
Birds of Texas and Adjacent States—*R.T. Peterson*
Birds of the West Indies—*Bond*
Eastern Birds' Nests—*Harrison*
Hawks—*Clark and Wheeler*
Hummingbirds—Williamson
Mexican Birds—*R.T. Peterson and Chalif*
Warblers—Dunn and Garrett
Western Birds—*R.T. Peterson*
Western Birds' Nests—*Harrison*
Backyard Bird Song—*Walton and Lawson*
Eastern Bird Songs —*Cornell Laboratory of Ornithology*
Eastern Birding by Ear—*Walton and Lawson*
More Birding by Ear: Eastern and Central—*Walton and Lawson*
Western Bird Songs—*Cornell Laboratory of Ornithology*
Western Birding by Ear—*Walton and Lawson*
Pacific Coast Fishes—*Eschmeyer, Herald, and Hammann*
Atlantic Coast Fishes—*Robins, Ray, and Douglass*
Freshwater Fishes (N. America north of Mexico)—*Page and Burr*
Insects (America north of Mexico)—*Borror and White*
Beetles—*White*
Eastern Butterflies—*Opler and Malikul*
Western Butterflies—*Opler and Wright*
Mammals—*Burt and Grossenheider*
Animal Tracks—*Murie*
Eastern Forests—*Kricher and Morrison*
California and Pacific Northwest Forests—Kricher and Morrison
Rocky Mountain and Southwest Forests—Kricher and Morrison
Venomous Animals and Poisonous Plants—Foster and Caras
Edible Wild Plants (e. and cen. N. America)—*L. Peterson*
Eastern Medicinal Plants and Herbs—*Foster and Duke*
Eastern Trees—*Petrides*
Ferns (ne. and cen. N. America)—*Cobb*
Mushrooms—*McKnight and McKnight*
Pacific States Wildflowers—*Niehaus and Ripper*
Western Medicinal Plants and Herbs—*Foster and Hobbs*
Rocky Mt. Wildflowers—*Craighead, Craighead, and Davis*
Trees and Shrubs—*Petrides*
Western Trees—Petrides
Wildflowers (ne. and n.-cen. N. America)—*R.T. Peterson and McKenny*
Southwest and Texas Wildflowers—*Niehaus, Ripper, and Savage*
Geology (e. N. America)—*Roberts*
Rocks and Minerals—*Pough*
Stars and Planets—*Pasachoff*
Atmosphere—*Schaefer and Day*
Eastern Reptiles and Amphibians—*Conant and Collins*
Western Reptiles and Amphibians—*Stebbins*
Shells of the Atlantic and Gulf Coasts, W. Indies—*Morris*
Pacific Coast Shells (including Hawaii)—*Morris*
Atlantic Seashore—*Gosner*
Coral Reefs (Caribbean and Florida)—*Kaplan*
Southeastern and Caribbean Seashores—*Kaplan*

A Field Guide to
Pacific States
Wildflowers

Washington, Oregon, California and adjacent areas

Theodore F. Niehaus

Illustrations by
Charles L. Ripper

*Sponsored by the National Audubon Society,
the National Wildlife Federation,
and the Roger Tory Peterson Institute*

HOUGHTON MIFFLIN COMPANY BOSTON NEW YORK

For information about permission to reproduce selections from
this book, write to Permissions, Houghton Mifflin Company,
215 Park Avenue South,New York, New York 10003

Visit our Web site: www.houghtonmifflinbooks.com.

PETERSON FIELD GUIDES and PETERSON FIELD GUIDE SERIES
are registered trademarks of Houghton Mifflin company.

Library of Congress Cataloging-in-Publication Data

Niehaus, Theodore F.
A field guide to Pacific States wildflowers.

(The Peterson field guide series.)
Includes index.
1. Wildflowers — Pacific States — Identification.
I. Ripper, Charles L.   II. Title.
QK143.N5   582'.13'0979   76-5873
ISBN 0-395-21624-9
ISBN 0-395-91095-1 (pbk.)

Printed in the United States of America

EB 28 27 26 25 24 23 22 21 20 19

Contents

Editor's Note

MANY YEARS AGO, in the mid-forties, Margaret McKenny and I began our collaboration of a *Field Guide to the Wildflowers of Northeastern and North-central North America*. It proved to be a staggering commitment that was to take me over tens of thousands of miles of back-country roads in search of flowering plants from which I made more than 1500 drawings—1344 of which appeared in the book, first published in 1968.

Therefore I am well aware of the extremely demanding work that has gone into this *Field Guide to Pacific States Wildflowers* by Theodore Niehaus and Charles Ripper. It involved more than 100,000 miles of travel; this included extended backpack trips into remote mountain regions that could not be reached by vehicle or by horse. This book is the closely integrated work of two veteran naturalists—Dr. Niehaus, a Ph. D. with a degree in taxonomic botany from the University of California and Charles (Chuck) Ripper, a professional biological illustrator, well known for his wildlife and botanical paintings.

Like the other volumes in the Field Guide Series this book is based on the "Peterson System," with species likely to be confused placed near each other for quick comparison and their key characters or "field marks" indicated by little arrows on the illustrations. Taken as a whole it is, in a sense, a pictorial key, consistent with the fundamental philosophy of the other Field Guides, which is based on readily noticed visual impressions rather than on technical or phylogenetic features.

This flower guide is patterned similarly to its eastern counterpart, stressing (1) color, (2) general shape or structure, and (3) distinctions between similar species—the field marks. The text is placed opposite the pictures; thus all pertinent information about a plant is confined within one double spread, eliminating the necessity of time consuming cross-references. It differs from the eastern book in having four pages of front matter that describe the plant regions of the Pacific states, and a key to the families which presents the family symbols that are used throughout the book.

The Pacific states, because of the wide variety of environments—mountains, valleys, plains, deserts, and the sea—has a greater wealth of wildflowers than any other area in the United States. This pocket guide cannot cover them all; it describes nearly 1500 species—the ones you are most likely to find in your travels within these three favored states.

ROGER TORY PETERSON

Introduction

THE PACIFIC STATES AREA, as considered here, extends from southern British Columbia south to and including northern Baja California and from the Pacific Ocean east to the foothills of the Rocky Mountains in Idaho and Utah, and barely into western Arizona from California (see map on page x).

For our purposes, wildflowers are plants with a main above-ground growth and death occurring in one growing season and without a woody stem, although a very few (Penstemon, Eriogonum, etc.) have a low aboveground stem that is woody. Except for cacti, considered to be shrubs and thoroughly covered in this *Field Guide,* shrubs and trees are not included; lack of space made this impossible.

The user of this guide will find each geographical plant community and its subhabitats well represented as to species. Selection was a complex process; every known flowering plant species in the area was given careful consideration. It was found that some species considered uncommon by various sources were in fact common and widespread; these were added to this *Field Guide.*

Intensive field study was conducted over three growing years. A program of visiting each plant region (see pp. xi–xiv) and all of its plant community types and subdivisions was conducted from early January until late fall, each area being revisited every two or three weeks to see each species come into flower. Of the 1492 species and subspecies in this guide, 1482 were observed growing in nature. Each species encountered during the field study was photographed in color as a whole plant; the small parts were then recorded in closeups. No one photograph can show all the important identifying features of most plants, but photographs can be of great value to an artist. My able partner Charles Ripper prepared his drawings and paintings by projecting the plant images to precise scale. Note the size scale at the lower right-hand corners of the illustration pages. A total of 1502 illustrations representing the common species in 77 different plant families were made. All families with wildflowers of possible interest are covered.

Each species description in the text consists of the (1) common name, (2) scientific name, (3) descriptive text, (4) region where found, and (5) flowering time.

Plant Names. Common names are sometimes debatable, because no system for common plant names exists. Some species have 15 to 20 different local names; on the other hand, 5 or 6 totally unrelated plants may have the same name. The genus name may be used as a common name for only one species in the genus, the rest remaining unnamed, so that many species have never been given a common name. Every source for common names was consulted, including all popular and scientific books for

vii

the United States and many European sources. Those given here are the most widely used or were judged most appropriate to the species; of necessity, some new names were also coined.

The scientific name for each species represents the latest information available from all sources. Where controversy exists, the best solution for this guide has been used.

Descriptive Text. The preparation of each species description required extensive study of many sources. These included floras, scientific papers (very old through very recent), consultation with scientists specializing in certain species or groups, study of thousands of museum specimens, and direct field study of living plants. Many new field observations are included here. Visual features most useful for species identification are italicized.

Region Where Found. The geographic regions are shown on the map on page x and described on pages xi–xiv.

Flowering Times. These are intended as a general guide; earlier times are for lower elevations and the southernmost areas.

Measurements. The measurement given for a species represents the length of the stem (which is not always the height of the plant). These are in U.S. units. It is now the policy of the *Field Guides* to provide metric measurements as well, in line with our gradual conversion to the metric system in the United States; although space limitations prevent their inclusion here, a U.S./metric equivalents rule is provided on page x.

Wildflower Identification Methods

Two systems are available to the user: (1) picture matching, using color and general shape, and (2) a key that guides the reader to an area of a few pages where picture matching takes over.

Picture Matching. Field marks—the exact distinctions between similar species—are emphasized both by arrows in the illustration and italics in the text description opposite. A few species, although giving a slight impression of being different, are very hard to distinguish visually, since the critical differences are microscopic or otherwise do not lend themselves to illustration.

Breakdown by flower color is used in many scientific keys. Some species have more than one color phase, so illustrations for these are repeated wherever possible. Text pages have cross references where similar but differently colored specimens are found. Borderline colors are often difficult to categorize, especially in the lavender-red and violet-blue areas. The terms red-purple and blue-purple used here will help the reader in color interpretations; most of the plants in this color area belong to the red-purple category. If a flower has two main colors, look under both color areas. It is well, if using this method, to remember that all plant species are as variable as the human species; an individual with a different number of petals or one that is an albino is not necessarily a new species but rather an example of extreme variation.

Key to Families. The system of keys beginning on page xv will lead the user to the family of the wildflower in question. The plant family pages are then used for visual matching. The key will also prove useful to those teaching field courses in plant identification.

The plant families are presented on the basis of identification by quick visual recognition. That is, each family description contains the few general recognition features (field marks) that most persons use for field identification. The most useful features are italicized. Many of these family field marks are also used for text page headings (e.g., Pealike Flowers—Pea Family). The page headings of the family key, pp. xv–xxxii, can also help narrow down the families under consideration to a very few. Once family recognition is learned, one can go anywhere in the world and be at home with any wildflower book, as the world's number of plant families is only about 280—and the family grouping may be nearly the same as in this *Field Guide.* The plant family symbols represent a condensed visual summary of the important family field marks and should aid fast family recognition.

Many friends, professional colleagues, and institutions have helped to produce this book. Space permits only a few to be acknowledged directly. My wife Jean's cheerful help as a field-trip driver and camp manager is deeply appreciated. Permission for extensive use of specimens, libraries, and picture collections at both the Jepson Herbarium and the University Herbarium at the University of California, Berkeley, is especially acknowledged. Other sources of pictures and specimens include: California Academy of Sciences in San Francisco; Santa Barbara Botanic Garden; Rancho Santa Ana Botanic Garden at Claremont; University of California at Los Angeles; Museum of Natural History, San Diego; University of Oregon; University of Washington; and members of the Alpine Garden Club of British Columbia, the Flat Earth Club, and the California Native Plant Society. The native plant section at the University of California Botanic Gardens (Berkeley), where hundreds of California native wildflowers are grown each year, was a mecca. Mr. Wayne Roderick, in charge of this section, was especially helpful, as was Mr. James Roof at Tilden Botanic Garden in Berkeley. Others who helped directly are Everett Evans, Lawrence Heckard, Alice Howard, Lincoln Constance, Forest and Mary Sheehan, Susan Watson, Jim Mac-Phail, Bob Woodward, Thelma Chapman, Colletta Lawler, Pierre Fischer, and Jacqueline Broughton. The careful work and constructive criticisms by my partner Charles Ripper, and by Roger Tory Peterson and Helen Phillips, Paul Brooks, and others at Houghton Mifflin Co. were also a great help. The plant family symbols, with a few additions for the Pacific States region, are from *A Field Guide to Wildflowers* (Eastern) by permission of Roger Tory Peterson.

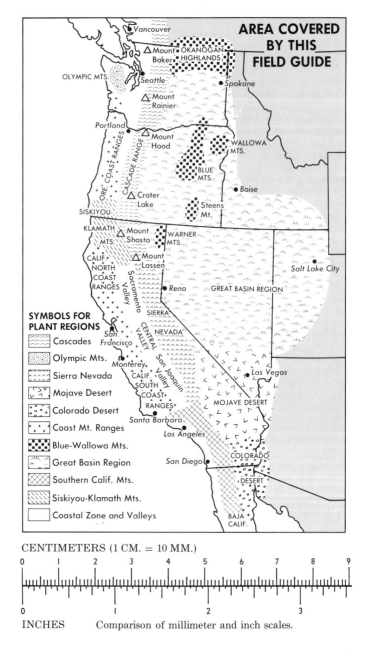

AREA COVERED BY THIS FIELD GUIDE

Vancouver
△ Mount Baker
OLYMPIC MTS.
OKANOGAN HIGHLANDS
Seattle
● Spokane
△ Mount Rainier
Portland
△ Mount Hood
ORE. COAST RANGES
CASCADE RANGE
WALLOWA MTS.
BLUE MTS.
● Boise
△ Crater Lake
SISKIYOU
Steens Mt.
KLAMATH MTS.
△ Mount Shasta
WARNER MTS.
CALIF. NORTH COAST RANGES
△ Mount Lassen
Sacramento Valley
● Reno
GREAT BASIN REGION
● Salt Lake City
SIERRA
San Francisco
NEVADA
CENTRAL VALLEY
Monterey
CALIF. SOUTH COAST RANGES
San Joaquin Valley
● Las Vegas
MOJAVE DESERT
Santa Barbara
Los Angeles
San Diego
COLORADO DESERT
BAJA CALIF.

SYMBOLS FOR PLANT REGIONS

- Cascades
- Olympic Mts.
- Sierra Nevada
- Mojave Desert
- Colorado Desert
- Coast Mt. Ranges
- Blue-Wallowa Mts.
- Great Basin Region
- Southern Calif. Mts.
- Siskiyou-Klamath Mts.
- Coastal Zone and Valleys

CENTIMETERS (1 CM. = 10 MM.)

0 1 2 3 4 5 6 7 8 9

0   1   2   3

INCHES   Comparison of millimeter and inch scales.

Plant Regions of the Pacific States

THE PACIFIC STATES AREA has the greatest number of flowering plant species in the United States because of the concentration, in small geographical areas, of many different ecological habitats. Mountain ranges, valleys, seacoast, and deserts are each subdivided into various habitats by short-distance extremes in soil types, altitude, climate, and other factors.

The plant regions of the Pacific States, as shown on the map opposite, are generalized areas within which many species are found exclusively or are most common. Each plant region has several plant-community zones, often related to altitude. In the Cascade–Sierra Nevada Mountain Axis, for example, if you travel east from Sacramento to the crest of the Sierra Nevada, you pass upward through Valley Grassland, Oak Woodland, Conifer Forest (with three or four subzones), and Alpine plant communities.

Each of the plant regions is strongly influenced by north-south and east-west factors of rainfall, warmth, proximity to ocean or interior, and latitude. They are also influenced by the kind of parent rock material, kinds of animals, steepness of terrain, and periodic fires. Many of the wildflower species are winter annuals, that is, they start growing with the first fall rain and flower the following spring. Regional ancestral flora unit influences include the northern Mexican forest from the south, Arctic tundra and northern forests from the north, and the Rocky Mountain forests from the east.

1. Pacific Coastal Strip. This is a narrow area along the entire Pacific Coast, consisting of often very narrow but different plant communities. These are Coastal Beach and Dunes, Coastal Prairies, Coastal Salt Marsh, Coastal Scrub, Closed-Cone Pine Forest, and Coastal Conifer Forest. Climate remains moderate throughout the year, with wildflowers blooming from January to October, and a few can always be found even through December. A narrow band of summer fog covers the entire length of the Pacific Coast strip and brings up to 15 inches of precipitation as "summer fog drip." Many plant species are the same for the entire length of the coast. In addition, at least 3 distinct and sharp species "break points" are present. To the north or south of such a point, a related sister species of the same genus is usually found as a replacement for one that has reached its limit of range. These special species ranges are: (a) British Columbia coast south to Coos Bay, Oregon, (b) California North Coast area: Coos Bay south to the north side of San Francisco Bay, (c) south side of San Francisco Bay south to Monterey Bay, and (d) Monterey Bay south to Baja California.

2. Olympic Mountains. This area of high rugged peaks is on the Olympic Peninsula of Washington. Composed of two outer belts of volcanic peaks and an inner core of equally rugged sedimentary peaks. The Mixed Conifer Forest community covers the area from sea level to the subalpine zone. Subalpine and alpine meadows (parks) occur along the high narrow ridge lines. The majority of special plant species found only in the Olympic Mountains occur in the subalpine and alpine zones. Flowering season is from April to August. The alpine zone is at peak flowering from late July through August.

3. Coast Mountain Ranges. Relatively old sedimentary mountain ranges with long north-south ridges and long narrow valleys, the valleys following the earthquake fault lines. Based on kind of plant species present, three different coast range sections are used in this guide to aid in their location. (a) Oregon Coast Ranges: a narrow range extending northward along the Oregon coast to and barely across the Columbia River into Washington. Entirely of the Mixed Conifer Forest. (b) Calif. North Coast Ranges: north-south mountains from Eureka, Calif. area south to the north side of San Francisco Bay. The Siskiyou and Klamath mountains are between this area and the Oregon Coast Ranges. (c) Calif. South Coast Ranges: north-south mountains from the south side of San Francisco Bay south to Santa Barbara, Calif., where they merge with the Southern Calif. Mts. (which see). A special dry desert climate occurs on the inland side of the South Coast Ranges due to a rain shadow effect, and many Mojave Desert species extend into the area.

The coast ranges in general are very moist on the coast side and become quite dry on the inland side. From the coast inland, Coastal Scrub, Coastal Mixed Conifer Forest, Oak Woodland, and Hard Chaparral plant communities are present. The blue-green rock Serpentine covers extensive areas, forming "Serpentine Barrens" where only a small number of plant species manage to live; serpentine soil chemically prohibits plant growth. A few special plant species have managed to adapt to this situation, and plant hunters often seek out the serpentine areas as many of the rarer species are present on this soil type. Serpentine areas are found in the other plant regions as well.

4. Siskiyou-Klamath Mountains. A series of steep jumbled west to east mountains, mostly running from the Pacific Ocean and intersecting with the Cascade Mountain Range in the southwestern Oregon area. A very ancient and complicated geological area with many special rock and soil types, including limestone and serpentine areas. Almost the entire area is of the Mixed Conifer Forest community with a few tiny areas of subalpine. Rich in local wildflower species at all elevations. Most of the other species are a mixture of Coast Range, Sierra, and Cascade origins.

5. Southern California Mountains. A series of mountain ranges which form a loose ring on the northern, eastern, and southern sides of the Los Angeles basin. They continue southward east of San Diego into Baja, California. All of these mountains are of granitic rocks. The lower coastal slopes are Coastal Sage Chaparral, with a narrow Mixed Conifer Forest along the crest. A few tiny Alpine areas are on the highest peaks. The Juniper-Piñon Forest community occuring along the eastern desert slopes. Elements from the South Coast Ranges, Sierra Nevada, and northern Mexican mountain wildflowers are to be found. Along the northern portion of these mountains both Mojave Desert and Great Basin plant species can be found westward nearly to the Santa Barbara area. Chaparral fires are a normal ecological feature, some wildflower species actually requiring fires to germinate and flower. The Fire Poppy, for example, appears only the first year after a fire in tremendous flame-orange masses. Other species appear only the second or third year after a fire, not to be seen again for many years until another fire occurs.

6. Central Valley of California. A long north-south valley between the Coast Ranges and Sierra Nevada. Originally of Valley Grassland, Oak Woodland, and Freshwater Marsh communities, but now almost entirely converted to agriculture. The vernal pool flora is unique, found only in California and adjacent parts of Oregon; vernal pools consist of low 1- or 2-ft. depressions which fill with winter and spring rains. Wildflower species found in these vernal pools grow under the water during the winter, and when they dry out in the spring months present massive fields of gold with each pool also having distinct 1- or 2-in. rings of separate flower colors from different wildflower species. These wildflower species are highly specialized and are rarely to be found elsewhere. Land leveling for agriculture is rapidly pushing these species to the brink of extinction.

7. Cascade–Sierra Nevada Mountain Axis. The Sierra Nevada portion, from Kern Canyon area north to the Mount Lassen area, is of granitic origin with a thin lava cap on the crest in the northern half. It is a high north-south mountain range with a long gradually sloping west side and a sharp east cliff-like dropoff. Plant communities from west to east are: Valley Grassland, Oak Woodland, Conifer Forest (with several subzones), Mountain Chaparral, Alpine and Juniper-Piñon Forest. The Cascade portion from Mount Lassen north to British Columbia is of volcanic origin from 250 to 300 volcanos. Plant communities from west to east are Maple Woodland, Conifer Forest, Alpine, and Juniper Forest.

8. Great Basin Region. A vast area of sagebrush plains and many small rugged mountains is between the Cascade–Sierra

Nevada Mts. and the Rockies to the east. Plant communities include Alkali Sink Scrub, Sagebrush Scrub, Juniper-Piñon Forest, Conifer Forest, and Alpine. This region is rich in wildflower species, with many appearing in April and May at the lower elevations. (This is a time of cold winds, so that the area is shunned by most persons, but it is actually a very good time for wildflowers.) A portion of easternmost Washington and ne. Oregon consists of the Paluose Prairies community; nearly all of the Paluose flora has been eliminated by agriculture.

9. Blue-Wallowa Mountains. Several different high mountain ranges in northeastern Oregon occurring as high islands in the Great Basin region. Other smaller areas included here are the Warner Mountains of ne. Calif., Steens Mountain of Oregon, and the Okanagan Highlands across the ne. top of Washington. Conifer Forest and tiny Alpine communities are present. Many local species are unique to these mountain ranges. The flora of the lower areas is a mixture of Sierra Nevada and Cascade species with some Rocky Mountain species. In the highest regions the flora is almost entirely from the Rocky Mountain region.

10. Mojave-Colorado Deserts. Two different deserts with many species in common. (1) The Mojave Desert is generally higher in elevation with Creosote Bush Scrub, Sand Dune, Joshua Tree Woodland and Juniper-Piñon Forest communities. Many wildflower species are unique to the western edge of the Mojave Desert. Many are being threatened by extinction by the rapid expansion of new towns. Main flowering season: April and May. (2) The Colorado Desert is at much lower elevations and is an extension of the Sonora Desert of Mexico. Main flowering season: February, March, and early April. Spring wildflower seasons vary in the extreme from none in very dry winters to lush in very wet winters. The lush desert wildflower display occurs rarely—once in 25 to 50 years. These lush years usually occur in the spring following torrential rains in October from Gulf of California hurricanes. By good fortune one of these rare lush springs occurred during the field research for this guide.

Family Descriptions and Key

A PLANT FAMILY is a large group of species that all share the same general traits. The key given here immediately reduces the family possibilities of an unidentified plant to a few, based on such characteristics as, for example, petal number. The portion of the key found on any given page leads only to families found on the same or facing pages, so that page turning is unnecessary. At the end of the family description are inclusive text page numbers for the species in that family treated in this *Field Guide*.

The family descriptions state the visual characteristics necessary for quick field identification of a plant family. Remember that the text page heading in this key which lists the group traits of the families on a page, represents a part of those family characters. The family symbol is a visual representation of the characters. Many learn to know the families on sight for rapid narrowing down to identify the species.

How to Use the Key. By following these four steps you will be led to the name of any wildflower you wish to identify.

1. Learn the plant-part names shown in the endpapers.
2. Look at the flower and note its shape, color, arrangement, etc. How many petals? Are they free from each other or fused? Are they arranged regularly or irregularly? Is the ovary in superior or inferior position? What shape is each flower part?
3. The key consists of numbered pairs of contrasting statements. Choose the one appropriate to the flower part considered.
4. At the end of the statement chosen, note the *See* reference which guides you to the next pair of statements. Continue until a plant family is named. Note the family symbol and the pages covering that family. Look on these pages for your flower.

Key to Families

1a. Flowers without petals or not apparent. See 5 on p. xvi.
1b. Flowers with petals. See 2.

2a. Petals 3 or 6. See 15 on p. xviii.
2b. Petals 4 or 5 or numerous. See 3.

3a. Petals numerous. See 92 on p. xxxii.
3b. Petals 4 or 5. See 4.

4a. Petals 4. See 26 on p. xx.
4b. Petals 5. See 37 on p. xxii.

Petals Absent or Not Apparent

(Families keyed below are described on this or facing page.)

5a. Plants of marshes or ponds. See 6.
5b. Plants of dry land or parasitic. See 9.

6a. Flowers in a white spikelike torch. **Saururaceae.**
6b. Flowers *not* in a torchlike arrangement. See 7.

7a. Flowers in a brown sausage-like cylinder. **Typhaceae.**
7b. Flowers in round balls or with a spathe. See 8.

8a. Flowers in round balls, pond plant. **Sparganiaceae.**
8b. Flowers surrounded by a spathe. **Araceae.**

9a. Plant with copious milky juice, ovary hanging to one side of flower. **Euphorbiaceae.**
9b. Plants without milky juice, ovary erect. See 10.

10a. Parasitic plants, stems orange or green. See 11.
10b. Plants not parasitic. See 12.

11a. Orange threadlike parasitic stems. **Cuscutaceae.**
11b. Orange or green twiggy, parasitic stems. **Loranthaceae.**

12a. Leaf of 3 broad fanlike leaflets. **Berberidaceae.**
12b. Leaves entire (whole). See 13.

13a. Tiny green flowers on short strings beneath leaves. Severe sting when the plant is touched. **Urticaceae.**
13b. Tiny green or reddish flowers in clusters. See 14.

14a. Plant surface scurfy, bracts rounded. **Chenopodiaceae.**
14b. Plant surface smooth, bracts pointed. **Amaranthaceae.**

 LIZARD-TAIL FAMILY (Saururaceae). Leaves simple and alternately arranged. Flowers in dense spike or raceme. Flower parts free. Sepals and petals absent. Stamens 6–8, pistils 3–4, free or fused. White p. 42.

 CATTAIL FAMILY (Typhaceae). Tall marsh plants in dense stands. Leaves straplike. Stiff rodlike stem with a thick cylindrical (sausagelike) brown spike of numerous minute female flowers tightly packed together. A slender tail of paler male flowers above. Brown p. 400.

 BUR-REED FAMILY (Sparganiaceae). Pond plants. Flowers in *round globe-like heads*. Heads unisexual, the lower female and upper male. Individual flowers on plan of 3's. No petals present. Leaves linear, grasslike. White p. 2.

Petals Absent or Not Apparent (*contd.*)

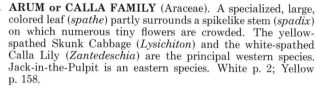

ARUM or CALLA FAMILY (Araceae). A specialized, large, colored leaf (*spathe*) partly surrounds a spikelike stem (*spadix*) on which numerous tiny flowers are crowded. The yellow-spathed Skunk Cabbage (*Lysichiton*) and the white-spathed Calla Lily (*Zantedeschia*) are the principal western species. Jack-in-the-Pulpit is an eastern species. White p. 2; Yellow p. 158.

SPURGE FAMILY (Euphorbiaceae). Usually with a thick milky sap. The flower consists of (1) *colored bracts,* which appear to be petals (the red bracts of the familiar *Poinsettia* are an example); (2) a central cluster of stamens and glands; and (3) *a 3-lobed ovary,* adjacent to the stamens but *hanging to one side.* White p. 100; Green p. 398.

DODDER FAMILY (Cuscutaceae). *Yellow* or *orange* parasitic *twining vines.* Leaves reduced to minute scales. Flowers tiny; waxy-white bell- or urn-shaped; 4 or 5 lobes. Related to the Morning Glory Family. Orange p. 226.

MISTLETOE FAMILY (Loranthaceae). Twiggy stems in parasitic clusters on host plant. Stems with or without leaves. Flowers minute. Fleshy, pink berries. Green p. 396.

BARBERRY FAMILY (Berberidaceae). Flowers regular, tiny, without petals in a pencil-sized spike *or* with 6 separate petals in 2 circles and reflexed backward. Stamens 6. Ovary superior. Leaves pinnate. White p. 42; Yellow p. 158.

NETTLE FAMILY (Urticaceae). In our area mostly with stinging hairs. Leaves opposite. Tiny greenish flowers without petals, in small stringy clusters. Calyx 4-parted, stamens 4. Green p. 398.

GOOSEFOOT FAMILY (Chenopodiaceae). Weedy herbs, often with *mealy, scurfy-white, dandruff-like* surfaces. Greenish flowers, very small, no petals present. Flowers in dense spike-like clusters. The garden vegetables spinach and beets belong to this family. Green p. 396–98.

AMARANTH FAMILY (Amaranthaceae). Weedy herbs; inconspicuous flowers in spikes or clusters. *Each flower* subtended by *3 sterile membraneous bracts* that are spiny. Plants are not mealy as in the Goosefoot Family. The garden ornamental Cockscomb belongs to this family. Green p. 398.

Petals 3 or 6
(Families keyed below are described on this or facing page.)

15a. Ovary in superior position. See 16.
15b. Ovary in inferior position. See 23.

16a. Floating plants, flowers purple. **Pontederiaceae.**
16b. Plants not floating on water. See 17.

17a. Plants of marshy places. See 18.
17b. Plants of dry or non-marshy places. See 19.

18a. Tiny green flowers in a spike. **Juncaginaceae.**
18b. White flowers in a branching pyramid. **Alismataceae.**

19a. Petals swept backwards. **Berberidaceae.** See p. xvii.
19b. Petals not swept backwards. See 20.

20a. Stamens numerous, milky sap, sepals falling off flower when it opens. **Papaveraceae.**
20b. Stamens 3, 6, or 9. See 21.

21a. Flowers small, in clusters. **Polygonaceae.**
21b. Flowers fairly large, Lily- or Amaryllis-like. See 22.

22a. Flowers in racemes, panicles, or spikes. **Liliaceae.**
22b. Flowers in an umbel with papery bracts. **Amaryllidaceae.**

23a. Petals in irregular arrangement. **Orchidaceae.**
23b. Petals in regular arrangement. See 24.

24a. Leaves swordlike, emerging from one another. **Iridaceae.**
24b. Leaves heart-shaped or lancelike. See 25.

25a. Leaves heart-shaped. **Aristolochiaceae.**
25b. Leaves lancelike. Long flower spikes. **Lythraceae.**

PICKEREL WEED FAMILY (Pontederiaceae). Marsh plants. Flowers on a plan of 3's. Flower spike subtended by a spathe. 6 large violet petals fused in a tube only near base, one *upper petal with a yellow* center. Blue p. 382.

ARROW-WEED FAMILY (Juncaginaceae). Salt marsh plants. Fleshy grasslike leaves. Flowers in *dense elongated spikes.* Flowers with 3 or 6 greenish sepal or petal-like segments. Fruits cylinder-shaped. Green p. 390.

WATER PLANTAIN FAMILY (Alismataceae). Freshwater marsh plants. Sepals 3. *3 large white petals, free.* 6 or more stamens. Fruit a collection of single-seeded akenes. White p. 2.

Petals 3 or 6 (*contd.*)

 POPPY FAMILY (Papaveraceae). Flowers regular. Parts free. *Sepals 2 or 3 and caducous* (falling off when flower opens). showy petals 4 or 6. *Stamens numerous.* Ovary superior. Yellowish *milky sap.* White p. 22; Orange p. 224.

 BUCKWHEAT FAMILY (Polygonaceae). Leaves alternate with a papery sheath (ocrea) around the swollen node ("knots"). *Or* if ocreae absent (*Eriogonum*) flowers in involucrate (invol) clusters. Numerous small flowers, each consisting of 4, 5, or 6 green or colored *petal-like* sepals. No true petals present. Stamens 6 or 9. Superior ovary with a 2- or 3-parted style. Fruit a 3-sided achene, often with 3 papery winglike margins. White pp. 34–38; Yellow pp. 134–38; Red pp. 276–78.

 LILY FAMILY (Liliaceae). Sepals and petals in 3's and *similarly colored.* Stamens 3 or 6. Ovary superior. Flowers arranged in racemes, panicles, or spikes. White pp. 4–16; Yellow pp. 122–24; Orange pp. 228–30; Red pp. 252–56; Blue p. 352. Brown-Green pp. 388–90.

 AMARYLLIS FAMILY (Amaryllidaceae). Similar to Lily Family but flowers arranged on *leafless stalks* (scapes) in a terminal *umbel with papery bracts.* White p. 18; Yellow p. 124; Red pp. 254–62; Blue p. 352.

 ORCHID FAMILY (Orchidaceae). Flowers *irregular-shaped.* Sepals similar in shape. Petals 3, 2 are similar-shaped, lateral petals and a 3rd lower and larger—the *Lip Petal.* Ovary *inferior.* Leaves entire, parallel veined. White p. 20; Orange p. 230; Brown-Green pp. 390–92.

 IRIS FAMILY (Iridaceae). Leaves flat, *swordlike,* and *flatly packed edge to edge* (equitant). Flowers regular-shaped. Parts in 3's. Two flower plans: (1) 3 broad petal-like sepals and 3 narrow erect petals (*Iris*); (2) both sepals and petals equal sized and colored, in a flat circle of 6. Ovary *inferior.* Yellow p. 126; Red p. 254; Blue p. 350.

 BIRTHWORT FAMILY (Aristolochiaceae). Large heart-shaped leaves. Red-brown flowers with *3 petal-like sepals* that flare out from a swollen cuplike (semi-inferior) ovary. No petals. Stamens 12. Brown p. 400.

 LOOSESTRIFE FAMILY (Lythraceae). Flowers regular-shaped. Sepals and petals 4 or 6, free. Ovary within a *6-ribbed cylinderlike* calyx (appearing as if an inferior ovary). Style 1, stigma 2-lobed. Steeplelike racemes. Red p. 274.

Petals 4

(Families keyed below are on this or facing page.)

26a. Ovary with superior position. See 27.
26b. Ovary with inferior position. See 35.

27a. Petals free from each other. See 28.
27b. Petals fused at least near base. See 33.

28a. Leaves and stems succulent. **Crassulaceae.** See p. xxv.
28b. Leaves and stems thin, not succulent. See 29.

29a. Sepals 2 (falling off early in one family). See 30.
29b. Sepals 4. See 31.

30a. Flower regular-shaped, stamens numerous, milky sap. **Papaveraceae.** See p. xix.
30b. Flower irregular-shaped and flattened. Stamens 4 or 6. **Fumariaceae.**

31a. Petals in a maltese cross. See 32.
31b. Petals in tiny urns. Fruit, angled akenes. **Polygonaceae.** See p. xix.

32a. Leaves palmately compound, skunky odor. **Capparidaceae.**
32b. Leaves various, not palmately compound. **Cruciferae.**

33a. Flowers papery brown, in spikes. **Plantaginaceae.**
33b. Flowers green, red, or blue. See 34.

34a. Stamens alternate to petals. Corolla without a constriction. **Gentianaceae.**
34b. Stamens opposite to petal lobes (often long and protruding), Corolla tube constricted near base. **Nyctaginaceae.**

35a. Ovary of two rounded spiny lobes. **Rubiaceae.**
35b. Ovary elongated or of one round lobe. See 36.

36a. 4 petals large or small, no central tiny flowers. Conspicuous elongated inferior ovary. **Onagraceae.**
36b. 4 large white "petals" with a center of tiny yellow flowers. **Cornaceae.**

 BLEEDING HEART FAMILY (Fumariaceae). Leaves highly divided into lacy segments. Sepals 2, small and falling off early. Petals 4, *flattened* into an elongated heart-shaped or spurred sac. Stamens 4 and individually free, or 6 and united in 2 sets. Ovary superior. White p. 42; Yellow p. 158; Red p. 280.

Petals 4 (*contd.*)

 CAPER FAMILY (Capp?aridaceae). Similar to Cruciferae Family below, but note the following differences. Leaves usually *palmately compound.* Ovary *banana-like* with a *long thin pedicel-like* base that is attached to a very long pedicel. Skunklike odor when handled. Yellow p. 140.

 MUSTARD FAMILY (Cruciferae). Leaves alternate. Urnlike flowers in a *regular maltese cross shape* of 4 equal-lengthed sepals and petals. *Stamens 6* (2 are attached at a lower level). The seedpod is a *silique or sicile* (only found in this family). A few genera have a cylindrical nonopening pod (*Raphanus, Cakile, Chorispora*). White pp. 24–30; Yellow pp. 140–48; Orange p. 224; Red pp. 266–68.

 PLANTAIN FAMILY (Plantaginaceae). Numerous brownish flowers in a dense *thumblike spike* on a long *leafless stalk.* Each flower of 4 sepals, 4 united tiny brown petals (corolla semitransparent, dry, and papery), and 2 stamens. Leaves in a basal rosette. Brown p. 396.

 GENTIAN FAMILY (Gentianaceae). Sepals 4 or 5, united. Petals 4 or 5, fused at base, forming a flattened bowl or an elongated vase. Stamens 4 or 5, fused to corolla wall and alternate to petals. Ovary superior, style 1, entire. Leaves opposite. White p. 100; Red p. 304; Blue pp. 342–44; Green p. 394.

 FOUR O'CLOCK FAMILY (Nyctaginaceae). Flowers in *umbels* or solitary. Leafy bracts below the umbel free or fused into large calyxlike cups. Funnel-like corollas (actually colored sepals) with 4 or 5 petal lobes and the *tube base is constricted.* No true petals present. Ovary superior. Pistil 1. White p. 100; Yellow p. 120; Red p. 300.

 BEDSTRAW OR MADDER FAMILY (Rubiaceae). 4 minute sepals. Petals 4, *in a tiny cross.* Stamens 4 and alternate to petals. Ovary *inferior,* becoming *twin* rounded seeds. Stems square and rough prickled. Leaves in whorls or pairs. White p. 100.

 EVENING PRIMROSE FAMILY (Onagraceae). Flower parts in 4's, free. *Long slender inferior ovary.* Style 1, the stigma either a 4-branched cross or bulblike. Pollen *enmeshed in cobwebby threads.* White p. 32; Yellow pp. 150–52; Red pp. 270–74.

 DOGWOOD FAMILY (Cornaceae). *4 large showy white bracts* often mistaken as petals surround a cluster of tiny yellow flowers with inferior ovaries. Style 1. White p. 100.

Petals 5

37a. Each petal *completely free* from others. See 38.
37b. Petals fused into a tube or slightly fused only at their bases. See 63 on page xxvii.

38a. Petals in irregular-shaped arrangement. See 39.
38b. Petals in regular-shaped arrangement. See 42 on p. xxiii.

Petals 5, Completely Free, Irregular Arrangement

(Families keyed below all described on this page.)

39a. Flowers with a banner or lip petal. See 40.
39b. Flowers with a long spurred base. See 41.

40a. Flowers pealike, leaves compound. **Leguminosae.**
40b. Flowers violet-like, leaves mostly entire. **Violaceae.**

41a. Leaf umbrellalike. **Tropaeolaceae.**
41b. Leaf *not* umbrellalike. **Ranunculaceae.** See page xxv.

 PEA FAMILY (Leguminosae). The *pealike* flower shape and the *peapod* (Legume capsule) are found only in this family. Flowers irregular-shaped. 5 petals: One large and broad upper petal—*Banner Petal*. Two similar shaped side petals—*Wing Petals*. Two lower petals joined to form a canoelike keel—*Keel Petals*. Leaves usually alternate arrangement and compound, with *stipules* at the petiole base. Terminal leaflet replaced by a tendril in some genera. White pp. 94–96; Yellow pp. 178–82; Orange p. 224; Red pp. 318–26; Blue pp. 376–80.

 VIOLET FAMILY (Violaceae). Flower parts on a plan of 5's. Irregular-shaped. The *Violet-like* flowers consist of 2 upper petals, 2 lateral petals, and a lower single lip petal. Ovary superior. The pistil with a distinctive thickened head and a short beak. White p. 52; Yellow pp. 162–64; Blue p. 358.

 NASTURTIUM FAMILY (Tropaeolaceae). Flower irregular-shaped. Leaves alternately arranged, often umbrellalike. Sepals 5, one with a *long spur*. Petals 5, free. Stamens 8. Ovary superior. Orange p. 226.

Petals 5, Completely Free, Regular Shape, Ovary Superior

(Families keyed below all described on this page.
Also more families with heading characters
above are on next two pages.)

42a. Sepals 2. **Portulacaceae.**
42b. Sepals more than 2. See 43.

43a. Leaf tubular, cobralike appearance or leaf blades flat with red glandular hairs. See 44.
43b. Leaf *not* as in 43a. See 45.

44a. Leaf tubular, raised cobra appearance. **Sarraceniaceae.**
44b. Leaf flat with red glandular hairs. **Droseraceae.**

45a. Leaf and stem white to red. **Pyrolaceae.**
45b. Leaves green. See 46.

46a. Ovary in superior position. See 47.
46b. Ovary semi-inferior or inferior position. See 59 on p. xxvi.

47a. Style and stigma beaklike (elongated) *or* stamens in elongated fused column. See 48 on p. xxiv.
47b. Style *not* beaklike or with stamens *not* fused. See 50 on p. xxiv.

 PURSLANE FAMILY (Portulacaceae). *Sepals 2.* Leaves entire, often linear and *thick fleshy-like* with a *smooth yellow-green* or dark green surface. Petals 5 to many (3–16). Stamens 5 to many. Ovary superior. Orange p. 226; Red pp. 292–94.

 PITCHER PLANT FAMILY (Sarraceniaceae). Insectivorous plants growing in bogs. Leaves tubular and hollow. In our area, appearing as a raised cobra. Flower nodding on a leafless stem. Sepals and petals 5, free. Stamens many. White p. 46.

 SUNDEW FAMILY (Droseraceae). Insectivorous herbs growing in bogs. Leaves in a flat rosette, upper surfaces covered with *sticky red club-shaped glands.* Sepals and petals 5, free. Leafless flower stems (scapes). White p. 46.

 WINTERGREEN FAMILY (Pyrolaceae). Low evergreen plants or saprophytes (red or white). Sepals and petals 5, petals distinct or united near bases. 10 elongated *sausage-like anthers* opening by terminal pores or by longitudinal slits. Style 1 with a *caplike stigma.* Flowers regular-shaped. Ovary superior. The distinct subfamily *Montropoideae* consists of fleshy white to red saprophytes. Petals (4), 5 or (6) and forming an *urnlike corolla.* White pp. 46–48; Red p. 296.

Petals 5, Completely Free, Regular Shape, Ovary Superior

(Families keyed below are described
on this or facing page.)

48a. Stamens 5–10, free from each other. See 49.
48b. Stamens numerous fused into a column. **Malvaceae.**

49a. Flowers pale to dark pink. **Geraniaceae.**
49b. Flowers yellow. **Zygophyllaceae.**

50a. Stem joints swollen and with a papery sheath. Flowers greenish, stamens 3–9. **Polygonaceae.** See page xix.
50b. Stem joints bare, flowers colored (not green). See 51.

51a. Stamens more than 20. See 52.
51b. Stamens 4, 5, 10, or 20. See 53.

52a. Leaves in distinct opposite pairs to top of stem. Stamens in 3 or 4 fused bundles. **Hypericaceae.**
52b. Leaves usually alternate or basal only. All stamens completely individual to base. **Ranunculaceae.**

53a. Pistils (style 1 each) 4 or 5, nearly separate. Leaves thick and succulent. **Crassulaceae.**
53b. Pistils 1 or 2 or numerous. See 54.

54a. Pistils 2, forming 2 divergent beaks (rarely 3 or 4). **Saxifragaceae.** See page xxvi.
54b. Pistil 1 or numerous (not 2). See 55.

55a. Leaf petiole base with a pair of stipules. **Rosaceae.** See page xxvi.
55b. Leaf petiole base without stipules. See 56.

56a. Fruit of 5 pea-sized nutlets (or fewer). **Limnanthaceae.**
56b. Fruit a capsule. See 57.

57a. Stigma caplike. **Pyrolaceae.** See page xxiii.
57b. Stigma 1 to 5 linear lobes, never caplike. See 58.

58a. Leaves opposite or whorled, often sticky-haired. **Caryophyllaceae.**
58b. Leaves alternate, surfaces smooth. **Linaceae.**

 MALLOW FAMILY (Malvaceae). Flowers regular. Leaves often *maplelike.* Showy *hollyhock-like flowers* of 5 broad petals, free or slightly fused. Filaments (basal thread portion) of the *numerous stamens fused into a column* around the elongated styles. The blunt pointed style tips protruding above the cluster of *free anthers.* Fruit *separating* into *nutlike carpels.* White p. 44; Pink-red pp. 286–90.

Petals 5, Completely Free,
Regular Shape, Ovary Superior (*contd.*)

 GERANIUM FAMILY (Geraniaceae). Flower parts in 5's, stamens 10, free. Ovary superior. *Styles elongated and beaklike.* When the 5 seeds mature both the seed and elongated style separate as one unit with the style portion *coiling.* Red pp. 284–86.

 CALTROP FAMILY (Zygophyllaceae). Leaves *pinnate* with a pair of *stipules* at base of petioles. Flowers on a plan of 5's, stamens 10. Styles in a *short, erect column.* Ovary superior. Yellow p. 120.

 ST. JOHN'S WORT FAMILY (Hypericaceae). Leaves in *opposite pairs to top of stem,* often with dark or translucent dots. Flowers regular. Sepals and petals 5, free. *Stamens numerous,* united at bases into *bunches.* Yellow p. 160.

 BUTTERCUP FAMILY (Ranunculaceae). Flowers regular shape or irregular (with a spur or spurs in *Delphinium, Aconitum,* and *Aquilegia*). Flower parts free. Sepals and petals usually 5 to many. Sepals petal-like with petals absent in *Thalictrum* and *Trautvettaria.* Stamens usually *numerous.* Fruits often a cluster of 1-celled akenes or a follicle pod (*Delphinium*), occasionally a berry (*Actaea*). White pp. 40–42; Yellow pp. 154–58; Orange p. 226; Red pp. 280–82; Blue pp. 354–56, 382; Green p. 404.

 SEDUM FAMILY (Crassulaceae). Leaves and stems fleshy. Sepals, petals 5. Stamens 5 or 10. In some species all parts 3 or 4's. Petals often forming an *elongated urn.* Ovary segments barely adhering to each other. Yellow pp. 164–66; Red p. 310.

 MEADOWFOAM FAMILY (Limnanthaceae). Low herbs of open moist places. Leaves alternately arranged, pinnately divided into linear segments. Flowers regular shape on a plan of 3's or 5's, parts free. Ovary superior. Fruit usually *5 large nutlike seeds* (occasionally fewer present). White p. 50.

 PINK FAMILY (Caryophyllaceae). Leaves mostly opposite. *Joints of stem often swollen.* Flowers regular-shaped. Sepals 4 or 5, free or united. Petals 4 or 5, very small or larger, *often notched or deeply divided.* Stamens 10 or fewer. White pp. 54–60; Red pp. 246, 282.

FLAX FAMILY (Linaceae). Slender-stemmed plants, often short threadlike linear leaves in alternate arrangement. Flower on a plan of 5's, parts free. Stamens alternate to petals. White p. 52; Blue p. 382.

Petals 5, Completely Free, Regular Shape, Ovary Inferior

(Families keyed below are described on this page.)

59a. Flowers in racemes, panicles, or spikes. See 60.
59b. Flowers in umbels. See 62.

60a. Styles 2, forming 2 divergent beaks (occasionally 3 or 4). **Saxifragaceae.**
60b. Style 1 or numerous (not 2). See 61.

61a. Leaf petiole base with a pair of stipules. **Rosaceae.**
61b. Leaf petiole base without stipules. **Loasaceae.**

62a. Styles 2, the base swollen into humps. **Umbelliferae.**
62b. Style 1 or 5, base not swollen. **Araliaceae.**

 SAXIFRAGE FAMILY (Saxifragaceae). Flowers regular. Sepals and petals 5, often *dainty or threadlike*. Stamens 5 or 10. Semi-inferior ovary of *2 carpels* barely fused to each other, giving a *forked hornlike* appearance. Leaves often *maplelike* with *scattered erect hairs*. White pp. 84–90, 100; Green p. 402.

 ROSE FAMILY (Rosaceae). Flowers regular. Sepals and petals 5, free. *Stamens numerous.* Ovary semi-inferior, usually *saucerlike or cuplike* with upper surface often *shiny or glassy.* Fruit a group of akenes, a pome (apple), a drupe (prune), or an aggregate of tiny drupelets (raspberry). Leaves often compound. A *pair of prominent stipules* usually present at base of leaf petiole. White p. 92; Yellow pp. 174–76; Red p. 310; Brown p. 404.

 LOASA FAMILY (Loasaceae). Sepals 5, Petals 5 to 10, *stamens numerous.* Flower parts attached on top of the *long inferior ovary.* Leaves covered with short barbed hairs (Thus *clinging tightly* to passers-by.). White p. 44; Yellow p. 160.

 CARROT FAMILY (Umbelliferae). Herbs with umbrellalike clusters (*umbels*) of numerous *tiny 5-petaled flowers.* Leaves often compound. Flowers small, of 5 free petals and stamens. Ovary inferior with *2 styles.* Style *bases swollen* forming a stylopodium. Fruit a dry *schizocarp of 2 halves,* found only in this family. White pp. 64–68; Yellow pp. 168–70; Red p. 302; Green p. 404.

 GINSENG FAMILY (Araliaceae). Ours an immense herb of shady places. Tiny flowers in round umbels. Each flower of 5 tiny free petals, stamens 5 and alternate to petals. Ovary more or less inferior with *1 or 5 styles* (base not swollen). Fruit a small fleshy berry. White p. 64.

5 United Petals

63a. Ovary in superior position. See 64.
63b. Ovary in inferior position. See 85 on page xxx.

64a. Flowers 2-lipped (irregular-shaped). See 65.
64b. Flowers round (regular-shaped). See 69 on page xxviii.

5 United Petals, Irregular Shape, Ovary Superior

(Families keyed below are described on this page.)

65a. Ovary of 4 nutlets, stems square. See 66.
65b. Ovary a capsule, stems rounded (a few angled). See 67.

66a. Ovary clearly 4-lobed. Often minty odor. **Labiatae.**
66b. Ovary not lobed, but later separating as 4 nutlets. Plant without strong mint odor. **Verbenaceae.**

67a. Stems with green foliage. See 68.
67b. Stems *without* green foliage. **Orobanchaceae.**

68a. One spurred flower on leafless stem. **Lentibulariaceae.**
68b. Flowers never single. Stems leafy. **Scrophulariaceae.**

 MINT FAMILY (Labiatae). Stems *square,* leaves *opposite.* Petals 5, in a 2-lipped corolla. Stamens 4 or 2. Style 1, tip unequally bilobed. Ovary of *4 nutlets.* Often a mintlike odor. White p. 82; Red pp. 312–14; Blue p. 374.

 VERVAIN FAMILY (Verbenaceae). Resembling Mint Family above. Flowers *slightly 2-lipped.* Ovary slightly *4-lobed.* Style 1 with *tip entire.* Without mintlike odors. Blue p. 374.

 BROOMRAPE FAMILY (Orobanchaceae). Similar to Snapdragon Family below. Low fleshy herbs *without chlorophyll.* Root parasites. White p. 82; Blue-Purple p. 338.

 BLADDERWORT FAMILY (Lentibulariaceae). Plants of ponds or damp places. Sepals 5, united. 5 united petals in a 2-lipped corolla with a spur. Stamens 2. Blue p. 338.

SNAPDRAGON FAMILY (Scrophulariaceae). Sepals 4 or 5. Petals 4 or 5, united in a *2-lipped corolla.* Stamens 4 (5 or 2) with a sterile remnant of a 5th present. Ovary 2-celled, style 1. Fruit a *capsule.* Several corolla shapes present: (1) Wide tube with 2 distinct lips. (2) Narrow pipelike tube with upper lip forming an arching pointed spout. (3) Corolla nearly regular-shaped. Stems *round.* Yellow pp. 112–18; Red pp. 234–44, 310; Blue pp. 336–38, 372.

5 United Petals, Regular Shape, Ovary Superior

(Families keyed below are described on facing page.)

69a. Stamens 10 or more. See 70.
69b. Stamens 5 to 8. See 73.

70a. Fused column of many stamens. **Malvaceae.** See p. xxiv.
70b. Stamens 10 (never in a fused column). See 71.

71a. Fleshy leaves, pistils 5. **Crassulaceae.** See p. xxv.
71b. Leaves ordinarily thin, ovary a capsule. See 72.

72a. Each leaf of 3 heart-shaped leaflets. **Oxalidaceae.**
72b. Leaf of 1 blade or scale. **Pyrolaceae.** See p. xxiii.

73a. Plant tissue with thick milky sap. See 74 and 83B.
73b. Plant tissue with ordinary watery sap. See 75.

74a. Flowers in umbels, starlike. **Asclepiadaceae.**
74b. Flowers in racemes, panicles, or solitary. **Apocynaceae.**

75a. Stems and leaves yellow-green or white. See 76.
75b. Stems and leaves green. See 77.

76a. Trailing yellow-orange stems. **Cuscutaceae.** See p. xvii.
76b. Round or cone clusters of purple flowers. **Lennoaceae.**

77a. Corolla base constricted. **Nyctaginaceae.** See p. xxi.
77b. Corolla tube base without constriction. See 78.

78a. Stamens 5 and opposite the 5 petal lobes. See 79.
78b. Stamens 5 and alternate to the 5 petal lobes. See 80.

79a. Pinwheel or shooting-star flowers. **Primulaceae.**
79b. Tubular flowers in headlike cluster. **Plumbaginaceae.**

80a. Flowers in coiled one-sided cymes or solitary. See 81.
80b. Flowers arranged in racemes, panicles, or spikes. See 82.

81a. Fruit 2 or 4 distinct nutlets, style 1. **Boraginaceae.**
81b. Fruit a capsule, style 2-lobed. **Hydrophyllaceae.**

82a. Styles 3, cleft, ovary 3-celled. **Polemoniaceae.**
82b. Style 1 or 2, ovary 1- or 2-celled. See 83.

83a. Style tip 1, entire. See 84.
83b. Style tip 2-lobed, stems vinelike. **Convolvulaceae.**

84a. Leaves in opposite arrangement. **Gentianaceae.** See p. xxi.
84b. Leaves in alternate arrangement. **Solanaceae.**

5 United Petals, Regular Shape, Ovary Superior (*contd.*)

 WOOD SORREL FAMILY (Oxalidaceae). Compound *clover-like leaves*. Flower funnel-like, stamens 10. Fruit an elongated *explosive* capsule. Yellow p. 164; Red p. 282.

 MILKWEED FAMILY (Asclepiadaceae). Thick *milky sap. Flower structure unique* with 5 swept back petals and 5 outer cups that often have a little curving horn on the central column. Flowers in *umbels*. White p. 62; Red p. 298.

 DOGBANE FAMILY (Apocynaceae). Thick *milky sap*. Flower plan of 5's. Corolla urnlike. Red p. 298; Blue p. 382.

 LENNOA FAMILY (Lennoaceae). Petals 5–8 in purplish tubular corolla. Stamens 5–8. Stigmas caplike. Blue p. 382.

 PRIMROSE FAMILY (Primulaceae). Flower plan of 5's. *Stamens opposite* petals. Style 1. Flower a pinwheel or shooting-starlike. White p. 100; Red pp. 246, 304; Blue p. 342.

 LEADWORT FAMILY (Plumbaginaceae). Sepals 5, fused and *folded like a fan*. 5 petals or nearly free, stamens opposite the petals. Styles 5, free or united. Red p. 282.

 FORGET-ME-NOT FAMILY (Boraginaceae). Flower plan of 5's. Corolla a trumpet or elongated tube. Stamens alternate to petals. Style 1 with *1 or 2 lobes*. Fruit *4 hard nutlets*. Flowers in a *1-sided coil*. White p. 78; Yellow p. 172; Orange p. 226; Red p. 308; Blue pp. 340–42.

 PHLOX FAMILY (Polemoniaceae). Flower plan of 5's. Corolla pinwheel-like or trumpet-like. Stamens alternate to petals. *Style 3-cleft*. White p. 72; Yellow p. 172; Orange p. 226; Red pp. 248–50, 306; Blue pp. 360–64.

 WATERLEAF FAMILY (Hydrophyllaceae). Flower plan of 5's. Small *bell-like* corollas. Stamens whiskerlike. Style 1. *2 caplike stigmas*. Flowers in a *coiled* cyme. White pp. 74–76; Yellow p. 172; Red p. 308; Blue pp. 366–70.

 MORNING-GLORY FAMILY (Convolvulaceae). Flower plan of 5's. Corolla *bell-like, twisted* in bud. Stamens alternate to petals. Stigmas 2. White p. 70; Pink p. 308.

 NIGHTSHADE FAMILY (Solanaceae). Flower plan of 5's. Flower a trumpet or flattened star with projecting beak. Stamens alternate to petals. Style 1. Fruit, berries, or capsules. White p. 80; Yellow p. 172; Blue p. 382.

5 United Petals, Ovary Inferior

(Families keyed below are described
on this or facing page.)

85a. Corolla regular-shaped. See 86.
85b. Corolla irregular-shaped (2-lipped or flat). See 89.

86a. Vines with tendrils. **Cucurbitaceae.**
86b. Stem erect or prostrate, without tendrils. See 87.

87a. Flowers in racemes, spikes, or solitary. See 88.
87b. Numerous flowers in heads, sunflower-like. Each flower
tubular (some with outer ray flowers). **Compositae.**

88a. Flowers pink, in twin pairs. **Caprifoliaceae.**
88b. Flowers blue. **Campanulaceae.**

89a. Flowers in racemes, panicles, or loose spikes. See 90.
89b. Numerous flowers in flat or cone-shaped head. See 91.

90a. Corolla base spurred, stamens 1–3. **Valerianaceae.**
90b. Corolla not spurred, stamens 5. **Campanulaceae.**

91a. Flower head a spiny cone, stamens free. **Dipsacaceae.**
91b. Flower head of numerous flat straplike corollas (tubular
disk flowers often present.). **Compositae.**

 CUCUMBER FAMILY (Cucurbitaceae). Vines with or without tendrils. Flowers unisexual. Female flower with an *inferior*
ovary. Melonlike fruits. Flower on a plan of 5's. Stamens often
in a fused column. White p. 98; Yellow p. 120.

 HONEYSUCKLE FAMILY (Caprifoliaceae). Regular shape.
Sepals 5. Long *funnel-like* flowers in *twin pairs*. Stamens 4.
Ovary *inferior*. Leaves opposite. Pink p. 316.

 BLUEBELL FAMILY (Campanulaceae). Regular *or* irregular
shape (1) Bluebell subfamily—Campanuloideae. Sepals 5,
petals 5 united as bowls or tubes. Stamens 5, fused in a
distinctive *baseball bat* structure. Ovary *inferior*. (2) Lobelia
subfamily—Lobelioideae. Similar to Bluebell subfamily, but
corolla strongly 2-lipped. Red p. 316; Blue pp. 346–48.

 VALERIAN FAMILY (Valerianaceae). Irregular-shaped.
Sepals obscure. Corolla tubelike often with a *spur or inflated
basal bulge*. Stamens 3 or 1. Ovary *inferior*. Fruit naked.
Leaves opposite. White p. 100; Pink p. 316.

 TEASEL FAMILY (Dipsacaceae). Flowers in *dense head*.
Calyx cuplike with tips forming bristles. Irregular corolla 4- or
5-lobed. Stamens 4. Ovary *inferior*. Pink p. 316.

5 United Petals, Ovary Inferior; Sunflowers

 SUNFLOWER FAMILY (Compositae). A Sunflower is a tightly *packed head of numerous small flowers.* The individual flowers of a head are of two types: (1) RAY FLOWERS with a *flattened straplike* corolla, and (2) DISK FLOWERS with a *round tubular* corolla. Three flower head combinations of these 2 flower types are possible. An individual flower consists of: an *inferior* single-seeded ovary (akene); an outer set of awns, feathery bristles, or scalelike *pappus* (sepals); a tubular (disk flowers) or straplike (ray flowers) corolla of fused petals; a column of stamens (filaments free, but anther portion fused into a tube); and a 2-lobed style. Below the head are leafy bracts (phyllaries). The family is subdivided into tribes (subfamilies). See key below. White pp. 102–8; Yellow pp. 184–220; Orange p. 226; Red pp. 328–32; Blue p. 384; Green-Brown p. 404.

Key to Compositae Tribes

1a. Flower head composed *only of straplike ray flowers.* Each ray corolla tipped by *5 teeth. Milky sap.* Chicory Tribe —Cichorieae. White p. 102; Yellow pp. 216–20; Orange p. 226; Red p. 330; Blue p. 384.

1b. Flower head all disk flowers or a combination of disk and ray flowers (Each ray corolla tipped by *3 teeth*). See 2.

2a. Plants spiny, *thistlelike.* Flower head *only of disk flowers.* Each corolla *deeply divided* into narrow lobes. Thistle Tribe—Cynareae. White p. 108; Yellow p. 210; Red pp. 328–30; Blue p. 384.

2b. Plant rarely spiny. Head of disk flowers only *or* of disk and ray flowers. Corolla not deeply cleft. See 3.

3a. Flower head bracts (phyllaries) greenish. See 4.

3b. Flower head bracts papery or translucent. Plants white woolly or if green with a disagreeable odor. See 8.

4a. Papery scales around *some or all* flowers in head and attached *below akene* (seed-ovary) *base.* See 5.

4b. Papery scales *absent* from all flowers in head. See 6.

5a. One papery scale *below all disk* flowers in head. Each ray flower subtended but not enclosed. Sunflower Tribe —Heliantheae. White p. 104; Yellow pp. 184–88.

5b. Papery scales *only in one circle* between the outer row of ray flowers and the inner zone of disk flowers. Each ray flower *enclosed* by an outer green bract. Plants often with unpleasant resinous *sticky hairs.* Tarweed Tribe —Madiinae. White p. 104; Yellow pp. 190–94.

6a. Pappus (sepals) at *top* of akene (seed) of bristles (in 1–2 series of unequal length), or awns, scales, or often none. See 7.

6b. Pappus (sepals) at *top* of akene (seed) of *soft spiderweblike* or feathery (plumose) bristles. Flower head phyllaries usually in *1-row,* if more the outer row very short. Senecio Tribe—Senecioneae. White p. 106; Yellow pp. 204–208; Orange p. 226; Red p. 330.

7a. Flower head phyllaries (bracts) in 1 or 2 rows of equal lengths, *never* imbricate (*not* overlapping like shingles). Woolly Sunflower Tribe—Helenieae. Yellow pp. 196–202.

7b. Flower head phyllaries (bracts) in several to many rows of graduated lengths, *imbricate* (overlapping like shingles). Aster Tribe—Astereae. White pp. 102, 108; Yellow pp. 212–14; Red p. 332; Blue p. 384.

8a. Plants *white woolly.* Flower heads of *numerous* rows of *papery translucent* phyllaries (bracts). Heads *only* of tiny disk flowers. Anther sac bases *tailed.* Everlasting Tribe —Inuleae. White p. 108; Yellow p. 210; Red p. 330; Green p. 404.

8b. Plants green. Leaves lacy with a strong *disagreeable odor.* Flower head with or without a few rows of thin, papery bracts. Anther sac bases blunt. Mayweed Tribe— Anthemideae. White p. 108; Yellow p. 210.

Petals Numerous, Regular Shape

(Families keyed below are described on this page.)

92a. Pond plants. **Nymphaeaceae.**
92b. Land plants. See 93.

93a. Leaves ordinary flat type. **Ranunculaceae.** See p. xxv.
93b. Leaves absent or strongly angular. See 94.

94a. Cactus-like with spine clusters. **Cactaceae.**
94b. Plant with succulent angular leaves. **Aizoaceae.**

WATER LILY FAMILY (Nymphaeaceae). Pond plants with large floating leaves. Large showy flowers. All flower parts numerous. White p. 2; Yellow p. 158.

CACTUS FAMILY (Cactaceae). Thick spiny plants, leafless. Cuplike flowers of numerous petals and stamens. Ovary inferior. Identity often based on *number and arrangement of each spine cluster.* Yellow pp. 128–32; Red p. 264.

CARPETWEED FAMILY (Aizoaceae). Leaves *thick, succulent and angular.* Petals and stamens numerous. Ovary a thick cuplike tube (inferior ovary). Yellow p. 120.

White or
Whitish Flowers

A large category in which most species are clearly white, but also including flowers that are mostly white or give a whitish impression (such as those spotted or tinted with yellow, red, blue, or green). If your flower is not in this section, check under the other colors. When possible, the group characteristics given in the text page titles are repeated in each color section, and in the same order. Where the flowers on a page look nearly the same but your sample does not fit, you can also use the cross reference given for other colors.

3 OR NUMEROUS PETALS: MARSH PLANTS

CALLA LILY Alien   *Zantedeschia aethiopica*
ARUM FAMILY See also p. Y 158.   (Araceae)
Note the large creamy-white funnel surrounding a narrow orange-yellow spike of tiny compacted flowers. Large, fleshy, arrowhead-shaped leaves. Fragrant. 2–4 ft. Wet disturbed places. Mostly along Calif. coast.   ALL YEAR

BUR REED   *Sparganium simplex*
BUR-REED FAMILY   (Sparganiaceae)
Note the *round balls* of flowers along a usually floating stem. All the linear grasslike leaves usually float gracefully in the same direction. 2–4 ft. Shallow water of ponds. Pacific States.   JULY–OCT.

FRINGED WATER PLANTAIN
          Machaerocarpus californicus
WATER PLANTAIN FAMILY   (Alismataceae)
Note the *sharply toothed* petal tips. The oblong, parallel-veined leaves rise separately from the leafless flower stem. ½–1½ ft. Sloughs and marshes. Cen. Calif. and Great Basin.   APRIL–AUG.

DUCK POTATO   *Sagittaria latifolia*
WATER PLANTAIN FAMILY   (Alismataceae)
The strongly *arrowhead-shaped,* parallel-veined leaves are variable in width. The 3-petaled flowers are in whorls of 3 along the leafless flower stem. 1–4 ft. Pond edges. Pacific States.   JULY–SEPT.

COMMON WATER PLANTAIN
          Alisma plantago-aquatica
WATER PLANTAIN FAMILY   (Alismataceae)
The 3-petaled flowers are *smooth-edged,* in umbels along a leafless flower stem and with an overall pyramid shape. Seed capsule buttonlike. Leaves oblong to oval. 2–4 ft. Pond edges. Pacific States.   JUNE–SEPT.

FRAGRANT WATER LILY Alien   *Nymphaea odorata*
WATER LILY FAMILY See also p. Y 158.   (Nymphaeaceae)
The large flowers are white and fragrant. Large floating leaves. Shallow lakes. Wash. and Ore.   JULY–OCT.

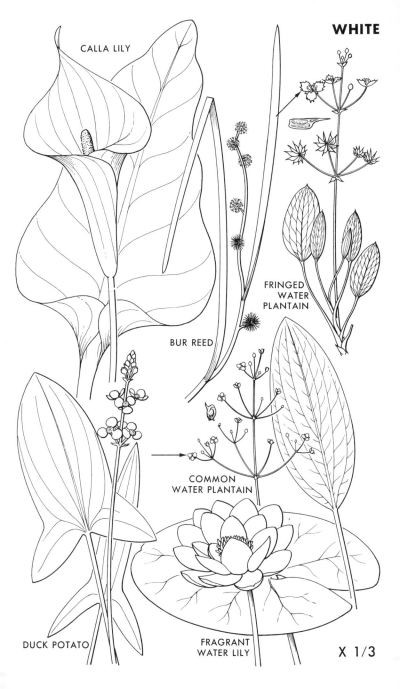

WHITE

CALLA LILY

FRINGED
WATER
PLANTAIN

BUR REED

COMMON
WATER PLANTAIN

DUCK POTATO

FRAGRANT
WATER LILY

X 1/3

3 OR 6 PETALS; FLOWERS HANGING

LILY FAMILY (Liliaceae)
See also pp. W 4–16; Y 122–24; O 228–30; R 252–56;
B 352; G 388–90.

SMITH'S FAIRYBELL *Disporum smithii*
The hanging *cylindrical* flowers are in terminal clusters.
Stigma *3-lobed.* The ovate leaves are attached to the stem by
clasping bases. 1–3 ft. Moist shady woods near the coast. Cen.
Calif. north to B.C. MARCH–JUNE

HOOKER'S FAIRYBELL *Disporum hookeri*
Similar to Smith's Fairybell. The flowers are *funnel-like* and
have an *entire stigma.* 1–3 ft. Shady woods away from coast.
Sierra Nevada and Calif. North Coast Ranges to B.C.
MARCH–MAY

CLASPING TWISTED STALK *Streptopus amplexifolius*
Note the sharply twisted, *right-angled pedicel* from which
hangs a single *bell-like* flower under each leaf. The parallel-
veined leaves are oval, the base clasping the well-branched
stem. Flowers white or tinted greenish. 1–2½ ft. Very
common. Moist shady woods. N. Calif. to B.C. MAY–JULY

ROSY TWISTED STALK *Streptopus roseus*
Note the *nearly straight* pedicels. Single, very small, bell-like
flowers hang under the unbranched stem. The white flowers are
usually streaked a reddish purple. ½–1 ft. Very common in
shady moist woods. Ore. Coast Ranges, Cascades to B.C.
JUNE–JULY

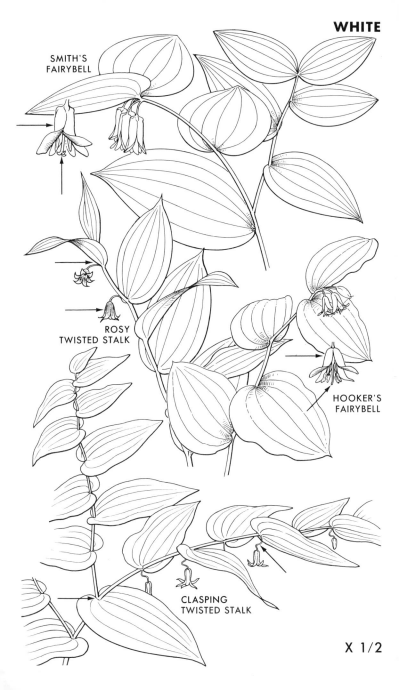

WHITE

SMITH'S
FAIRYBELL

ROSY
TWISTED STALK

HOOKER'S
FAIRYBELL

CLASPING
TWISTED STALK

X 1/2

3, 4, OR 6 PETALS; FLOWERS SMALL STARS

LILY FAMILY (Liliaceae)
See also pp. W 4–16; Y 122–24; O 228–30; R 252–56;
B 352; G 388–90.

BRANCHED SOLOMON'S SEAL   *Smilacina racemosa*
Numerous starlike flowers in a *well-branched* racemose inflorescence. Many parallel-veined leaves clothe the arching stem. Berries red, with occasional purple spots. 1–3 ft. Shady woods. Mts. of Pacific States.   MARCH–JULY

STAR SOLOMON'S SEAL   *Smilacina stellata*
Similar to Branched Solomon's-Seal. 3–15 flowers on an *unbranched* inflorescence. Berries red-purple, becoming black. 1–2 ft. Damp woods. Pacific States.   MARCH–JUNE

FALSE LILY OF THE VALLEY *Maianthemum dilatatum*
Note the parallel-veined, *heart-shaped* leaves. Tiny flowers with 4 petals. One of the few species that break the rule of 3's or 6's in the Lily Family. 6–15 in. Moist shady woods. Calif. North Coast north to B.C.   MAY–JUNE

BEAR GRASS   *Xerophyllum tenax*
The large dense *spikelike brush* of numerous small flowers is well above the large clump of wiry grasslike leaves. 1–5 ft. Shady forests. Cen. Calif. north to B.C.   MAY–AUG.

DEATH CAMAS   *Zigadenus venenosus*
The numerous flowers are in a thick spike. Stamens longer than petals. Petal tips rounded. The yellowish gland on each petal is rounded. Linear leaves. Bulb coat black. 1–2 ft. Moist places. Pacific States.   MAY–JULY

FREMONT'S CAMAS   *Zigadenus fremontii*
Flowers in a loose spike. Stamens not longer than petals. Petal tips pointed. The yellowish petal gland flattened along top. 1–3 ft. Thickets below 3500 ft. Calif. and s. Ore. Coast Ranges.
MARCH–MAY

DESERT CAMAS   *Zigadenus brevibracteatus*
Cream flowers form an *open well-branched* inflorescence. The yellow-green petal gland is a flattened double yoke. The petals alternate in shape. Stamens shorter than petals. 1–2 ft. Sandy flats. Mojave Desert, Calif. South Coast Ranges.   APRIL–MAY

ELEGANT CAMAS   *Zigadenus elegans*
The gland on each petal a *deep 2-pronged yoke*. Stamens same length as petals. Racemose inflorescence. Many habitats. Mts. of Great Basin, Cascades north to B.C.   JUNE–AUG.

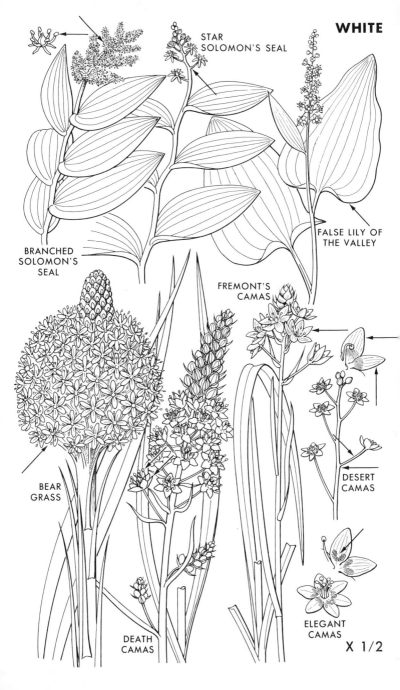

WHITE

STAR SOLOMON'S SEAL

FALSE LILY OF THE VALLEY

BRANCHED SOLOMON'S SEAL

FREMONT'S CAMAS

BEAR GRASS

DESERT CAMAS

DEATH CAMAS

ELEGANT CAMAS

X 1/2

3 OR 6 PETALS; LILYLIKE

Lily Family (Liliaceae)
See also pp. W 4–16; Y 122–24; O 228–30; R 252–56;
B 352; G 388–90.

WASHINGTON LILY *Lilium washingtonianum*
The flower tube is ⅔ petal length before curving at tips, usually
3–5 in. long. White with purple dots, becoming pink with age in
some areas. Fragrant. Leaves whorled. 2–8 ft. Dry forests.
Sierra Nevada, Siskiyous, and north to Mt. Hood, Ore.
July–Aug.

DESERT LILY *Hesperocallis undulata*
Flowers trumpetlike, similar to true lilies. Leaves *wavy-margined* and arranged alternately. 1–6 ft. Sandy flats.
Mojave, Colorado Deserts. March–May

CHAPARRAL LILY *Lilium rubescens*
The flower tube is ½ or less the petal length, 1–3 in. White with
purple dots at first, aging to a dark wine color. Leaves whorled.
Fragrant. 2–5 ft. Dry wooded slopes. Calif. North Coast
Ranges. June–July

QUEEN CUP *Clintonia uniflora*
Note the single, upright, *cuplike* flower per stem. Several
oblong leaves 4–6 in., parallel veined. 6–12 in. Shady woods.
Sierra Nevada north to B.C. May–July

SAND LILY *Leucocrinum montanum*
Flowers *starlike* with a long tube, tufted among long linear
leaves. Fragrant. 2–6 in. Meadows and flats. East of
Cascades–Sierra Nevada; Sierra Co., Calif., north to Ore.
April–June

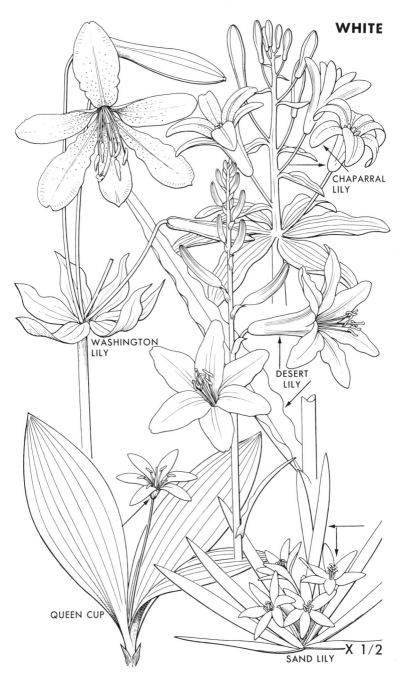

WHITE

CHAPARRAL
LILY

WASHINGTON
LILY

DESERT
LILY

QUEEN CUP

SAND LILY

X 1/2

3 OR 6 PETALS: FAWN LILIES

Lily Family (Liliaceae)
See also pp. W 4–16; Y 122–24; O 228–30; R 252–56;
B 352; G 388–90.

CALIFORNIA FAWN LILY   *Erythronium californicum*
Stigma lobes *stubby,* stamen filament tapered at tip. Creamy
flower with pale greenish-yellow base and a band of yellow-
orange. Fawn-spotted leaves. $\frac{1}{2}$–1 ft. Below 4000 ft. Calif.
North Coast Ranges.   MARCH–MAY

SIERRA FAWN LILY   *Erythronium multiscapoideum*
Similar to California Fawn Lily. Stigma lobes *threadlike.*
Delicate fragrance. $\frac{1}{2}$–1 ft. Semishade of shrubs. Western
foothills of Sierra Nevada.   MARCH–MAY

PLAINLEAF FAWN LILY   *Erythronium purpurascens*
Leaves yellow-green, *not spotted,* edges turned up and wavy-
margined. Creamy flowers with a yellowish base, turning
purplish with age. Flowering as snow melts. 3–8 in. Damp
woods 4000–8000 ft. Sierra Nevada.   MAY–AUG.

GLACIER FAWN LILY   *Erythronium montanum*
Petals *pure white* with a bright yellow basal band. Bright green
oblong leaves without spots. Flowers immediately after snow
melts. $\frac{1}{2}$–2 ft. Damp mt. meadows near timberline. Mt. Hood,
Ore., north to B.C.   JUNE–SEPT.

OREGON FAWN LILY   *Erythronium oregonum*
Upper *half* of stamen filament is much thinner. Petal tips
twisted, white to pale pink, bases yellow inside and reddish
brown outside. Fawn-spotted leaves. $\frac{1}{2}$–1 ft. Openings in
woods at lower elevations. Nw. Calif. and west of Cascades.
                                             APRIL–MAY

LEMON FAWN LILY   *Erythronium citrinum*
Petals creamy with a lemon-yellow base. Stigma *entire.*
Fawn-spotted leaves. 4–12 in. Shady woods below 4000 ft. Nw.
Calif. and sw. Ore.   MARCH–APRIL

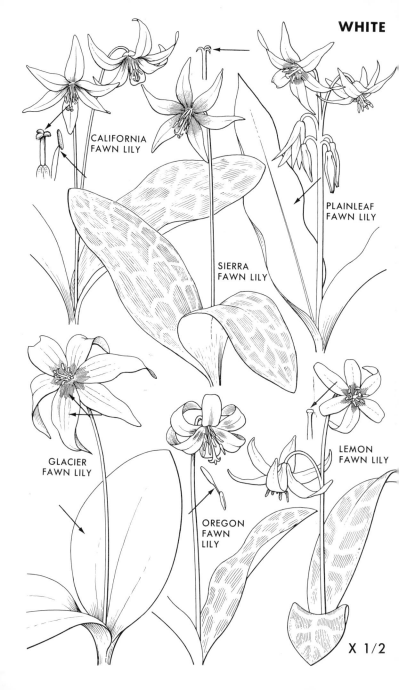

WHITE

CALIFORNIA
FAWN LILY

SIERRA
FAWN LILY

PLAINLEAF
FAWN LILY

GLACIER
FAWN LILY

OREGON
FAWN
LILY

LEMON
FAWN LILY

X 1/2

3 OR 6 PETALS; FLOWERS IN PANICLES

LILY FAMILY (Liliaceae)
See also pp. W 4–16; Y 122–24; O 228–30;
R 252–56; B 352; G 388–90.

CALIFORNIA CORN LILY *Veratrum californicum*
Tall *cornlike stalk* with many large parallel-veined leaves in an alternate arrangement. Flowers in a terminal panicle. 6 smooth-edged petals, each with a green V-shaped spot at the base. 3–6 ft. Mt. meadows. Calif. JUNE–AUG.

FRINGED CORN LILY *Veratrum fimbriatum*
Note the *fringed* petals. Flowers in thick cones. Leaves and stem as in California Corn Lily. 3–6 ft. Wet meadows. Central portion of Calif. North Coast. JULY–SEPT.

SISKIYOU CORN LILY *Veratrum insolitum*
Similar to California Corn Lily. All flower parts and stem covered by *short velvety hairs*. 3–4 ft. Prairies and openings in thickets. Nw. Calif. and sw. Ore. JUNE–SEPT.

WESTERN TOFIELDIA *Tofieldia glutinosa*
Small white flowers in a *terminal cluster*. The leafless flower stem is covered with minute, reddish, glandular hairs. Linear basal leaves. 1–3 ft. Wet meadows, bogs. Sierra Nevada; Calif. North Coast Ranges north to B.C. JUNE–AUG.

WHITE SCHOENOLIRION *Schoenolirion album*
Stamen *filaments smooth*. Flowers white, tinted green or pink. Leaves basal, linear. 1–5 ft. Meadows of n. Calif. to s. Ore. JUNE–JULY

WAVY-LEAF SOAP PLANT *Chlorogalum pomeridianum*
Large basal rosette of *wavy-margined* linear leaves. The white linear flower petals with green or purple midveins are often completely curled. A single stout and leafless flower stem. Flowers open in the early evening and close in the morning. The large bulb is surrounded by a pad of coarse fibers. 1–7 ft. Dry open hills. Calif. MARCH–JULY

NARROWLEAF SOAP PLANT
Chlorogalum angustifolium
Leaf margins *straight-edged*. Flowers bell-like, petals white with a greenish-yellow midvein. Bulb covered with delicate fibers. 1–2 ft. Dry grasslands and woodlands. Central Valley of Calif. APRIL–JULY

HARTWEG'S ODONTOSTOMUM
Odontostomum hartwegii
The petal tips *sweep backward* in the white to yellowish tubular flowers. Linear basal leaves. 5–12 in. Grassy foothills. Cen. Calif. APRIL–MAY

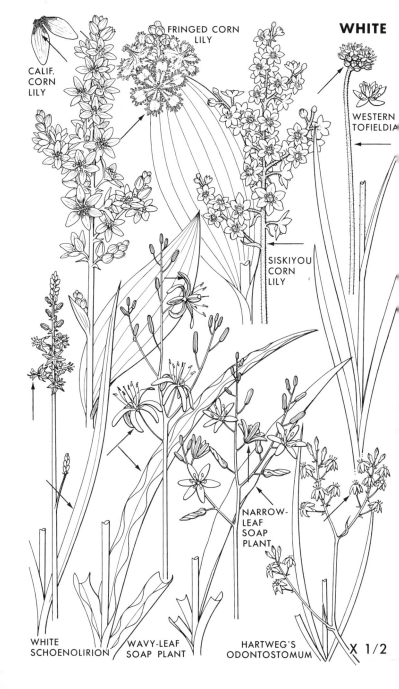

CALIF.
CORN
LILY

FRINGED CORN
LILY

WHITE

WESTERN
TOFIELDIA

SISKIYOU
CORN
LILY

NARROW-
LEAF
SOAP
PLANT

WHITE
SCHOENOLIRION

WAVY-LEAF
SOAP PLANT

HARTWEG'S
ODONTOSTOMUM

X 1/2

3 PETALS: SMALL MARIPOSA TULIPS

LILY FAMILY (Liliaceae)
See also pp. W 4–16; Y 122–24; O 228–30;
R 252–56; B 352; G 388–90.

LYALL'S STAR TULIP　　　　　　*Calochortus lyallii*
Petals narrow *lancelike,* the lower edges strongly *fringed,* white
except for dark *purple horseshoe* mark at base. Eastern slope
of Cascades in Wash. and B.C.　　　　　　MAY–JULY

WHITE GLOBE LILY　　　　　　*Calochortus albus*
Note the *hanging* lanternlike flowers. The white flowers are
tinted a light pink in some areas. Grasslike leaves. $\frac{1}{2}$–$2\frac{1}{2}$ ft.
Shady thickets. Cen. Calif.　　　　　　APRIL–JUNE

TOLMIE'S PUSSY EARS　　　　　　*Calochortus tolmiei*
The *entire petal surface* hairy, edges *not fringed.* Petal tips
rounded. Flowers white, often tinted rose to purple. 4–15 in.
West of Cascades–Sierra Nevada.　　　　　　APRIL–JULY

ELEGANT CATS EAR　　　　　　*Calochortus elegans*
Anthers *spear-shaped,* with a long *thin point projecting* from
the tips. Petal hairy over most of surface, except *tip* usually
hairless, side edges fringed. Flowers white, often tinted a faint
blue. A naked purple crescent at base of petal. Petal tips
pointed. Stem barely above ground, 2–6 in. Mt. slopes.
N. Calif. and north to se. Wash.　　　　　　MAY–JULY

BEAVERTAIL CATS EAR　　　　　　*Calochortus coeruleus*
Very similar to Elegant Cats Ear. Anthers large and *oblong,* tip
blunt, with or without a short tip. Flowers white to pale blue.
Common in woods at low elevations. Sierra Nevada, Calif.
North Coast Ranges.　　　　　　MAY–JULY

NAKED CATS EAR　　　　　　*Calochortus nudus*
Petals *round-tipped,* nearly *naked,* with a few long hairs above
the gland. Gland transverse or arched upward, bordered with a
fringed membrane. Flower white to pale lavender. 4–12 in.
Meadows and forest openings, 4000–7500 ft. N. Sierra Nevada,
Siskiyous.　　　　　　MAY–JULY

LESSER STAR TULIP　　　　　　*Calochortus minimus*
Petal tip *triangular-pointed.* Petal hairless or nearly so. Gland
transverse. 4–8 in. Grassy openings in woods. Western slope of
Sierra Nevada.　　　　　　MAY–AUG.

OAKLAND STAR TULIP　　　　　　*Calochortus umbellatus*
Petal tip *square-edged,* naked except for short hairs around
edge of transverse gland near base. Flowers white to pale
lavender, purple spot often present near gland edge. 3–12 in.
Clearings. Coast Ranges of cen. Calif.　　　　　　MARCH–MAY

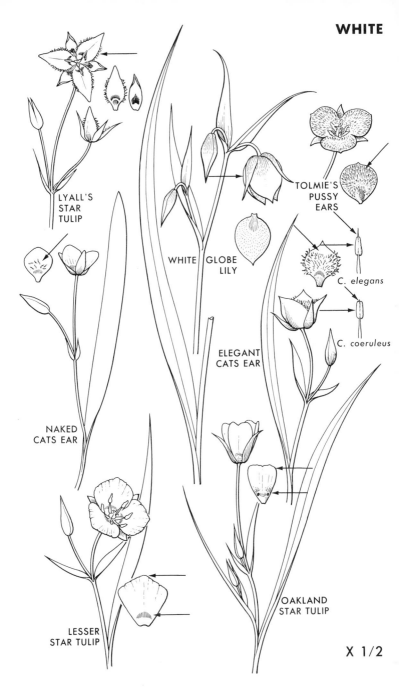

WHITE

LYALL'S
STAR
TULIP

TOLMIE'S
PUSSY
EARS

WHITE GLOBE
LILY

C. elegans

C. coeruleus

ELEGANT
CATS EAR

NAKED
CATS EAR

OAKLAND
STAR TULIP

LESSER
STAR TULIP

X 1/2

3 PETALS: LARGE MARIPOSA TULIPS

LILY FAMILY (Liliaceae)
See also pp. W 4–16; Y 122–24; O 228–30;
R 252–56; B 352; G 388–90.

SQUARE MARIPOSA TULIP   *Calochortus venustus*
Note the *rectangular* yellow spot at the petal base, a pale red spot in upper petal center, and a lower dark red one with a yellowish border. Petals white, red in some areas. 4–12 in. Sierra Nevada, Calif. South Coast Ranges.   MAY–JULY

CATALINA MARIPOSA TULIP   *Calochortus catalinae*
Note the *squarish* yellow gland with a few long hairs, surrounded by a rounded dark purple spot. $\frac{1}{2}$–2 ft. Grassy places near coast. Cen. Calif. to Baja.   MARCH–MAY

LEICHTLIN'S MARIPOSA TULIP *Calochortus leichtlinii*
The *triangular* yellow-haired basal spot has a dark purplish-red spot above it. Flowers white, tinted smoky blue. Open places. Sierra Nevada to ne. Calif.   JUNE–AUG.

SUPERB MARIPOSA TULIP   *Calochortus superbus*
Note the reddish-haired *inverted V* near the petal base, with a yellow-bordered brown-purple spot above it. Petals penciled with purple near bases. 1–2 ft. Open places. Calif.   MAY–JULY

DUNN'S MARIPOSA TULIP   *Calochortus dunnii*
Note curved reddish-brown spot above the horseshoe-shaped mat of short yellowish hairs. Dry rocky slopes. Mts. east of San Diego; Baja.   JUNE

SEGO LILY   *Calochortus nuttallii*
Note the yellow *rounded spot* with a purple-red horseshoe mark above it at the petal base. Utah state flower. 8–16 in. Open places. Great Basin, Mojave Desert.   MAY–AUG.

HOWELL'S MARIPOSA TULIP   *Calochortus howellii*
Large rounded petals with short *smoky-brown hairs* scattered over surface, becoming very dense above the greenish gland. 1–2 ft. Hot rocky places. Sw. Ore.   JUNE–JULY

BIG POD MARIPOSA TULIP   *Calochortus eurycarpus*
Note the large, rounded to squarish, purple *spot on upper petal* above a greenish area. Basal gland area yellow with long cobwebby hairs. 1–2 ft. Great Basin.   JUNE–AUG.

LOBB'S MARIPOSA TULIP   *Calochortus subalpinus*
The white chalicelike flower has a *golden interior* of long hairs. A slightly arching gland near petal base. 2–12 in. Subalpine meadows. Cen. Cascades.   JUNE–AUG.

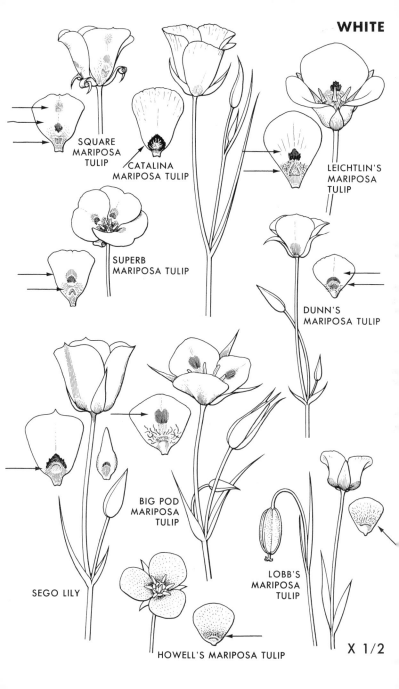

WHITE

SQUARE
MARIPOSA
TULIP

CATALINA
MARIPOSA TULIP

LEICHTLIN'S
MARIPOSA
TULIP

SUPERB
MARIPOSA TULIP

DUNN'S
MARIPOSA TULIP

BIG POD
MARIPOSA
TULIP

SEGO LILY

LOBB'S
MARIPOSA
TULIP

HOWELL'S MARIPOSA TULIP

X 1/2

3 PETALS; UMBEL ON LEAFLESS STEM

AMARYLLIS FAMILY (Amaryllidaceae)
See also pp. Y 124; R 254-62; B 352.

PAPER ONION   *Allium amplectens*
Note the umbel of numerous white *papery flowers* on a tall leafless stem. Leaves often dried up at flowering time. Onion odor. ½–2 ft. Common in hot dry openings below 6000 ft. West of Sierra Nevada in Calif., occasionally in Ore. and Wash.
MARCH–JUNE

SIERRA ONION   *Allium obtusum*
Note the *1 flat leaf* that is longer than the flower stem. The several to many flowers are white to greenish with a purplish-red midrib. Onion odor. 1–3 in. Gravelly subalpine, alpine slopes. Sierra Nevada.   MAY–JULY

RED-SKINNED ONION   *Allium haematochiton*
Petals broadly oval. Onion odor. Dry places. 4–12 in. Calif. South Coast Ranges, south to Baja.   MARCH–MAY

COMMON MUILLA   *Muilla maritima*
The 3 oval, shiny petals are *slightly united* near the base. 4–70 flowers per umbel, white to greenish with a brownish midrib. Leaves linear. No onion odor. ½–2 ft. Grassy places. Calif.
MARCH–JUNE

WHITE HYACINTH   *Triteleia hyacinthina*
Note the *united flower tube* below the spreading petal tips. Flowers white or tinted blue. Petal midribs green. Each umbel has numerous flowers. No onion odor. ½–2 ft. Common in many places. Pacific States.   MARCH–AUG.

LONG-RAYED HYACINTH   *Triteleia peduncularis*
The umbrellalike flower *pedicels are very long,* 3–10 or more times the length of the white to pale blue flowers. ½–3 ft. Wet streambanks, marshes. Calif. North Coast Ranges, south to Monterey, Calif.   MAY–JULY

GLASSY HYACINTH   *Triteleia lilacina*
Similar to White Hyacinth above. Inner surface of the petals with a glassy shine from *tiny glasslike beads.* Petal tips appear pointed by folding of petal edges. ½–2 ft. Volcanic tabletops of Central Valley of Calif.   APRIL–MAY

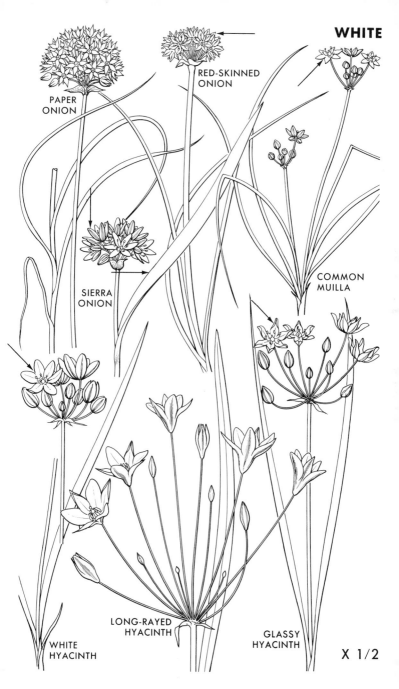

WHITE

PAPER
ONION

RED-SKINNED
ONION

SIERRA
ONION

COMMON
MUILLA

WHITE
HYACINTH

LONG-RAYED
HYACINTH

GLASSY
HYACINTH

X 1/2

3 PETALS; BILATERAL SYMMETRY:
ORCHIDS

ORCHID FAMILY (Orchidaceae)
See also pp. O 230; G 390–92.

SIERRA CRANE ORCHID,   *Habenaria dilatata*
CASCADE CRANE ORCHID
Pure white flowers with a *long curving spur*. Numerous flowers in a spike. Sierra Crane Orchid (ssp. *leucostachys*) with spur petal *much longer* than lip petal is common in Calif., while the Cascade Crane Orchid (ssp. *elegans*) with spur and lip petals of *equal* length occurs from Ore. to B.C. 1–4 ft. Very common in wet springy places.   MAY–AUG.

GREENE'S COASTAL HABENARIA   *Habenaria greenei*
Note the thick *cone-shaped* spike of flowers. The greenish spur petal straight, slightly longer than the lip petal. Thickets. 1–3 ft. Along immediate Pacific Coast.   JULY–SEPT.

ELEGANT HABENARIA   *Habenaria elegans*
Each of the white to greenish flowers has a long, slender, *straight spur*. Numerous flowers in a spike. The 2–4 lancelike leaves usually dried up by flowering time. 1–2 ft. Dry woods. Pacific States.   MAY–SEPT.

ROUND-LEAVED ORCHID   *Habenaria orbiculata*
Note the 2 large *rounded leaves* at the base of the leafless flower stem. The long curving spur equals or is longer than the lip petal. Flowers white to greenish. ½–2 ft. Mossy forests. Cascades to B.C.   JUNE–AUG.

HOODED LADIES TRESSES   *Spiranthes romanzoffiana*
The lip petal is *constricted near the tip*. Flower spike a dense spiral much like a woman's braided hair. 4–20 in. Wet streambanks, meadows. Pacific States.   JUNE–AUG.

WESTERN LADIES TRESSES   *Spiranthes porrifolia*
Similar to Hooded Ladies Tresses. The lip petal is triangular to oval, with 2 prominent protuberances at the base. ½–2 ft. Wet springy places. Pacific States.   JULY–AUG.

PHANTOM ORCHID   *Eburophyton austinae*
Entire plant white to yellowish. 1–2 ft. A saprophyte that grows in deep humus under shady conifers. Mts. of Pacific States.   MAY–JULY

RATTLESNAKE ORCHID   *Goodyera oblongifolia*
The *skin pattern* of a *rattlesnake* is simulated by a central strip of mottled white on the dark green, oblong leaves. Leaves in a basal rosette. A few white to greenish tubular flowers on a leafless stem. 1–3 ft. Dry shady woods. Pacific States.
         JULY–SEPT.

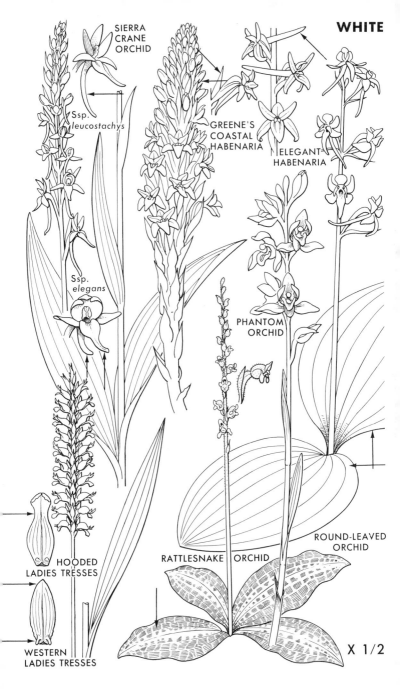

WHITE

SIERRA CRANE ORCHID

Ssp. *leucostachys*

GREENE'S COASTAL HABENARIA

ELEGANT HABENARIA

Ssp. *elegans*

PHANTOM ORCHID

HOODED LADIES TRESSES

ROUND-LEAVED ORCHID

WESTERN LADIES TRESSES

RATTLESNAKE ORCHID

X 1/2

6 SHOWY PETALS; MILKY SAP: POPPIES

POPPY FAMILY (Papaveraceae)
See also p. O 224.

MATILIJA POPPY *Romneya coulteri*
Note the smooth, bluish-green, partly divided leaves on the tall clustered stems. Flowers 3–6 in. across with 6 white crinkly petals, many yellow stamens. Deliciously fragrant. 3–7 ft. Dry washes, canyons of s. Calif. MAY–JULY

PYGMY POPPY *Canbya candida*
Note small tuft of short, linear, *hairless* leaves with long slender flower stems. Waxy-white flowers with 6 petals. Tiny plants. 1–3 in. Sandy places. Western edge of Mojave Desert north to Great Basin in Ore. APRIL–JUNE

CREAM CUPS *Platystemon californicus*
The 6 creamy petals have a bright yellow basal spot. Petal color can vary in some plants from pure yellow to reddish. The elongated flower stems have conspicuous long hairs. Leaves linear in a basal cluster. Milky sap. Entire fields may become cream-colored from this plant in early spring. 4–12 in. Open fields. Calif. to w. Baja. MARCH–JULY

PRICKLY POPPY *Argemone munita*
Note the numerous *yellow spines* on the stems and leaves. Large, white, 6-petaled flowers with a dense yellow center of stamens. 2–5 ft. Dry disturbed places. Calif. MARCH–AUG.

WHITE

MATILIJA POPPY

PYGMY POPPY

× 1

CREAM CUPS

PRICKLY POPPY

X 1/2

4-PETALED MALTESE CROSS;
OVAL SEEDPODS

MUSTARD FAMILY (Cruciferae)
See also pp. W 24–30; Y 140–48; O 224; R 266–68.

FREMONT'S PEPPERGRASS   *Lepidium fremontii*
Large, rounded, *bushlike,* with numerous flowering branches.
Leaves linear or pinnatified into a few linear lobes. Base of
stem somewhat woody. Seedpod flattened into 2 winglike
portions. ½–2 ft. Common. Mojave, Colorado Deserts.

MARCH–MAY

FLATPOD   *Idahoa scapigera*
The threadlike flower stem with a *solitary* flattened disklike
pod. Flowers inconspicuous. A basal cluster of oval to comb-
shaped leaves. 1–6 in. Flats that flood. Great Basin to cen.
Calif.   FEB.–APRIL

POORMANS PEPPERGRASS Alien   *Lepidium campestre*
Seedpods oval, with a notch between the upper 2 halves. Basal
leaves nearly entire but with toothed lobes along lower portion
of the blade. ½–2 ft. Disturbed places. Pacific States.

MARCH–AUG.

HOARY CRESS Alien   *Cardaria draba*
The seedpods are *kidney-shaped* in outline. Flowers are a
gray-white. Oval gray leaves, petioled at stem base, but becoming arrowhead-shaped and clasping on upper stem. 1–2 ft.
Disturbed places. Pacific States.   MARCH–JUNE

SPECTACLE POD   *Dithyrea californica*
Note the 2 diverging *winglike* pods, somewhat thickened and
with a *corky margin.* Numerous pods crowded together.
Leaves basal. 4–12 in. Common in sandy places. Mojave,
Colorado Deserts, Calif. South Coast Ranges.   MARCH–MAY

FORKED PEPPERGRASS   *Lepidium oxycarpum*
Note the *2 sharp points* of each seedpod. Seedpods numerous
above the linear leaves, which occasionally have toothed
margins. 1–8 in. Open flats. Cen. Calif. coast and west side of
Central Valley of Calif.   MARCH–MAY

SHINING PEPPERGRASS   *Lepidium nitidum*
Seedpods smooth and *shiny ovals.* Leaves linear, with sharp
margin points. Stems well branched. 2–15 in. Common in
open places. Pacific States.   FEB.–MAY

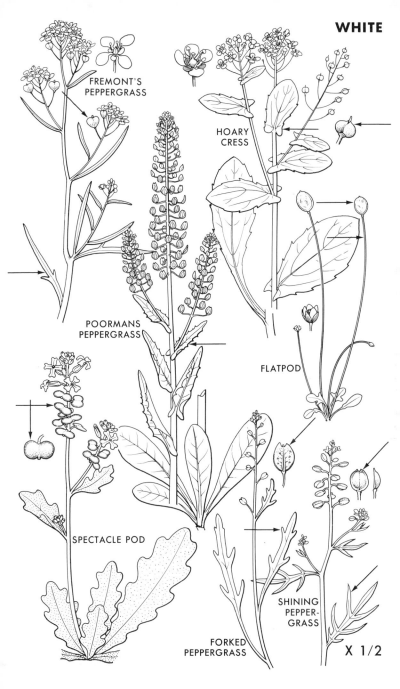

WHITE

FREMONT'S PEPPERGRASS

HOARY CRESS

POORMANS PEPPERGRASS

FLATPOD

SPECTACLE POD

SHINING PEPPER-GRASS

FORKED PEPPERGRASS

X 1/2

4-PETALED MALTESE CROSS;
OVAL SEEDPODS

MUSTARD FAMILY (Cruciferae)
See also pp. W 24–30; Y 140–48; O 224; R 266–68.

SHEPHERDS PURSE Alien   *Capsella bursa-pastoris*
Note the flat *heart-shaped seedpods*. If inverted they resemble
a shepherd's purse. Flowers tiny. Basal leaves dandelionlike,
becoming reduced upward. ½–2 ft. Common. Pacific States.
ALL YEAR

BREWER'S WHITLOW GRASS   *Draba breweri*
The flattened seedpods are oblong, twisted, and hairy. Tiny
flowers above a tuft of gray linear leaves. 1–4 in. Alpine
meadows. Sierra Nevada to Mt. Shasta.   JULY–AUG.

FIELD PENNYCRESS Alien   *Thlaspi arvense*
Note the round *penny-sized* seedpods. Stem leaves narrow and
spearlike. ½–2 ft. Pacific States.   MAY–SEPT.

LACE POD   *Thysanocarpus curvipes*
Note the round single-seeded pods hanging from a curved
pedicel. Each flattened seed is surrounded by a thin papery
margin with *thick* radiating ribs. Best observed when back-
lighted. Leaves basal or along lower stem, slender arrowhead-
like. Plant parts with hairs. One of first spring plants. ½–3 ft.
Open grassy slopes, very common. Pacific States.   FEB.–JUNE

SPOKE POD   *Thysanocarpus radians*
Similar to Lace Pod. Pods with *thin* radiating ribs. Plant parts
hairless. ½–2 ft. Grassy places. Cen. Calif. to s. Ore.
MARCH–MAY

SWEET ALYSSUM Alien   *Lobularia maritima*
Note the numerous small white flowers in thick *thumblike*
branches; entire plant a small cushiony mass. Seedpods oval,
leaves linear. 1–10 in. Frequent along coast. Pacific States.
ALL YEAR

FENDLER'S PENNYCRESS   *Thlaspi fendleri*
Flowers in dense *headlike clusters.* Seedpods triangular. Stem
leaves arrowheadlike, with a dense cluster of spoonshaped
leaves below. ½–2 ft. Pacific States.   APRIL–AUG.

SPRING WHITLOW GRASS Alien   *Draba verna*
Note the elongated oval seedpods on long thin pedicels. Tiny
white *bilobed petals.* The oval glandular leaves are in a
basal cluster. 1–3 in. Pacific States.   FEB.–MAY

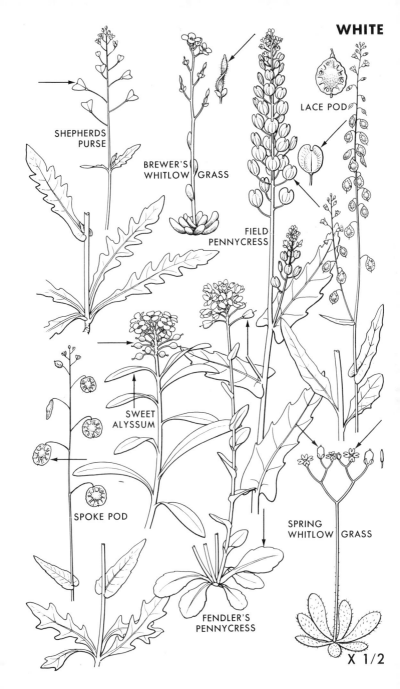

WHITE

SHEPHERDS PURSE

BREWER'S WHITLOW GRASS

LACE POD

FIELD PENNYCRESS

SWEET ALYSSUM

SPOKE POD

FENDLER'S PENNYCRESS

SPRING WHITLOW GRASS

X 1/2

4-PETALED MALTESE CROSS;
LINEAR SEEDPODS

MUSTARD FAMILY (Cruciferae)
See also pp. W 24–30; Y 140–48; O 224; R 266–68.

HAIRY CAULANTHUS   *Caulanthus pilosus*
All plant parts *densely long-haired*. The flower is a green to
purplish urn of sepals with 4 whitish and somewhat crisped
petals. Basal rosette of leaves dandelionlike with long petioles,
becoming linear on the stem. Seedpods long, linear. 1–3 ft.
Dry open places. Great Basin and south to northern edge of
Mojave Desert.   MAY–JULY

DESERT CANDLE   *Caulanthus inflatus*
The smooth yellow-green stems are strongly *inflated to re-
semble candles*. Leaves oblong to oval and clasping the stem.
Small white flowers in terminal tuft, purple before opening.
Stout linear seedpods. 1–3 ft. Open flats and thickets. Calif.
South Coast Ranges east to w. Mojave Desert.   MARCH–MAY

WILD RADISH Alien   *Raphanus sativus*
Seedpod a fat *cylinder with constrictions* between each seed.
Flowers pale white to various shades of pink and yellow. All
colors usually found at the same location. Broad pinnate leaves
along stem. 1–4 ft. Common in disturbed places. Pacific
States.   FEB.–JULY

DRUMMOND'S ROCK CRESS   *Arabis drummondii*
Seedpods *crowded and erect*. Flowers white to pinkish. Basal
leaves lancelike, with a narrowing basal portion. Leaves
become slender arrowheads clasping the upper stem. Hairless
to few-haired. 1–3 ft. Open mt. slopes. Pacific States.
                                        MAY–JULY

RECTER'S ROCK CRESS   *Arabis rectissima*
Note that *both* the flowers and seedpods are *reflexed downward*. Petals white to pinkish. Leaves bristly-haired, spatula-
like at the stem base and becoming slim arrowheads that clasp
the upper stem. 1–3 ft. Dry open places in woods at mid-mt.
elevations. Calif. to Ore.   MAY–JULY

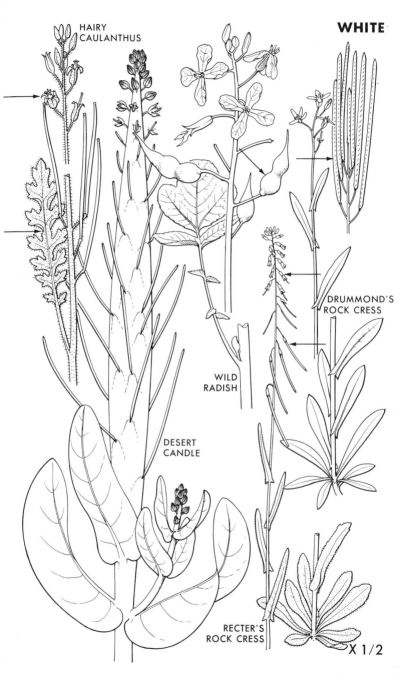

HAIRY
CAULANTHUS

WHITE

DRUMMOND'S
ROCK CRESS

WILD
RADISH

DESERT
CANDLE

RECTER'S
ROCK CRESS

X 1/2

4-PETALED MALTESE CROSS;
LINEAR SEEDPODS

Mustard Family (Cruciferae)
See also pp. W 24–30; Y 140–48; O 224; R 266–68.

CALIFORNIA MUSTARD   *Thelypodium lasiophyllum*
The *broad* leaves *sharply toothed.* Seedpods whiskerlike and
strongly reflexed downward. The white to yellow flowers are in
terminal spikes on well-branched stems. ½–4 ft. Below 5000 ft.
West of Cascades–Sierra Nevada.   March–June

WHOLE-LEAF MUSTARD   *Thelypodium integrifolium*
Numerous long, narrow seedpods give a *brushlike* appearance
to the plant. The white to bluish or pinkish flowers are in
terminal clusters. The large oblong leaves are in a basal
rosette. Stem leaves short and linear. 3–6 ft. Great Basin,
western edge of Mojave Desert.   June–Oct.

WHITE WATERCRESS   *Rorippa nasturtium-aquaticum*
Alien
Sprawling succulent stems with pinnate leaves, each leaf con-
sisting of 3–9 oval leaflets. Tiny flowers in terminal clusters.
Pungent taste. 1–2 ft. Common in quietly running water.
Pacific States.   All Year

LYALL'S BITTERCRESS   *Cardamine lyallii*
The leaves are *rounded to kidney-shaped* and scattered along
the erect stem. Dense terminal racemes of flowers, becoming
elongated as the linear seedpods develop. ½–2 ft. Mt. meadows
and streambanks. N. Sierra Nevada to B.C.   June–Aug.

BREWER'S BITTERCRESS   *Cardamine breweri*
Note the fleshy *3-lobed leaves,* consisting of 2 small opposite-
paired leaflets and a larger terminal leaflet. Flowers small.
Seedpods linear. ½–2 ft. Wet springy areas or streambanks.
Pacific States.   April–Aug.

WESTERN BITTERCRESS   *Cardamine oligosperma*
The pinnate leaves have 5–9 rounded leaflets. Most of the
leaves are in a loose basal rosette. Flowers 2–10 per raceme.
Linear seedpods. 4–12 in. Open damp places. Pacific States.
   March–July

MILKMAIDS   *Dentaria californica*
The flowering stem has mostly pinnate leaves with 3 *linear
leaflets.* Flowers white to pale pink. A solitary fleshy leaf with
a rounded outline marks this plant from the first fall rains until
the flowering stem develops. One of first spring wildflowers.
4–15 in. Shady woods. Many places west of deserts in Calif.
   Feb.–May

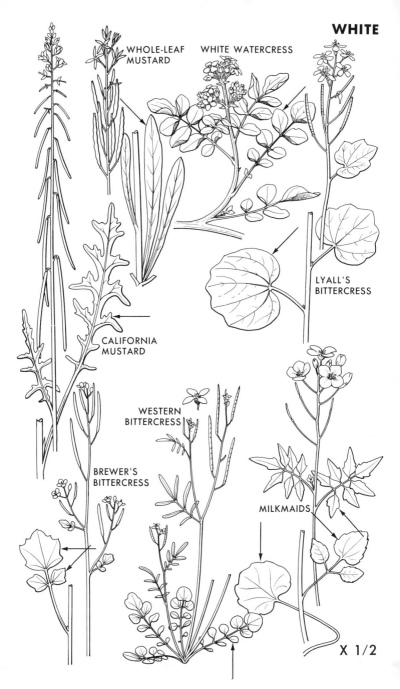

WHOLE-LEAF
MUSTARD

WHITE WATERCRESS

LYALL'S
BITTERCRESS

CALIFORNIA
MUSTARD

WESTERN
BITTERCRESS

BREWER'S
BITTERCRESS

MILKMAIDS

X 1/2

4 SHOWY PETALS ON TOP OF OVARY

Evening-Primrose Family (Onagraceae)
See also pp. Y 150–52; R 270–74.

WHITEPOLE EVENING PRIMROSE *Oenothera pallida*
Linear leaves less than $\frac{3}{8}$ in. wide. Large flower on erect stems.
$\frac{1}{2}$–3 ft. Dunes. Great Basin.   May–July

BIRDCAGE EVENING PRIMROSE *Oenothera deltoides*
Stems with a *peeling epidermis*. Leaves spatula-shaped on an
erect stem. Large petals. Evening flowering. The dead stems
resemble a birdcage. 2–12 in. Sandy places. Great Basin to
Mojave, Colorado Deserts.   March–July

CALIFORNIA EVENING PRIMROSE
Oenothera californica
Leaves with wavy margins, on an erect stem. Stem epidermis
not peeling. Large flowers, aging pink. $\frac{1}{4}$–2 ft. Sandy places.
S. Calif.   April–June

TUFTED EVENING PRIMROSE *Oenothera caespitosa*
Linear leaves with lobed margins, in a flat rosette. Stem
epidermis smooth. Large flowers, aging pink. 0.1–8 in. Dry
slopes. Mts. of s. Calif. north to Wash. on eastern side of
Cascades–Sierra Nevada.   April–Aug.

BOOTH'S EVENING PRIMROSE *Camissonia boothii*
Note that the *bright* green leaves are *spotted* with red and are
in a basal cluster below the stem. Smallish flowers in a compact
spikelike cluster. Stem epidermis peeling or shredding. 3–12 in.
Rocky soils. Calif. South Coast Ranges; Mojave, Colorado
Deserts.   March–June

BROWN-EYED EVENING PRIMROSE
Camissonia clavaeformis
A *brown spot* is often present at the petal base. Flowers with
rounded petals in a cluster above the basal rosette of oval,
strongly toothed leaves. Seed capsules club-shaped with a
definite pedicel. $\frac{1}{4}$–$\frac{1}{2}$ ft. Sandy soils. Great Basin in Ore.
south to Mojave, Colorado Deserts.   March–May

NUTTALL'S GAYOPHYTUM *Gayophytum nuttallii*
Note the fine *threadlike stems* and leaves, often well-branched
with minute white flowers that dry pink or red. $\frac{1}{4}$–2 ft.
Common in dry places. Pacific States.   June–Sept.

STICKY FIREWEED *Epilobium glandulosum*
Many small flowers (less than $\frac{1}{2}$ in.) on long ovaries. Flowers
vary from white to pink. Stem minutely sticky-haired. Opposite lancelike leaves with minutely sawtoothed margins. Moist
places in mts. Sierra Nevada to B.C.   June–Aug.

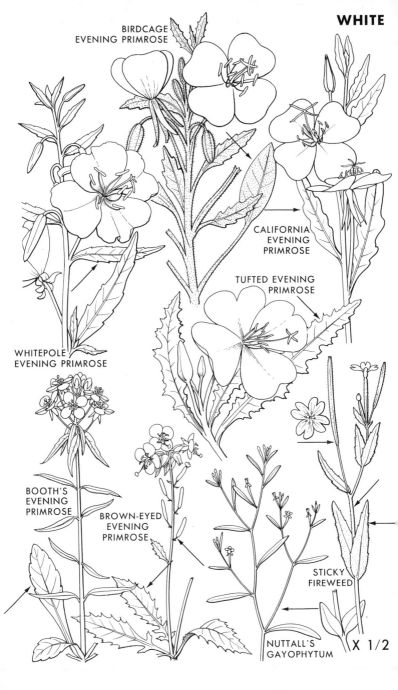

WHITE

BIRDCAGE EVENING PRIMROSE

CALIFORNIA EVENING PRIMROSE

TUFTED EVENING PRIMROSE

WHITEPOLE EVENING PRIMROSE

BOOTH'S EVENING PRIMROSE

BROWN-EYED EVENING PRIMROSE

STICKY FIREWEED

NUTTALL'S GAYOPHYTUM

X 1/2

4 OR 5 PETALS; TINY TUBULAR
FLOWERS IN CLUSTERS

Buckwheat Family (Polygonaceae)
See also pp. W 34–38; Y 134–38; R 276–78.

WESTERN BISTORT   *Polygonum bistortoides*
Note the *rounded ball* of small flowers on a *wiry* leafless stem
well above the leaves. Basal leaves broad, lancelike, and
petioled. ½–2 ft. Wet mt. meadows to coastal marshes. Pacific
States.   June–Sept.

WILLOW SMARTWEED   *Polygonum lapathifolium*
Note the rounded, *smooth-edged* papery bracts that surround
the stem immediately above where each leaf is attached.
Leaves willowlike. Flowers white to pinkish in long, dense,
spikelike clusters. 2–5 ft. Moist places. Pacific States.
      June–Oct.

LADYS THUMB   *Polygonum persicaria*
Similar to Willow Smartweed, but the papery stem bracts are
fringed. Flower clusters somewhat thumblike. 1–5 ft.
Common in moist places at lower elevations. Pacific States.
      March–Nov.

NEWBERRY'S KNOTWEED   *Polygonum newberryi*
The leaves *broadly oblong* to *triangular* along a usually
sprawling stem. Flowers white to greenish or pinkish. ½–2 ft.
Rocky alpine and subalpine slopes. Sierra Nevada north to
Wash.   June–Sept.

ALPINE KNOTWEED   *Polygonum phytolaccaefolium*
The tall erect stems with large lanceolate leaves (5–6 in. long).
3–6 ft. Moist to later dry, rocky, subalpine and alpine
meadows. Sierra Nevada north to B.C.   June–Sept.

YARD KNOTWEED Alien   *Polygonum aviculare*
The small, sprawling, wiry stems have numerous *tiny, blue-
green,* lancelike leaves with silvery bracts at their bases. Tiny
white, pale green, or pink flowers. 1–2 ft. Very common.
Pacific States.   All Year

DOUGLAS'S KNOTWEED   *Polygonum douglasii*
Stems *erect. Narrow linear* leaves with basal papery bracts.
Flowers white to greenish or reddish, in loosely flowered
racemes. Dry mt. meadows. Pacific States.   June–Sept.

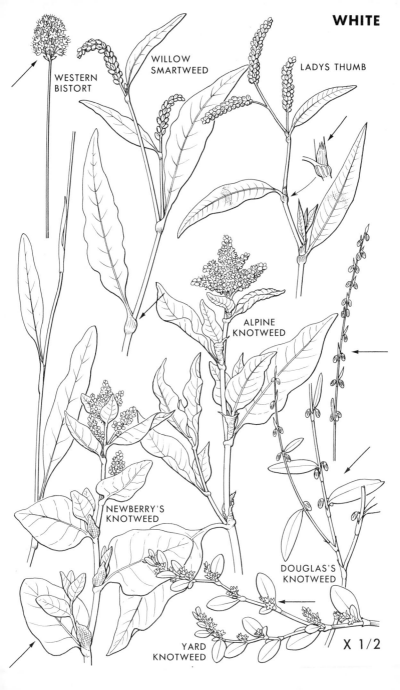

WHITE

WESTERN
BISTORT

WILLOW
SMARTWEED

LADYS THUMB

ALPINE
KNOTWEED

NEWBERRY'S
KNOTWEED

DOUGLAS'S
KNOTWEED

YARD
KNOTWEED

X 1/2

4 OR 6 PETALS; TINY TUBULAR
FLOWERS IN CLUSTERS

BUCKWHEAT FAMILY (Polygonaceae)
See also pp. W 34–38; Y 134–38; R 276–78.

BRITTLE SPINEFLOWER *Chorizanthe brevicornu*
Flowers within a *narrowly elongated cylinder* with ribs and 6 curved spines at the top. Linear leaves. 2–8 in. Gravelly slopes. Great Basin; Mojave, Colorado Deserts.
MARCH–JULY

ROUNDLEAF SPINEFLOWER *Oxytheca perfoliata*
Similar to Triangle Spineflower but the stem leaves *rounded.* The flowers 4-lobed halfway down the tube. 2–12 in. Sandy places. Mojave Desert and edge of Great Basin. APRIL–JULY

TRIANGLE SPINEFLOWER *Chorizanthe perfoliata*
Stem leaves *3-cornered,* surrounding the stem, while the basal rosette is of linear leaves. Flower a twisted 4-angled tube with 4 curved spines. 6–12 in. Dry flats. Calif. South Coast Ranges, Mojave Desert. APRIL–JUNE

THURBER'S SPINEFLOWER *Chorizanthe thurberi*
Numerous cylindrical flowers with 3 inflated basal *buttress-like sacs;* 5 short teeth at top and a small horn on each buttress sac. Spatula-like leaves. 2–8 in. Common in sandy places. Deserts and Calif. South Coast Ranges. APRIL–JUNE

NODDING ERIOGONUM *Eriogonum cernuum*
Flowers *nodding* or pendulant, white to rose-tinted. Petals rectangular with wavy margins. Rounded leaves. 4–12 in. Eastern side of Cascades–Sierra Nevada; Great Basin.
JUNE–SEPT.

ANGLESTEM ERIOGONUM *Eriogonum angulosum*
The erect, *angled* stem whitish-haired. Basal leaves broadly *lanceolate* with *wavy* margins. A few linear leaves along the open-branched stems. Flower clusters in a broad bowl of rounded bracts. Each flower white and rose. 4–12 in. Sandy soils. Calif. and Great Basin. JUNE–JULY

PYROLA-LEAVED ERIOGONUM
Eriogonum pyrolaefolium
The shiny, dark green, oval to spatula-shaped leaves are in a flat basal cluster. A dense cluster of white flowers (aging reddish) and immediately below are 2 lancelike bracts. 1–6 in. Gravelly alpine slopes. N. Calif. to B.C. JULY–AUG.

SPURRY ERIOGONUM *Eriogonum spergulinum*
Note the 2 or 3 whorls of *thin linear leaves* along the well-branched stem and the broadly opened flowers on long *thread-like pedicels.* Flowers white with rose midribs. 4–20 in. Dry mt. slopes. Cen. Wash. to s.-cen. Calif. JUNE–SEPT.

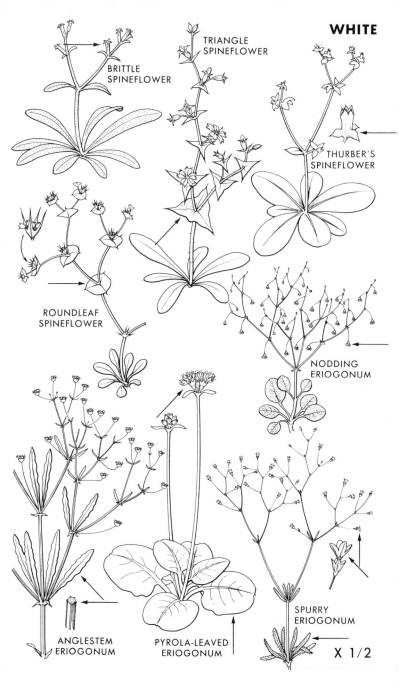

WHITE

BRITTLE SPINEFLOWER

TRIANGLE SPINEFLOWER

THURBER'S SPINEFLOWER

ROUNDLEAF SPINEFLOWER

NODDING ERIOGONUM

ANGLESTEM ERIOGONUM

PYROLA-LEAVED ERIOGONUM

SPURRY ERIOGONUM

X 1/2

4 OR 6 PETALS; TINY TUBULAR
FLOWERS IN CLUSTERS

BUCKWHEAT FAMILY (Polygonaceae)
See also pp. W 34–38; Y 134–38; R 276–78.

NAKED ERIOGONUM *Eriogonum nudum*
Tall *naked* stems. A flat basal cluster of dark green, oval leaves
below the stems. Each leaf *long-petioled* and with clumps of
white woolly hair. Flower cluster bracts oblong. Flowers white
to pale pink or pale yellow. Petals broadly oblong. ½–3 ft.
Very common in dry open places. Pacific States. MAY–NOV.

ONION-HEAD ERIOGONUM *Eriogonum latens*
The large *round head* of numerous small white flowers is on a
long leafless stem. It resembles the flower head of the garden
onion. The rectangular to oval leaf blades and elongated
petiole covered by dense velvety gray hairs. 1–2 ft. Rocky
slopes. Eastern side of Sierra Nevada, adjacent White Mts.
JULY–SEPT.

COAST ERIOGONUM *Eriogonum latifolium*
Leaves in cluster near base of stems, each leaf blade *oblong* and
wavy-margined, densely white woolly underneath. Upper
stems leafless. Flowers white to rose. 1–2 ft. Cliffs along coast.
Cen. Calif. coast to Ore. JUNE–SEPT.

TALL ERIOGONUM *Eriogonum elatum*
The large greenish *arrowheadlike* leaves mostly basal. Flower
stems open and loosely branched. Each flower cream, aging
reddish. 1–3 ft. Dry open places. Great Basin and northern
edge of Mojave Desert. JUNE–SEPT.

LONG-STEMMED ERIOGONUM *Eriogonum elongatum*
At intervals along the gray erect stems are *whorls* of *gray
lanceolate leaves.* Flowers white or tinted rose. 1–4 ft. Dry
rocky slopes. Calif. South Coast Ranges to Baja. AUG.–NOV.

SLENDER ERIOGONUM *Eriogonum viridescens*
The white to pinkish flower clusters are on long *threadlike*
pedicels. Lancelike grayish leaves are at *each* branching point
on stem. The basal rosette leaves are oval to rounded. 4–12 in.
Dry plains. W. Mojave Desert and southern edges of Central
Valley of Calif. MAY–OCT.

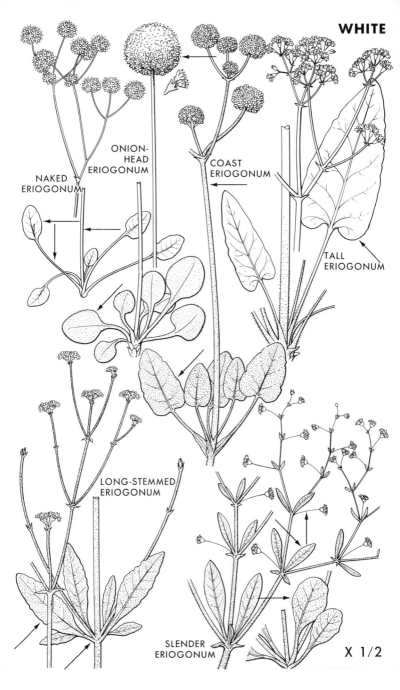

WHITE

NAKED
ERIOGONUM

ONION-
HEAD
ERIOGONUM

COAST
ERIOGONUM

TALL
ERIOGONUM

LONG-STEMMED
ERIOGONUM

SLENDER
ERIOGONUM

X 1/2

5 TO MANY PETALS;
NUMEROUS STAMENS

BUTTERCUP FAMILY (Ranunculaceae)
See also pp. W 42; Y 154-58; O 226;
R 280-82; B 354-56, 382; G 404.

MARSH MARIGOLD *Caltha leptosepala*
Note the fleshy, *round* to *kidney-shaped* leaves. Large solitary
flowers on leafless stems well above the leaves. 6–12 in. Wet
mt. marshes. Pacific States. MAY–AUG.

WESTERN BANEBERRY *Actaea rubra*
Leaves pinnate with the lateral leaflets narrow and toothed,
while the terminal leaflet is *maple-like*. Small flowers in
terminal clusters. Shiny red or white berries. 1–3 ft. Moist mt.
forests, streambanks. Pacific States. MAY–JULY

WESTERN PASQUE FLOWER *Anemone occidentalis*
Large *bowl-like* flowers cream to yellow-green. Pinnate leaves
divided into many lacy linear segments. Later the numerous
long-tailed seeds resemble an *upturned mop*. ½–2 ft. Subalpine and alpine rocky slopes. Sierra Nevada and north to
B.C. MAY–SEPT.

DRUMMOND'S ANEMONE *Anemone drummondii*
Flowers in a *flat wheel*. Petals white with a fluorescent blue
tint on their backs. Pinnate leaves with short linear segments.
4–12 in. Open slopes, mid-altitude to alpine. Sierra Nevada,
nw. Calif. north to B.C. MAY–AUG.

COLUMBIA WINDFLOWER *Anemone deltoidea*
Single slender stems with a solitary leaf of *3 oval leaflets* below
the solitary white flower. 4–12 in. Dry conifer forests.
Nw. Calif. to w. Wash. APRIL–JULY

WESTERN WOOD ANEMONE *Anemone lyallii*
Slender stems with pinnate leaves of 3 leaflets. Each main leaf
is *long-petioled*. 4–12 in. Moist forests at low elevations. West
of Cascades south to cen. Calif. APRIL–JULY

COVILLE'S COLUMBINE *Aquilegia pubescens*
Large, upright to nodding, *5-spurred* flowers. Petals white with
tints of blue, pink, or yellow. Pinnate leaves of 3 or 9 leaflets.
½–2½ ft. Alpine rockpiles and cliffs. Sierra Nevada.
JUNE–AUG.

AMERICAN GLOBEFLOWER *Trollius laxus*
Solitary flowers on a *leafy stem*. Leaves divided into 5 fingerlike
lobes, each lobe of 3 smaller segments. Flowers as snow melts.
½–1½ ft. Wet alpine meadows. Wash. and B.C. MAY–AUG.

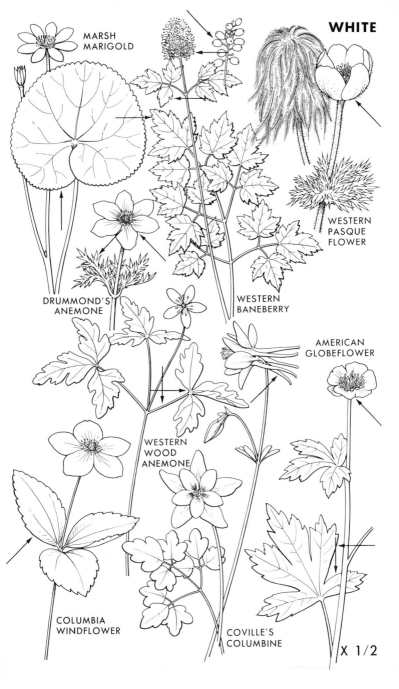

MARSH MARIGOLD

WHITE

WESTERN PASQUE FLOWER

DRUMMOND'S ANEMONE

WESTERN BANEBERRY

AMERICAN GLOBEFLOWER

WESTERN WOOD ANEMONE

COLUMBIA WINDFLOWER

COVILLE'S COLUMBINE

X 1/2

4, 5, OR 6 PETALS;
NUMEROUS STAMENS

BUTTERCUP FAMILY (Ranunculaceae)
See also pp. W 40; Y 154–58; O 226;
R 280–82; B 354–56, 382; G 404.

LOBB'S BUTTERCUP *Ranunculus lobbii*
The floating leaves are of *3 oblong lobes* and the submerged ones are *threadlike*. Flowers 5-petaled. Floating stems to 3 ft. Shallow water. Lowlands of Pacific States. FEB.–MAY

WATER BUTTERCUP *Ranunculus aquatilis*
Entirely of submerged leaves divided into many *threadlike filaments*. Flowers 5-petaled. Submerged floating stems 1–5 ft. Ponds and slow streams. Pacific States. APRIL–AUG.

WATERFALL BUTTERCUP *Ranunculus hystriculus*
Fleshy *maple-like leaves*. 5 white to pale yellow petals. 6–18 in. Growing about rocky cliffs where sprayed by waterfalls. Sierra Nevada. APRIL–JUNE

BARBERRY FAMILY (Berberidaceae)
See also p. Y 158.

VANILLA LEAF *Achlys triphylla*
The *single large pinnate* leaf has a rounded outline but is composed of 3 leaflets. Numerous small flowers are in a slender spike. 10–20 in. Moist forests. B.C. south to n. Calif. on western side of Cascades. APRIL–JULY

NORTHERN INSIDE-OUT FLOWER
Vancouveria hexandra
Flower petals *swept backward*. Flower pedicel *hairless*. The squarish pinnate leaflets numerous. 4–15 in. Deep shade. Western side of Cascades to nw. Calif. MAY–JULY

REDWOOD INSIDE-OUT FLOWER
(not shown) *Vancouveria planipetala*
Similar to preceding, but flower *pedicels glandular*-haired. ½–2 ft. Redwood forests. Calif. to sw. Ore. MAY–JUNE

LIZARD TAIL FAMILY (Saururaceae)

YERBA MANSA *Anemopsis californica*
The many small flowers are in a *tall cone* above a circle of petal-like *white bracts*. Leaf blades oblong to oval. 2–6 in. ½–2 ft. Alkaline and saline marshes. Mostly Calif.
MARCH–SEPT.

BLEEDING HEART FAMILY (Fumariaceae)
See also pp. Y 158; R 280.

DUTCHMANS BREECHES *Dicentra cucullaria*
Note the nodding, white to pale pink, *2-spurred* flowers resembling tiny pairs of upside-down pantaloons. Pinnate leaves divided into linear segments. 8–16 in. Moist woods. Mts. of e. Ore. and Wash., Columbia River. MARCH–MAY

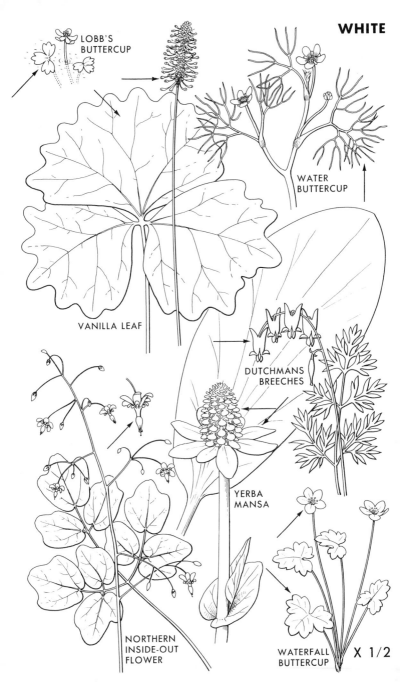

WHITE

LOBB'S BUTTERCUP

WATER BUTTERCUP

VANILLA LEAF

DUTCHMANS BREECHES

YERBA MANSA

NORTHERN INSIDE-OUT FLOWER

WATERFALL BUTTERCUP

X 1/2

5 PETALS; NUMEROUS STAMENS

Mallow Family (Malvaceae)
See also pp. 286–90.

CALIFORNIA HIBISCUS   *Hibiscus californicus*
Large white flowers have a *red spot* in the interior. Stamens are combined into an elongated central shaft. Leaves heart-shaped. 3–6 ft. Moist riverbanks. Delta region of Central Valley of Calif.   Aug.–Sept.

MAPLE-LEAVED SIDALCEA   *Sidalcea malachroides*
Note the *maple-like* leaves. Flowers in dense spikelike clusters. Stamens combined into a central column. 2–5 ft. Disturbed places along the coast. Monterey, Calif. to s. Ore.   May–July

ALKALI MALLOW   *Sida hederacea*
Note the *rounded* to *kidney-shaped* leaves along the *prostrate* stem, all short velvety-haired. Creamy, bowl-shaped flowers with the stamens fused into a central column. 4–15 in. Dry places. Calif. and Great Basin.   May–Oct.

Loasa Family (Loasaceae)
See also p. Y 160.

WHITE-BRACTED STICKLEAF   *Mentzelia involucrata*
Leaves somewhat triangular with *many coarse teeth.* The satiny-cream to pale-yellow flowers are solitary and cuplike on top of an inferior ovary. Stems and leaves strongly haired. 4–12 in. Rocky places. Mojave, Colorado Deserts.   Jan.–May

DESERT ROCK NETTLE   *Eucnide urens*
Leaves *rounded* with coarse teeth and are covered with velvety white hairs. Large cuplike creamy flowers on top of an inferior ovary. Rounded bushlike plants. 1–2 ft. Dry rocky places. Mojave Desert.   April–June

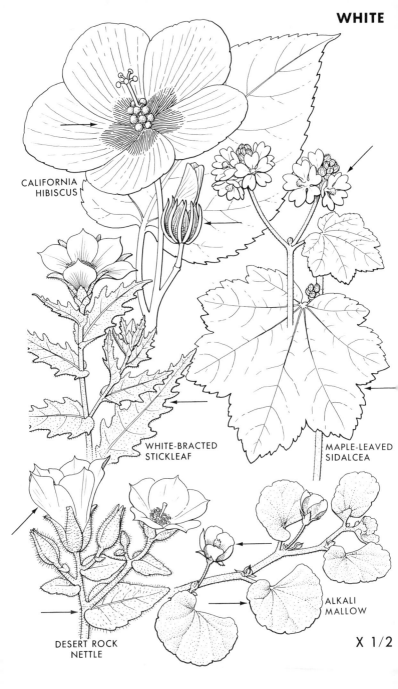

CALIFORNIA
HIBISCUS

WHITE-BRACTED
STICKLEAF

MAPLE-LEAVED
SIDALCEA

DESERT ROCK
NETTLE

ALKALI
MALLOW

X 1/2

5 PETALS; SPECIALIZED LEAVES; INSECTIVOROUS OR SAPROPHYTIC

SUNDEW FAMILY (Droseraceae)

ROUNDLEAF SUNDEW *Drosera rotundifolia*
The surfaces of the *rounded leaf blades* are covered with many red-stalked hairs with glandular tips. Small insects become trapped in the hairs and are digested for their nitrogen content. A slender stalk above the leaves has small white flowers. 2–12 in. Mossy bogs. Pacific States. JUNE–SEPT.

LINEARLEAF SUNDEW *Drosera anglica*
Similar to Roundleaf Sundew. Leaves *oblong to linear.* 2–12 in. Mossy bogs. B.C. to Ore.; rare in Calif. JUNE–AUG.

PITCHER PLANT FAMILY (Sarraceniaceae)

CALIFORNIA PITCHER PLANT
Darlingtonia californica
Note the raised *cobralike* appearance of the leaves with 2 mustache-like appendages. Insects are trapped inside the hollow leaves and provide additional nitrogen for the plant. Single nodding flowers with creamy sepals and dark red petals. ½–2 ft. Acid marshes. Siskiyous of sw. Ore. to n. Sierra Nevada. APRIL–JUNE

WINTERGREEN FAMILY (Pyrolaceae)
See also pp. W 48; R 296.

INDIAN PIPE *Monotropa uniflora*
Note the translucent waxy-white stems and the *single, nodding,* bell-like flower. The white to pink flowers turn black with age. Leaves small colorless scales. A saprophyte using decaying leaves for food. 4–12 in. Dark moist woods. Calif. North Coast Ranges north to B.C. JUNE–AUG.

AMERICAN PINE SAP *Monotropa hypopithys*
Note the *several* nodding, waxy-white to yellowish, bell-like flowers. Occasionally red in our area. A saprophyte in dark conifer forests. 2–10 in. Nw. Calif. to B.C. MAY–AUG.

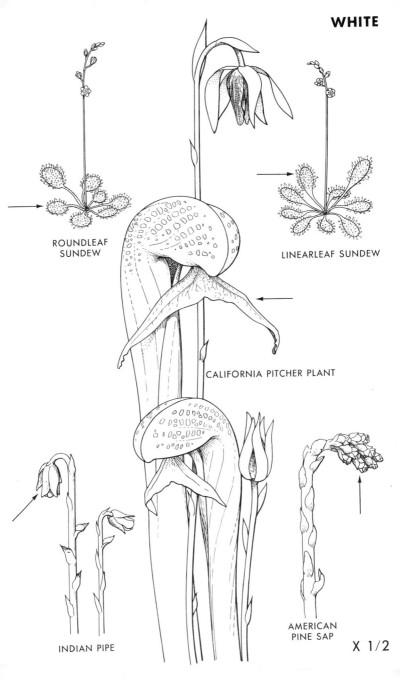

WHITE

ROUNDLEAF
SUNDEW

LINEARLEAF SUNDEW

CALIFORNIA PITCHER PLANT

INDIAN PIPE

AMERICAN
PINE SAP

X 1/2

5 PETALS; FLOWERS NODDING, WAXY

WINTERGREEN FAMILY (Pyrolaceae)
See also pp. W 46; R 296.

LITTLE PRINCES PINE   *Chimaphila menziesii*
Note the *lancelike* to linear leaves with small sharp teeth. The
1–3 waxy *crownlike* flowers becoming pinkish with age. Shady
conifer woods. Mts. of Pacific States.   JUNE–AUG.

WHITE-VEINED WINTERGREEN   *Pyrola picta*
Note the *white-veined* leaves, broadly oval in shape. The
waxy-white flowers have the styles *bent* to 1 side. 4–8 in. Dry
shady forests. Mts. of Pacific States.   JUNE–AUG.

ONE-SIDED WINTERGREEN   *Pyrola secunda*
The white to greenish flowers are arranged *along 1 side* of the
erect to drooping flower stem. The oval leaves a shiny green.
4–8 in. Dry shady forests. Mts. of Pacific States.   JUNE–SEPT.

ONE-FLOWERED MONESES   *Moneses uniflora*
Note the *single,* nodding, waxy-white to pale pink flower on a
2–4 in. leafless stem above the oval leaves with small sharp
teeth. 2–5 in. Rotting wood humus of cool shady forests. Mts.
of Pacific States.   MAY–JULY

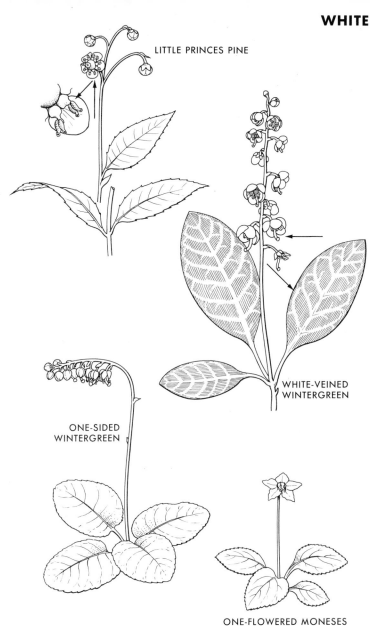

LITTLE PRINCES PINE

WHITE-VEINED
WINTERGREEN

ONE-SIDED
WINTERGREEN

ONE-FLOWERED MONESES

X 1/2

5 SHOWY PETALS; 5 NUTLIKE SEEDS

Meadow Foam Family (Limnanthaceae)
All species of Meadow Foam develop 3–5 large
nutlike seeds. The various species are found
in wet to moist depressions in open fields.

WHITE MEADOW FOAM　　　　　*Limnanthes alba*
The flower is bowl-shaped. The sepals have long, fine, white
hairs on the inner surface. The hairy linear leaves divided 1 or 2
times. Petals white, aging pink. 4–12 in. Central Valley of
Calif.　　　　　　　　　　　　　　　　　　　　April–June

SLENDER MEADOW FOAM　　　　*Limnanthes gracilis*
Flowers bowl-shaped and petals *without colored veins.* Stems
and leaves hairless. The 5 pinnate leaflets each divided into 3–5
oblong segments. 4–8 in. Lake shores, meadows. Mts. east of
San Diego, Calif.　　　　　　　　　　　　　　　April–May

MOUNTAIN MEADOW FOAM　　　*Limnanthes montana*
Flowers bell-shaped, each petal without colored veins or hairs.
Sepals hairy. The pinnate leaves divided into 3–5 oblong or
toothed segments. 4–8 in. Southern foothills of w. Sierra
Nevada.　　　　　　　　　　　　　　　　　　　March–May

DOUGLAS'S MEADOW FOAM　　　*Limnanthes douglasii*
Flowers bowl-shaped with the *inner portion yellow* in ssp.
douglasii, and each petal has a U-*shaped band* of short hairs at
the base of the inner surface. Each pinnate leaf is divided into
5–11 leaflets which may be entire or 3–5 toothed. 4–15 in. Calif.
Coast Ranges and western foothills of Sierra Nevada. Other
subspecies that vary from these features are: (1) ssp. *nivea* has
dark, prominent, purple veins in the petals; Calif. Coast
Ranges; (2) ssp. *rosea* has pink veins in the petals and the
entire petal ages to rose; grassland ponds along western base of
Sierra Nevada; (3) ssp. *sulphurea* (not shown) has bright
yellow petals; found only at Point Reyes Natl. Seashore, Calif.
　　　　　　　　　　　　　　　　　　　　　　March–May

WOOLLY MEADOW FOAM　　　　*Limnanthes floccosa*
White *woolly hairs* on *all* plant parts. Sepals and petals are of
equal length. Leaves with 5–7 pinnate leaflets, each leaflet
simple to 3-parted in lance-elliptic segments. Petals white
aging to pink. 2–8 in. N. Central Valley of Calif. to s. Ore.
　　　　　　　　　　　　　　　　　　　　　　March–May

STRIPED MEADOW FOAM　　　　*Limnanthes striata*
Flower bell-shaped, each petal with brown-purple veins and *2
rows of hairs* at the inner base. 4–12 in. At low elevations in
the northern half of w. Sierra Nevada foothills. March–May

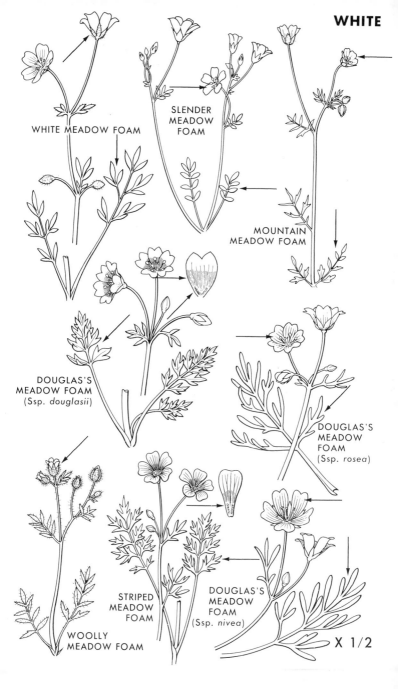

WHITE

WHITE MEADOW FOAM

SLENDER MEADOW FOAM

MOUNTAIN MEADOW FOAM

DOUGLAS'S MEADOW FOAM
(Ssp. *douglasii*)

DOUGLAS'S MEADOW FOAM
(Ssp. *rosea*)

WOOLLY MEADOW FOAM

STRIPED MEADOW FOAM

DOUGLAS'S MEADOW FOAM
(Ssp. *nivea*)

X 1/2

5 PETALS; EQUAL SYMMETRY: TINY FLAX
5 PETALS; BILATERAL SYMMETRY: VIOLETS

FLAX FAMILY (Linaceae)
See also p. B 382.

THREADSTEM FLAX *Hesperolinon micranthum*
Note the widely branching, *threadlike stems* with many small
5-petaled flowers. Flowers white to pale pink. Leaves linear
and threadlike. 2–15 in. Common on hot open slopes. Calif.
and Ore. MAY–JULY

VIOLET FAMILY (Violaceae)
See also pp. Y 162–64, B 358.

TWO-EYED VIOLET *Viola ocellata*
The 2 side petals of the white flower each have near the base a
small *purple eyespot* and yellow banding. The lower lip petal is
purple-veined. Backs of the 2 upper petals are a deep purple.
Leaves nearly triangular with strongly toothed margins.
4–12 in. Rocky banks. Calif. Coast Ranges north to s. Ore.
APRIL–JUNE

CANADA VIOLET *Viola canadensis*
Note the *broadly triangular* lip petal and that the 2 upper
petals are *widely separated* and *not* reflexed backward. The
middle pair of petals are upright. Petals yellow-based, the
lower 3 with some purple speckles. All petals purple-tinted on
the back. Flowers long-stemmed. Leaves heart-shaped.
4–15 in. Moist woods. Ore. to B.C. MAY–JULY

WEDGE-LEAVED VIOLET *Viola cuneata*
Note the *wedge-shaped* leaf base. The white flowers have
purple eyespots on the 2 side petals but *no yellow banding* as in
the Two-eyed Violet. Petal backs purplish throughout except
for the yellow spur. 2–8 in. Damp open woods. Calif. North
Coast and Siskiyous into Ore. MARCH–JUNE

MACLOSKEY'S VIOLET *Viola macloskeyi*
Note the 2 upper petals are *reflexed backward* and the tips are
close to each other, while the middle 2 are turned *downward*.
Flower with purple veins in the lower 3 petals. The flowers are
stemless. Leaves rounded to kidney-shaped. 1–5 in. Open wet
meadows. Mts. of Pacific States. MAY–AUG.

WHITE

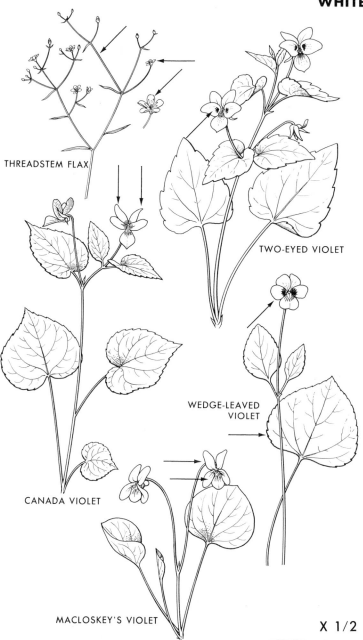

THREADSTEM FLAX

TWO-EYED VIOLET

CANADA VIOLET

WEDGE-LEAVED VIOLET

MACLOSKEY'S VIOLET

X 1/2

5 DEEPLY CLEFT PETALS; SEPALS FREE

PINK FAMILY (Caryophyllaceae)
See also pp. W 56–60; R 246, 282.

COMMON CHICKWEED Alien   *Stellaria media*
Note the *single line* of hairs running down *1 side* of the stem.
Leaves *oval*. Petals 2-parted, shorter than the sepals. ½–1½ ft.
Common. Pacific States.   FEB.–OCT.

STICKY STARWORT   *Stellaria jamesiana*
Petals triangular in outline with the tips squared and with a
short V notch. Long linear leaf pairs. Sticky-stemmed.
4–12 in. Mt. forests. Pacific States.   MAY–JULY

LONG-STALKED STARWORT   *Stellaria longipes*
Stems erect with *lance-linear* leaves. Flowers solitary on *long
pedicels*. Petals 2-parted. Sepals and petals of equal length.
4–12 in. Mt. meadows. Pacific States.   MAY–AUG.

BEACH STARWORT   *Stellaria littoralis*
Leaves broadly triangular to oval. Each petal bilobed nearly to
base. Sticky-stemmed. ½–2 ft. Sand dunes along coast. San
Francisco north to Ore. border.   MARCH–JULY

JAGGED CHICKWEED Alien   *Holosteum umbellatum*
Stem erect with a dense *umbrellalike* flower cluster. Petal tips
jagged. Leaves linear in a basal rosette. 3–12 in. Shady places.
Mostly e. Wash. and Ore.   APRIL–JUNE

LARGE MOUSE EAR Alien   *Cerastium vulgatum*
The oval leaves hairy and *stalkless*. Stems sticky-haired.
Petals broadly notched. Sepals and petals of equal length.
4–15 in. Common in lawns. Pacific States.   FEB.–NOV.

STICKY MOUSE EAR Alien   *Cerastium viscosum*
Sepals *sharply pointed* from long sticky hairs. Petals notched,
often shorter than the sepals. Leaves oval. Stem erect, sticky-
haired. 4–12 in. Pacific States.   FEB.–JUNE

UMBRELLA CHICKWEED   *Stellaria umbellata*
Small flowers on *long pedicels* in a loose umbrella. Petals
minute or absent. Stems long and usually sprawling. Great
Basin and south to Calif., where occasional.   APRIL–AUG.

CORN SPURRY Alien   *Spergula arvensis*
Linear leaves in *whorls*. Flowers inconspicuous. 4–15 in.
Disturbed places. West of Cascades–Sierra Nevada.
                                                 ALL YEAR

MEADOW CHICKWEED   *Cerastium arvense*
Leaves *linear*. Petals broad, sharply notched. Sepals shorter
than petals. 4–12 in. Pacific States.   FEB.–OCT.

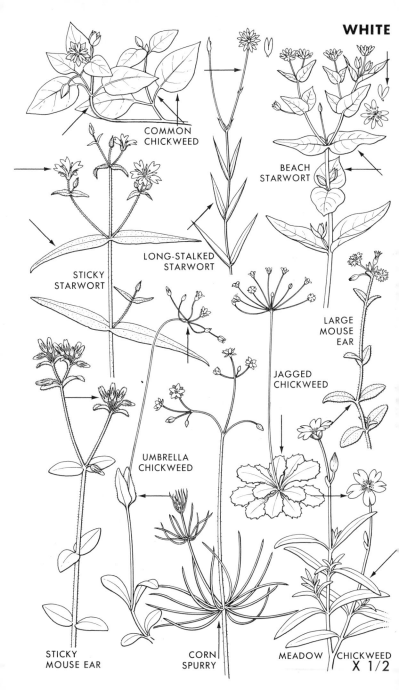

WHITE

COMMON CHICKWEED

BEACH STARWORT

LONG-STALKED STARWORT

STICKY STARWORT

LARGE MOUSE EAR

JAGGED CHICKWEED

UMBRELLA CHICKWEED

STICKY MOUSE EAR

CORN SPURRY

MEADOW CHICKWEED
X 1/2

5 LINEAR PETALS; SEPALS FREE

PINK FAMILY (Caryophyllaceae)
See also pp. W 54–60; R 246, 282.

NUTTALL'S SANDWORT *Arenaria nuttallii*
Both sepals and petals are *elongated* and *sharp pointed*. Sepal backs with 3 green lines, but at times appearing as 1. Plant a low cushion with flat leaves crowded along the stem. 2–6 in. Dry sandy places. Pacific States. MAY–AUG.

BEAUTIFUL SANDWORT *Arenaria capillaris*
Leaves narrow, *grasslike*. Sepals short, squat, and with multiple lines on the back, 2 of which are very distinct. Broad, slightly bilobed petals. Grows in low mats. 1–2 ft. Rocky places. Cascades and Olympic Mts. JUNE–AUG.

BALLHEAD SANDWORT *Arenaria congesta*
Flowers in *headlike* clusters. 4–12 in. Rocky slopes. Desert to alpine zone. Mostly Cascades–Sierra Nevada. JUNE–AUG.

MOJAVE SANDWORT *Arenaria macradenia*
Base of sepal backs *bulged*. Plants tall with relatively long leaves. 4–18 in. All s. Calif. APRIL–JULY

NEEDLELEAF SANDWORT *Arenaria aculeata*
Petals narrowly bilobed, sepals triangular with 3 lines close to each other on the back. 4–10 in. Great Basin. MAY–JULY

ALPINE SANDWORT *Arenaria obtusiloba*
Similar to Nuttall's Sandwort. Sepals rounded with *purplish tips* and 3 lines on the backs. Petals bilobed. 1–3 in. Alpine rocky places. Pacific States. JUNE–SEPT.

RUBY SANDWORT *Arenaria rubella*
Similar to Nuttall's Sandwort. Sepals oval, but pointed and with 3 lines on the backs. Petals rounded. 1–4 in. Dry alpine slopes. Pacific States. JUNE–AUG.

KING'S SANDWORT *Arenaria kingii*
Sepal backs have a central dark line within a green area, the green area with outer papery margins. Petals rounded. 4–8 in. Common. Rocky slopes. Sierra Nevada, Great Basin.
JUNE–AUG.

RYDBERG'S SANDWORT *Arenaria confusa*
Leaves *short but broad*. Sepals triangular with 1 line on the backs. Petals narrow. 4–12 in. Mts. of s. Calif. JULY–AUG.

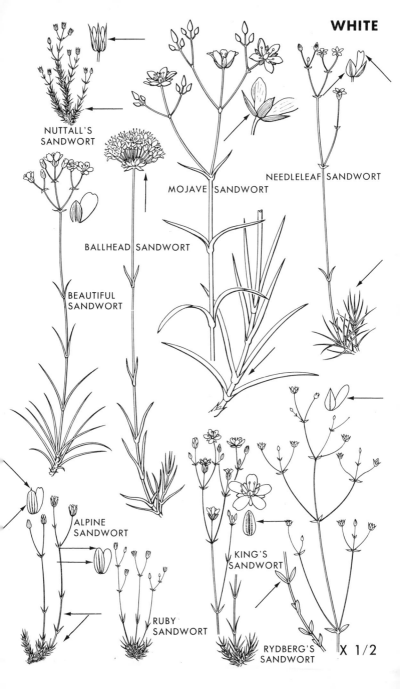

WHITE

NUTTALL'S
SANDWORT

MOJAVE SANDWORT

NEEDLELEAF SANDWORT

BALLHEAD SANDWORT

BEAUTIFUL
SANDWORT

ALPINE
SANDWORT

RUBY
SANDWORT

KING'S
SANDWORT

RYDBERG'S
SANDWORT

X 1/2

5 CLEFT PETALS; TUBULAR CALYX

PINK FAMILY (Caryophyllaceae)
See also pp. W 54-60; R 246, 282.

Note: Most Catchflys flower as the afternoon shadows begin, and are whitish. Become pinkish and wither when struck by morning sun. Sticky-haired, often catching small flies.

MOUNTAIN CATCHFLY *Silene montana*
Each petal tip is divided into *4 subequal linear* segments, while the inner teeth are of many threads. White or aging pink. $\frac{1}{2}$-1$\frac{1}{2}$ ft. Dry slopes 4000–10,000 ft. Sierra Nevada to s. Ore.
JUNE–AUG.

DOUGLAS'S CATCHFLY *Silene douglasii*
Flowers cream, becoming pink or purple tinted. Each petal *barely bilobed,* its 2 inner teeth linear. 4–15 in. Open slopes at mid-elevations in the mts. Pacific States. MAY–AUG.

BABYS BREATH Alien *Gypsophila paniculata*
Stems well-branched with numerous *tiny* rounded *bowl-like* flowers. Flowers have an unpleasant sour odor. Leaves linear. 1–3 ft. Dry areas. Great Basin. JUNE–AUG.

PARRY'S CATCHFLY *Silene parryi*
Each petal tip is divided into 4 *rounded lobes,* the inner 2 being somewhat larger. The inner 2 teeth on the petal are short but broad and with a wavy margin. Flowers white, but aging to a dark red. Mts. of Ore. to B.C. JULY–AUG.

SCOULER'S CATCHFLY *Silene scouleri*
Note the *triangular* greenish sepal tips on the tubular calyx. Petals white or tinted green or pink, each tip divided into 4 lobes with the center 2 much larger. Petal tip lobing varies from the coast to inland forms. The 2 *broad* inner toothlike appendages may be entire or of several lobes. The gray, velvety, spatula-shaped leaves are mostly basal. $\frac{1}{2}$-3 ft. Coastal bluffs to forest openings. Cen. Calif. north to B.C.
MAY–AUG.

MENZIES' CATCHFLY *Silene menziesii*
Flowers white. Each petal is of 2 broad diverging and rounded lobes. The inner petal teeth are small or absent. 2–8 in. Openings in damp woods. Mts. of Pacific States. MAY–AUG.

BRIDGES' CATCHFLY *Silene bridgesii*
Flowers dirty white. Each petal tip has 2 equal lobes. The inner 2 petal teeth linear or slightly irregular. $\frac{1}{2}$-1$\frac{1}{2}$ ft. Dry open slopes below 8000 ft. Sierra Nevada north to Mt. Shasta.
JUNE–JULY

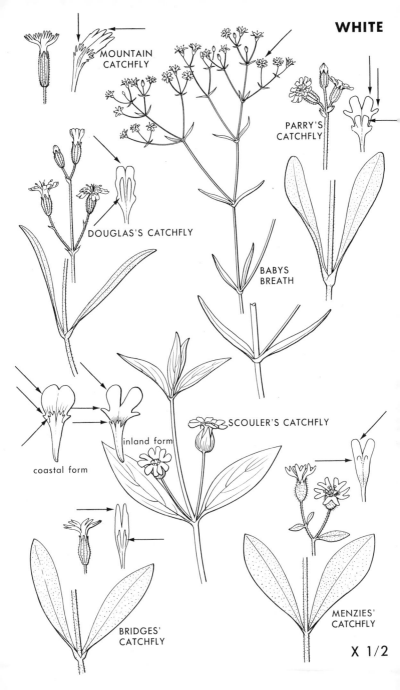

WHITE

MOUNTAIN CATCHFLY

PARRY'S CATCHFLY

DOUGLAS'S CATCHFLY

BABYS BREATH

coastal form

inland form

SCOULER'S CATCHFLY

BRIDGES' CATCHFLY

MENZIES' CATCHFLY

X 1/2

5 CLEFT PETALS; TUBULAR CALYX

PINK FAMILY (Caryophyllaceae)
See also pp. W 54–60; R 246, 282.

Note: Most Catchflys flower as the afternoon shadows begin, and are whitish. Become pinkish and wither when struck by morning sun. Sticky-haired, often catching small flies.

OREGON CATCHFLY   *Silene oregana*
Each petal tip is divided into 4 narrow lobes, with the 2 inner ones *longer* and *forked*. The inner 4 petal teeth are linear. Flowers white, aging pink. 1–2 ft. Open woods.   JUNE–SEPT.

GRAY'S CATCHFLY   *Silene grayi*
Similar to Sargent's Catchfly. Each petal tip 4-lobed; the inner 2 are broad, while the *outer* 2 are *shorter* and *linear*. Flowers white, becoming rosy with age. 4–10 in. Alpine slopes. Mts. of n. Calif. and s. Ore.   JULY–AUG.

HOOKER'S INDIAN PINK   *Silene hookeri*
The long linear petal tips are divided into 4 deep lobes with the inner 2 somewhat broader. The inner petal has 2 broad tooth-like appendages. Flowers white or pink in a few areas. Open woods. Nw. Calif., s. Ore.   APRIL–JUNE

EVENING LYCHNIS Alien   *Lychnis alba*
The large white pinwheel flowers have deeply bilobed tips. Opens in late afternoon. 2–4 ft. Disturbed places, grainfields. Pacific States.   JUNE–AUG.

BELL CATCHFLY   *Silene campanulata*
Note the *broad, oval,* sticky leaves. Flowers nodding, the calyx enlarged and *bell-like*. Each petal tip of 4 sections, each further divided to make 8 *linear lobes.* 4–12 in. Thickets. N. Calif., s. Ore.   MAY–AUG.

SARGENT'S CATCHFLY   *Silene sargentii*
Each petal tip with 4 lobes; the 2 inner ones *broad* and the 2 outer lobes *shorter* and *pointed.* The calyx a long linear tube with purplish ribs. Flowers white, aging pink. 1–5 in. Alpine slopes. Sierra Nevada.   JULY–AUG.

LEMMON'S CATCHFLY   *Silene lemmonii*
Flowers *nodding.* Petal tips divided into 4 linear lobes with 4 inner short linear teeth. Flowers white or tinted yellowish to pink. $\frac{1}{2}$–$1\frac{1}{2}$ ft. Common. Open woods. Mts. of Calif. and s. Ore.   JUNE–AUG.

COMMON CATCHFLY Alien   *Silene gallica*
Flowers white or tinted pink, each petal tip is *rounded* with 2 inner toothlike appendages. Calyx tube with 10 purplish ribs. 4–20 in. Common. Pacific States.   FEB.–JULY

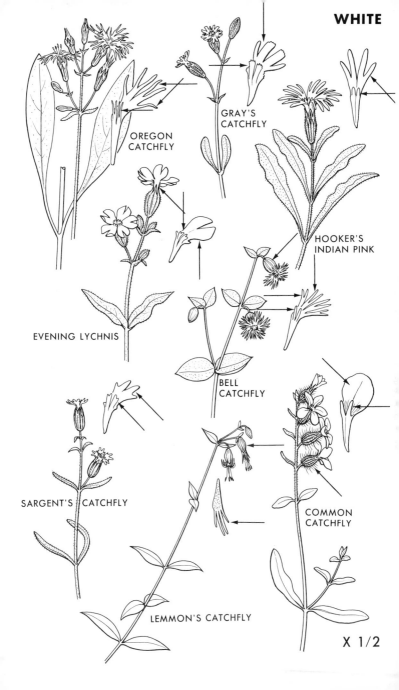

WHITE

OREGON CATCHFLY

GRAY'S CATCHFLY

HOOKER'S INDIAN PINK

EVENING LYCHNIS

BELL CATCHFLY

SARGENT'S CATCHFLY

COMMON CATCHFLY

LEMMON'S CATCHFLY

X 1/2

5 PETALS; FLOWERS IN UMBEL CLUSTER; MILKY SAP

Milkweed Family (Asclepiadaceae)
See also p. R 298.

SHOWY MILKWEED *Asclepias speciosa*
Note the long *curving toothlike hoods,* creamy or tinted pink. A curved horn protrudes toward the central column. White velvety leaves are oval to oblong in opposite pairs. 1–4 ft. Common. Calif. and Great Basin. May–Aug.

NARROW-LEAVED MILKWEED *Asclepias fascicularis*
The long *linear leaves* in whorls of 3–6 are generally hairless and folded upward. Flowers white to greenish- or purple-tinted. 2–4 ft. Dry places. Pacific States. June–Sept.

HUMBOLDT MILKWEED *Asclepias cryptoceras*
Stem *prostrate.* The opposite-paired, fleshy leaves are rounded to oval. The hoods rounded, the 2 inner *edges raised into slender points.* Flowers white to greenish. 4–12 in. Gravelly slopes. Great Basin. April–June

WOOLLY MILKWEED *Asclepias vestita*
Both leaves and stem white woolly-haired. Each rounded hood has a *short, blunt peg* protruding. The long oblong leaves in opposite pairs. ½–2 ft. Dry fields. S. Central Valley of Calif. and w. Mojave Desert. May–June

INDIAN MILKWEED *Asclepias eriocarpa*
White woolly leaves *lancelike,* in whorls of 3–4, rarely in opposite pairs. Each hood has a *slender* pointed *horn curving* inward. Flowers creamy, or tinted purple. 1–4 ft. Dry fields. Calif. June–Aug.

DESERT MILKWEED *Asclepias erosa*
The hoods rounded with a strongly curved horn protruding. The *opposite pairs* of *leaves* are broadly oblong to oval. 2–3 ft. S. Central Valley of Calif. and Mojave, Colorado Deserts. May–July

RUSH MILKWEED *Asclepias subulata*
Note the *narrow toothlike petals.* Flower clusters on whitish rushlike stems which have *no leaves.* 1–6 ft. Mojave, Colorado Deserts to Baja. March–Dec.

SMOOTH MILKVINE *Sarcostemma hirtellum*
Note the *twining vine* with the umbrellalike clusters of flowers that have *hairless* petal edges. Leaves linear, silvery-haired. Flowers white to greenish-yellow. 3–7 ft. Common in washes. Mojave, Colorado Deserts. March–May

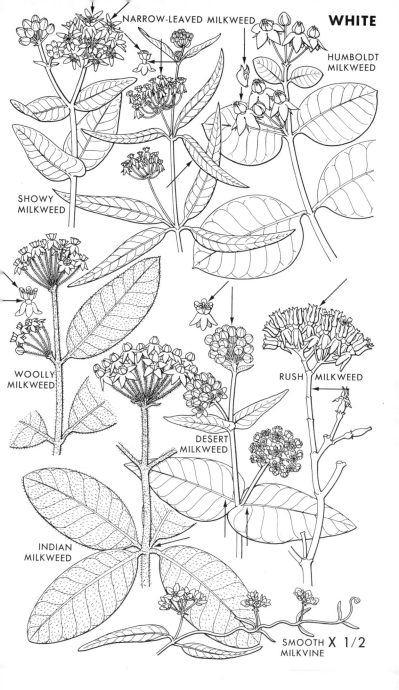

NARROW-LEAVED MILKWEED

WHITE

HUMBOLDT
MILKWEED

SHOWY
MILKWEED

WOOLLY
MILKWEED

RUSH MILKWEED

DESERT
MILKWEED

INDIAN
MILKWEED

SMOOTH **X 1/2**
MILKVINE

5 TINY PETALS; FLOWERS IN UMBEL: GIANT PLANTS

CALIFORNIA SPIKENARD   *Aralia californica*
GINSENG FAMILY   (Araliaceae)
Note the *ball-like umbels* of flowers in branching racemes at the top of very large fleshy stems with huge pinnate leaves (1–3 ft. long) and oval leaflets. Common in shady places along streams. 3–9 ft. Calif. and s. Ore.   JUNE–AUG.

CARROT FAMILY (Umbelliferae)
See also pp. W 66–68; Y 168–70; R 302; G 404.

POISON HEMLOCK Alien   *Conium maculatum*
The single towering stem is *spotted with purple.* Leaves fernlike. Very poisonous. 2–10 ft. Common in disturbed places. West of Cascades–Sierra Nevada.   MARCH–SEPT.

QUEEN ANNE'S LACE Alien   *Daucus carota*
Flowers in a *flat umbel.* Older flower clusters cuplike *"bird's nests."* Immediately below the flower umbel are stiff *3-forked* bracts. Leaves finely subdivided. Strong carrotlike odor. 1–3 ft. Open places. Pacific States.   ALL YEAR

HENDERSON'S ANGELICA   *Angelica hendersonii*
Stout-stemmed with the pinnate leaves divided 2–3 times into large somewhat *rounded leaflets* with finely toothed margins. Inflated basal leaf sheath 4–10 in. long. Flower petal *back hairy.* Fruits elongated, with 2 broad wings and 3 slightly raised ribs on the seed body. 1–3 ft. Coastal bluffs and dunes. Wash. to Calif.   JUNE–AUG.

WESTERN OXYPOLIS   *Oxypolis occidentalis*
Stem simple or few-branched with the pinnate leaves divided into *oblong leaflets.* Seeds elongated, with 2 broad wings. 2–4 ft. Streamsides and wet places in mts. San Bernardino Mts. of s. Calif. north to Ore.   JULY–AUG.

COW PARSNIP   *Heracleum lanatum*
The huge leaves are divided into *maple-like leaflets* that are often 1–2 ft. broad. Flower umbels ½–1 ft. wide on tall, stout, hollow stems. 3–8 ft. Moist thickets. Common along Pacific Coast.   MARCH–SEPT.

DOUGLAS'S WATER HEMLOCK   *Cicuta douglasii*
Note the stout hollow stems with the 1–3 times divided, pinnate leaves 1–1½ ft. long. Each leaflet narrowly lancelike with *sawtoothed edges.* Flowers in a flat-topped umbel. Fruits round with low corky ribs, the ribs broader than the intervals. Poisonous. 2–7 ft. Marshy places. Pacific States.   JUNE–SEPT.

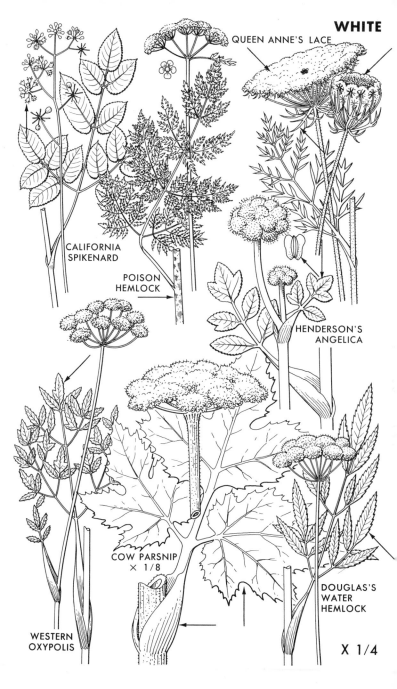

WHITE

QUEEN ANNE'S LACE

CALIFORNIA
SPIKENARD

POISON
HEMLOCK

HENDERSON'S
ANGELICA

COW PARSNIP
× 1/8

WESTERN
OXYPOLIS

DOUGLAS'S
WATER
HEMLOCK

X 1/4

5 TINY PETALS; FLOWERS IN UMBEL; SHORT, LACY, OR CUT LEAFLET LOBES

CARROT FAMILY (Umbelliferae)
See also pp. W 64–68; Y 168–70; R 302; G 404.

CELERY Alien   *Apium graveolens*
Pinnate leaves divided 3 times into toothed leaflets. The
flowers are in a rounded cluster. Fruits oblong with 5–15
narrow, slightly raised ribs. Strong celery odor. 2–4 ft.
Common in wet places at low elevations in Calif.   MAY–JULY

BEACH SILVERTOP   *Glehnia leiocarpa*
Note the *prostrate* rosette of pinnate leaves; each leaflet is
broadly oval with some velvety hairs. Fruits with many broad
wings. Coastal dunes. Calif. North Coast to B.C.   MAY–JUNE

AMERICAN OENANTHE   *Oenanthe sarmentosa*
Stems succulent, often reclining. The younger shoots are
curled, appearing almost *tendril-like.* Leaves divided once into
broad leaflets. Fruit broad with slightly raised ribs. 2–5 ft.
Marshes. West of Cascades–Sierra Nevada.   JUNE–OCT.

SHEPHERDS NEEDLE Alien   *Scandix pecten-veneris*
Note the many long *needlelike fruits* which appear soon after
the small white flowers. Leaves pinnate, divided 2–3 times into
fine linear segments. ½–1 ft. Disturbed places. Pacific States.
APRIL–JULY

CELERY-LEAVED LOVAGE   *Ligusticum apiifolium*
Similar to Celery. But the leaves are with *deeper cut* notches
and *without* broad areas of leaf blade. 1–5 ft. Shady thickets.
Western half of Pacific States.   JUNE–JULY

GRAY'S LOVAGE   *Ligusticum grayi*
Stems smooth with most of the pinnate leaves near the base.
Each leaflet is deeply divided once and *tipped by 2–3 teeth.*
½–2 ft. Dry mt. meadows. Pacific States.   JUNE–SEPT.

CANBY'S LOMATIUM   *Lomatium canbyi*
A low plant with *fine, lacy,* compound leaves. The oval seeds
have papery margins half as wide as the seed body. 4–8 in.
Rocky places. Great Basin.   MARCH–MAY

MARTINDALE'S LOMATIUM   *Lomatium martindalei*
Note the low cluster of pinnate leaves with the final leaflet
division having toothed margins. Fruits elongated with *thin
raised wings* as wide as the fruit body. 4–8 in. Rocky slopes at
high elevations. Coast Range and Cascades in Ore. north to
B.C.   MAY–AUG.

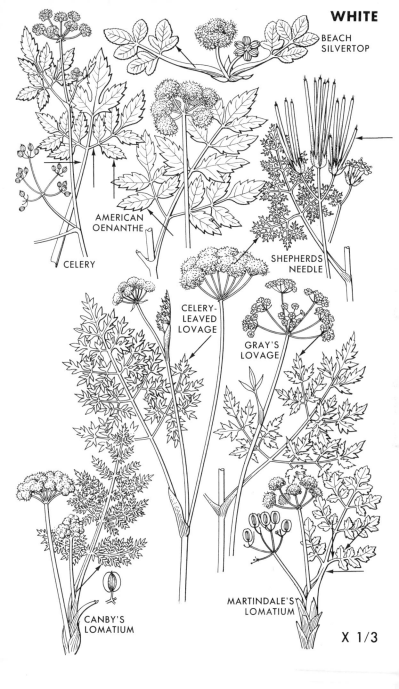

WHITE

BEACH
SILVERTOP

CELERY

AMERICAN
OENANTHE

SHEPHERDS
NEEDLE

CELERY-
LEAVED
LOVAGE

GRAY'S
LOVAGE

CANBY'S
LOMATIUM

MARTINDALE'S
LOMATIUM

X 1/3

5 TINY PETALS; FLOWERS IN UMBEL; SLENDER, SMOOTH-EDGED LEAFLETS

CARROT FAMILY (Umbelliferae)
See also W 64–66; Y 168–70; R 302; G 404.

RANGERS BUTTON *Sphenosciadium capitellatum*
Note the well separated *buttonlike* umbels of numerous small flowers. Large pinnate leaves. The leaflets are nearly linear with a few teeth on the upper half. 2–5 ft. Mt. marshes. Mts. of Calif. Ore., and Nevada. JULY–AUG.

PARISH'S YAMPAH *Perideridia parishii*
Leaves very simple, usually of 1 leaflet or occasionally up to 3 simple leaflets. The roots are elongated tapers. The roots of all Yampahs are edible and were an important Indian food. 1–3 ft. Damp mt. meadows. Mts. of Calif. and sw. Ore. JULY–SEPT.

KELLOGG'S YAMPAH *Perideridia kelloggii*
Stems stout with most of the pinnate leaves basal. Each leaf divided once or twice into linear, fernlike leaflets. The main leaflets *appear to rise* from the inflated leaf sheath. The roots are elongated tapers with a *wide swelling* near the lower tips. 2–5 ft. Open places below 4000 ft. Calif. Coast Ranges and western foothills of Sierra Nevada. JULY–AUG.

BOLANDER'S YAMPAH *Perideridia bolanderi*
Similar to Gairdner's Yampah below. Leaflets highly divided into short segments. Short fat radishlike root. ½–3 ft. Dry open rocky places. Sierra Nevada, Cascades in Ore. and Great Basin. MAY–AUG.

GAIRDNER'S YAMPAH *Perideridia gairdneri*
Stems slender with the pinnate leaves divided 1 or 2 times into similar linear-shaped divisions. Fruits *rounded.* 1–4 ft. Meadows at low to middle elevations. Pacific States. JUNE–AUG.

OREGON YAMPAH *Perideridia oregana*
Similar to Gairdner's Yampah. The 3 terminal leaflets often of equal length. Fruits elongated. Sausagelike roots. 1–2 ft. Open rocky meadows. Calif. and Ore. Coast Ranges; Cascades in Calif. through Ore. JUNE–AUG.

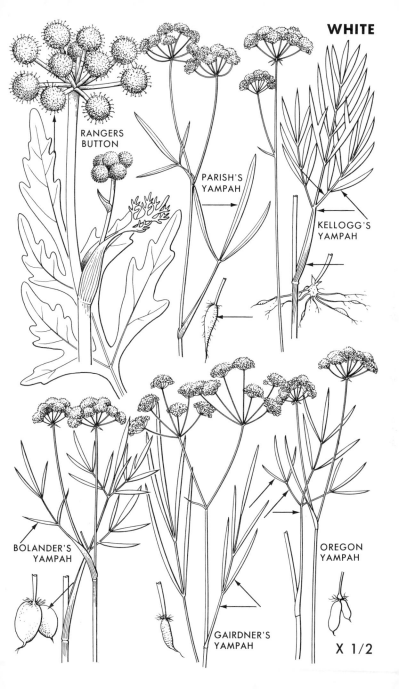

WHITE

RANGERS
BUTTON

PARISH'S
YAMPAH

KELLOGG'S
YAMPAH

BOLANDER'S
YAMPAH

OREGON
YAMPAH

GAIRDNER'S
YAMPAH

X 1/2

5-PETALED SHOWY TRUMPETS ON VINES

MORNING GLORY FAMILY (Convolvulaceae)
See also p. R 308.

FIELD BINDWEED Alien — *Convolvulus arvensis*
Note the *arrowhead* leaf shape with *sharp-pointed* lobes. Small white or pink-tinted flowers ($\frac{1}{2}$–$1\frac{1}{2}$ in.) on trailing stem. Disturbed places. Pacific States. APRIL–OCT.

PIUTE MORNING GLORY — *Calystegia longipes*
Note the narrow *awl-like* leaves remote from the flower, which is on an erect stem. Vine 1–3 ft. Dry slopes. Southern half of Calif. MAY–JULY

SONORA MORNING GLORY — *Calystegia fulcrata*
Note the *small arrowhead* leaf at the *base* of each flower as well as on the vine. Dry mt. slopes. Calif. MAY–AUG.

HEDGE MORNING GLORY — *Calystegia sepium*
Note the arrowhead leaves with *blunt lobes* on the long twining vine. Flowers white to pinkish. Marshes. Lowlands of Pacific States. MAY–SEPT.

WESTERN MORNING GLORY — *Calystegia occidentalis*
Leaves arrowhead-shaped, each basal lobe *2-pointed.* Flowers white, aging purplish. Cen. Calif. to Ore. MAY–JULY

OREGON MORNING GLORY — *Calystegia nyctagineus*
Immediately below each flower are *broad bracts* that *conceal* the calyx. Leaves *triangular* with *rounded* lobes. Flowers cream or tinted pink. Pine forests. N. Sierra Nevada to s. Wash. JUNE–AUG.

SOUTHERN CALIFORNIA MORNING GLORY
Calystegia aridus
Triangular leaves with basal lobes *accentuated* and with a *white velvety* surface. Creamy flowers on long vines. Dry slopes. S. Calif. MAY–JUNE

MODOC MORNING GLORY — *Calystegia polymorpha*
(not shown)
Much like the preceding species, but the flowers are white with a *yellow interior* and short stem (1–2 ft.). Often on serpentine rock. N. Calif. and s. Ore. JUNE–JULY

SIERRA MORNING GLORY — *Calystegia malacophylla*
Leaves triangular with *sharp 3-pointed* basal lobes and dense grayish hairs. Short stem (4–12 in.). Dry slopes. Calif. Coast Ranges and Sierra Nevada. APRIL–AUG.

HILL MORNING GLORY — *Calystegia subacaulis*
Grayish heart-shaped leaves in *stemless cluster.* Flowers cream with purple tint. Dry areas. Cen. Calif. APRIL–JUNE

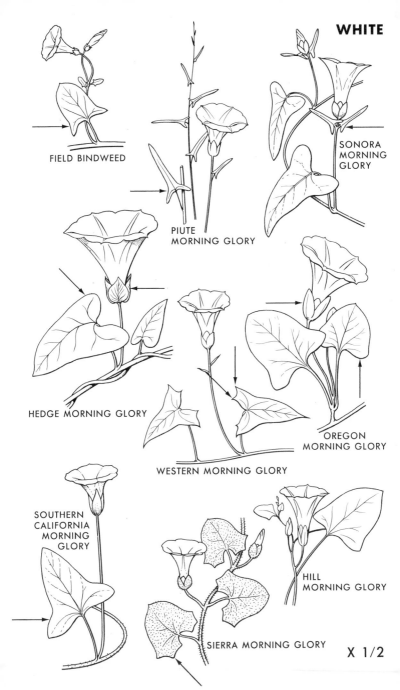

WHITE

FIELD BINDWEED

PIUTE MORNING GLORY

SONORA MORNING GLORY

HEDGE MORNING GLORY

WESTERN MORNING GLORY

OREGON MORNING GLORY

SOUTHERN CALIFORNIA MORNING GLORY

SIERRA MORNING GLORY

HILL MORNING GLORY

X 1/2

5 PETALS; SMALL UPRIGHT TRUMPETS

PHLOX FAMILY (Polemoniaceae)
See also pp. Y 172; O 226;
R 248–50, 306; B 360–64.

BALLHEAD IPOMOPSIS *Ipomopsis congesta*
Flowers in *headlike* clusters. Forklike leaves. 4–10 in. Open
slopes. Great Basin, eastern side Sierra Nevada. JUNE–AUG.

HARKNESS LINANTHUS *Linanthus harknessii*
The *short* funnel-shaped flowers are white to pale blue and
barely exceed the sepals. Each leaf 3- to 5-cleft. 2–6 in. Open
places. Pacific States, except s. Calif. JUNE–AUG.

SAN GABRIEL LINANTHUS *Linanthus concinnus*
Low tufted plant with a large white funnel-shaped flower.
Each petal has *2 short dark lines* near its base. 1–2 in. Dry
rocky slopes. San Gabriel Mts. in Calif. MAY–JULY

FLAX-FLOWERED LINANTHUS *Linanthus liniflorus*
Each flower on a *long pedicel.* The funnel-shaped flower tube is
hidden within the sepals. The stems tend to branch in pairs.
4–20 in. Great Basin and Calif. APRIL–JULY

NUTTALL'S LINANTHUS *Linanthus nuttallii*
Flowers funnel-shaped with a yellow tube. *No membrane*
between the sepals. 4–8 in. Mts. Pacific States. MAY–AUG.

BAKER'S LINANTHUS *Linanthus bakeri*
Similar to Flax-flowered Linanthus, but the yellow flower tube
well extended above the sepals before becoming funnel-shaped.
2–8 in. Cen. Calif. to Wash. MARCH–JUNE

EVENING SNOW *Linanthus dichotomus*
Large snowy white flowers *without pedicels.* Sepals joined by
transluscent membranes except the *tips, which are free.* The
flowers open at dusk, giving a snowy appearance to a field.
2–8 in. Foothills. Calif. APRIL–JUNE

PARRY'S LINANTHUS *Linanthus parryae*
Tiny upright trumpet flowers have 2 tiny, *arching, kidneylike,
purple* lines below each petal within corolla throat. 1–2 in.
W. Mojave Desert, and west to Calif. South Coast Ranges.
MARCH–MAY

GRAND LINANTHUS *Linanthus grandiflorus*
The *broad* funnel flower tube is *well extended* from the white-
haired calyx. 4–20 in. Calif. Goast Ranges. APRIL–JULY

HOOD'S PHLOX *Phlox hoodii*
A low cushion plant with tiny *spine-tipped* leaves and white to
lilac flowers. Rocky places. Great Basin mts. MAY–JULY

72

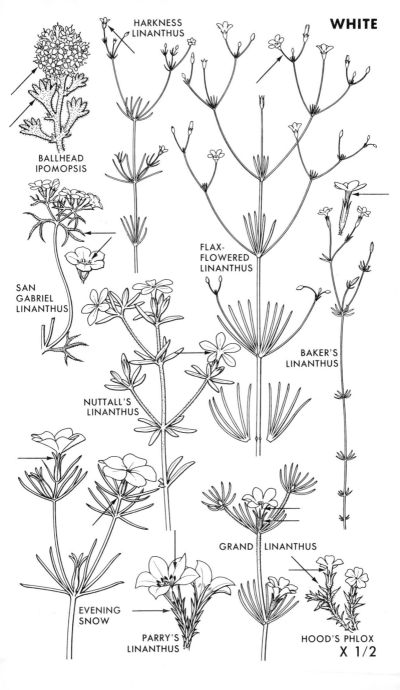

WHITE

BALLHEAD
IPOMOPSIS

HARKNESS
LINANTHUS

FLAX-
FLOWERED
LINANTHUS

BAKER'S
LINANTHUS

SAN
GABRIEL
LINANTHUS

NUTTALL'S
LINANTHUS

EVENING
SNOW

GRAND LINANTHUS

PARRY'S
LINANTHUS

HOOD'S PHLOX
X 1/2

5 UNITED PETALS IN BOWLS OR BELLS; FLOWERS IN COILED CLUSTERS

WATERLEAF FAMILY (Hydrophyllaceae)
See also pp. W 76; Y 172; R 308; B 366-70.

PACIFIC WATERLEAF *Hydrophyllum tenuipes*
Each pinnate leaf has 5 lancelike and toothed leaflets. Often the upper 3 are joined and each of the lower 2 is forked. White to greenish flowers. ½–2 ft. Shady woods along coast. N. Calif. to Wash. APRIL–JUNE

FENDLER'S WATERLEAF *Hydrophyllum fendleri*
Similar to Pacific Waterleaf. Each pinnate leaf of 7–9 leaflets. Each lateral leaflet tends to be *bilobed.* ½–2 ft. Shady woods. N. Calif. to B.C. MAY–AUG.

SMALL-FLOWERED NEMOPHILA *Nemophila parviflora*
The small white to blue-tinted flowers *barely exceed* the *sepals.* The pinnate leaves are oppositely arranged. ½–2 ft. Shady slopes. Mts. at moderate elevations. Pacific States except s. Calif. APRIL–JUNE

WHITE FIESTA FLOWER *Pholistoma membranaceum*
Note the *ladderlike* pinnate leaves have 5–9 broadly linear leaflets. The broad bowl-like flowers have a purple spot on each petal lobe. The sprawling stem has reverse prickles. 1–2 ft. Shady places. Southern ⅔ of Calif. MARCH–MAY

SIERRA NEMOPHILA *Nemophila spatulata*
Note the *spatula-shaped leaves* with 3–5 teeth. Small, white to pale blue, bowl-shaped flowers may have purple spots on each petal lobe. Stems prostrate. 4–8 in. Mt. meadows. S. Calif. Mts., Sierra Nevada. MAY–JULY

CALIFORNIA HESPEROCHIRON
Hesperochiron californicus
The white *bowl-shaped* flowers are *nestled* among a *low tuft* of narrowly oblong leaves. 1–2 in. Moist places. Sierra Nevada south to S. Calif. Mts., and Great Basin. APRIL–JULY

SUKSDORF'S ROMANZOFFIA *Romanzoffia suksdorfii*
Flowers funnel-like with a yellow band inside. 4–12 in. Wet cliffs below 2500 ft. Monterey, Calif., north to Ore. along the coast. APRIL–MAY

MEADOW NEMOPHILA *Nemophila pedunculata*
Leaves all opposite. Each flower on a peduncle as long as the adjacent leaf. The tiny white bell-like flowers have a bluish spot on each petal, and the sepals are lancelike. 4–12 in. Pacific States. APRIL–AUG.

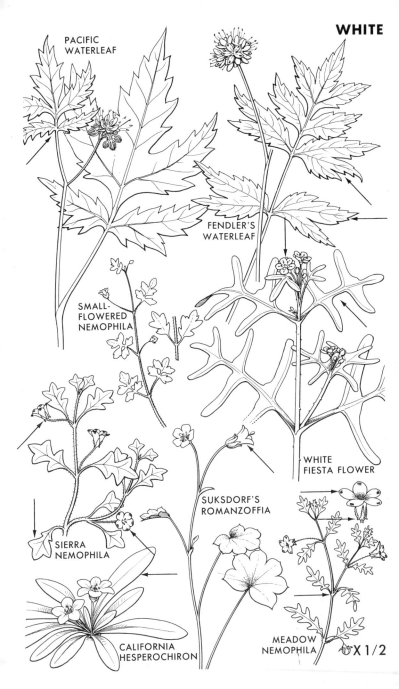

WHITE

PACIFIC WATERLEAF

FENDLER'S WATERLEAF

SMALL-FLOWERED NEMOPHILA

WHITE FIESTA FLOWER

SIERRA NEMOPHILA

SUKSDORF'S ROMANZOFFIA

CALIFORNIA HESPEROCHIRON

MEADOW NEMOPHILA

X 1/2

5 UNITED PETALS IN BOWLS OR BELLS; FLOWERS IN COILED CLUSTERS

WATERLEAF FAMILY (Hydrophyllaceae)
See also pp. W 74; Y 172; R 308; B 366-70.

COMMON EUCRYPTA   *Eucrypta chrysanthemifolia*
The small *open* bell-like flowers are white to yellowish and are in a loosely coiled cluster. *Lacy* pinnate leaves. Sticky stems. Pleasantly scented. ½-2 ft. Shady places. Cen. Calif. and south to Baja.   MARCH–MAY

STINGING PHACELIA   *Phacelia malvifolia*
Note the *maple-like* leaves. Flowers dull white. Stems and leaves with many stinging hairs. 1-3 ft. Moist gravelly places below 3000 ft. San Luis Obispo, Calif. and north along the coast to Ore.   APRIL–JULY

CATERPILLAR PHACELIA   *Phacelia cicutaria*
Each leaf has *oblong to lancelike* leaflets with *toothed* margins. Flowers dirty white or pale yellow. Stems erect or more often leaning against dry rocky banks. 1-3 ft. Sierra Nevada foothills; Calif. South Coast Ranges to Baja.   MARCH–MAY

IMBRICATE PHACELIA   *Phacelia imbricata*
Note that each grayish leaf is divided into 5-9 *acutely cleft leaflets*. Leaves mostly basal. Simple erect stems with stinging hairs. 1-2 ft. Dry rocky places. Foothills of Sierra Nevada and Calif. Coast Ranges to Baja.   APRIL–JULY

TALL PHACELIA   *Phacelia procera*
The large entire leaves have *sharp* and *deeply cut* lobes. Flowers white to greenish-brown in thick coils. Erect stems. 2-6 ft. Mt. meadows. Cen. Calif. to Wash.   JUNE–AUG.

SHORT-LOBED PHACELIA   *Phacelia brachyloba*
The sawtoothed linear leaves are in a basal rosette. Flowers white to pale pink with a yellow tube. Stamens erect. Hairs stinging. ½-2 ft. Cen. Calif. to Baja.   MAY–JUNE

SILVERLEAF PHACELIA   *Phacelia hastata*
Leaves *lancelike* and silvery gray. Numerous white to lavender tinted, bell-like flowers in coils. 1-2 ft. Dry rocky places. Pacific States.   MAY–AUG.

VARI-LEAF PHACELIA   *Phacelia heterophylla*
Leaves *3-lobed,* consisting of a large terminal leaflet and 2 smaller divergent leaflets. Flowers white to greenish-yellow on a single, erect, *columnlike* stem. 1-4 ft. Rocky places below 7000 ft. Cen. Calif. to B.C.   MAY–JULY

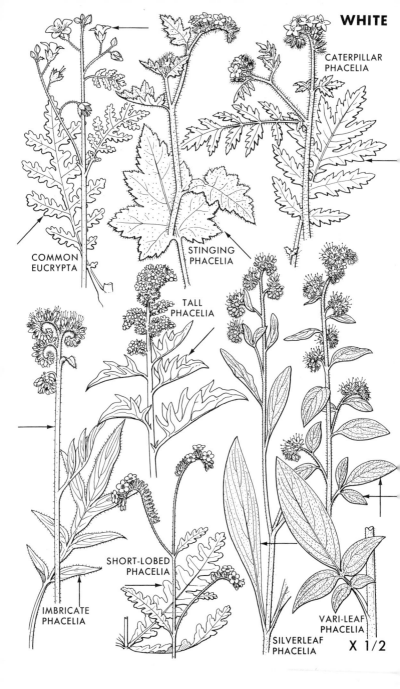

WHITE

CATERPILLAR
PHACELIA

COMMON
EUCRYPTA

STINGING
PHACELIA

TALL
PHACELIA

IMBRICATE
PHACELIA

SHORT-LOBED
PHACELIA

VARI-LEAF
PHACELIA

SILVERLEAF
PHACELIA

X 1/2

5-PETALED PINWHEELS IN COILED CLUSTERS; 4 NUTLIKE SEEDS

FORGET-ME-NOT FAMILY (Boraginaceae)
See also pp. Y 172; O 226; R 308; B 340–42.

POPCORN FLOWER   *Plagiobothrys nothofulvus*
Note that basal rosette of linear leaves has *pale yellow hairs.*
Many strongly coiled flower sprays. The 4 teardrop seeds
somewhat *gnarled* in appearance. ½–2 ft. Very common in
Calif. Occasionally northward.   MARCH–MAY

COMMON CRYPTANTHA   *Cryptantha intermedia*
Similar to Popcorn Flower, but has *white hairs.* The 4 tear-
drop-shaped seeds have a *rounded bumpy* surface. ½–2 ft. Dry
open slopes. Common. Pacific States.   MAY–SEPT.

SALT HELIOTROPE   *Heliotropium curassavicum*
Tiny flowers are in long curved sprays, white to bluish. The
low, matlike, fleshy stems are smooth and covered with a bluish
wax. 6–18 in. Drying flood plains. Great Basin and also
throughout Calif.   MARCH–MAY

CALIFORNIA STICKSEED   *Hackelia californica*
The *entire* surface of each teardrop seed is covered by numerous
stout spines. Each spine is topped by tiny hooks. *Broad* lancelike leaves. Flowers have a toothlike projection opposite each
petal lobe. 1–3 ft. Open forests. Calif. North Coast Ranges,
Sierra Nevada north to Ore.   JUNE–AUG.

BRISTLY PECTOCARYA   *Pectocarya setosa*
Note the 4 divergent *rounded* seeds with many short, hooked
hairs and a few longer spines below. 2–8 in. Sandy places below
6000 ft. Mostly in Calif.   APRIL–MAY

SLENDER PECTOCARYA   *Pectocarya linearis*
The tiny flowers soon develop into *4 linear, twisted,* spiny seeds
diverging from each other. 4–12 in. Open places below 3000 ft.
Southern ⅔ of Calif.   MARCH–MAY

NODDING STICKSEED   *Hackelia deflexa*
Similar to California Stickseed. Each teardrop seed has *only a
fringe* of hook-tipped spines. The linear leaves are very narrow
and short. 1–3 ft. Sagebrush or open woods. Great Basin in
Wash. and B.C.   MAY–JULY

SIERRA CRYPTANTHA   *Crypthantha nubigena*
Many flowers in a *clublike* cluster. Stem leaves clothed with
many sharp hairs. 2–8 in. Alpine rocky slopes. Sierra Nevada
and high mts. of Ore. Great Basin.   JULY–AUG.

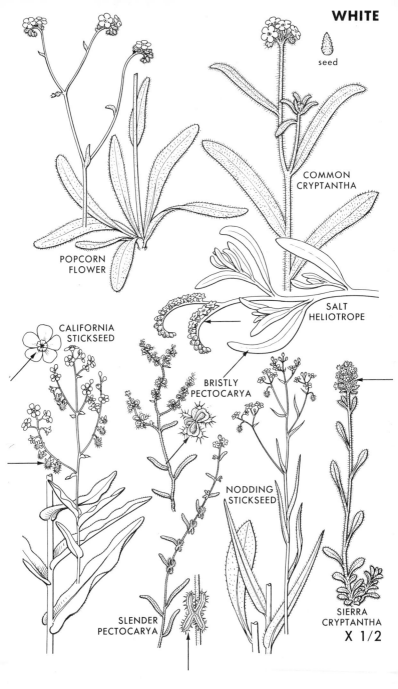

WHITE

seed

COMMON
CRYPTANTHA

POPCORN
FLOWER

SALT
HELIOTROPE

CALIFORNIA
STICKSEED

BRISTLY
PECTOCARYA

NODDING
STICKSEED

SLENDER
PECTOCARYA

SIERRA
CRYPTANTHA
X 1/2

5 UNITED PETALS; LARGE TRUMPETS OR FLAT STARLIKE FLOWERS

NIGHTSHADE FAMILY (Solanaceae)
See also pp. Y 172; B 382.

DWARF CHAMAESARACHA *Chamaesaracha nana*
Note the *5 green spots* at the petal bases of the white *starlike* flowers. Leaves oval and smooth-edged. Berries dull white to yellowish. 2–10 in. Dry open places. Great Basin in Ore. and Calif. MAY–JULY

WRIGHT'S GROUND CHERRY *Physalis acutifolia*
The disklike flowers white with an *inner ring* of yellow. The calyx becomes an inflated papery bladder covering the seed capsule. Leaves lanceolate. 1–3 ft. Disturbed places. All of s. Calif. JULY–OCT.

WHITE NIGHTSHADE Alien *Solanum nodiflorum*
Note the *yellow beak* of stamens projecting from the starlike, white to purple-tinted petals. Leaves triangular. Fruit a shiny black berry. 1–2 ft. Disturbed places. Calif. APRIL–NOV.

JIMSONWEED *Datura meteloides*
Note the very large trumpetlike flowers (4–8 in. long). Calyx tubular. Leaves grayish and unequally oval. 2–5 ft. Dry open places. Pacific States. APRIL–OCT.

DESERT TOBACCO *Nicotiana trigonophylla*
The white to greenish, trumpetlike flowers are *short*-tubed. Also note the oval leaves with the 2 *earlike* basal lobes that clasp the stem. Plants sticky-haired. 1–3 ft. Grows along the drip line of rocks. Mojave, Colorado Deserts. MARCH–JUNE

INDIAN TOBACCO *Nicotiana bigelovii*
Long slender trumpetlike flowers with *long petals*. Leaves oblong to oval with the blade portion *extending to base* of the petiole. Sticky-haired and bad smelling. 1–4 ft. Dry valleys. S. Ore. south to San Diego, Calif. west of the deserts.
MAY–OCT.

COYOTE TOBACCO *Nicotiana attenuata*
The *long* slender trumpetlike flowers have *short petals*. Leaves lanceolate to ovate with a *definite petiole*. Sticky-haired and bad smelling. 1–6 ft. Disturbed places. Great Basin and northern ⅔ of Calif. MAY–OCT.

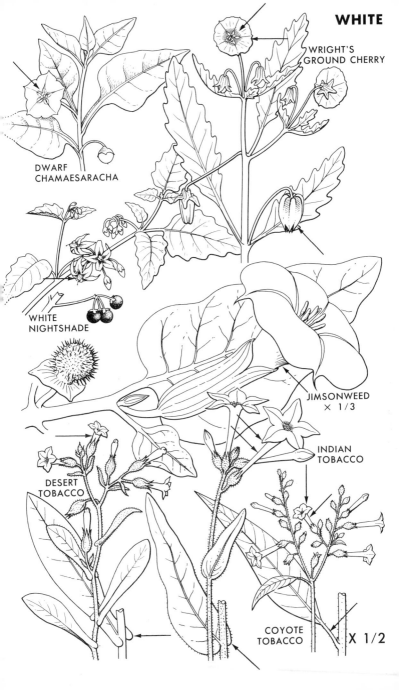

WHITE

WRIGHT'S
GROUND CHERRY

DWARF
CHAMAESARACHA

WHITE
NIGHTSHADE

JIMSONWEED
× 1/3

DESERT
TOBACCO

INDIAN
TOBACCO

COYOTE
TOBACCO

X 1/2

5-PETALED, 2-LIPPED TUBULAR FLOWERS
SQUARE OR ROUND STEMS

Mint Family (Labiatae)
See also pp. R 312–14; B 374.

CALIFORNIA SKULLCAP   *Scutellaria californica*
Note that the long tubular flowers are in pairs at each pair of
opposite leaves. The calyx has a *skullcap-like* crest on the
upper side. Flowers white to pale yellow. Leaves linear,
oblong. 4–12 in. Dry thickets. Cen. Calif. north to Siskiyous.
JUNE–JULY

HOREHOUND Alien   *Marrubium vulgare*
Note the numerous tiny flowers in *doughnut-like* circles around
the square stem. Also note the pairs of gray oval leaves have a
crinkly surface. Stem white, woolly. 1–3 ft. Very common in
disturbed places. Pacific States.   ALL YEAR

SIERRA MINT   *Pycnanthemum californicum*
Note the strong 4-column arrangement of triangular leaves.
Flowers in clusters above each pair of leaves, white with reddish
spots. Strong odor. 2–3 ft. Along drying streambanks. Calif.
JUNE–SEPT.

DESERT PENNYROYAL   *Monardella exilis*
Note the large *white- and green*-veined bracts surrounding the
terminal cluster of numerous small tubular flowers. 3–16 in.
Sandy plains. W. Mojave Desert.   MAY–JUNE

YERBA BUENA   *Satureja douglasii*
Note the trailing square stem with oval leaves and small, white
or purple-tinted, 2-lipped tubular flowers. ½–2 ft. Shady low-
elevation woods. West of Cascades and south along the various
Coast Ranges to s. Calif.   APRIL–SEPT.

AFRICAN SAGE Alien   *Salvia aethiopis*
Note the large *hooked* upper corolla lip of each flower. The
white to pale yellow flowers are in whorls surrounded by large
cuplike bracts. Stems branching in pairs, with each succeeding
pair at right angles to the previous set, giving a *pyramid* shape
to the plant. The leaves gray-haired and mostly basal. Strong
disagreeable odor. 1–3 ft. Scattered localities in Great Basin.
JUNE–JULY

Broomrape Family (Orobanchaceae)
See also p. B 338.

GRAY'S BROOMRAPE   *Orobanche grayana*
The round short stem has numerous 2-lipped tubular flowers
each on *very long* round pedicels. Flowers white to pale yellow
or purplish. 2–5 in. Under shrubs. Pacific States.
JUNE–SEPT.

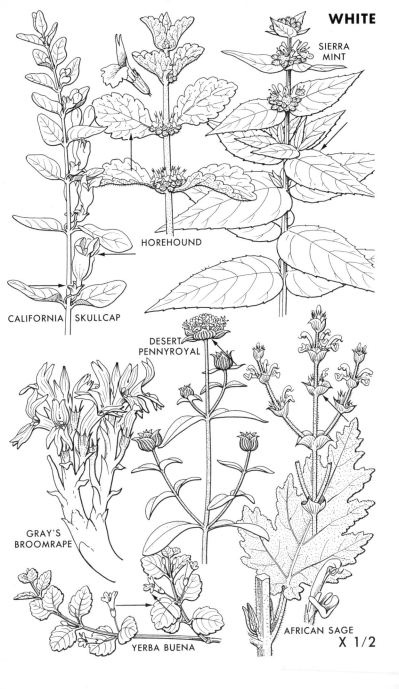

WHITE

SIERRA
MINT

HOREHOUND

CALIFORNIA SKULLCAP

DESERT
PENNYROYAL

GRAY'S
BROOMRAPE

YERBA BUENA

AFRICAN SAGE

X 1/2

5 DAINTY PETALS; 2 HORNLIKE STYLES
5 STAMENS; MAPLE-LIKE LEAVES

SAXIFRAGE FAMILY (Saxifragaceae)
See also pp. W 84–90, 100; G 402.

SMOOTH GRASS OF PARNASSUS *Parnassia palustris*
Note that each of the oval petals has a *smooth margin*. Near the petal base is a fringe of threadlike glands with globular tips. Shiny, dark green, delta-shaped leaves. 1–2 ft. Wet meadows, or marshy springs. Pacific States. JULY–OCT.

FRINGED GRASS OF PARNASSUS
Parnassia fimbriata
Similar to preceding, but the *petal* edges *fringed* and the leaves kidney-shaped. The fringed gland at each petal base with *stubby* lobes. 1–2 ft. Wet places. N. Calif. to B.C.
JULY–SEPT.

MOUNTAIN BOYKINIA *Boykinia major*
Note the *broad oval* petals. Flowers in dense clusters well above the large maple-like leaves. 1–3 ft. Mt. meadows and streambanks. Cen. Calif. north to Wash. Ssp. *intermedia* (not shown) has elongated oval petals. Cen. Ore. coast to Olympic Peninsula. JUNE–SEPT.

COAST BOYKINIA *Boykinia elata*
The numerous flowers have *lancelike petals*. Leaves maple-like with 5–7 lobes; long *spidery stipules* at the petiole base. The glandular-haired stems are from a scaly, exposed rootstock. ½–2 ft. Moist shady woods. Mts. of Pacific States.
JUNE–AUG.

PACIFIC MITELLA *Mitella trifida*
Each slender-based petal broadens into a *thick 3-pronged* fork. The flowers are on a spike above the maple-like leaves. Plants from a scaly rootstock. 8–15 in. Shaded woods. Mts. of n. Calif. to B.C. MAY–JULY

CROSS-SHAPED MITELLA *Mitella stauropetala*
Similar to Pacific Mitella. Each of the *threadlike* petals divided into 3 equal *pitchfork-like* divisions. 1–2 ft. Shady woods. Mts. of e. Ore. and Wash. MAY–JUNE

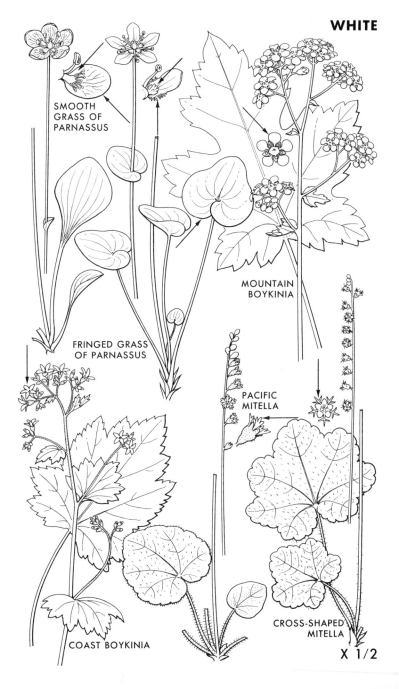

SMOOTH GRASS OF PARNASSUS

MOUNTAIN BOYKINIA

FRINGED GRASS OF PARNASSUS

PACIFIC MITELLA

COAST BOYKINIA

CROSS-SHAPED MITELLA

X 1/2

5 DAINTY PETALS; 2 HORNLIKE STYLES
5 STAMENS; MAPLE-LIKE LEAVES

SAXIFRAGE FAMILY (Saxifragaceae)
See also pp. W 84–90, 100; G 402.

CREVICE HEUCHERA   *Heuchera micrantha*
The 2-lobed leaf stipules at the base of the leaf petiole have a fringe of long hairs. Flowers tiny and numerous. Leaves maple-like. 1–2½ ft. Moist rocks and cliffs. Cen. Calif. to B.C.
MAY–AUG.

GREEN-TINTED HEUCHERA   *Heuchera chlorantha*
The tiny white to greenish flowers are in dense *spikelike panicles.* The stipules at the leaf petiole base are tapered and hairless. Stems and leaves have conspicuous brown hairs. 1–3 ft. Various habitats. West of Cascades in Ore. and north to B.C.   MAY–AUG.

JACK O' THE ROCKS   *Heuchera rubescens*
Note the *flat margin edges* of the maple-like leaves. The numerous tiny flowers are white to pale pink in loose racemes. 4–12 in. Dry rocky slopes. Mts. of Sierra Nevada and Mojave Desert.   MAY–AUG.

POKER HEUCHERA   *Heuchera cylindrica*
Note the *thick pokerlike* spike of creamy bell-like flowers well above the maple-like leaves. 1–3 ft. Frequent on rocky slopes. Eastern side of Cascades, Great Basin.   APRIL–AUG.

ALPINE HEUCHERA   *Heuchera glabra*
At the bottom of the leaf petiole are the 2-lobed stipules with a fringe of *only a few short hairs.* Both the stems and leaf petioles are essentially hairless. The numerous tiny flowers are in a loose panicle. 1–2 ft. Streambanks and wet cliffs. Cascades and Olympic Mts. of Wash.   JUNE–AUG.

ELMERA   *Elmera racemosa*
Note the *white bell-like calyx* from which the tiny linear petals emerge. Each petal has 5 short fingerlike lobes. Leaves kidney-shaped with toothed margins. 4–10 in. Subalpine and alpine rocky ledges. Mts. of Wash.   JUNE–AUG.

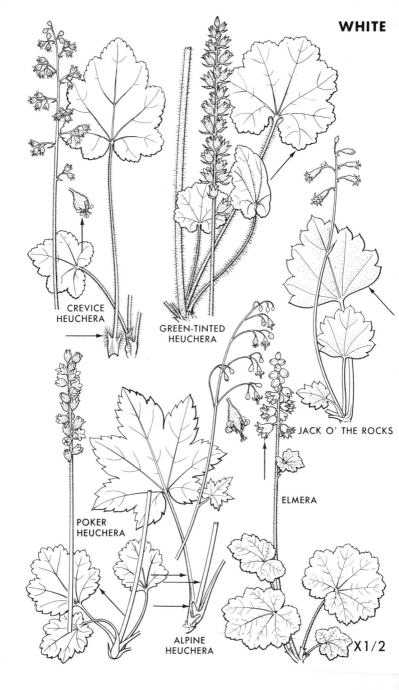

WHITE

CREVICE
HEUCHERA

GREEN-TINTED
HEUCHERA

JACK O' THE ROCKS

POKER
HEUCHERA

ELMERA

ALPINE
HEUCHERA

X1/2

5 DAINTY PETALS; 2 HORNLIKE STYLES
10 STAMENS; LEAVES VARIOUS

SAXIFRAGE FAMILY (Saxifragaceae)
See also pp. W 84–90, 100; G 402.

PRAIRIE STAR *Lithophragma parviflora*
The basal leaves are *deeply divided* 3–5 times. Each of the white to pinkish petals is divided into 3 linear lobes. The flowers are on leafless spikes. 9–14 in. Open grassy places. Pacific States. MARCH–JUNE

WOODLAND STAR *Lithophragma affine*
Similar to Prairie Star. The basal leaves are rounded and nearly *without* any divisions. Petals deeply notched. ½–2 ft. Grassy places. Calif. to s. Ore. MARCH–MAY

SINGLE SUGAR SCOOP *Tiarella unifoliata*
Each leaf is *one single* maple-like unit. The long stamens are conspicuously whiskerlike and are well beyond the slender coiled petals. Seed capsule resembles a sugar scoop. 4–20 in. Shady woods below 3500 ft. Monterey, Calif., and north up the coast to Wash. MAY–AUG.

TRIPLE SUGAR SCOOP *Tiarella trifoliata*
Similar to Single Sugar Scoop. Differs by having each leaf *divided into 3 leaflets*. ½–2 ft. Moist woods. West of Cascades in Ore. to B.C. MAY–AUG.

LEATHER-LEAVED SAXIFRAGE *Leptarrhena pyrolifolia*
Flowers are in a *terminal cluster* well above the basal rosette of bright green, leathery, oval leaves. ½–2 ft. Wet meadows, streambanks. Mts. of Pacific States. JUNE–AUG.

UMBRELLA PLANT *Peltiphyllum peltatum*
The leaf blade is an *immense umbrella* (1–2 ft. wide) on a stout succulent petiole arising from a large fleshy rhizome that crawls over wet rocks. Flowers white to pink. 1–4 ft. On rocks within flowing mt. streams. Sw. Ore. to the Sierra Nevada.

APRIL–JULY

OREGON SAXIFRAGE *Saxifraga oregana*
Flowers in clusters above the basal rosette of *spatula-shaped* leaves (1–6 in. long). Petals oval. 1–3 ft. Wet meadows and bogs. Sierra Nevada to w. Wash. MAY–AUG.

SIERRA SAXIFRAGE *Saxifraga aprica*
The tiny white flowers have round petals and are in a *rounded terminal cluster*. The basal rosette leaves oval. Entire plant surface tends to be purplish. 1–5 in. Very common in moist alpine meadows. Sierra Nevada to sw. Ore. MAY–AUG.

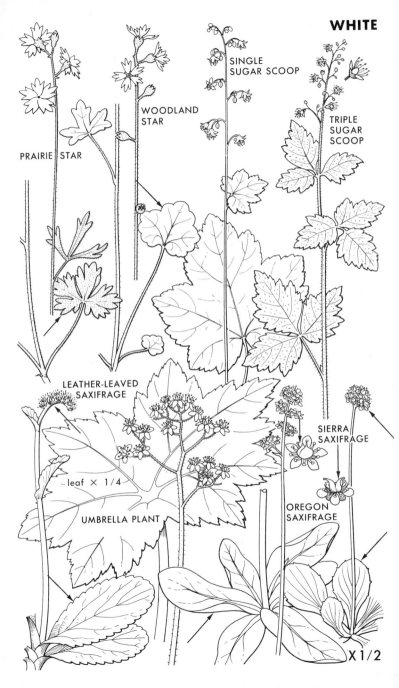

WHITE

SINGLE
SUGAR SCOOP

WOODLAND
STAR

TRIPLE
SUGAR
SCOOP

PRAIRIE STAR

LEATHER-LEAVED
SAXIFRAGE

leaf × 1/4

SIERRA
SAXIFRAGE

UMBRELLA PLANT

OREGON
SAXIFRAGE

× 1/2

5 DAINTY PETALS; 2 HORNLIKE STYLES
5 OR 10 STAMENS; LEAVES VARIOUS

SAXIFRAGE FAMILY (Saxifragaceae)
See also pp. W 84–88, 100; G 402.

TUFTED SAXIFRAGE *Saxifraga caespitosa*
Note the small, *narrow, trilobed* (sometimes 5) *leaves* are in tiny basal tufts. Flowers somewhat bowl-shaped with rounded petals. 2–12 in. Rocky crevices. Ore. to B.C. APRIL–SEPT.

MERTENS' SAXIFRAGE *Saxifraga mertensiana*
The large rounded leaves have equal *rectangular* lobes, each with 3 smaller triangular lobes. Narrow white petals. 6–12 in. Wet banks. Mts. of cen. Calif. to B.C. FEB.–AUG.

RUSTY SAXIFRAGE *Saxifraga ferruginea*
The flower has *2 kinds of petals:* 3 *broad* ones, each with 2 yellow-orange spots; and 2 *narrow* petals without markings. Straplike leaves with occasional jagged teeth. ½–2 ft. Wet banks. Mts. of n. Calif. to B.C. JUNE–AUG.

SPOTTED SAXIFRAGE *Saxifraga bronchialis*
Each petal has *numerous* yellow and orange spots. The tiny lancelike leaves have short bristles along the margins. 2–12 in. Many habitats. Ore. to B.C. JUNE–AUG.

TOLMIE'S SAXIFRAGE *Saxifraga tolmiei*
Basal leaves are *tiny, smooth, and round.* Flowers on a leafless red stem. Petals oval. White clublike stamens. 1–6 in. Mt. meadows. Cen. Calif. to B.C. JULY–AUG.

BROOK SAXIFRAGE *Saxifraga punctata*
Note the round to kidney-shaped leaves with triangular toothed margins. Each petal has 2 yellow dots. ½–1½ ft. Mt. streambanks. Pacific States. JULY–AUG.

LYALL'S SAXIFRAGE *Saxifraga lyallii*
Note the *fanlike leaf blade* on a tapering petiole. Petals with 2 yellow dots. 4–15 in. Damp meadows. N. Cascades in Wash. to B.C. JULY–AUG.

BUD SAXIFRAGE *Saxifraga bryophora*
The flower is often replaced by a *miniature plantlet.* Petals have 2 yellow spots. Straplike leaves have scattered hairs. 2–8 in. Subalpine, alpine meadows. Sierra Nevada.
JULY–AUG.

CALIFORNIA SAXIFRAGE *Saxifraga californica*
The *5 stamens* are opposite the rounded petals. Basal rosette of oblong leaves. Leafless flower stem. 4–12 in. Shady banks at low elevations. Calif., Ore. FEB.–JUNE

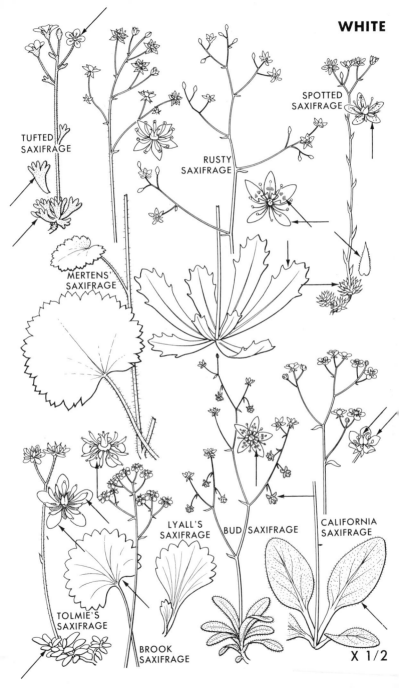

WHITE

TUFTED
SAXIFRAGE

RUSTY
SAXIFRAGE

SPOTTED
SAXIFRAGE

MERTENS'
SAXIFRAGE

TOLMIE'S
SAXIFRAGE

LYALL'S
SAXIFRAGE

BROOK
SAXIFRAGE

BUD SAXIFRAGE

CALIFORNIA
SAXIFRAGE

X 1/2

5 PETALS; MANY STAMENS; PINNATE LEAVES WITH 2 STIPULES AT BASE

Rose Family (Rosaceae)
See also pp. Y 174–76; R 310; Br 404.

THREE-TOOTHED HORKELIA   *Horkelia tridentata*
Silvery-haired pinnate leaflets, each tip *3-toothed.* 6–12 in.
Woods. Sierra Nevada to sw. Ore.   May–July

BALLHEAD HORKELIA   *Horkelia congesta*
Similar to preceding. Flowers in dense *headlike* clusters.
6–20 in. Openings in woods. W. Ore.   April–June

DUSKY HORKELIA   *Horkelia fusca*
Note the long, *featherlike,* pinnate leaves, each leaflet of 2–3
linear segments. $\frac{1}{4}$–2 ft. Woods and meadows. Sierra Nevada
to cen. Wash., Great Basin.   May–July

DWARF BRAMBLE   *Rubus pedatus*
Each erect stem has 1–3 *palmate* leaves with 3–5 *fingerlike*
leaflets and 1 flower. Moist woods. Ore. to B.C.   May–July

STICKY CINQUEFOIL   *Potentilla glandulosa*
Pinnate leaves have 5–9 strongly toothed leaflets. Flowers
creamy to light yellow. Sticky stems. 1–3 ft. Very common.
Many habitats. Pacific States.   May–Aug.

BEACH STRAWBERRY   *Fragaria chiloensis*
Note the 3 broadly oval leaflets have *rounded bases.* Leaf
surface *shiny green.* Berries tasteless. Only near the immediate
coast. Pacific States.   April–Aug.

VIRGINIA STRAWBERRY   *Fragaria virginiana*
Note the 3 broadly oblong leaflets have *straight wedgelike*
bases. Leaf surface *blue-green.* Delicious edible strawberries.
Open woods, meadows. Pacific States.   March–Aug.

PARTRIDGE FOOT   *Luetkea pectinata*
Each leaf is divided like a *partridge foot.* Short erect stem.
2–6 in. Alpine slopes. N. Calif. to B.C.   July–Sept.

MOUSE TAIL IVESIA   *Ivesia santolinoides*
Gray *mousetail-like leaves* in a basal rosette. Tall threadlike
flowering stem. $\frac{1}{2}$–2 ft. Mt. slopes 5000 to 10,000 ft. Cen.
Sierra Nevada south to San Jacinto Mts.   June–Aug.

GOATSBEARD   *Aruncus vulgaris*
Numerous small white flowers in *long narrow sprays.* Leaves
are divided 2–3 times into large oblong leaflets. 3–6 ft. Shady
woods. N. Calif. to B.C.   May–July

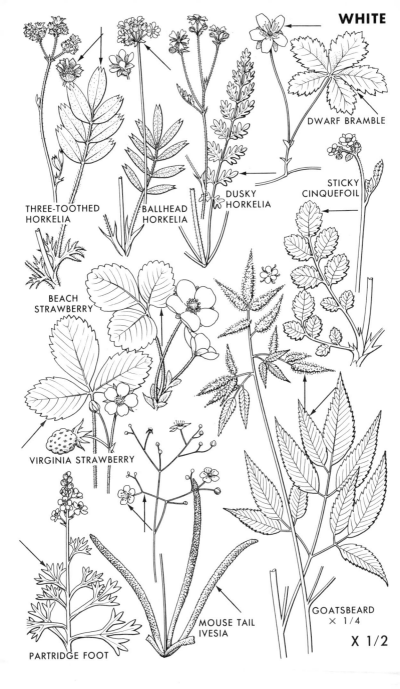

WHITE

DWARF BRAMBLE

STICKY
CINQUEFOIL

THREE-TOOTHED
HORKELIA

BALLHEAD
HORKELIA

DUSKY
HORKELIA

BEACH
STRAWBERRY

VIRGINIA STRAWBERRY

PARTRIDGE FOOT

MOUSE TAIL
IVESIA

GOATSBEARD
× 1/4

× 1/2

PEALIKE FLOWERS; LEAFLETS IN PAIRS

PEA FAMILY (Leguminosae)
See also pp. W 94–96; Y 178–82; O 224;
R 318–26; B 376–80.

WHITE DWARF LOCOWEED   *Astragalus didymocarpus*
The pinnate leaves have 7–17 *square-tipped* leaflets, each with
a *notch*. Flowers in dense, oblong to oval heads. Seedpods are
small rounded wrinkled sacs. 2–12 in. Grassy places. Calif.
South Coast Ranges; Mojave, Colorado Deserts.   FEB.–MAY

ROGUE RIVER LOCOWEED   *Astragalus accidens*
Note the 15–27 leaflets are each square-tipped but *not* notched.
7–15 flowered spike. Inflated seedpods oblong with a thin
curved beak. 1–1½ ft. Thickets. N. Central Valley of Calif. to
sw. Ore.   APRIL–JULY

NUTTALL'S LOCOWEED   *Astragalus nuttallii*
Note the 23–43 *silvery*-haired leaflets. Flowers nodding, white
or tinted lilac. Inflated oblong seedpods with short triangular
beaks. 1–3 ft. Coastal dunes and bluffs. Cen. Calif. Coast.
JAN.–OCT.

THREAD-LEAVED LOCOWEED   *Astragalus filipes*
Note the 6–19 grayish leaflets which are *linear and sharp-
pointed*. Racemes 3- to 10-flowered. Seedpods linear. ½–2 ft.
Many habitats. Great Basin.   MAY–JULY

COMMON FALSE LOCOWEED   *Oxytropis campestris*
Note the *bottlebrush* spike of flowers well above the leaves. All
plant parts covered with silvery hairs. A highly variable species. 6–24 in. E. Ore. to B.C.   MAY–JULY

NEVADA PEA   *Lathyrus lanszwertii*
Note the *terminal tendril* above the 6–12 linear leaflets. Flow-
ers with occasional reddish veins. Stems sprawling. 1–3 ft.
Sagebrush or open woods. Eastern side of Sierra Nevada and
Great Basin.   MAY–JULY

POMONA LOCOWEED   *Astragalus pomonensis*
Seedpods are short *sausage-like* with a *bent tip*. The 25–41
leaflets are bright green. Racemes 10- to 25-flowered. 1–3 ft.
Valleys and hillsides. San Luis Obispo, Calif., south to San
Bernardino area.   MARCH–MAY

AMERICAN LICORICE   *Glycyrrhiza lepidota*
Note the oblong capsules have *hooked hairs*. The numerous
white to pale yellow flowers are in an erect *brushlike head*.
Leaflets lancelike. 1–4 ft. Disturbed places. Pacific States.
MAY–AUG.

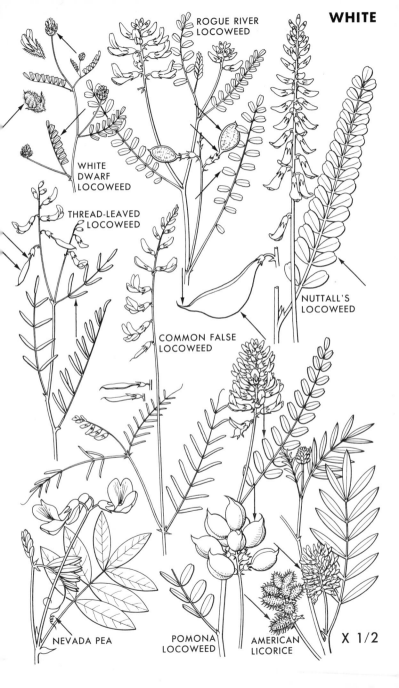

WHITE

ROGUE RIVER
LOCOWEED

WHITE
DWARF
LOCOWEED

THREAD-LEAVED
LOCOWEED

NUTTALL'S
LOCOWEED

COMMON FALSE
LOCOWEED

NEVADA PEA

POMONA
LOCOWEED

AMERICAN
LICORICE

X 1/2

PEALIKE FLOWERS; 3–8 FINGERLIKE LEAFLETS: LUPINES, CLOVERS

PEA FAMILY (Leguminosae)
See also pp. W 94; Y 178–82; O 224;
R 318–26; B 376–80.

WHITEWHORL LUPINE *Lupinus densiflorus*
The flowers are in *whorls* along the long flower spike. A complicated species with white flowers that vary to pink or reddish in some areas. 7–9 palmate leaflets. 1–3 ft. Grassy fields. Foothills of Calif. APRIL–JUNE

PINE LUPINE *Lupinus albicaulis*
Flowers *without a definite* arrangement on the long flower spike. Petals white to purple-tinted. Center of banner petal yellow. 5–9 palmate leaflets. 1–3 ft. Open slopes. Entire area west of Cascades–Sierra Nevada. MAY–AUG.

WHITE SWEET CLOVER *Melilotus albus*
Numerous small pealike flowers in *spikelike* racemes. Palmate leaflets 3. Strong sweet odor. 3–7 ft. Disturbed places. Pacific States. MAY–OCT.

LONG-STALKED CLOVER *Trifolium longipes*
The flowers are in a *dense rounded head.* No bract below the flower head. Calyx teeth *long and hairy-margined.* The 3 palmate leaflets long and narrow with toothed edges. 2–15 in. Moist places in the mts. Pacific States. MAY–SEPT.

WHITE LAWN CLOVER Alien *Trifolium repens*
Note that the 3 palmate leaflets are *oval but larger* at the tip end. Calyx teeth short. Flowers in a rounded head without a papery bract under it. 4–12 in. Lawns and meadows. Pacific States. ALL YEAR

SHASTA CLOVER *Trifolium productum*
Note that long narrow pealike flowers are *reverse-* (downward) pointed in a dense head on a long stem. The 3 palmate leaflets are sharp spearhead-shaped with sawtooth edges. 4–16 in. Woods and meadows. Cen. Sierra Nevada to Ore. MAY–AUG.

MOUNTAIN CARPET CLOVER *Trifolium monanthum*
The long tubular creamy flowers with a purple-tipped keel are *long-stemmed.* The 3 leaflets oval. This clover grows in very low dense carpets. Common in open wet places. Sierra Nevada south to S. Calif. Mts. JUNE–OCT.

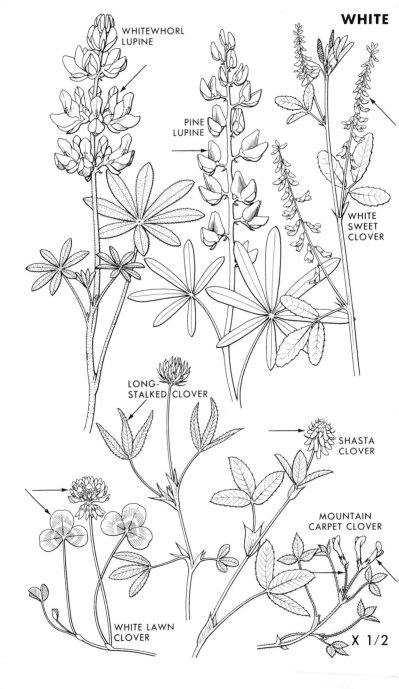

WHITE

WHITEWHORL
LUPINE

PINE
LUPINE

WHITE
SWEET
CLOVER

LONG-
STALKED CLOVER

SHASTA
CLOVER

MOUNTAIN
CARPET CLOVER

WHITE LAWN
CLOVER

X 1/2

5-PETALED STARS; VINES WITH SMALL SPINY MELONS

CUCUMBER FAMILY (Cucurbitaceae)
See also p. Y 120.

In the Cucumber Family the male and female flowers are separate from each other, but on the same vine. Fruit a usually small melon, surface smooth or spiny, native species not edible. All species of *Marah* have an immense manlike underground tuber.

COAST MANROOT *Marah oreganus*
Note the leaves have 5-7 shallow but sharp-pointed lobes. Male flowers small and bell-like. The melon is rounded with a nearly smooth surface. Vines 3-20 ft. Slopes below 6000 ft. San Francisco area north to B.C. on west side of Cascades; rarely east along Columbia and Snake Rivers. MARCH–JUNE

SIERRA MANROOT *Marah horridus*
Note that leaf has 5-7 deep lobes and the general margin has many jagged points. Male flowers bell-shaped. The melon is *oblong* with a dense spiny covering, 2-4 seeded. Vines 3-12 ft. Dry slopes below 3000 ft. W. Sierra Nevada foothills south to Los Angeles area. MARCH–APRIL

BRANDEGEA *Brandegea bigelovii*
Note the simple 3-5 triangular lobes of each leaf. The tiny (¼ in. or less) spiny melon is narrowly oblong. Small, flat, starlike flowers. Vines 3-10 ft. Along desert washes. Colorado and e. Mojave Deserts. MARCH–APRIL

CALIFORNIA MANROOT *Marah fabaceus*
The large *entire leaves* have 5-7 pointed lobes and a U-shaped base. Male flowers flat stars. The melon is *globe*-shaped with many surface spines. 4 large seeds to each melon. Vines 6-20 ft. Shrubby places below 5000 ft. W. Sierra Nevada and Calif. Coast Ranges. FEB.–APRIL

TAW MANROOT *Marah watsonii*
The 5-lobed leaves have the *outer lobe enlarged* and rounded, margins smooth. The leaves are waxy blue underneath. The melon is *globular and few-spined,* 2-seeded. Vines 3-10 ft. Below 3000 ft. Around edges of Sacramento Valley portion of the Central Valley of Calif. MARCH–APRIL

CUCAMONGA MANROOT *Marah macrocarpus*
Note the deeply lobed leaves have sharp-pointed tips. The male flower is a flat star. The melon is *oblong and densely spiny.* Each melon usually contains 5 or more large seeds. Vines 5-20 ft. Dry slopes below 3000 ft. Santa Barbara, Calif., and south to Baja. JAN.–APRIL

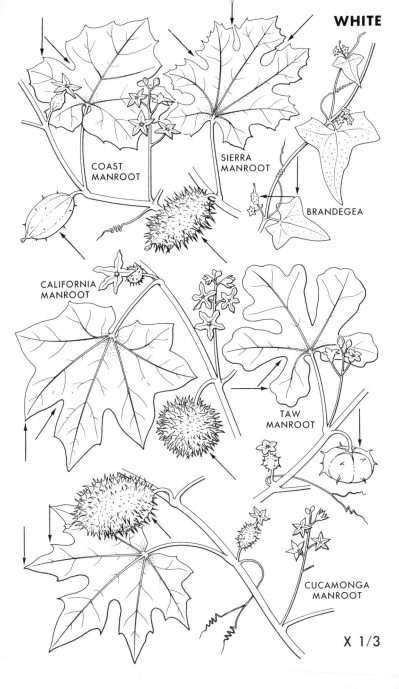

WHITE

COAST MANROOT

SIERRA MANROOT

BRANDEGEA

CALIFORNIA MANROOT

TAW MANROOT

CUCAMONGA MANROOT

X 1/3

MISCELLANEOUS WHITE FLOWERS

YERBA DE SELVA   *Whipplea modesta*
SAXIFRAGE FAMILY   (Saxifragaceae)
See also pp. W 84–90; G 402.
Small *headlike clusters* of tiny petal-less flowers. Forms a dense ground cover. Very common. Cen. Calif. in Coast Ranges north to Olympic Peninsula.   APRIL–JUNE

MOUNTAIN VALERIAN   *Valeriana sitchensis*
VALERIAN FAMILY See also p. R 316.   (Valerianaceae)
Tubular flowers have a *1-sided bulge*. Leaves pinnate. 1–4 ft. Mt. meadows. Nw. Calif. north to B.C.   JULY–SEPT.

BEDSTRAW   *Galium aparine*
BEDSTRAW FAMILY   (Rubiaceae)
4-angled spiny stems have *whorls* of leaves. Tiny flowers. Spiny *twin* seeds. 1–5 ft. Pacific States.   MARCH–JULY

ARCTIC STARFLOWER   *Trientalis arctica*
PRIMROSE FAMILY   (Primulaceae)
See also pp. R 246, 304; B 342.
Terminal umbrellalike cluster of oval leaves and *additional* ones *along* the stem. Flat star-shaped flowers. 2–8 in. Swamps. West of Cascades.   MAY–AUG.

WHITE SHOOTING STAR   *Dodecatheon dentatum*
PRIMROSE FAMILY   (Primulaceae)
See also pp. R 246, 304; B 342.
The creamy white *petals* are *swept backward* into a shooting star. A yellow band around corolla tube. Anthers deep red. $\frac{1}{2}$–1$\frac{1}{2}$ ft. Damp slopes, streambanks. Cascades.   MAY–JULY

THYME-LEAF SPURGE   *Euphorbia serpyllifolia*
SPURGE FAMILY See also p. G 398.   (Euphorbiaceae)
The white flower glands give the appearance of *small white eyes*. Thymelike leaves have minutely toothed tips. Milky sap. 1–12 in. Disturbed places. Pacific States.   MAY–OCT.

BUCKBEAN   *Menyanthes trifoliata*
GENTIAN FAMILY   (Gentianaceae)
See also pp. R 304; B 342–44; G 394.
Starlike petal lobes have *dense hair*. Trifoliate leaves. 4–12 in. Mt. bogs. Sierra Nevada north to B.C.   MAY–AUG.

DESERT WISHBONE BUSH   *Mirabilis bigelovii*
FOUR O' CLOCK FAMILY   (Nyctaginaceae)
See also pp. Y 120; R 300.
Flowers white or tinted pink with *bilobed petal tips*. Oval to kidney-shaped leaves on sticky stems. 1–2 ft. Rocky slopes. Mojave, Colorado Deserts.   MARCH–JUNE, OCT.–NOV.

BUNCHBERRY   *Cornus canadensis*
DOGWOOD FAMILY   (Cornaceae)
Umbrellalike leaf whorl with a large 4-petaled flower. Red berries. 2–8 in. Woods. N. Calif. to B.C.   MAY–JULY

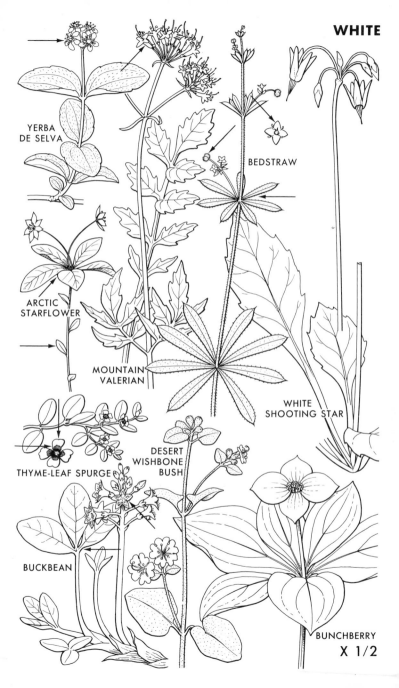

WHITE

YERBA
DE SELVA

BEDSTRAW

ARCTIC
STARFLOWER

MOUNTAIN
VALERIAN

WHITE
SHOOTING STAR

THYME-LEAF SPURGE

DESERT
WISHBONE
BUSH

BUCKBEAN

BUNCHBERRY
X 1/2

DAISIES OR DANDELIONLIKE FLOWERS

SUNFLOWER FAMILY (Compositae)
See also pp. W 102-8; Y 184-220; O 226;
R 328-32; B 384; G 404.

EATON'S DAISY *Erigeron eatonii*
Disk flowers are in a *raised crown*. Leaves linear. 3-12 in. In mts. Cascades–Sierra Nevada; Great Basin. MAY–JULY

COULTER'S DAISY *Erigeron coulteri*
Broad lancelike leaves have *clasping bases*. 1-4 ft. Mt. streambanks, meadows. Sierra Nevada to ne. Ore.
JUNE–AUG.

PHILADELPHIA DAISY *Erigeron philadelphicus*
Each flower head has *hundreds of fine* ray florets. 1-4 ft. Common in moist open fields. Pacific States. MARCH–JULY

OLYMPIC ASTER *Aster paucicapitatus*
Solitary flower head has about *13 white ray flowers*. Alternate leaves. ½-2 ft. Olympic Mts., Wash. AUG.-SEPT.

TWIGGY WREATH PLANT *Stephanomeria virgata*
The all ray-flowered flower head has 4-15 reddish-backed florets. Highly branched, leafless stems. Seed smooth-sided. 2-7 ft. Common. Calif. to sw. Ore. JULY–SEPT.

SMALL WREATH PLANT *Stephanomeria exigua*
(not shown)
Similar to above. Seeds grooved. Pacific States. MAY–OCT.

NEW MEXICO PLUMESEED *Rafinesquia neo-mexicana*
Dandelionlike leaves. Each seed topped by a beak and plumelike pappus. Ray flowers only. Milky sap. 2-5 ft. Mts. of Calif.
APRIL–JULY

TOBACCO WEED *Atrichoseris platyphylla*
The *spotted* leaves are in a basal rosette. Seeds awnless. Ray flowers only. Milky sap. Fragrant. 1-6 ft. Sandy washes. Mojave, Colorado Deserts. MARCH–MAY

WHITE HAWKWEED *Hieracium albiflorum*
The ray-flowered heads are *few-haired* and well separated by open branching. Conspicuously long-haired. Milky sap. 1-3 ft. Forest openings. Mts. of Pacific States. JUNE–AUG.

WESTERN HAWKWEED *Hieracium albertinum*
(not shown)
Similar to White Hawkweed. Flower heads are *clustered* and *strongly haired*. 1-6 in. East of Cascades. JUNE–AUG.

CUT-LEAVED DAISY *Erigeron compositus*
A low plant with *fan-shaped* leaves, each with cut lobes. 1-10 in. Rocky ridges. Calif. mts. to Wash. MAY–AUG.

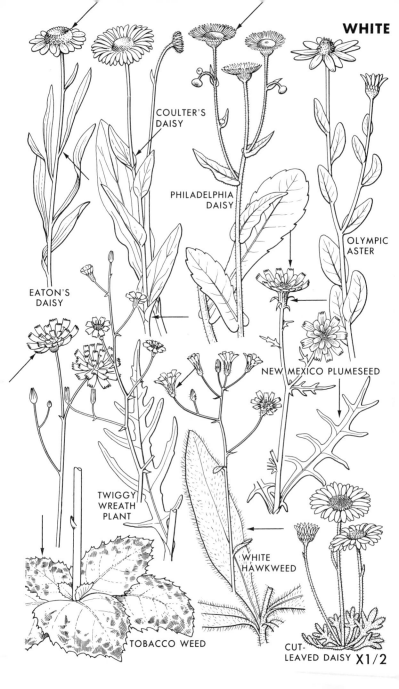

WHITE

COULTER'S DAISY

PHILADELPHIA DAISY

OLYMPIC ASTER

EATON'S DAISY

NEW MEXICO PLUMESEED

TWIGGY WREATH PLANT

WHITE HAWKWEED

TOBACCO WEED

CUT-LEAVED DAISY X1/2

STICKY TARWEEDS; SUNFLOWERS

SUNFLOWER FAMILY (Compositae)
See also pp. W 102–8; Y 184–220; O 226;
R 328–32; B 384; G 404.

STICKY CALYCADENIA *Calycadenia multiglandulosa*
Ray flower corolla broadly rounded with 2 *large outer* teeth
and a *single narrow* central tooth. Also with or without a red
eyespot at its base. Flower heads clustered. Plants hairy, with
sticky tack or T-shaped glands mixed in. ½–2½ ft. Meadow
edges. Sierra Nevada foothills.   JUNE–SEPT.

SOFT CALYCADENIA   *Calycadenia mollis*
Similar to Sticky Calycadenia. Ray flower has *3 equal and
nearly free lobes.* Also yellow and rose flowered forms.
½–2½ ft. Common in open places. W. Sierra Nevada foothills,
Calif. Coast Ranges.   MAY–OCT.

ROUGH EYELASH   *Blepharipappus scaber*
The 3-toothed ray flower has 3 *purple veins* on its back. Short
linear leaves. Pappus linear with a fringe of eyelash-like hairs.
4–12 in. Common. Great Basin.   APRIL–AUG.

SIERRA LAYIA   *Layia pentachaeta*
Basal and stem leaves *both* narrowly linear with *elongated*
pairs of lobes. Broad oval ray flowers have 3 equal teeth.
Sticky-haired. ½–3 ft. Common on grassy slopes below
3000 ft. Foothills of Sierra Nevada, southwestern margin of
Central Valley.   MARCH–MAY

WHITE LAYIA   *Layia glandulosa*
Basal leaves linear with *1-4 pairs of short* lobes, stem leaves
entire. Ray flower tip has 3 equal teeth. Sticky-haired. ½–2 ft.
Common. Pacific States.   MARCH–JUNE

HAYFIELD TARWEED   *Hemizonia luzulaefolia*
Each ray flower long, linear, 3-toothed, the *inner tooth nar-
rower.* Inner disk flower *anthers black,* giving the flower a
speckled appearance. Stem and leaves sticky-haired. ½–3 ft.
Grasslands, open woodlands. Central Valley of Calif., Calif.
Coast Ranges.   APRIL–NOV.

WHITE MULE EARS   *Wyethia helianthoides*
Note the *massively enlarged* sunflowerlike head. 1–2½ ft.
Moist meadows. Great Basin.   MAY–JUNE

PINK-RAYED CROWN   *Syntrichopappus lemmonii*
Ray flowers 6–8, uppersides with *pale yellow base,* undersides
rose-colored with bright red veins. Leaves linear on an erect
reddish stem. 1–4 in. Sandy slopes 3000–5000 ft. Western margin of Mojave Desert.   APRIL–MAY

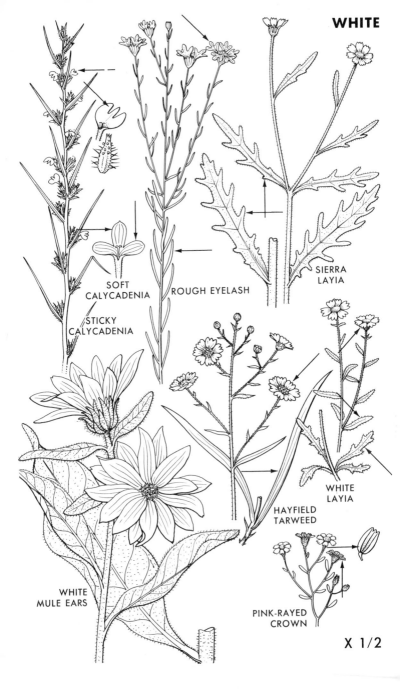

WHITE

SOFT
CALYCADENIA

STICKY
CALYCADENIA

ROUGH EYELASH

SIERRA
LAYIA

WHITE
LAYIA

HAYFIELD
TARWEED

WHITE
MULE EARS

PINK-RAYED
CROWN

X 1/2

PINCUSHIONS; WOOLLY SUNFLOWERS

SUNFLOWER FAMILY (Compositae)
See also pp. W 102–8; Y 184–220; O 226; R 328–32;
B 384; G 404.

EMORY'S ROCK DAISY *Perityle emoryi*
Note the broadly triangular leaves with deeply toothed margins. 3–15 in. All S. Calif. FEB.–MAY

WHITE WOOLLY DAISY *Antheropeas lanosum*
Flower heads ½–2 in. broad. The white ray flowers often have red veins. The linear leaves have a cottony covering. 1–6 in. Sandy places. Mojave, Colorado Deserts. FEB.–MAY

WESTERN COLTSFOOT *Petasites palmatus*
Terminal *cluster* of white to pinkish flowers on a single fat stem. Basal leaves broadly triangular. ½–2 ft. Shady woods, streambanks. All coastal mts., Cascades. MARCH–JULY

TRAIL PLANT *Adenocaulon bicolor*
Note the basal rosette of *triangular leaves* with a thin white cottony covering below a single tall leafless flower stem. 1–5 small flowers, soon becoming sticky clinging seeds. 1–3 ft. Shady forests. Pacific States. JUNE–SEPT.

FREMONT'S PINCUSHION *Chaenactis fremontii*
The *green leaves divided* into a few linear lobes. Pincushion-like disk flower heads. Each seed topped by *4 lancelike* bristles. ¼–1¼ ft. Common on sandy slopes. Mojave, Colorado Deserts; southern end of Central Valley of Calif.
MARCH–MAY

DUSTY MAIDEN *Chaenactis douglasii*
Cottony, *lacy pinnate leaves* below the white or pink-tinted pincushions. Each seed topped by ca. 10 *oblong* bristles. ½–1½ ft. Dry mt. slopes. Pacific States. MAY–SEPT.

PEBBLE PINCUSHION *Chaenactis carphoclinia*
Seeds topped by 4 *spine-tipped* bristles. Lacy pinnate leaves. ¼–1¼ ft. Common on hot desert pavements. Mojave, Colorado Deserts. MARCH–MAY

ESTEVE'S PINCUSHION *Chaenactis stevioides*
The grayish leaves divided twice into *numerous short, thick segments.* Seeds topped by 4 flattened bristles with short triangular tips. 2–10 in. Sandy places below 5000 ft. Mojave, Colorado Deserts; s. Central Valley of Calif. MARCH–MAY

SPANISH NEEDLES *Palofoxia arida*
Leaves *linear.* On top of each seed are *needlelike* bristles with a central midrib. Pincushion-like flower heads. ½–3 ft. Sandy washes. Mojave, Colorado Deserts. JAN.–SEPT.

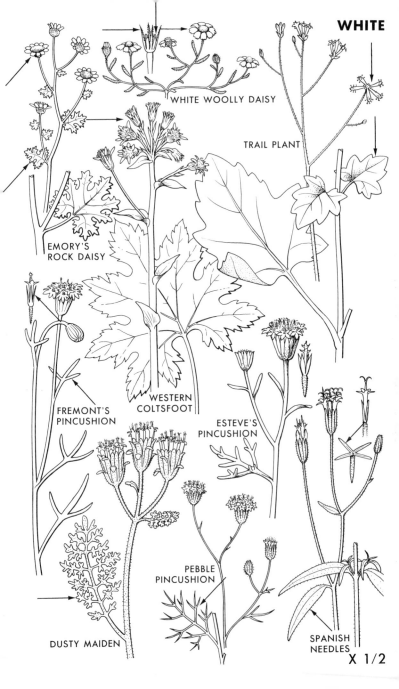

WHITE

WHITE WOOLLY DAISY

TRAIL PLANT

EMORY'S
ROCK DAISY

FREMONT'S
PINCUSHION

WESTERN
COLTSFOOT

ESTEVE'S
PINCUSHION

PEBBLE
PINCUSHION

DUSTY MAIDEN

SPANISH
NEEDLES

X 1/2

DAISIES, THISTLES, EVERLASTINGS, SMELLY MAYWEEDS

SUNFLOWER FAMILY (Compositae)
See also pp. W 102–6; Y 184–220; O 226; R 328–32;
B 384; G 404.

OX EYE DAISY Alien   *Chrysanthemum leucanthemum*
Large *daisylike flowers*. Lower stem leaves spoon-shaped with
a toothed margin around the spoon bowl. 1–3 ft. Disturbed
places at all altitudes. Pacific States.   MAY–OCT.

ENGLISH DAISY Alien   *Bellis perennis*
Small *aster-like flowers* with many thin ray florets, white or
tinted pink. Leaves spoon-shaped. Prostrate. Mostly in lawns,
pastures. Pacific States.   ALL YEAR

MOJAVE DESERT STAR   *Monoptilon bellioides*
A small *mound of aster-like* flowers above the linear leaves.
Common on sandy plains. Mojave, Colorado Deserts.
      FEB.–MAY

DOG FENNEL Alien   *Anthemis cotula*
Note the *lacy leaves* divided 2–3 times into narrow segments.
Many flowers at the top of a well-branched stem. Strong bad
smell if handled. ½–3 ft. Pacific States.   APRIL–OCT.

COMMON YARROW   *Achillea millefolium*
The leaves linear with numerous, very short, *highly dissected
leaflets*. Flowers in *flat-topped* clusters. Stem covered with
white cottony hairs. Strong unpleasant odor. 1–3 ft. Sea level
to alpine. Pacific States.   MARCH–NOV.

PEREGRINE THISTLE   *Cirsium cymosum*
Erect stem. Flower heads cream to pale brown. 2–5 ft.
Meadows, woodlands. Cen. Calif. to cen. Ore.   JUNE–SEPT.

DRUMMOND'S THISTLE   *Cirsium drummondii*
Spiny white to pinkish *flower heads nestled* in a *flat* rosette of
spiny leaves. West of Cascades–Sierra Nevada.   JUNE–AUG.

ELK THISTLE (not shown)   *Cirsium foliosum*
Similar to Drummond's Thistle. High mts. and plains from
Cascades–Sierra Nevada east through Great Basin.
      JUNE–AUG.

ALPINE EVERLASTING   *Antennaria alpina*
Gray linear leaves in *tufted mats*. Papery flower heads on
leafless stem. 1–6 in. Alpine. Pacific States.   JULY–OCT.

NARROWLEAF EVERLASTING *Antennaria stenophylla*
Grayish linear leaves *scattered up* stem. Flowers are in an
elongated cone. 2–12 in. Great Basin in Wash.   MAY–JULY

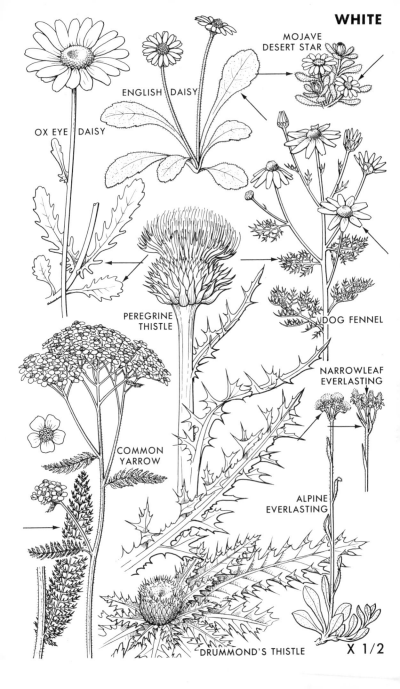

WHITE

MOJAVE
DESERT STAR

ENGLISH DAISY

OX EYE DAISY

PEREGRINE
THISTLE

DOG FENNEL

NARROWLEAF
EVERLASTING

COMMON
YARROW

ALPINE
EVERLASTING

DRUMMOND'S THISTLE

X 1/2

Yellow
Flowers

Yellow flowers separate out fairly easily. Pale yellow, cream, or greenish-yellow flowers merge into the Whites or Greens; if in doubt look here and also in White or Green. When possible, the group characteristics given in the text page titles are repeated in each color section, and in the same order. Where the flowers on a page look nearly the same but your sample does not fit, you can also use the cross references given for other colors.

5 PETALS; 2-LIPPED TUBULAR FLOWERS

SNAPDRAGON FAMILY (Scrophulariaceae)
See also pp. Y 114–18; R 234–44, 310; B 336–38, 372.

MUSK FLOWER   *Mimulus moschatus*
Flower and pedicel length *together is shorter* than adjacent petiole *and* leaf blade. Plants creeping. Feels cold and wet to the touch. Compare with next species to avoid confusion. 2–12 in. Moist places. Pacific States.   MAY–AUG.

FLORIFEROUS MONKEY FLOWER
                                 Mimulus floribundus
Similar to Musk Flower. Flower and pedicel length *together longer than* the adjacent petiole *and* triangular leaf blade. ½–2 ft. Moist places. Pacific States.   APRIL–OCT.

PRIMROSE MONKEY FLOWER   *Mimulus primuloides*
The *long threadlike pedicel* places the single flower well above a rosette of oval leaves. 1–4 in. Common; wet meadows. Pacific States.   MARCH–JUNE

CHICKWEED MONKEY FLOWER   *Mimulus alsinoides*
The tiny yellow flower has a *large central red spot* on the lower lip. 2–12 in. Wet mossy cliffs at low elevations. West of Cascades and south to nw. Calif.   MARCH–JUNE

YELLOW & WHITE MONKEY FLOWER
                                    Mimulus bicolor
The upper 2 petals are white and the lower 3 are yellow with red dots. 4–12 in. Moist banks below 6000 ft. Western slope Sierra Nevada and north to Trinity alps.   APRIL–JUNE

TOOTHED MONKEY FLOWER   *Mimulus dentatus*
Each flower has a distinct rounded fatness. Leaves bright green and toothed. 4–12 in. Wet woods. Northwestern coastal region of Calif. and north to Olympic Peninsula, Wash.   MAY–SEPT.

SEEP-SPRING MONKEY FLOWER   *Mimulus guttatus*
The fleshy stem has *smooth* leaves. Flowers are in definite racemes and have pedicels shorter than the corolla. Highly variable in size: 2 in.–3 ft. Common in wet places at lower and mid-mt. elevations. Pacific States.   MARCH–SEPT.

MOUNTAIN MONKEY FLOWER   *Mimulus tilingii*
Similar to preceding. Large flowers are above the leaves on pedicels that are *usually longer* than the corolla. Leaves nearly hidden. Each plant appears to be a *tuft* of yellow flowers. Wet alpine slopes. Pacific States.   JUNE–SEPT.

WIDE-THROAT MONKEY FLOWER   *Mimulus brevipes*
Flowers have a *wide-open throat* and a *very short* corolla tube. Lancelike leaves. 1–3 ft. S. Calif. Mts.   APRIL–JULY

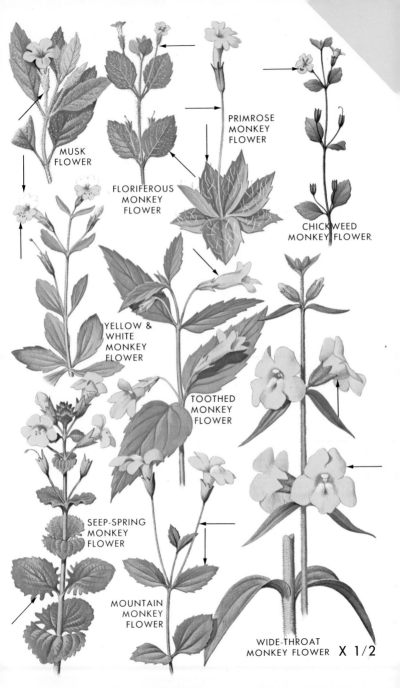

MUSK
FLOWER

PRIMROSE
MONKEY
FLOWER

FLORIFEROUS
MONKEY
FLOWER

CHICKWEED
MONKEY FLOWER

YELLOW &
WHITE
MONKEY
FLOWER

TOOTHED
MONKEY
FLOWER

SEEP-SPRING
MONKEY
FLOWER

MOUNTAIN
MONKEY
FLOWER

WIDE-THROAT
MONKEY FLOWER **X 1/2**

5 PETALS; 2-LIPPED TUBULAR FLOWERS

SNAPDRAGON FAMILY (Scrophulariaceae)
See also pp. Y 112–18; R 234–44, 310; B 336–38, 372.

FIELD OWL CLOVER *Orthocarpus campestris*
Stem leaves and flower bracts are *all linear* and *without* any lobes. Flowers bright yellow and well extended from the hairy calyx. All flower bracts completely *green.* 4–10 in. Moist depressions. Cen. Calif. to s. Ore. APRIL–JULY

CREAM SACS *Orthocarpus lithospermoides*
The flower corolla has *tiny bracts* and *calyx.* All flower bracts completely *green.* The *central leaf petiole quite broad* with thin threadlike lobes. Flowers are clear yellow to cream, becoming pink with age in some areas. ½–2 ft. Open grassy places. Cen. Calif. to s. Ore. APRIL–JUNE

HAIRY OWL CLOVER *Orthocarpus hispidus*
Small flower tube is yellow or white and barely extended beyond the *large threadlike lobes* of each flower bract. All flower bracts completely *green.* Stem leaves threadlike. 4–16 in. Moist fields. Pacific States. MAY–AUG.

BUTTER AND EGGS *Orthocarpus erianthus*
The white corolla tube has a distinct *right-angled jog,* a red-purple hooked beak, and 3 yellow sacs. The upper leaves and bracts are *purple-tipped.* 2–14 in. Often in great masses within grasslands. Calif. to s. Ore. MARCH–MAY

YELLOW RATTLE *Rhinanthus crista-galli*
The large *inflated calyx* has a *tiny* flower emerging from it. The flower has 3 lower sacs and a short, curved beak petal above. Sawtoothed, narrowly triangular leaves. ½–3 ft. Moist fields and slopes. Nw. Ore. to B.C. JUNE–AUG.

NARROW-LEAVED OWL CLOVER
Orthocarpus attenuatus
Corolla sacs *not inflated,* pale yellow, rarely dotted. Flower *bract tips white.* Stem leaves linear, the upper with 1 pair of threadlike lobes. 4–12 in. Grassy places. West of Cascades–Sierra Nevada, and S. Calif. Mts. MARCH–JUNE

PALLID OWL CLOVER *Orthocarpus linearilobus*
The 3 corolla *sacs are yellow* with red-purple spots. The *flower bract tips are white.* Lower stem leaves linear, the upper have 2–3 pairs of threadlike lobes. 4–12 in. Grassy places. Western slope of Sierra Nevada. APRIL–JUNE

GHOST FLOWER *Mohavea confertiflora*
Pale yellowish *cuplike flowers* are purple-dotted. 4–12 in. Sandy places. Mojave, Colorado Deserts to Baja. MARCH–APRIL

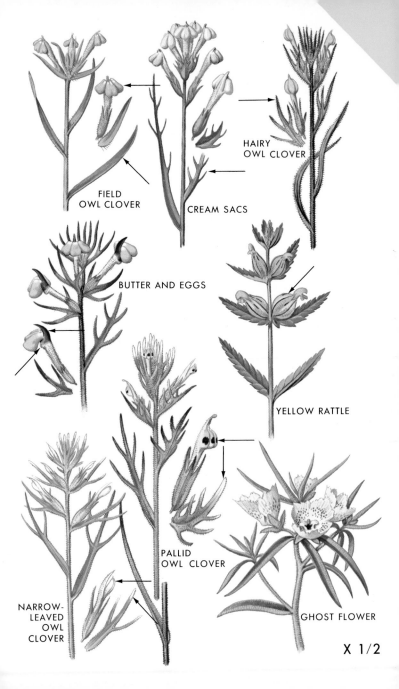

FIELD OWL CLOVER

CREAM SACS

HAIRY OWL CLOVER

BUTTER AND EGGS

YELLOW RATTLE

NARROW-LEAVED OWL CLOVER

PALLID OWL CLOVER

GHOST FLOWER

X 1/2

5 PETALS; 2-LIPPED FLOWERS

SNAPDRAGON FAMILY (Scrophulariaceae)
See also pp. Y 112–18; R 234–44, 310; B 336–38, 372.

WIGHT'S PAINTBRUSH   *Castilleja wightii*
The colored flower bract leaves have 3 nearly equal rounded
lobes. The lobe tips are a deep cream-yellow or dull red. The
spoutlike corolla tube has a blunt nose. Lower stem leaves
linear, while the upper have 3 sharp-pointed lobes. 1–3 ft. Dry
banks near coast. Santa Barbara, Calif., north to Wash. along
coast.   MARCH–JULY

THOMPSON'S PAINTBRUSH   *Castilleja thompsonii*
The *upper colored flower bract* leaves have 5 *linear* lobes and
are yellow-tipped. The spoutlike flower tube is greenish yellow. The *trilobed* stem leaves have narrow linear lobes.
4–16 in. Dry slopes. Common. Great Basin.   MAY–JULY

WALLOWA PAINTBRUSH   *Castilleja chrysantha*
The *oval flower bracts* and the square-tipped corolla are both a
pale yellow-green. Stem leaves linear or 3-pointed. 4–12 in.
Most common species in alpine and subalpine meadows of the
Wallowa and Blue Mts. of Ore.   JUNE–SEPT.

COBWEBBY PAINTBRUSH   *Castilleja arachnoidea*
The flower spike has a *thick, tight, rounded* appearance. The
colored flower bracts are trilobed, with a wide round-tipped
central lobe. Stem leaves are trilobed and troughlike. The
entire plant is heavily covered with *spiderweb* hairs. 4–12 in.
Ridges and slopes. Mts. of n. Calif. and sw. Ore. JUNE–AUG.

DALMATIAN TOADFLAX Alien   *Linaria dalmatica*
The erect spikes have *snapdragonlike* flowers with a *pointed
spur.* The stem leaves are oval and blue-green. 2–5 ft. Fields
and roadsides. Pacific States.   MAY–AUG.

WOOLLY MULLEIN Alien   *Verbascum thapsus*
Note the large, *soft, white-woolly* leaves extending up the single
coarse stem. The terminal spike has numerous small, slightly
bilateral-shaped yellow flowers. 2–6 ft. Common in disturbed
places. Pacific States.   JUNE–SEPT.

MOTH MULLEIN Alien   *Verbascum blattaria*
The large, flat, slightly bilateral-shaped flowers are a bright
yellow or white on tall spikes. The straplike leaves are bright
green. 1–4 ft. Disturbed places. Pacific States.   MAY–OCT.

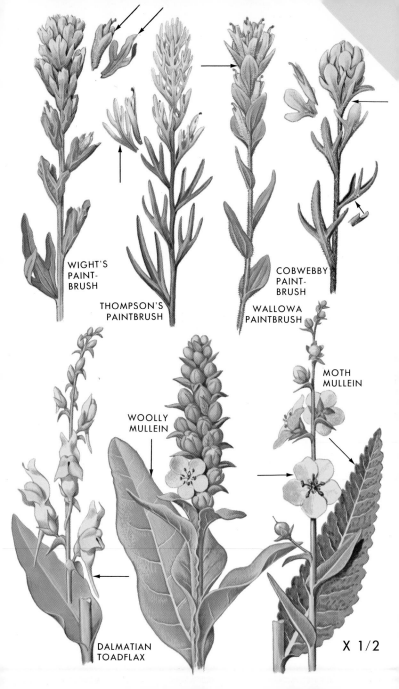

WIGHT'S PAINT-BRUSH

THOMPSON'S PAINTBRUSH

COBWEBBY PAINT-BRUSH

WALLOWA PAINTBRUSH

WOOLLY MULLEIN

MOTH MULLEIN

DALMATIAN TOADFLAX

X 1/2

5 PETALS; 2-LIPPED TUBULAR FLOWERS

Snapdragon Family (Scrophulariaceae)
See also pp. Y 112–16; R 234–44, 310; B 336–38, 372.

HOT ROCK PENSTEMON   *Penstemon deustus*
The short, tan to yellow, tubular flower has *distinct red lines* on the petal lobes. The lancelike leaves have sharply jagged edges and are in opposite pairs. Somewhat bushy. ½–2 ft. Rocky places. Cen. Wash. to cen. Calif.   **May–July**

YELLOW PENSTEMON   *Penstemon confertus*
The pale, creamy-yellow flowers *without markings* are in dense whorls. The upper stem leaves are narrowly linear and smooth-edged, while the lower have large marginal teeth and are blue-green. ½–2 ft. Great Basin of Wash. and nw. Ore.
    May–Aug.

COILED LOUSEWORT   *Pedicularis contorta*
The pale yellow flower has a coiled or curved beak surrounded by a large rounded hood. Arranged in spikes. The long-petioled leaves have many opposite pairs of sawtoothed leaflets. ½–2 ft. Mt. meadows. N. Calif. to Wash.
    June–Aug.

TOWERING LOUSEWORT   *Pedicularis bracteosa*
The short, *linear, round-beaked* flowers are in dense towering spikes. Flowers are pale yellow with reddish tints, or in some areas are dark red. Calyx tips linear. The large, triangular-outlined leaves have many opposite-paired, linear leaflets. 2–3 ft. Damp mt. meadows. N. Calif. to B.C., and Great Basin.   **June–Aug.**

STICKY CHINESE HOUSES   *Collinsia tinctoria*
The flowers are arranged in *pagoda-like* whorls. The light yellow to greenish-white flowers have purple dots or lines and a *large lower lip*. Oval leaves in opposite pairs. ½–2 ft. Dry open places below 6000 ft. W. Sierra Nevada, Calif. North Coast Ranges.   **May–Aug.**

DWARF LOUSEWORT   *Pedicularis semibarbata*
The *low flat whorl* of pinnate leaves has a dense short spike of linear, beaked flowers *hidden* within the rosette. Flowers are yellow with reddish tints. The pinnate leaflets have a second pair at right angles. 2–6 in. Common; shady *dry* conifer forests. Mts. of Calif.   **May–July**

MOUNT RAINIER LOUSEWORT
      Pedicularis rainierensis
The pinnate leaves are both in a basal rosette and scattered along the short stem. Flower pale yellow. Calyx tips *rounded*. 1–3 ft. Alpine and subalpine meadows. Mt. Rainier National Park, Wash.   **July–Aug.**

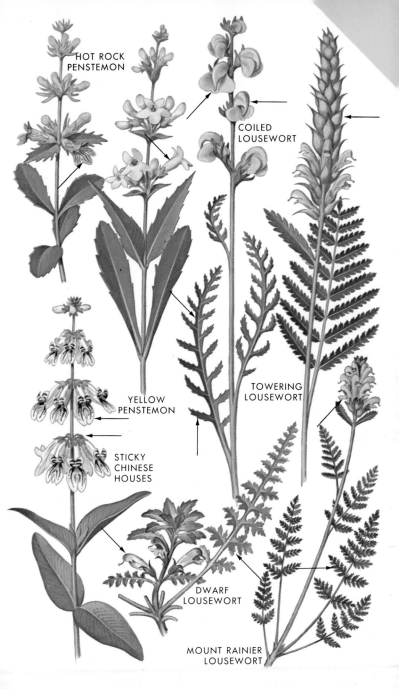

HOT ROCK
PENSTEMON

COILED
LOUSEWORT

YELLOW
PENSTEMON

STICKY
CHINESE
HOUSES

TOWERING
LOUSEWORT

DWARF
LOUSEWORT

MOUNT RAINIER
LOUSEWORT

5 PETALS; VINELIKE STEMS

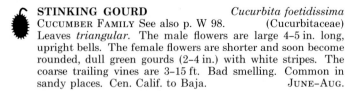

STINKING GOURD   *Cucurbita foetidissima*
CUCUMBER FAMILY See also p. W 98.   (Cucurbitaceae)
Leaves *triangular*. The male flowers are large 4–5 in. long, upright bells. The female flowers are shorter and soon become rounded, dull green gourds (2–4 in.) with white stripes. The coarse trailing vines are 3–15 ft. Bad smelling. Common in sandy places. Cen. Calif. to Baja.   JUNE–AUG.

FINGER-LEAVED GOURD   *Cucurbita digitata*
CUCUMBER FAMILY See also p. W 98.   (Cucurbitaceae)
Note the *narrow 5-fingered* leaf has a central white strip. Flowers and gourds as above. Vines 3–15 ft. Sandy places. Occasional, s. Calif.   AUG.–OCT.

COYOTE GOURD   *Cucurbita palmata*
CUCUMBER FAMILY See also p. W 98.   (Cucurbitaceae)
Note the *palmate 5-lobed* leaf. Flowers, gourds, and vines as above. Dry sandy flats. Cen. and s. Calif.   APRIL–SEPT.

PUNCTURE VINE Alien   *Tribulus terrestris*
CALTROP FAMILY   (Zygophyllaceae)
Note the oppositely paired *pinnate leaves* are along a weak, sprawling stem. Flowers yellow-orange, becoming a *starlike spiny seedpod*. Disturbed places. Pacific States. APRIL–OCT.

NEW ZEALAND SPINACH Alien
     Tetragonia tetragonioides
CARPET WEED FAMILY   (Aizoaceae)
The triangular succulent leaves along the trailing stem are *bright green* and have *sparkling crystalline vesicles*. A single yellow-green flower occurs on the top side of each leaf petiole base. Beaches, salt marshes. Calif. and Ore. coasts.
     APRIL–SEPT.

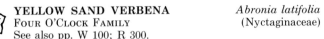

YELLOW ICE PLANT Alien   *Mesembryanthemum edule*
CARPET WEED FAMILY   (Aizoaceae)
Fat, succulent *3-sided leaves* occur along a long trailing stem. Each yellow flower has *numerous* petals which dry pink. Ovary inferior. Sand dunes, banks. Coastal region of Pacific States.
     APRIL–OCT.

YELLOW SAND VERBENA   *Abronia latifolia*
FOUR O'CLOCK FAMILY   (Nyctaginaceae)
See also pp. W 100; R 300.
The *thick, succulent,* round to kidney-shaped leaves are oppositely paired on a trailing glandular-haired stem. The numerous tubular flowers are in an *umbel*. Prostrate stems. Coastal beaches of Pacific States.   MAY–OCT.

STINKING GOURD

FINGER-LEAVED GOURD

COYOTE GOURD

NEW ZEALAND SPINACH

YELLOW ICE PLANT

YELLOW SAND VERBENA

PUNCTURE VINE

X 1/2

3 PETALS: MARIPOSA TULIPS

LILY FAMILY (Liliaceae)
See also pp. W 4–16; Y 122–24; O 228–30; R 252–56;
B 352; G 388–90.

GOLDENBOWL MARIPOSA TULIP
Calochortus concolor
Large golden bowl-like flowers have a *red-brown rounded* area
at the petal base surrounding a gland area with a thick *hornlike
projection* of hairs. Long yellow hairs also present. 1–2 ft. San
Bernardino Mts., Calif., to Baja. MAY–JULY

TIBURON MARIPOSA TULIP *Calochortus tiburonensis*
The pale yellow petals are *triangular pointed* and have a
central inverted V of red-brown. *Entire* inner petal surface
covered with long, pale-yellow hairs. 1–2 ft. Serpentine slopes.
Tiburon Ridge, San Francisco Bay area. Mid-JUNE

CLUB-HAIRED MARIPOSA TULIP
Calochortus clavatus
Note the *jagged, transverse* red-brown line on the lemon-
yellow petals. Club-shaped hairs on inner petal. 1½–3 ft.
Rocky slopes below 4000 ft. W. Sierra Nevada foothills, Calif.
South Coast Ranges to Los Angeles. MAY–JUNE

GOLDEN FAIRY LANTERN *Calochortus amabilis*
The *nodding,* somewhat *triangular* flowers are a deep clear
yellow. Petal edges fringed. ½–2 ft. Shady thickets, woods.
Calif. North Coast Ranges. APRIL–JUNE

SAN LUIS OBISPO MARIPOSA TULIP
Calochortus obispoensis
The *flat starlike* flower has narrow *lancelike* petals tipped with
long purple-brown hairs. Long needlelike sepals. 1–2 ft. Hills
in San Luis Obispo, Calif. area. MAY–JUNE

GOLD NUGGETS *Calochortus luteus*
Each bright yellow petal has a *central red-brown spot* on the
inner surface. Occurs in large golden masses. ½–2 ft. Open
fields below 3000 ft. Calif. Coast Ranges and w. Sierra Nevada foothills. APRIL–JUNE

YELLOW STAR TULIP *Calochortus monophyllus*
Small upright flowers whose inner surfaces are *yellow-haired*
and *without* other colors. 3–8 in. Woodlands. Western foothills of n. Sierra Nevada. APRIL–MAY

WEED'S MARIPOSA TULIP *Calochortus weedii*
The yellow-orange flowers are *flecked* red-brown inside and are
also *margined* outside with red-brown. The inner petal surface
has long yellow hairs and a round reddish gland from which a
horn of yellow hairs projects. 1–3 ft. Rocky soil. Coastal hills,
Monterey to San Diego, Calif. MAY–JULY

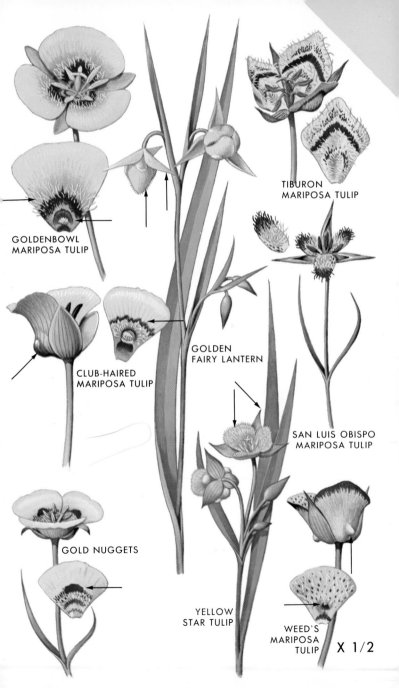

GOLDENBOWL
MARIPOSA TULIP

TIBURON
MARIPOSA TULIP

CLUB-HAIRED
MARIPOSA TULIP

GOLDEN
FAIRY LANTERN

SAN LUIS OBISPO
MARIPOSA TULIP

GOLD NUGGETS

YELLOW
STAR TULIP

WEED'S
MARIPOSA
TULIP

X 1/2

3 OR 6 PETALS; RACEMES OR UMBELS

LILY FAMILY (Liliaceae)
See also pp. W 4–16; Y 122; O 228–30; R 252–56;
B 352; G 388–90.

YELLOW FAWN LILY *Erythronium grandiflorum*
Large, bright yellow, *nodding, starlike* flowers on a leafless stem. Bright green leaves. 4–12 in. Common. N. Calif. to B.C., and Great Basin; rare in Sierra Nevada. MARCH–MAY

YELLOW BELLS *Fritillaria pudica*
1–3 strongly *nodding yellow bells* are above the linear leaves. 2–12 in. Open places. Great Basin. MARCH–JUNE

LEMON LILY *Lilium parryi*
The 1 to few (rarely to 25) clear waxy, lemon-yellow *trumpet-like* flowers have occasional maroon spots. Fragrant. Stem has linear leaves. 2–5 ft. Wet springy places 4000–9000 ft. Mts. of s. Calif. JULY–AUG.

CALIFORNIA BOG ASPHODEL *Narthecium californicum*
The thick stamen *filaments woolly-haired*. Small starlike flowers are in a *brushlike* cluster. 1–2 ft. Wet meadows. Sw. Ore., Calif. North Coast Ranges, Sierra Nevada. JULY–AUG.

AMARYLLIS FAMILY (Amaryllidaceae)
See also pp. W 18; R 254–62; B 352.

GOLDEN STARS *Bloomeria crocea*
A sunburst of 6 golden *linear* petals *separate to bases.* Long *threadlike* filaments. Flowers in an umbel. 2–24 in. Woodlands. Calif. South Coast Ranges to Baja. APRIL–JUNE

PRETTY FACE *Triteleia ixioides*
Note that the stamens are attached in the *center* of a *forked ribbonlike filament.* Petals fused below into a tube. Flowers in umbels. 2–24 in. Three subspecies: (1) COAST P.F.-ssp. *ixioides* has bright golden yellow flowers that age purplish. Strictly in coastal hills from San Francisco south to San Luis Obispo, Calif. MAY–AUG. (2) FOOTHILL P.F.-ssp. *scabra* flowers are *flat wheels* of pale creamy yellow. Petal segments broad. Grasslands, woodlands. Western foothills of Sierra Nevada. MARCH–JUNE. (3) MOUNTAIN P.F.-ssp. *analina* flowers are smaller and dark yellow with purple veins. Mt. meadows and shady forests. Siskiyous of s. Ore. south through Sierra Nevada. MAY–AUG.

HENDERSON'S STARS *Triteleia hendersonii*
The pale yellow petal segments have dark *blue stripes* and are united below in a short tube. Stamen *filaments linear.* Flowers in an umbel. 4–12 in. Shady woods. Sw. Ore. and Klamath River area of n. Calif. MAY–JUNE

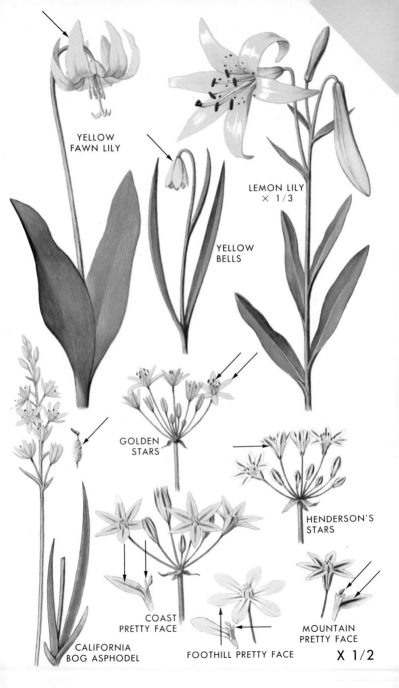

YELLOW
FAWN LILY

LEMON LILY
× 1/3

YELLOW
BELLS

GOLDEN
STARS

HENDERSON'S
STARS

CALIFORNIA
BOG ASPHODEL

COAST
PRETTY FACE

FOOTHILL PRETTY FACE

MOUNTAIN
PRETTY FACE

X 1/2

3 OR 6 PETALS; FLAT IRIS-LIKE LEAVES

Iris Family (Iridaceae)
See also pp. R 254; B 350.

HARTWEG'S IRIS   *Iris hartwegii*
Short stout corolla tube above ovary. Pedicel below ovary *very long.* Petals *narrow,* pale yellow. 2–16 in. W. Sierra Nevada foothills; S. Calif. Mts. (where blue-flowered). May–June

FERNALD'S IRIS   *Iris fernaldii*
Corolla tube above the ovary *very long,* funnel-like near the top. Pedicel below the ovary very short. Flowers soft creamy yellow, indistinctly veined. ½–1½ ft. Shady woods. Cen. Calif. Coast Ranges. April–May

SISKIYOU IRIS   *Iris bracteata*
Corolla tube is *short and narrow* above the ovary, *long-* pediceled (2–3 in.) below. Petals light yellow with red-brown veins. 8–12 in. Pine woods. Siskiyous, s. Ore. May–June

BOWL-TUBED IRIS   *Iris macrosiphon*
Corolla tube above the ovary *very long* and has a *bowl-shaped* enlargement at the top. Pedicel below ovary short. Flower color variable: yellow, creamy-white, and various shades of blue. ½–1½ ft. Open places or woods. Calif. Coast Ranges and w. Sierra Nevada foothills. April–June

CALIF. GOLDEN-EYED GRASS
                                              Sisyrinchium californicum
Bright yellow *6-petaled* flowers with 5–7 dark veins. Tufted, flat, dull green leaves. ½–2 ft. Wet places along coast. West of Cascades, south along coast to cen. Calif. May–June

ELEMER'S YELLOW-EYED GRASS
(not shown)   *Sisyrinchium elmeri*
Similar to preceding. Flowers yellow-orange, dark veined. 2–8 in. Interior mt. meadows. Calif. July–Aug.

DOUGLAS'S IRIS   *Iris douglasiana*
Top of ovary *nipplelike.* Both the corolla tube above the ovary and the pedicel below are of *nearly equal length* (1–2 in.). Petals pale creamy yellow to dark blue. Coastal hills. S. Ore. south to Santa Barbara, Calif. Jan.–May

GOLDEN IRIS   *Iris innominata*
Corolla tube above ovary *short* (1 in.), funnel-like at the top. Pedicel below ovary *short.* Petals bright yellow to blue-purple. ½–2 ft. Sw. Ore., adjacent Calif. May–June

YELLOW-LEAVED IRIS   *Iris chrysophylla*
Corolla tube *very long, tapering* to ovary below. Pedicel below ovary *short.* Petals white with a central yellow area and *bright red-brown veins.* 2–8 in. Open woods. West of Cascades in Ore., barely into Calif. May–July

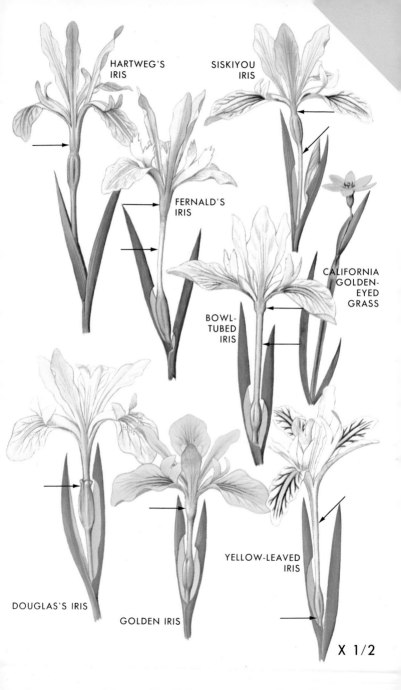

HARTWEG'S IRIS

SISKIYOU IRIS

FERNALD'S IRIS

CALIFORNIA GOLDEN-EYED GRASS

BOWL-TUBED IRIS

DOUGLAS'S IRIS

GOLDEN IRIS

YELLOW-LEAVED IRIS

X 1/2

MANY PETALS: PRICKLY PEAR CACTUS

Cactus Family (Cactaceae)
See also pp. Y 130–32; R 264.

PANCAKE PRICKLY PEAR   *Opuntia chlorotica*
The *treelike trunk has* large yellow-green *pancake* pads. Each
spine cluster has 3–6 main *all-yellow spines* and is *deflexed* to
one side ($^{3}\!/_{4}$–$1\,^{1}\!/_{4}$ in. long). Each spine cluster is surrounded by a
round fringe of very short spinelets. 3–8 ft. Rocky walls.
Mojave, Colorado Deserts.   May–June

PYGMY PRICKLY PEAR   *Opuntia fragilis*
Tiny ($^{1}\!/_{2}$–2 in.), dark green, globular stem pads. Each round
stem bump has 1–5 slender, white to brown spines $^{1}\!/_{8}$ to 1 in.
long. Forms low mats. Dry places. Great Basin. May–June

GRIZZLY BEAR CACTUS   *Opuntia erinacea*
The *oblong, flat green* pads have *numerous long* gray whiskerlike spines (1–$2\,^{1}\!/_{2}$ in.). Flowers yellow, aging pink. In low
clumps. 1–2 ft. Rocky slopes. S. Sierra Nevada flank to mts. of
Mojave Desert.   May–June

INDIAN FIG Alien   *Opuntia ficus-indica*
Treelike, 8–15 ft. Large green oblong pads (1–2 ft.) are *usually
smooth* (spineless). Dry slopes. Los Angeles Basin and south to
Baja. Frequent garden plant.   May–June

PLAINS PRICKLY PEAR   *Opuntia polyacantha*
A *circle of gray woolly hair* surrounds each cluster of 5–11
spines ($^{1}\!/_{4}$–2 in.). Flat oblong stem pads (2–6 in.). Forms broad,
low mats 4–12 in. high. Dry slopes. Great Basin, and to B.C.
                    May–June

MESA PRICKLY PEAR   *Opuntia littoralis*
Pads waxy-blue covered and narrowly oblong (5–12 in.). Main
spines *round* in cross section. Within each spine cluster of 8–16
is 1 erect spine $^{1}\!/_{2}$–$1\,^{1}\!/_{2}$ in. long and 2 lateral ones nearly as long
but *bent* downward. Erect or spreading stems. 3–5 ft. Dry
washes. Along s. Calif. coast; western margin of Mojave,
Colorado Deserts.   May–June

COAST PRICKLY PEAR   *Opuntia oricola*
Similar to preceding. Each spine *flattened* in cross section.
Stem joints oblong. Treelike 3–10 ft. Occurring with coastal
sagebrush. Santa Barbara, Calif., to Baja.   May–June

ENGELMANN'S PRICKLY PEAR   *Opuntia phaeacantha*
Usually *3 main spines at right angles* per spine cluster. Spines
flattened in shape. Stem pads round to oblong in sprawling
right-angled stems. 1–4 ft. Common. E. Mojave Desert and
east.   May–June

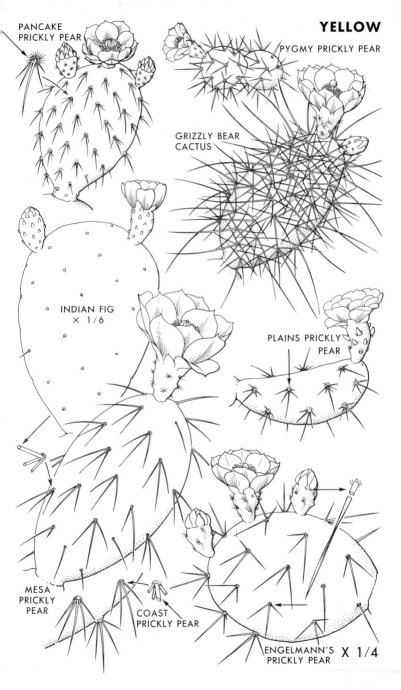

YELLOW

PANCAKE PRICKLY PEAR

PYGMY PRICKLY PEAR

GRIZZLY BEAR CACTUS

INDIAN FIG × 1/6

PLAINS PRICKLY PEAR

MESA PRICKLY PEAR

COAST PRICKLY PEAR

ENGELMANN'S PRICKLY PEAR × 1/4

MANY PETALS: CYLINDRICAL
CHOLLA CACTUS

CACTUS FAMILY (Cactaceae)
See also pp. Y 128–32; R 264.

TEDDY BEAR CHOLLA   *Opuntia bigelovii*
The single erect treelike trunk (2–5 ft.) has many *teddy-bear arms* clustered at the top. The stem joints are *densely packed with porcupine-like* white to pale yellow spines. Flowers yellow to pale green, rarely red-tinted. Each joint is only slightly attached, so those who carelessly brush by will have it "jump" — a painful experience. 2–5 ft. Well-drained slopes. Mojave, Colorado Deserts.   APRIL–MAY

DEVILS CHOLLA   *Opuntia stanlyi*
The short, raised stem bumps are about ½ in. long and high, but are nearly concealed by *stout, broad, flattened* spines *without* a papery sheath. One spine is central, with a ring of shorter spines. Stem pads are slender cylinders 1–4 in. long and 1–1½ in. thick. Flowers yellow or with a red tint. Low creeping mats. Dry flats above 3000 ft. Mts. of Mojave Desert.
                                      MAY–JUNE

SILVER CHOLLA   *Opuntia echinocarpa*
The *short, round* stem bumps ¼–½ in. long and 1 in. wide with a cluster of 3–10 long spines *with silvery papery sheaths.* Stem pads are slender, 4–8 in. long and 1 in. wide. The greenish-yellow flowers have some of the outer petals streaked with red. Erect, highly branched stem. 2–4 ft. Washes, mesas. Mojave, Colorado Deserts.   APRIL–MAY

DIAMOND CHOLLA   *Opuntia ramosissima*
Note the *diamond-like* surface pattern on the thin pencil-like cylindrical stem pads and the *long solitary* yellow spines. Flowers yellow-green or tinted red. Bushy or treelike, 1–5 ft. Mojave, Colorado Deserts.   APRIL–MAY

BUCKHORN CHOLLA   *Opuntia acanthocarpa*
Stem pads are slender cylinders 1 ft. long with *elongated* raised bumps about 1 in. long and ¼ in. wide. Each spine cluster has 10–12 long, stout (1–1¼ in.), straw-colored spines. Flowers yellow (or reddish in some areas). Open, well-branched plants 3–7 ft. Dry slopes. Mojave, Colorado Deserts.   MAY–JUNE

PARRY'S CANE CHOLLA   *Opuntia parryi*
Each spine cluster has *very short spines.* The cylinder-like stem pads are *nearly smooth* with prominently raised and narrowly elongated bumps about 1 in. long. Flowers yellow-green with the petal tips red-tinted. Stems few-branched, 2–8 ft. Common on gravelly slopes. Sw. corner Central Valley of Calif. to Colorado Desert.   MAY–JUNE

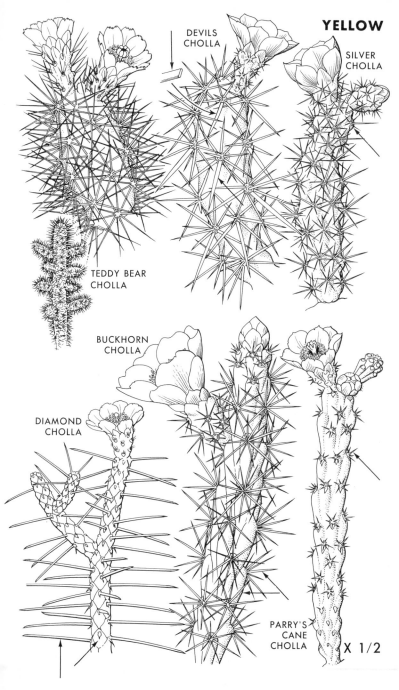

YELLOW

DEVILS
CHOLLA

SILVER
CHOLLA

TEDDY BEAR
CHOLLA

BUCKHORN
CHOLLA

DIAMOND
CHOLLA

PARRY'S
CANE
CHOLLA

X 1/2

MANY PETALS: CACTUS; 1 NONJOINTED BARREL- OR SNAKELIKE STEM

CACTUS FAMILY (Cactaceae)
See also pp. Y 128–30; R 264.

GOLDEN SNAKE CACTUS   *Bergerocactus emoryi*
The long *yellow snakelike* stems are prostrate to erect in usu-
ally dense clumps. Each stem has 15–25 ribs bearing a *dense
mat of ultralong* golden-yellow spines. 10–30 spines per cluster.
Flowers yellow-green. 3–9 ft. Dry cliffs, mesas near San Diego,
Calif. to Baja.   MAY–JUNE

RED BARREL CACTUS   *Ferocactus acanthodes*
The stem is a *single, large, elongated, barrel-like* cylinder
1–5 ft. tall. Each rib has spine clusters of flattened reddish
spines. Flowers yellow. 1–6 ft. Rocky walls and slopes.
Mojave, Colorado Deserts to Baja.   MARCH–MAY

COAST BARREL CACTUS   *Ferocactus viridescens*
Note the *large, single, round, barrel*-shaped stem is usually
broader than long. Stem 15–20 ribbed. Each spine cluster
usually has 4 short main spines per cluster in a maltese cross.
Flowers yellow-green with a central red stripe. Rocky hillsides.
Coastal hills. San Diego, Calif., area to Baja.

MOJAVE MOUND CACTUS   *Echinocactus polycephalus*
Note the *clump* of 10–20 *watermelon-sized* ribbed cylinders.
Flowers yellow with a *dense, woolly* outer covering. Each spine
cluster has 3–4 curved red-gray central spines and 6–8 shorter
ones below. ½–1½ ft. Rocky slopes. Mojave Desert.
                                                   APRIL–MAY

UNISEXUAL FISHHOOK CACTUS *Mammillaria dioica*
Each stem bump topped by a spine cluster of 5–15 bristles, the
one central spine a curved fishhook. The short, round-topped,
cylinder-like stem has many rounded bumps covering the surface. Flowers small, pale yellow or creamy, some with pink
midribs. Each plant usually of one sex (a few are both).
2–12 in. Sandy places. W. Colorado Desert to San Diego on
coast and south to Baja.   FEB.–APRIL

SIMPSON'S BALL CACTUS   *Pediocactus simpsonii*
Spines are in *radiating clusters* on *nipplelike* bumps which are
in 8–14 spiral rows. Each spine cluster has 8–13 *long,* straight,
yellow to red-brown ones and 10–25 *smaller* ones below.
Flowers yellow-green, white, or dark red. Small (3–8 in.),
round, melonlike stems, single or clustered.   MAY–JULY

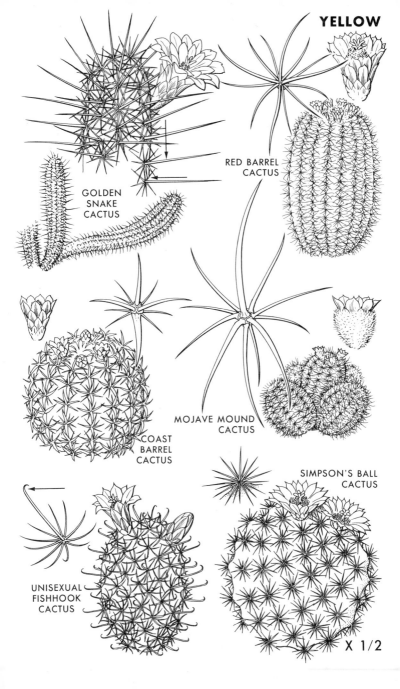

YELLOW

GOLDEN SNAKE CACTUS

RED BARREL CACTUS

COAST BARREL CACTUS

MOJAVE MOUND CACTUS

SIMPSON'S BALL CACTUS

UNISEXUAL FISHHOOK CACTUS

X 1/2

4 OR 6 PETALS; TINY TUBULAR FLOWERS IN CLUSTERS

BUCKWHEAT FAMILY (Polygonaceae)
See also pp. W 34–38; Y 136–38; R 276–78.

DEVILS SPINY HERB   *Chorizanthe rigida*
The small, tufted plant has broadly oval leaves and a cluster of spiny flowers. Each flower surrounded by 3 long spines. 1–4 in. Stony places. Mojave, Colorado Deserts.   MARCH–MAY

PUNY ERIOGONUM   *Eriogonum pusillum*
The gray spatula-like to spoonlike leaves are in a basal rosette. Stem leafless and well-branched. Flowers in few flowered umbels, pale yellow with red midribs. 4–12 in. Common on plains. Mojave Desert.   MARCH–JULY

ROCK ERIOGONUM   *Eriogonum saxatile*
The fat *wedgelike* and *white felt*-covered leaves are all in a basal rosette below the somewhat branched stems. Flowers in *loose whorls,* pale yellow to pale pink. 4–12 in. Rocky ridges. 4000–12,000 ft. Mts. of cen. and s. Calif.   MAY–JULY

SLENDER ERIOGONUM   *Eriogonum gracile*
The long erect upper branches have many well-spaced *whorls* of flowers *around the stem.* Basal leaves elongated, often dried at flowering time. Flowers pale yellow, pink, or white. 1–3 ft. Common in open woodland fields at low elevations. Cen. and s. Calif.   JULY–OCT.

KIDNEYLEAF ERIOGONUM   *Eriogonum reniforme*
All of the *felt-haired, kidney-shaped* leaves are in a flat basal rosette. The leafless stem branched in an orderly forking pattern. Each branchlet is tipped by a single umbel of yellow flowers. 2–12 in. Very common in sandy places. Mojave, Colorado Deserts to Baja.   MARCH–JUNE

DESERT TRUMPET   *Eriogonum inflatum*
Note the *inflated trumpet* at the top of *each* stem section of the well-branched, leafless stem. Oval to rounded green leaves with crisped margins are in a basal cluster. Flowers yellow with hairy red-brown midribs. 1–4 ft. Common in washes, mesas. Mojave, Colorado Deserts.   FEB.–OCT.

LITTLE TRUMPET ERIOGONUM   *Eriogonum trichopes*
Each of the numerous, *fine threadlike* stem branches has a single flower. The crinkled, green, oval to oblong leaves each have a long petiole and are all in a basal rosette. The lower central stem may become somewhat inflated into a trumpet. 1–2 ft. Very common in sandy places. Inner Calif. South Coast Ranges; Mojave, Colorado Deserts.   APRIL–AUG.

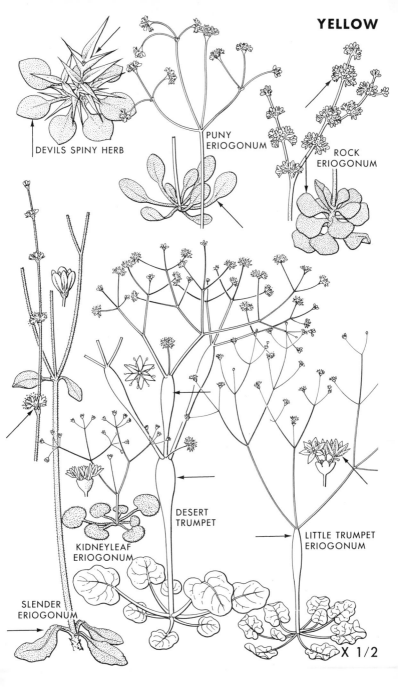

YELLOW

DEVILS SPINY HERB

PUNY ERIOGONUM

ROCK ERIOGONUM

KIDNEYLEAF ERIOGONUM

DESERT TRUMPET

LITTLE TRUMPET ERIOGONUM

SLENDER ERIOGONUM

X 1/2

4 OR 6 PETALS; TINY TUBULAR FLOWERS IN CLUSTERS

BUCKWHEAT FAMILY (Polygonaceae)
See also pp. W 34–38; Y 134–38; R 276–78.

MARUM-LEAVED ERIOGONUM *Eriogonum marifolium*
The oval leaves are downy-haired underneath and green above.
The leaves are in *tufts* at *each branching* point of the stem.
Umbel *bracts hairy* and *slightly toothed.* In mats. 2–8 in. Mt.
slopes. Cascades–Sierra Nevada. JULY–AUG.

BEAR VALLEY ERIOGONUM *Eriogonum ursinum*
Each of the *shiny green oval* basal leaves has a *sharp tip.* The
compound pale yellow flower umbels have leafy bracts at *both*
levels. ½–1½ ft. Rocky places at mid-mt. levels in the northern
half of Sierra Nevada. AUG.–SEPT.

OVAL-LEAVED ERIOGONUM *Eriogonum ovalifolium*
A dense basal *mat of tiny* white woolly *egg-shaped leaves.*
Flower stems protrude above in round heads of yellow, pink, or
white flowers. Umbel bracts are not visible. 4–8 in. Desert
slopes to alpine. Mts. of Pacific States. MAY–JULY

CUSHION ERIOGONUM *Eriogonum caespitosum*
A low, rounded cushion plant that has numerous *tiny, white-
haired, spatula*-shaped leaves. The flower stem is topped by a
single umbel of yellow to reddish, tubular, 6-petaled flowers.
Below the umbel is a *bract* with long *linear lobes reflexed
downward.* 1–4 in. Open rocky ridges. Sierra Nevada and
White Mts. north to se. Ore. MAY–JULY

FROSTY ERIOGONUM *Eriogonum incanum*
The *frosty gray* oblong to oval leaves have *long petioles* and are
entirely in basal mats. A whorl of 3–6 lancelike bracts occurs
just below the flower umbel. Each umbel bract *hairy* and
short-toothed. Flowers pale yellow. Mats 1–8 in. Rocky slopes
above 7000 ft. Sierra Nevada. JULY–AUG.

SULPHUR ERIOGONUM *Eriogonum umbellatum*
Spatula-shaped gray leaves with *long petioles* occur *both* in the
basal rosette and as *whorls at each* branching point. Flowers
sulphur-yellow, tinted red and in compound umbels with a
whorl of linear leaves *only* below the primary umbel. 4–12 in.
Very common. Mts. of Pacific States. JUNE–AUG.

LOBB'S ERIOGONUM *Eriogonum lobbii*
The entire plant is prostrate with a central rosette of *large,
gray, oval* leaves. The *long prostrate* stems have umbels of
yellow-orange flowers. Rocky ridges above 5000 ft. Calif.
North Coast Ranges; Sierra Nevada. JUNE–SEPT.

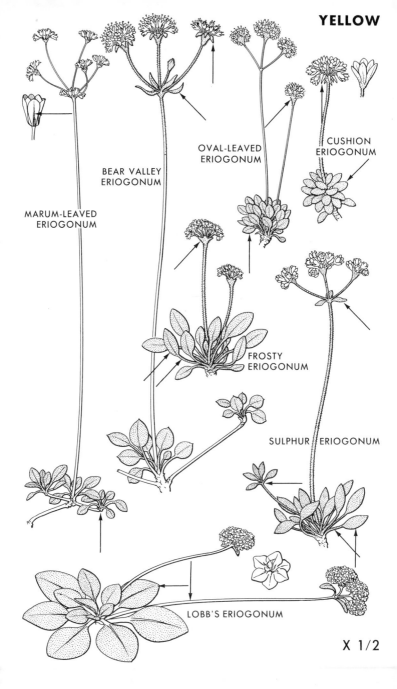

YELLOW

CUSHION
ERIOGONUM

OVAL-LEAVED
ERIOGONUM

BEAR VALLEY
ERIOGONUM

MARUM-LEAVED
ERIOGONUM

FROSTY
ERIOGONUM

SULPHUR ERIOGONUM

LOBB'S ERIOGONUM

X 1/2

4 OR 6 PETALS; TINY TUBULAR
FLOWERS IN CLUSTERS

BUCKWHEAT FAMILY (Polygonaceae)
See also pp. W 34–38; Y 134–38; R 276–78.

HERCULES ERIOGONUM   *Eriogonum heracleoides*
Basal rosette leaves *linear.* The erect flower stem has only one
whorl of linear leaves halfway up. Flowers creamy yellow, in
compound umbels that have leafy bracts at the base of the
main umbel. ½–2 ft. Open places. Great Basin.   MAY–JULY

JUNIPER ERIOGONUM   *Eriogonum collinum*
The small *heart-shaped* leaf blade is bright green and has a
long red petiole. Leaves are in a loose basal rosette. The erect
stems are branched above and have small terminal clusters of
pale yellow flowers. 1–3 ft. Occurs in Juniper forests. Calif.,
Nev., and Idaho in Great Basin.   JUNE–SEPT.

ROUNDHEAD ERIOGONUM
Eriogonum sphaerocephalum
Note the *hairy line* up the side of each petal. The bright,
sulphur-yellow flowers are in a *single* terminal umbel. A hairy,
oblong-lobed bract is just below the flower umbel. The gray
lancelike *leaves are in whorls* at each stem node, including one
halfway below the flowers. 2–8 in. Dry rocky places. Eastern
side Sierra Nevada; north to Great Basin.   MAY–JULY

ARROWLEAF ERIOGONUM   *Eriogonum compositum*
Most of the gray *arrowhead leaves* are in the basal cluster.
Leaflike bracts occur below the primary flower umbel. The
secondary flower umbels have short-toothed bracts below
them. Flowers pale yellow. ½–1½ ft. Dry rocky cliffs. Calif.
North Coast Ranges, Great Basin.   MAY–JULY

BLUE MOUNTAIN ERIOGONUM   *Eriogonum strictum*
The flower umbels are in a *compound umbel* on a long leafless
stem. The gray leaf blades are *rounded* and on a *long petiole.*
½–1 ft. Dry open places. Ne. Calif. to Wash. in Great Basin.
    MAY–AUG.

YELLOW ERIOGONUM   *Eriogonum flavum*
The *linear,* gray-haired leaves are in a basal rosette below the
leafless flower stem. The 4–6 leaflike bracts are immediately
below the many *headlike clusters* of pale to deep yellow
flowers, sometimes rose-tinted. Petal tips *rounded.* Mat plant.
Open rocky ridges. Great Basin.   JUNE–AUG.

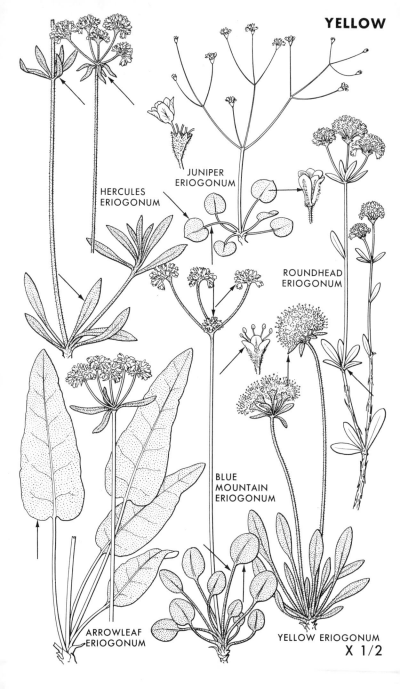

YELLOW

HERCULES
ERIOGONUM

JUNIPER
ERIOGONUM

ROUNDHEAD
ERIOGONUM

BLUE
MOUNTAIN
ERIOGONUM

ARROWLEAF
ERIOGONUM

YELLOW ERIOGONUM
X 1/2

4-PETALED MALTESE CROSS; SEEDPOD LINEAR

Mustard Family (Cruciferae)
See also pp. W 24–30; Y 142–48; O 224; R 266–68.

SHORTPOD MUSTARD Alien *Brassica geniculata*
The linear seedpods are *very short* ($\frac{1}{4}$ in.) and *pressed to stem,* usually 1-seeded. Upper leaves tiny. Basal leaves have a large terminal lobe and *many small lateral* ones. Flowers bright yellow. Stems smooth. 1–3 ft. Common. Calif. May–Oct.

FIELD MUSTARD Alien *Brassica campestris*
Both the lower *pinnate* leaves and the upper stem *arrowhead* ones *clasp the stem.* The elongated seedpods rounded. 1–4 ft. Common. Pacific States. Jan.–June

WILD RADISH Alien *Raphanus sativus*
Seedpod a fat *cylinder with constrictions* between each seed. Flowers yellow or other colors, all at same location. Broad pinnate leaves. 1–4 ft. Common. Pacific States. Feb.–July

TOWER MUSTARD *Arabis glabra*
Basal leaves are hairy and *linear* with a *reverse-toothed margin.* Smooth, slim *arrowlike* leaves clasp the slender towerlike stem. Small, pale yellow flowers. Slender upright seedpods. 2–6 ft. Openings below 7000 ft. Pacific States.
March–July

GOLDEN PRINCES PLUME *Stanleya pinnata*
The long linear petals have a *hairy* surface on the lower *inner* portion. Flowers are in a dense *terminal brushlike spike.* 1–5 ft. Desert slopes. Great Basin and Mojave, Colorado Deserts. April–Sept.

BLACK MUSTARD Alien *Brassica nigra*
The short seedpods ($\frac{3}{4}$ in.) are *erect or spreading,* several-seeded. Stems coarse-haired. Lower pinnate leaves have a large terminal lobe and small lateral ones. Flowers bright yellow. 2–8 ft. Common. Pacific States. April–Aug.

CALIFORNIA MUSTARD *Thelypodium lasiophyllum*
The *broad* leaves *sharply toothed.* The whiskerlike seedpods strongly *reflexed downward.* Pale yellow flowers are in terminal spikes. $\frac{1}{2}$–4 ft. Common below 5000 ft. West of Cascades–Sierra Nevada. March–June

YELLOW BEE PLANT *Cleome lutea*
Caper Family (Capparidaceae)
Each *palmate leaf* usually has 5 leaflets. The *flat banana-shaped* seedpods hang downward on long curving pedicels. 1–3 ft. Sandy places. Great Basin. May–Aug.

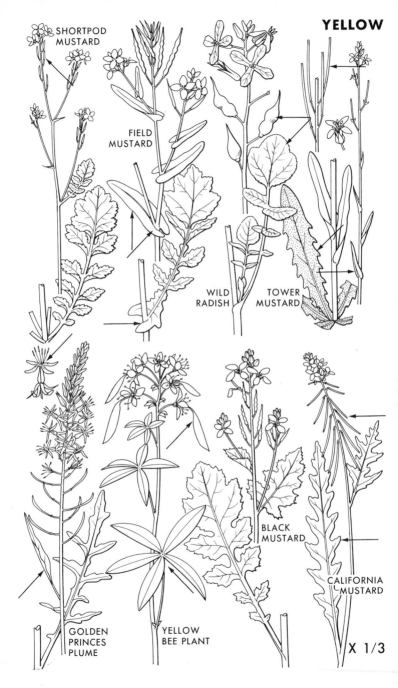

YELLOW

SHORTPOD MUSTARD

FIELD MUSTARD

WILD RADISH

TOWER MUSTARD

GOLDEN PRINCES PLUME

YELLOW BEE PLANT

BLACK MUSTARD

CALIFORNIA MUSTARD

X 1/3

4-PETALED MALTESE CROSS;
SEEDPOD LINEAR

MUSTARD FAMILY (Cruciferae)
See also pp. W 24–30; Y 140–48; O 224; R 266–68.

HEART-LEAVED JEWEL FLOWER
Streptanthus cordatus
The pointed sepals have a terminal *tuft of hairs*. The urn-shaped flowers have yellow or red-purple petals with white tips. Seedpods erect. Heart-shaped yellow-green leaves clasp the upper stem while the basal ones are toothed spatulas. 1–3 ft. Rocky slopes. Calif. desert mts. and north along Sierra Nevada to se. Ore.   MAY–JULY

MOUNTAIN JEWEL FLOWER   *Streptanthus tortuosus*
Similar to preceding. The red-purple pointed *sepal tips are bent downward* and are completely *hairless*. The urn-shaped flowers have yellow to red-purple veins. Seedpods horizontal. Heart-shaped stem leaves, basal ones spatula-shaped. ½–3 ft. Common. Hot rocky slopes. W. Sierra Nevada; Calif. Coast Ranges.   APRIL–AUG.

VARIABLE-LEAVED JEWEL FLOWER
Streptanthus diversifolius
Blue-green, heart-shaped leaves clasp the upper stem, but *vary to linear pinnate* lobed ones below. Flowers pale yellow. Seedpods strongly curved. ½–2 ft. Rocky slopes, volcanic tabletops. Sierra Nevada foothills.   APRIL–JULY

MILKWORT JEWEL FLOWER *Streptanthus polygaloides*
Leaves are *all linear* and undivided. Urn-shaped calyx yellow to purple. Petals yellow to nearly white. 1–3 ft. Dry open slopes. W. Sierra Nevada foothills.   MAY–JUNE

HAIRY CAULANTHUS   *Caulanthus pilosus*
All plant parts *densely long-haired*. Urn-shaped flowers have green to purple sepals and pale yellow to white crisped petals. Basal leaves dandelionlike with long petioles, becoming linear on the stem. 1–3 ft. Dry open places. Great Basin south to edge of Mojave Desert.   MAY–JULY

LONG-BEAKED STREPTANTHELLA
Streptanthella longirostris
Plant parts *all long and narrow* including the urn-like hairy calyx, yellow petals, and pendant seedpods. Leaves linear with pinnate lobes. Plant smooth, waxy blue. ½–2 ft. Common. Great Basin; Mojave, Colorado Deserts.   MARCH–APRIL

COOPER'S CAULANTHUS   *Caulanthus cooperi*
The *slender snakelike stem tip* has slim arrowhead leaves. Basal leaves spatula-like. Common. Growing within and through small shrubs. Plant hairless. ½–2 ft. Mojave, Colorado Deserts.   MARCH–APRIL

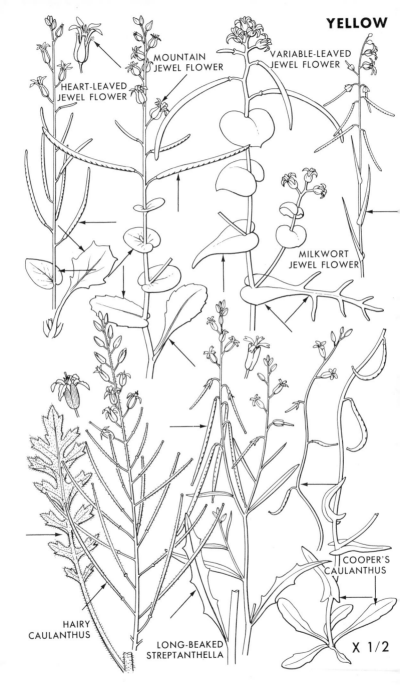

YELLOW

HEART-LEAVED JEWEL FLOWER

MOUNTAIN JEWEL FLOWER

VARIABLE-LEAVED JEWEL FLOWER

MILKWORT JEWEL FLOWER

HAIRY CAULANTHUS

LONG-BEAKED STREPTANTHELLA

COOPER'S CAULANTHUS

X 1/2

4-PETALED MALTESE CROSS;
SEEDPOD LINEAR

MUSTARD FAMILY (Cruciferae)
See also pp. W 24–30; Y 140–48; O 224; R 266–68.

WESTERN YELLOW CRESS *Rorippa curvisiliqua*
The yellow flowers soon become *short, curved,* linear pods
(½ in. or less). Stem well-branched with the leaves pinnatified
into many irregularly toothed leaflets. 4–12 in. Wet places.
Pacific States. APRIL–SEPT.

TUMBLING MUSTARD Alien *Sisymbrium altissimum*
The long (2–4 in.), slender seedpods have *pedicels as thick as
the pod* and spreading from stem. The pinnate leaves entirely
of narrow opposite lobes. Flowers pale yellow. 2–3 ft. Pacific
States. MAY–SEPT.

HEDGE MUSTARD Alien *Sisymbrium officinale*
Leaves and linear seedpods are *closely pressed* to the *thin wiry
stems.* Lower stem leaves have a large terminal leaflet and 1–4
pairs of linear leaflets. Small, pale yellow flowers. ½–3 ft.
Common. Pacific States. MARCH–SEPT.

AMERICAN WINTER CRESS *Barbarea orthoceras*
The basal pinnate leaves have a *large, rounded, terminal* lobe
and 1–2 pairs of linear leaflets. The upper pinnate leaves clasp
the stout succulent stem. The dense raceme of yellow flowers
becomes a looser spike of numerous long seedpods, 8–15 in.
Streambanks, springs, meadows. Pacific States.
MARCH–SEPT.

LONDON ROCKET Alien *Sisymbrium irio*
The *pedicel thinner* than the seed capsule above it. Basal
leaves have a broad semi-triangular tip portion and broad
lateral leaflets. 1–3 ft. Common in Calif. JAN.–MAY

WESTERN TANSY MUSTARD *Descurainia pinnata*
The *lacy leaves* have numerous short segments. Tiny bright
yellow flowers. The numerous short linear seedpods have *2
rows* of seeds and hang on threadlike pedicels. Seedpod short-
tipped. Plant has scattered stinging hairs. ½–2 ft. Common.
Pacific States. MARCH–JULY

MOUNTAIN TANSY MUSTARD *Descurainia richardsonii*
Similar to preceding. Seedpod has *1 row* of seeds and tip is long
and slender. 1–4 ft. Mts. of Pacific States. MAY–AUG.

DYERS WOAD *Isatis tinctoria*
Flowers are in a broad rounded inflorescence on a single tall
stem. Stem leaves arrowhead-shaped. Numerous *flat brown
sausagelike* seedpods all hang downward. A blue dye source.
2–4 ft. Common in n. Calif. hayfields. APRIL–AUG.

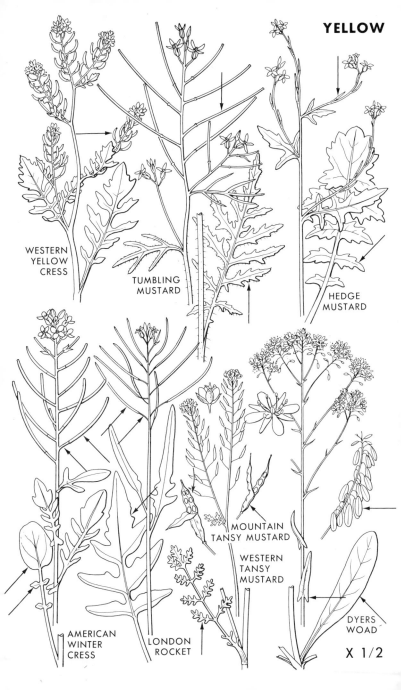

YELLOW

WESTERN
YELLOW
CRESS

TUMBLING
MUSTARD

HEDGE
MUSTARD

MOUNTAIN
TANSY MUSTARD

WESTERN
TANSY
MUSTARD

DYERS
WOAD

AMERICAN
WINTER
CRESS

LONDON
ROCKET

X 1/2

4-PETALED MALTESE CROSS;
SEEDPOD LINEAR

Mustard Family (Cruciferae)
See also pp. W 24–30; Y 140–48; O 224; R 266–68.

TUFTED WALLFLOWER *Erysimum suffrutescens*
The *numerous* gray, narrowly linear or *threadlike leaves* give a tufted appearance to the stems. Flowers bright yellow. Seedpods coarse, square in cross section. Coastal dunes. S. Calif. coast. Jan.–May

FRANCISCAN WALLFLOWER *Erysimum franciscanum*
Leaf blades broadly linear with *sharp and deep teeth.* Flowers cream, aging dark yellow. Seedpods crowded together and upright (1–4 in.), often tinted purple. 2–15 in. Rocky coastal hills. San Francisco north to sw. Ore. March–May

ROUGH WALLFLOWER *Erysimum asperum*
The *linear gray-haired* leaves have *smooth* edges. Seedpods ascending, square in cross section, not constricted between seeds. Flowers yellow, tinted orange or red. ½–3 ft. Great Basin and w. Ore. May–July

SHY WALLFLOWER *Erysimum inconspicuum*
Petals *small* (¼ in.), pale yellow. The narrow lancelike leaves are green- or white-haired. The ascending to erect seedpods (1–2 in.) are 4-sided. ½–2 ft. Great Basin. June–July

MENZIES' WALLFLOWER *Erysimum menziesii*
Stems in a *low clump.* Basal leaves green, *spatula-shaped* with a few obscure teeth. Flowers bright yellow. Large flattened seedpods (1–4 in.) are *stiffly at right angles* to stem. 2–8 in. Sand dunes of Calif. coast. March–May

WESTERN WALLFLOWER *Erysimum occidentale*
Bright yellow flowers. Smooth gray-green leaves. Seedpods *flattened,* without constrictions. Seeds with *papery margin.* 1–2 ft. Sagebrush flats. Great Basin. March–May

DOUGLAS'S WALLFLOWER *Erysimum capitatum*
The gray-haired basal leaves lancelike with toothed margins. Seedpods 2–4 in. long, somewhat 4-angled. Flowers yellow or orange. ½–3 ft. Below 8000 ft. Calif. March–July

SIERRA WALLFLOWER *Erysimum perenne*
Flowers bright yellow. Bright green spatula-shaped leaves. Seedpods *flattened and constricted* between seeds. ½–2 ft. Dry slopes. Sierra Nevada to Siskiyous. June–Aug.

CASCADE WALLFLOWER *Erysimum arenicola*
(not shown)
Similar to preceding. High Cascades–Olympic Mts.
June–Sept.

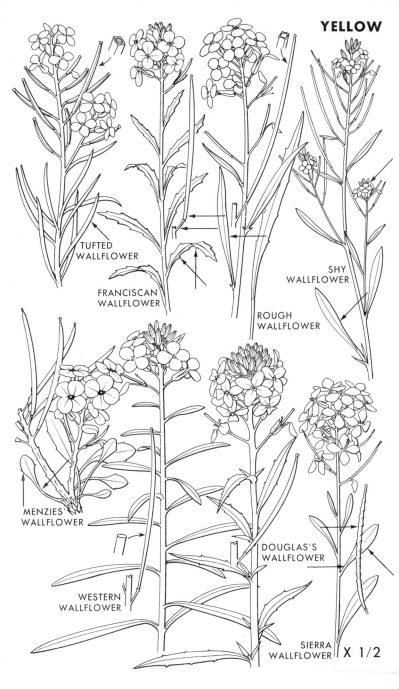

YELLOW

TUFTED
WALLFLOWER

FRANCISCAN
WALLFLOWER

ROUGH
WALLFLOWER

SHY
WALLFLOWER

MENZIES'
WALLFLOWER

WESTERN
WALLFLOWER

DOUGLAS'S
WALLFLOWER

SIERRA
WALLFLOWER   X 1/2

4-PETALED MALTESE CROSS;
SEEDPOD OVAL

MUSTARD FAMILY (Cruciferae)
See also pp. W 24–30; Y 140–46; O 224; R 266–68.

YELLOW PEPPERGRASS *Lepidium flavum*
The oval seedpod has a *2-horned* top. Smooth yellow-green stems are in prostrate mats. The linear leaves have irregularly lobed margins. Flowers sulphur-yellow. 2–12 in. Common on flats. Mojave, Colorado Deserts. MARCH–MAY

COMB DRABA *Draba oligosperma*
The low cushion plant has a dense mat of tufted linear leaves. Using a hand lens, *comb-shaped hairs* may be seen on the leaves. 3–15 yellow to off-white flowers. The seedpod is hairy and oblong to rounded. 1–4 in. Foothills to mostly alpine slopes. Sierra Nevada to B.C.; Great Basin. JULY–AUG.

LEMMON'S DRABA *Draba lemmonii*
The low *thumblike* clusters of yellow flowers become flattened, hairy, and *twisted* oblong pods. The small spatula-like leaves are all in a dense basal tuft. 1–5 in. Frequent on alpine rocky slopes. Sierra Nevada. JULY–AUG.

KING'S LESQUERELLA *Lesquerella kingii*
The sprawling stems radiate from the basal rosette of silvery-gray leaves that have long tapering petioles. Hairy *twin-round* seedpods. Rocky desert mt. slopes. Mojave Desert north to Wallowa mts. of ne. Ore. MARCH–JUNE

WESTERN LESQUERELLA *Lesquerella occidentalis*
Similar to preceding. Leaf blade oval on long petioles. 2–8 in. Dry mt. slopes. Sierra Nevada and Calif. North Coast Ranges to ne. Ore. APRIL–JULY

SHIELD PEPPERGRASS Alien *Lepidium perfoliatum*
Note the smooth *heart-shaped* leaves which *surround* the upper stem. Numerous tiny flowers become small rounded seedpods with a minute notch at the top. 9–20 in. Disturbed places. Pacific States. MARCH–JUNE

MINER'S PEPPER *Lepidium densiflorum*
The *linear* leaves have coarsely toothed margins. Plants hairy. Petals often absent. Seedpods rounded with a terminal notch. 1–2 ft. Common. Pacific States. APRIL–JUNE

OREGON DOUBLE BLADDER POD *Physaria oregana*
The *seedpod heart-shaped*. The elongated gray basal leaves have several large *squared margin lobes*. Flowers pale yellow. 2–8 in. Dry places at lower elevations. Blue Mts. and Snake River of se. Ore. APRIL–JUNE

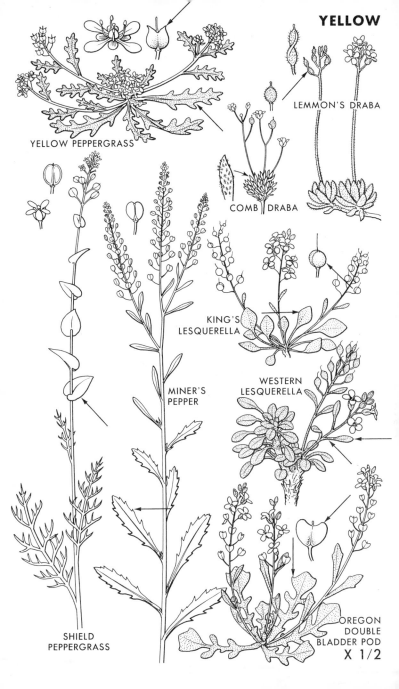

YELLOW

YELLOW PEPPERGRASS

LEMMON'S DRABA

COMB DRABA

KING'S LESQUERELLA

MINER'S PEPPER

WESTERN LESQUERELLA

SHIELD PEPPERGRASS

OREGON DOUBLE BLADDER POD
X 1/2

4 SHOWY PETALS ON TOP OF OVARY

Evening Primrose Family (Onagraceae)
See also pp. W 32; Y 152; R 270–74.

YELLOW FIREWEED   *Epilobium luteum*
Pale yellow petals on a *very long* ovary. Stigma flat, 4-lobed.
The oval to nearly triangular, bright green leaves are in oppo-
site pairs. $\frac{1}{2}$–$2\frac{1}{2}$ ft. Moist streambanks in mts. Cascades and
west in B.C. to Ore.   July–Sept.

SIERRA EVENING PRIMROSE   *Oenothera xylocarpa*
The softly haired leaves are partly pinnate with a large *terminal leaf blade* and short irregular lobes below. The large, bright
yellow petals are both wedge-shaped and notched. 4 linear
stigma lobes. Flat rosette. Dry flats 6000–10,000 ft. S. and
e. Sierra Nevada.   July–Aug.

COAST SUN CUP   *Camissonia ovata*
Cuplike flowers are nestled in the low circle of bright green
leaves that have *oval blades* on long petioles. Stigma tip
rounded. Open fields near the coast. San Luis Obispo, Calif.,
north to s. Ore.   March–June

NORTHERN SUN CUP   *Camissonia subacaulis*
(not shown)
Similar to Coast Sun Cup. Leaves lancelike. A strictly inland
species. Great Basin.   May–Aug.

HOOKER'S EVENING PRIMROSE   *Oenothera hookeri*
The *stout* single *erect stem* has many long lancelike leaves and
many large flowers (2–4 in. wide). Stigma of 4 linear lobes.
1–5 ft. Moist springy places. Pacific States.   June–Dec.

YELLOW DESERT EVENING PRIMROSE
                                       Oenothera primiveris
Large flat flowers with bilobed petals are above a flat circle of
gray leaves with broad pinnate lobes. Stigma of 4 linear lobes.
Dry flats. Mojave, Colorado Deserts.   March–May

TANSYLEAF SUN CUP   *Camissonia tanacetifolia*
The *cuplike flowers* have *round* petal tips and are on long
ovaries above the prostrate circle of *featherlike* leaves. Stigma
a round lobe. Flower 1–1$\frac{1}{2}$ in. wide. Meadows and flats.
N. Sierra Nevada; Great Basin.   May–Aug.

YELLOW WATER WEED   *Ludwigia peploides*
Note the *black glandular bumps* on the leaf bases and the
one-sided ovary below the large petals. A water-inhabiting
plant that has numerous shiny green lancelike leaves. Stem
floating, 1 to many ft. long. Slow streams, ponds. Lower
Columbia River in Wash. south to Baja.   June–Sept.

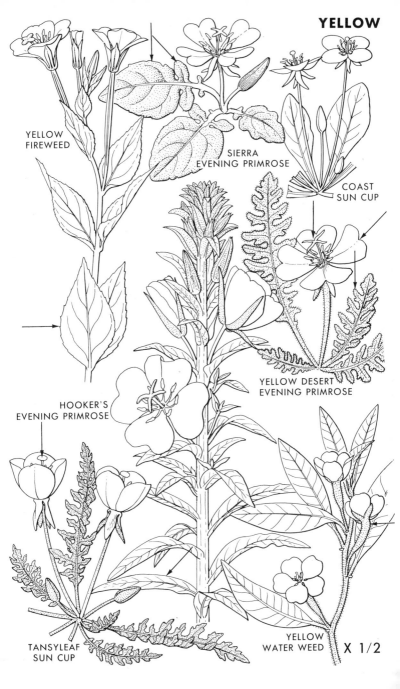

YELLOW

YELLOW
FIREWEED

SIERRA
EVENING PRIMROSE

COAST
SUN CUP

YELLOW DESERT
EVENING PRIMROSE

HOOKER'S
EVENING PRIMROSE

TANSYLEAF
SUN CUP

YELLOW
WATER WEED

X 1/2

4 SHOWY PETALS ON TOP OF OVARY

EVENING PRIMROSE FAMILY (Onagraceae)
See also pp. W 32; Y 150; R 270–74.

MUSTARD EVENING PRIMROSE

Camissonia californica

The erect plant resembles members of the Mustard Family. Leaves are narrowly lancelike with an irregularly toothed margin. Flowers ½–1 in. wide. *Sepals swept backward* and the petals may have red dots. Stigma a rounded head. 1–3 ft. Cen. and s. Calif. APRIL–MAY

BROWN-EYED EVENING PRIMROSE

Camissonia clavaeformis

The *rounded* petals often have a *basal brown spot.* Flowers in a thick cluster above the rosette of strongly toothed oval leaves. The club-shaped seedpod has a definite pedicel. ¼–½ ft. Common. Great Basin; Mojave, Colorado Deserts.
MARCH–MAY

MINIATURE EVENING PRIMROSE

Camissonia micrantha

The small prostrate stem has *tiny gray lancelike* leaves with *wavy* margins. Seedpods curved. Flowers tiny (¼ in.). 2–20 in. Very common. Cen. Calif. to Baja. MARCH–AUG.

YELLOW CUPS *Camissonia brevipes*

The green linear pinnate leaves have *red veins.* Flower stem curved over until flowering is completed. Flowers bright yellow. Stigma tip round. Seedpod has constrictions. 4–16 in. Slopes and washes. Mojave, Colorado Deserts. MARCH–MAY

HEARTLEAF EVENING PRIMROSE

Camissonia cardiophylla

The *heart-shaped* leaves have short sharp teeth. The erect stem has the terminal flower buds in a nodding curve. ½–2 ft. Flats and canyons. Mojave, Colorado Deserts. MARCH–MAY

FIELD EVENING PRIMROSE *Camissonia dentata*

Note the *curved snakelike* seedpods. Flowers small (¼–½ in. wide). The erect stem 1/16 in. wide or more, well branched, and has *long narrowly linear leaves* with toothed margins. Petal bases with or without red dots. Stigma tip a rounded lobe. 2–8 in. Dry flats below 5000 ft. Cen. and s. Calif.
MARCH–MAY

CONTORTED EVENING PRIMROSE

(not shown) *Camissonia contorta*

Similar to preceding. Flowers tiny (¼ in. or less), stem very thin (less than 1/16 in. wide). 2–9 in. Widespread. Pacific States. MAY–JUNE

BEACH EVENING PRIMROSE

Camissonia cheiranthifolia

The prostrate stems have *gray oval leaves.* Small yellow flowers are nestled among the leaves. Strictly on coastal sand dunes. S. Ore. south to Baja. APRIL–AUG.

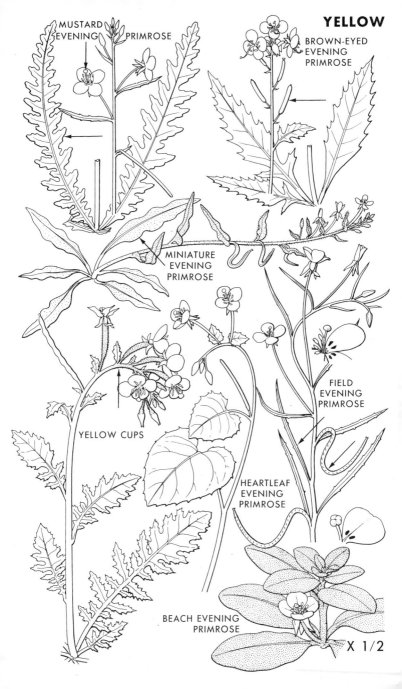

YELLOW

MUSTARD EVENING PRIMROSE

BROWN-EYED EVENING PRIMROSE

MINIATURE EVENING PRIMROSE

YELLOW CUPS

FIELD EVENING PRIMROSE

HEARTLEAF EVENING PRIMROSE

BEACH EVENING PRIMROSE

X 1/2

5 TO 12 GLOSSY PETALS; MANY STAMENS

BUTTERCUP FAMILY (Ranunculaceae)
See also pp. W 40–42; Y 154–58; O 226; R 280–82;
B 354–57, 382; G 404.

BIRDFOOT BUTTERCUP   *Ranunculus orthorhynchus*
Seeds have a *long straight beak*. Leaves birdsfoot-like. ½–2 ft.
Meadows, streambanks. Pacific States.   APRIL–JULY

CREEPING BUTTERCUP   *Ranunculus repens*
The pinnate leaf blade is strongly 3-parted into lobed sections.
Stems erect. Seedheads rounded, each smooth seed is oval with
a nearly straight beak. Plant parts hairy. 2–3 ft. Moist disturbed places. Pacific States.   MAY–AUG.

PRICKLESEED BUTTERCUP Alien
                            Ranunculus muricatus
Seeds flat ovals with a thick birdlike beak and the *seed walls
covered with many curved spines*. Shiny maplelike leaves.
½–2 ft. Wet places. Pacific States.   MAY–JUNE

MALE BUTTERCUP Alien   *Ranunculus testiculatus*
Tiny *gray* plants have linear pinnate leaves. Pale yellow
flowers urn-shaped. Each hairy seed has a slender central shaft
and 2 saclike bulges near the base. Seedhead cylindrical.
1–2 in. Very common. Great Basin.   MARCH–MAY

ESCHSCHOLTZ'S BUTTERCUP
                            Ranunculus eschscholtzii
The low, tufted plants have *very large petals*. The shiny green
leaves are rounded in outline but have 3 deeply parted segments. The oval seeds have a long straight beak. 1–6 in.
Alpine slopes. Mts. of Pacific States.   JUNE–AUG.

SAGEBRUSH BUTTERCUP   *Ranunculus glaberrimus*
The shiny green leaves resemble *broad butter forks* with 3 or 4
broad teeth. Upper stem leaves linear. Seeds slightly hairy.
Stems erect to prostrate. 2–10 in. Common on flats of Great
Basin. A second form with leaves all linear on eastern slopes of
Cascades–Sierra Nevada.   MARCH–JUNE

DESERT BUTTERCUP   *Ranunculus cymbalaria*
The shiny green leaves are *heart-shaped* with a *wavy margin*.
Seeds *oblong* and *ribbed,* the beak short and straight. Seed
head a *thumblike* cylinder. 5–12 petals. 2–12 in. Marshy meadows. Mojave Desert north to Great Basin.   JUNE–AUG.

WATER PLANTAIN BUTTERCUP
                            Ranunculus alismaefolius
The shiny green leaves are lancelike on semi-sprawling stems.
Seeds rounded with the almost straight *beak pointed outward*
at nearly a *right angle*. First plant to flower in wet high mt.
meadows. 1–3 ft. Pacific States.   MAY–JULY

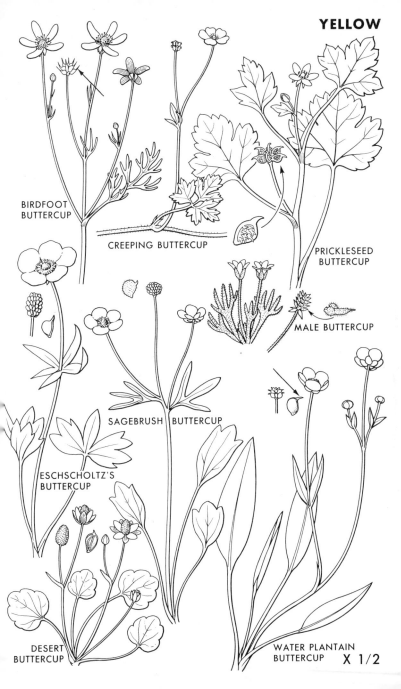

YELLOW

BIRDFOOT
BUTTERCUP

CREEPING BUTTERCUP

PRICKLESEED
BUTTERCUP

MALE BUTTERCUP

SAGEBRUSH BUTTERCUP

ESCHSCHOLTZ'S
BUTTERCUP

DESERT
BUTTERCUP

WATER PLANTAIN
BUTTERCUP X 1/2

BUTTERCUP FAMILY (Ranunculaceae)
See also pp. W 40–42; Y 154–58; O 226; R 280–82;
B 354–56, 382; G 404.

WOODLAND BUTTERCUP   *Ranunculus uncinatus*
Each petal an elongated oval. The trifoliate pinnate leaves are
often of sharp-pointed, partly linear lobes. Stems erect. Each
seed has a *hooked beak.* Seedhead globular. ½–3 ft. Moist
shady places. Pacific States.   APRIL–JULY

MACOUN'S BUTTERCUP   *Ranunculus macounii*
The petals are *short,* barely longer than the sepals. *Seedhead
elongated.* Each seed is a fat oval with a short curved beak.
Stem sprawling, rooting at the nodes. Leaves 3–5 parted.
1–3 ft. Marshy places. Great Basin.   MAY–JULY

TIMBERLINE BUTTERCUP   *Ranunculus verecundus*
The low, tufted plant has broad, partially divided, oval basal
leaves. Upper stem leaves linear. Seeds nearly oval with a
well-curved beak. Seedheads elongated cylinders. Plants
nearly smooth. 5–7 petals. 2–8 in. Alpine slopes. Cascades and
Blue Mts. of Ore.   JULY–AUG.

BLISTER BUTTERCUP Alien   *Ranunculus acris*
The hairy pinnate leaf blade is strongly 3-parted, each with
numerous short lobes. Seedheads rounded, each smooth seed is
oval and has a nearly straight beak. The erect stems and leaves
hairy. 2–3 ft. Moist disturbed places. N. Calif. to B.C.; Great
Basin.   MAY–AUG.

WESTERN BUTTERCUP   *Ranunculus occidentalis*
The *flat oval seeds* are smooth to slightly hairy and have a
strongly curved beak. Hemispheric seedheads. 5 petals. Sepals
reflexed. The widely spaced, 3-parted leaves are on erect, well-
branched stems. 1–2½ ft. Moist soil below 6000 ft. Pacific
States, except s. Calif.   APRIL–JUNE

CALIFORNIA BUTTERCUP   *Ranunculus californicus*
Note the *9–16 or more petals.* The fat oval seeds have a short,
stout curved beak. The erect stem is well-branched, and has
widely spaced, lightly paired, pinnate leaves. 1–2½ ft. Moist
slopes and meadows. Calif. foothills and mts.   FEB.–JULY

SACRAMENTO VALLEY BUTTERCUP
                              Ranunculus canus
Stems and leaves are covered by many long *white soft-silky
hairs.* Petals 5–10. Sepals reflexed. Seeds disklike, have a short
triangular beak with a curved tip. Leaves strongly 3–5 parted.
Stem erect. 1–3 ft. Open grasslands. Central Valley of Calif.
                                                  FEB.–MAY

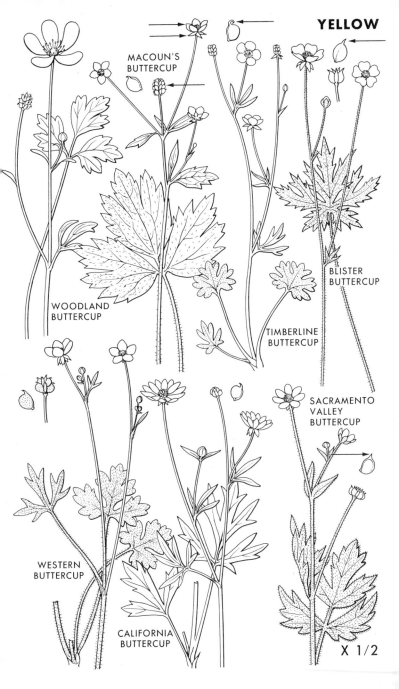

YELLOW

MACOUN'S
BUTTERCUP

BLISTER
BUTTERCUP

WOODLAND
BUTTERCUP

TIMBERLINE
BUTTERCUP

SACRAMENTO
VALLEY
BUTTERCUP

WESTERN
BUTTERCUP

CALIFORNIA
BUTTERCUP

X 1/2

2 TO 5 PETALS OR VARIOUSLY MODIFIED

BUTTERCUP FAMILY (Ranunculaceae)
See also pp. W 40–42; Y 154–58; O 226; R 280–82;
B 354–56, 382; G 404.

GOLDEN COLUMBINE *Aquilegia flavescens*
Note the *5 spurs* on the *nodding,* bright yellow flowers, but
tinted pink in some areas. The waxy-blue, pinnate leaves have
3 leaflets. 1–2½ ft. Moist mt. woods and meadows. Cascades,
Wallowa Mts. of Ore. JUNE–AUG.

FEW-FLOWERED MEADOW RUE

Thalictrum sparsiflorum
Note the numerous pendulous yellow-green flowers that have
white sepals resembling petals (no petals present). Pinnate
leaves divided 2–4 times. Stamens and pistils are *both* present
in the same flower. 1–3 ft. Moist thickets. 5000–12,000 ft. Mts.
of Pacific States. JULY–AUG.

FENDLER'S MEADOW RUE *Thalictrum fendleri*
Similar to preceding. But any one plant has *all male* (stamens
only) or *all female* (pistils only) flowers. No petals present.
3–5 ft. Moist places near streams. 4000–10,000 ft. Common.
Pacific States. MAY–AUG.

MISCELLANEOUS FAMILIES

YELLOW SKUNK CABBAGE *Lysichitum americanum*
ARUM FAMILY See also p. W 2. (Araceae)
Note the *large yellow envelope-like* spathe around the narrow
pokerlike spike of tiny flowers. Large oval leaves (1–5 ft. wide).
Strong skunky odor. 1–2 ft. Shady swamps. Nw. Calif. coast
to B.C. and east. APRIL–JULY

INDIAN POND LILY *Nuphar polysepalum*
WATER LILY FAMILY See also p. W 2. (Nymphaeaceae)
Note the large *floating* oval-shaped leaves and water lily–like
flowers. Shallow ponds. Calif. Coast Ranges, Sierra Nevada to
B.C. APRIL–SEPT.

FIRE HEARTS *Dicentra ochroleuca*
BLEEDING HEART FAMILY (Fumariaceae)
See also pp. W 42; R 280.
Long *flattened heartlike* flowers. Tall gray-green stems. Lacy
leaves. Common second and third years after a chaparral fire;
requires fire to grow. 3–9 ft. Calif. South Coast Ranges.

MAY–JULY

GOLDEN EAR DROPS *Dicentra chrysantha*
BLEEDING HEART FAMILY (Fumariaceae)
See also pp. W 42; R 280.
Somewhat elongated heart-shaped flowers. 2 reflexed petals.
Pinnate linear leaflets. Erect stems 1–5 ft. Frequent on recent
forest fire sites. Cen. Calif. to Baja. APRIL–SEPT.

GOLDEN INSIDE-OUT FLOWER

Vancouveria chrysantha
BARBERRY FAMILY See also p. 42. (Berberidaceae)
Flower petals swept backward. Squarish pinnate leaflets. 8–
16 in. Open areas below 400 ft. Nw. Calif. and sw. Ore. JUNE

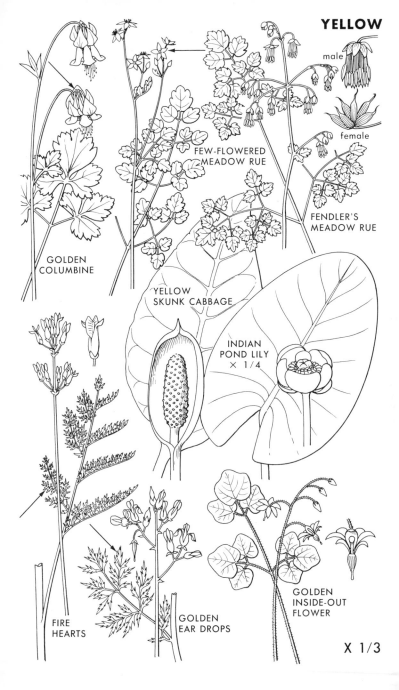

YELLOW

male

female

FEW-FLOWERED
MEADOW RUE

FENDLER'S
MEADOW RUE

GOLDEN
COLUMBINE

YELLOW
SKUNK CABBAGE

INDIAN
POND LILY
× 1/4

FIRE
HEARTS

GOLDEN
EAR DROPS

GOLDEN
INSIDE-OUT
FLOWER

X 1/3

5 PETALS; NUMEROUS BUSHY STAMENS

St. John's Wort Family (Hypericaceae)

KLAMATH WEED Alien   *Hypericum perforatum*
Note the *linear to lancelike sepals.* *Tall* wiry stems have paired linear leaves. Petals yellow-orange, sometimes black-dotted. 1–3 ft. Open fields. Pacific States.   JUNE–SEPT.

GOLD WIRE   *Hypericum concinnum*
Similar to Klamath Weed. Sepals *oval with a pointed* tip, margins black-dotted. Leaves lancelike, usually *folded upward.* Many wiry stems in a clump. 4–16 in. Brushy slopes. Calif. North Coast Ranges, w. Sierra Nevada.   MAY–JULY

SCOULER'S ST. JOHN'S WORT   *Hypericum formosum*
Note the *triangular to oval sepals without* a pointed tip. Petals sometimes black-dotted. The paired leaves *oblong* to oval, and *flat.* ½–2½ ft. Moist places. Coastal regions and mts. of Pacific States.   JUNE–SEPT.

TINKERS PENNY   *Hypericum anagalloides*
The *tiny stem* (1–3 in.) in creeping mats. Tiny, paired, oval to round leaves. Small yellow-orange flowers. Moist meadows. Sea level to high mts. Pacific States.   JUNE–AUG.

Loasa Family See also p. W 44. (Loasaceae)

WHITE-STEMMED STICKLEAF   *Mentzelia albicaulis*
Small flowered (¼–½ in.). The white shiny stems erect, with the linear to triangular leaves *strongly sawtoothed.* Petals on top of ovary. 4–15 in. Common. Great Basin, and south on deserts to Baja.   MARCH–JULY

NEVADA STICKLEAF   *Mentzelia dispersa*
Leaves narrowly linear *without a toothed margin.* Small flowered (¼ in.). Petals on top of ovary. Slender white stems. 4–12 in. Calif. and Great Basin.   MAY–AUG.

LINDLEY'S BLAZING STAR   *Mentzelia lindleyi*
Large flowered. The *nearly oval* golden-yellow petals have an orange-red base. Leaves *dandelionlike.* Petals on top of ovary. ½–2 ft. Rocky slopes below 3000 ft. Sierra Nevada foothills, Calif. South Coast Ranges.   MARCH–JUNE

GIANT BLAZING STAR   *Mentzelia laevicaulis*
Large (4–6 in. wide) pale yellow flowers. Lancelike petals on top of ovary. The *gray,* elongated, triangular leaves have raggedly toothed margins. Tall erect stems 1–5 ft. Common in open places. Calif. and Great Basin.   JUNE–OCT.

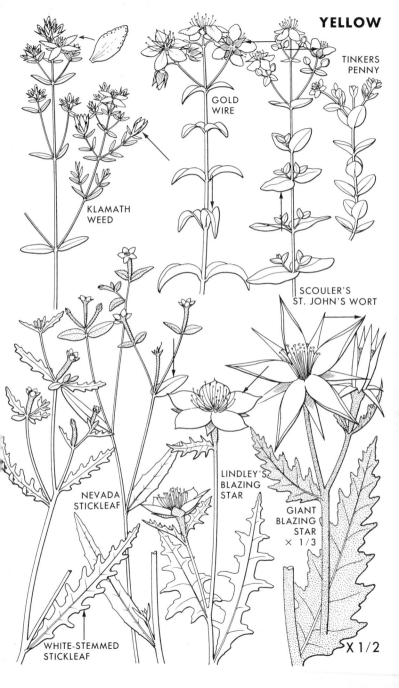

YELLOW

KLAMATH
WEED

GOLD
WIRE

TINKERS
PENNY

SCOULER'S
ST. JOHN'S WORT

NEVADA
STICKLEAF

LINDLEY'S
BLAZING
STAR

GIANT
BLAZING
STAR
× 1/3

WHITE-STEMMED
STICKLEAF

X 1/2

5 PETALS; BILATERAL SYMMETRY: VIOLETS

VIOLET FAMILY (Violaceae)
See also pp. W 52; Y 164; B 358.

DOUGLAS'S VIOLET *Viola douglasii*
Leaves highly divided into *numerous short linear lobes*. Large, bright yellow flowers. 2–6 in. Grassy places in woodlands or pine forests. Calif. Coast Ranges, w. Sierra Nevada foothills, and S. Calif. Mts. MARCH–MAY

PINE VIOLET *Viola lobata*
Each leaf is divided into 3–9 *broad fingerlike or moosehorn-like* lobes. Petals deep yellow with or without purple veins. 4–12 in. Common in dry open woods, 1000–6000 ft. Mts. of Calif. APRIL–JULY

SHELTON'S VIOLET *Viola sheltonii*
Note the dark green, *fan-shaped, pinnate* leaves. Each leaf is divided into 3 definite leaflets which are further subdivided. Nearly stemless. Petals deep lemon-yellow, the lower 3 veined brown-purple. 1–2 in. Open forest 2000–8000 ft. Mts. of Calif. and intermittently north. APRIL–JULY

CALIFORNIA GOLDEN VIOLET *Viola pedunculata*
The leaves *delta-shaped* to oval with toothed margins. Large flowered (1–2 in. wide), petals yellow-orange, the lower 3 veined dark brown and in a *rounded* pattern. 4–12 in. Grasslands below 2500 ft. Calif. Central Valley and Coast Ranges south to Baja. FEB.–APRIL

MOUNTAIN VIOLET *Viola purpurea*
The nearly *triangular leaves* have toothed margins, purple-tinted. Petals deep lemon-yellow, the lower 3 veined purple. 2–8 in. Dry mt. slopes. Pacific States. APRIL–AUG.

SMOOTH YELLOW VIOLET *Viola glabella*
Tall *erect stem has heart-shaped* leaves. Petals deep yellow with the lateral and lower ones variously purple-tinted. 4–12 in. Moist woods. Mts. of Pacific States. MARCH–JULY

NUTTALL'S VIOLET *Viola nuttallii*
Leaves lancelike to oval, hairy. Petals deep yellow with the lower 3 veined brown-purple. 1–3 in. Highly variable species. Dry mt. forests. Pacific States. APRIL–JULY

REDWOOD VIOLET *Viola sempervirens*
The *lower lip petal V-pointed*. Upper 4 petals point upward. Petals lemon-yellow, the lower 3 faintly purple-veined. Stems spreading by runners. Leaves rounded. 4–12 in. Shady woods. West of Cascades and south to Monterey, Calif. FEB.–APRIL

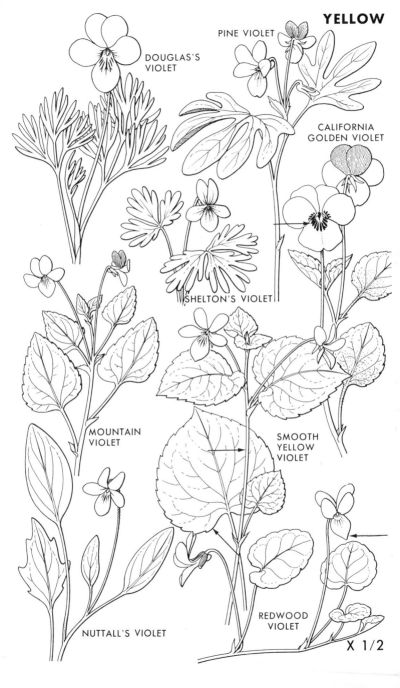

YELLOW

DOUGLAS'S VIOLET

PINE VIOLET

CALIFORNIA GOLDEN VIOLET

SHELTON'S VIOLET

MOUNTAIN VIOLET

SMOOTH YELLOW VIOLET

NUTTALL'S VIOLET

REDWOOD VIOLET

X 1/2

5 PETALS; BILATERAL SYMMETRY: VIOLETS
5 PETALS; TINY UPRIGHT URNS OR STARS

VIOLET FAMILY (Violaceae)
See also pp. W 52; Y 162; B 358.

GOLDEN SAGEBRUSH VIOLET   *Viola aurea*
The gray leaves are nearly round with *conspicuously sharp-pointed white tips.* Rosettes 1–2 in. Dry open places, often with sagebrush. Lake Tahoe, Calif., south in Great Basin to Mojave Desert, Mt. Pinos, and San Bernardino Mts. of s. Calif.   APRIL–JUNE

FELT VIOLET (not shown)   *Viola tomentosa*
Similar to preceding. Stem and leaves covered by a thin gray *coat of feltlike hairs.* 1–6 in. Dry open places along eastern slope of n. Sierra Nevada.   JUNE–AUG.

ROUNDLEAF VIOLET   *Viola orbiculata*
Leaves round, plants stemless. Round-tipped petals are bright yellow with dark markings on the lower 3. 1–2 in. Alpine slopes. Olympic Mts., Cascades, and east.   MAY–AUG.

WOOD SORREL FAMILY (Oxalidaceae)
See also p. R 282.

CREEPING WOOD SORREL Alien   *Oxalis corniculata*
Slender creeping stems *rooting at nodes.* Small (½ in.), deep yellow-orange flowers. Trifoliate leaves. 1–12 in. Very common in lawns, etc. Pacific States.   ALL YEAR

SUKSDORF'S WOOD SORREL   *Oxalis suksdorfii*
Slender trailing stem, *not rooting* at nodes. Large flowers (¾ in.). 4–12 in. West of Cascades to n. Calif.   MAY–JULY

BERMUDA SORREL Alien   *Oxalis pes-caprae*
Note the deep yellow *funnel-shaped* flowers on a tall leafless stem. Leaves cloverlike. 4–12 in. City areas at lower elevations. Pacific States.   NOV.–MARCH

SEDUM FAMILY (Crassulaceae)
See also pp. Y 166; R 310.

DWARF CLIFF SEDUM   *Parvisedum pumilum*
The *bootlace-like* stems topped by 2 or more graceful sprays of starlike flowers. 1–10 in. Rocky cliffs and vernal pools. Calif. Coast Ranges, lower Sierra Nevada.   MARCH–JUNE

PYGMY STONECROP   *Tillaea erecta*
The tiny plant (1–2 in.) has short, fleshy, oblong leaves in opposite pairs along the well-branched stem. Many tiny flowers, becoming red with age. Grows in masses on rocks and in grass. 1–2 in. Below 3000 ft. Ore., Calif.   FEB.–MAY

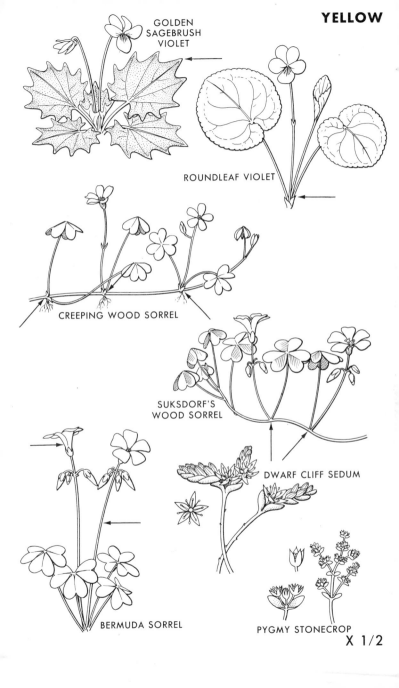

YELLOW

GOLDEN
SAGEBRUSH
VIOLET

ROUNDLEAF VIOLET

CREEPING WOOD SORREL

SUKSDORF'S
WOOD SORREL

DWARF CLIFF SEDUM

BERMUDA SORREL

PYGMY STONECROP

X 1/2

5 PETALS; URN OR STARLIKE FLOWERS

SEDUM FAMILY (Crassulaceae)
See also pp. Y 164; R 310.

Note that the flower stem of *Sedums* originates from the center
of the basal leaf rosette, while the flower stem of *Dudleyas*
comes from the side.

NARROW-PETALED SEDUM   *Sedum stenopetalum*
Leaves linear, but with a *distinct keel* on the lower side. The
older leaf edges become dried membranes before falling off.
Basal leaf cluster often absent. 2–8 in. Open rocky places.
Pacific States.   MAY–AUG.

LANCELEAF SEDUM   *Sedum lanceolatum*
Both the basal rosette and flower stem leaves are *similarly
linear and round.* 2–8 in. Rocky places. Pacific States.
                                                       JUNE–AUG.

POWDERY DUDLEYA   *Dudleya farinosa*
Rosette leaves oval with the *broadest end near the base,* often
densely covered with a white mealy wax. Triangular leaves
clasp the flower stem. Flowers pale lemon-yellow, oblong
petals. 4–16 in. Only on coastal cliffs. Calif. and s. Ore.
coasts.   MAY–SEPT.

SIERRA SEDUM   *Sedum obtusatum*
Basal rosette leaves spatula-like in erect, cupped *clusters.*
Petals lemon-yellow, fading to pink, united about $\frac{1}{4}$ of basal
portion. Petal tip *squared off.* Flower stem leaves different
from basal ones. 1–8 in. Rocky slopes 4000–13,000 ft. Sierra
Nevada to Siskiyous.   MAY–AUG.

CAÑON DUDLEYA   *Dudleya cymosa*
The oval rosette leaves are in a loose cluster. Flower stem
leaves lancelike. The flowers bright yellow to red, petal *lobes
narrowly lancelike.* 4–12 in. Hot rocky cliffs at lower elevations. W. Sierra Nevada, Calif. Coast Ranges.   APRIL–JULY

PANAMINT DUDLEYA   *Dudleya saxosa*
Rosette leaves pale green or blue, *narrowly lancelike* and
nearly round. The calyx red with oblong yellow petals, becoming red with age. 2–8 in. Dry rocky slopes. Desert mts. of
s. Calif.   APRIL–JUNE

PACIFIC SEDUM   *Sedum spathulifolium*
Spatula-like leaves are in *flat rosettes.* Numerous rosettes are
often connected by runnerlike stems. Petals entirely *free* from
each other. Flower stem leaves different from basal ones.
2–12 in. Open rocky slopes. West of Cascades–Sierra Nevada at
lower elevations.   MAY–AUG.

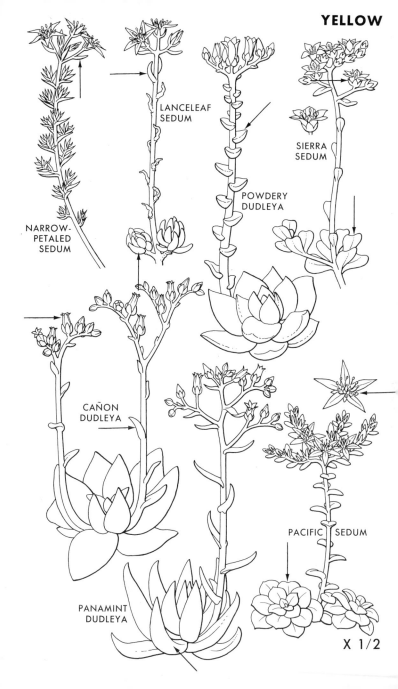

YELLOW

NARROW-
PETALED
SEDUM

LANCELEAF
SEDUM

POWDERY
DUDLEYA

SIERRA
SEDUM

CAÑON
DUDLEYA

PACIFIC SEDUM

PANAMINT
DUDLEYA

X 1/2

5 TINY PETALS; FLOWERS IN UMBEL

CARROT FAMILY (Umbelliferae)
See also pp. W 64–68; Y 170; R 302; G 404.

CARAWAY LEAF LOMATIUM *Lomatium caruifolium*
The leaves are divided into linear segments. Seeds are elongated with white lines on the seed body. Grassy places. ½–2 ft.
Calif. Coast Ranges.   MARCH–MAY

GIANT-SEEDED LOMATIUM *Lomatium macrocarpum*
Low pinnate leaves are divided 2–3 times into sharp-pointed linear segments. Tiny yellow, white, or red-purple flowers. *Long* (½–1 in.) *flattened* seeds have an outer wing narrower than the seed body. ½–2 ft. Dry rocky places. Cen. Calif. to B.C.   MARCH–JUNE

FERN-LEAVED LOMATIUM *Lomatium dissectum*
Stems *erect* and well-branched, the leaves mostly basal. Leaves broadly divided 2–4 times into linear oblong segments with rounded tips. Flowers yellow or red-purple. Short oval seeds (½–¾ in.) with narrow margin wings. 3–5 ft. Rocky places. Pacific States.   APRIL–JUNE

PESTLE LOMATIUM *Lomatium nudicaule*
Stem becoming an *enlarged pestle* just below the umbels. Leaves divided 1–2 times into *broad oval* leaflets. Seeds oblong (½ in.) with wings slightly less broad than the seed body. 1–2 ft. Common. Open slopes. Pacific States except s. Calif.
                                    APRIL–JUNE

COUS LOMATIUM *Lomatium cous*
The low leaf is divided 1–3 times with the final segments *short and round-tipped*. Flowers yellow to purple. Seeds narrow ovals (½ in.) with each wing nearly equal to seed body. 4–12 in. Dry rocky flats. E. Ore.   APRIL–JULY

FOOTHILL LOMATIUM *Lomatium utriculatum*
The outer wing margin is ⅔ length of each elongated seed. Leaves divided into linear segments. Grassy places. ½–2 ft. Many habitats below 6000 ft. Pacific States.   FEB.–MAY

LEWIS'S LOMATIUM *Lomatium triternatum*
Each leaf is divided 1–3 times with the final divisions of *long slender segments*. Seeds are long slender ovals with very narrow wings. ½–2 ft. Rocky soil. Cen. Calif. to B.C. and Great Basin.   APRIL–JULY

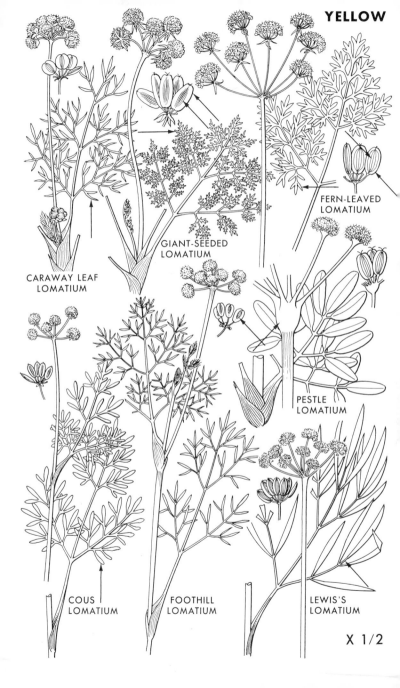

YELLOW

FERN-LEAVED
LOMATIUM

GIANT-SEEDED
LOMATIUM

CARAWAY LEAF
LOMATIUM

PESTLE
LOMATIUM

COUS
LOMATIUM

FOOTHILL
LOMATIUM

LEWIS'S
LOMATIUM

X 1/2

5 TINY PETALS; FLOWERS IN UMBEL

CARROT FAMILY (Umbelliferae)
See also pp. W 64–68; Y 168; R 302; G 404.

TEREBINTH PTERYXIA   *Pteryxia terebinthina*
A low plant of gray-green lacy leaves. The widely spreading umbel has smaller secondary umbels. Seeds oblong-oval, with many thin *wavy-margined membranes.* ½–2 ft. Dry slopes below 10,000 ft. Sierra Nevada, and Calif. North Coast Ranges to Siskiyous.   MAY–JUNE

POISON SANICLE   *Sanicula bipinnata*
Each leaflet slightly enlarged with rounded marginal teeth. Seeds rounded with bumplike hooked spines. ½–3 ft. Open places at lower elevations. Cen. and s. Calif.   APRIL–MAY

PURPLE SANICLE   *Sanicula bipinnatifida*
Leaf petiole *conspicuously broad* with a *spiny margin.* Flowers are in yellow (or red-purple) balls with long feathery stamens. Rounded spiny seeds. ½–2 ft. Common at low elevations. Yellow form most common on west slope of Sierra Nevada. West of Cascades–Sierra Nevada from B.C. to Baja.
       MARCH–MAY

PACIFIC SNAKEROOT   *Sanicula crassicaulis*
The erect stems have smooth *maplelike leaves* that have *spiny margins.* Flower umbel compound with 2–5 smaller ones. Oval seeds have spiny hooks. 1–3 ft. Shady woods below 5000 ft. West of Cascades and all of Calif.   MARCH–JUNE

HARTWEG'S TAUSCHIA   *Tauschia hartwegii*
The huge leaves (½–1 ft.) divided into partial leaflets. The flowering umbel on a tall leafless stem. 1–4 ft. Shady woods. Cen. and s. Calif.   MARCH–MAY

SWEET FENNEL Alien   *Foeniculum vulgare*
Tall *waxy-blue canelike* stems. Leaves divided into *threadlike* divisions. Sweet licorice odor when handled. 3–6 ft. Disturbed places where common. Pacific States.   MAY–DEC.

FOOTSTEPS OF SPRING   *Sanicula arctopoides*
Note the *flat* rosette of *pale yellow leaves* that are deeply 3-parted with numerous linear spinelike teeth. Rounded buttonlike flower umbels are nestled among the leaves. Seeds have spiny hooks. 2–8 in. Open coastal slopes below 1000 ft. Cen. Calif. along coast to cen. Wash.   MARCH–MAY

SIERRA SNAKEROOT   *Sanicula graveolens*
The erect stem has smooth *lacy linear* leaves. 10–15 flowers in a loose umbel. Seeds oval with spiny hooks. 2–16 in. Open woods. Mts. of Pacific States.   APRIL–JULY

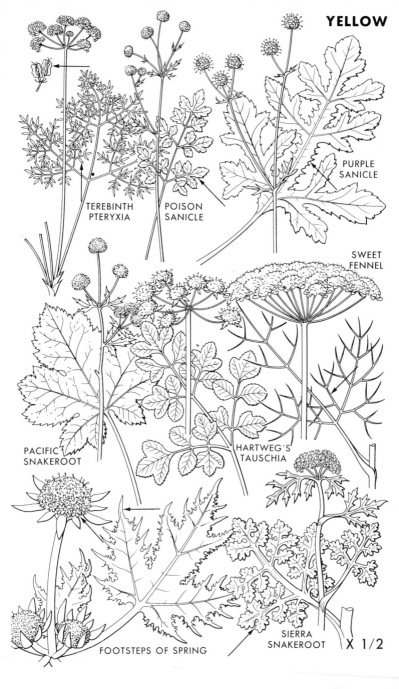

YELLOW

TEREBINTH PTERYXIA

POISON SANICLE

PURPLE SANICLE

SWEET FENNEL

PACIFIC SNAKEROOT

HARTWEG'S TAUSCHIA

FOOTSTEPS OF SPRING

SIERRA SNAKEROOT

X 1/2

5 PETALS UNITED AS TRUMPETS, BELLS, OR FLAT WHEELS

PHLOX FAMILY (Polemoniaceae)
See also pp. W 72; O 226; R 248–50, 306;
B 360–64.

DESERT GOLD   *Linanthus aurens*
Note the *golden upright funnel-like* flowers with an orange to brown-purple throat. Branched threadlike stems, each leaf cleft into 3–7 linear lobes. 2–6 in. Common in sandy areas. Mojave, Colorado Deserts.   MARCH–JUNE

WATERLEAF FAMILY (Hydrophyllaceae)
See also pp. W 74–76; R 308; B 366–70.

SAGEBRUSH BELLS   *Phacelia glandulifera*
Note the short golden funnel-like flowers are on long coiled sprays. Gray, pinnate, lobed leaves. 1–2 ft. Common on drying sagebrush flats. Great Basin.   MAY–JUNE

WHISPERING BELLS   *Emmenanthe penduliflora*
Note the pale yellow, *nodding, bell-like* flowers on the erect, glandular-haired stems. Leaves linear with sawtoothed edges. 4–20 in. Common. Southern ⅔ of Calif.   APRIL–JULY

FORGET-ME-NOT FAMILY (Boraginaceae)
See also pp. W 78; O 226, R 308; B 340–42.

CALIFORNIA PUCCOON   *Lithospermum californicum*
Numerous *large dark yellow* funnel-like flowers are in a *congested* cluster. A few scattered, broad, linear leaves on stem. 4 nutlike seeds per fruit. ½–1½ ft. Foothill woodlands. Cen. Calif. to Ore.   APRIL–JUNE

MOJAVE POPCORN FLOWER   *Cryptantha confertiflora*
Note the *clublike cluster of both* pale and dark yellow flowers mixed together. Each petal has a conspicuous *small inner toothlike* lobe. White bristly-haired leaves. 4 nutlike seeds. 6–24 in. Rocky limestone slopes. Eastern slopes Sierra Nevada; Mojave Desert, s. Great Basin.   MAY–JULY

WESTERN PUCCOON   *Lithospermum ruderale*
Note that the upper linear *leaves are crowded* together and *mixed with many small,* pale yellow, tubular flowers in a coil. Leaves have many spiny hairs. 4 nutlike seeds. ½–1¼ ft. Dry slopes. Mostly in Great Basin.   APRIL–JUNE

NIGHTSHADE FAMILY (Solanaceae)
See also pp. W 80; B 382.

TOMATILLO Alien   *Physalis philadelpica*
Note the *broad wheel-like* flowers have a *projecting column* of stamens. Leaf blades triangular. The calyx becoming an *inflated* papery urn around the purple berry. 1–3 ft. Disturbed places. Calif.   JUNE–SEPT.

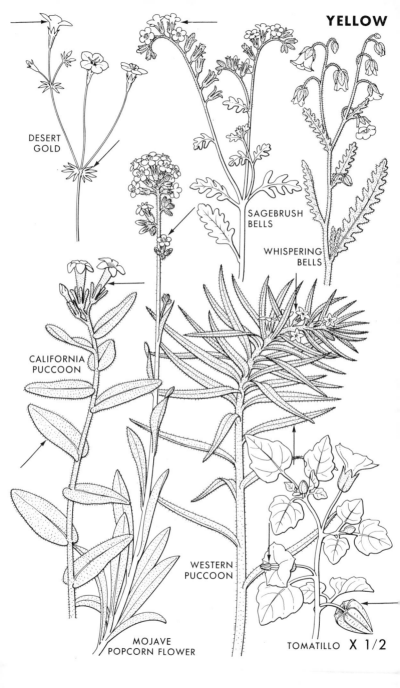

YELLOW

DESERT
GOLD

SAGEBRUSH
BELLS

WHISPERING
BELLS

CALIFORNIA
PUCCOON

WESTERN
PUCCOON

MOJAVE
POPCORN FLOWER

TOMATILLO **X 1/2**

5 PETALS; MANY STAMENS; PINNATE LEAVES WITH STIPULES AT BASE: CINQUEFOILS

ROSE FAMILY (Rosaceae)
Also pp. W 92; Y 176; R 310; Br 404.

PACIFIC SILVERWEED *Potentilla pacifica*
The *long, featherlike* leaves have 9–31 bright green leaflets. Strawberry-like runners spread this species. Coastal beaches, marshes. Pacific Coast. APRIL–AUG.

COMMON SILVERWEED *Potentilla anserina*
(not shown)
Similar to preceding. Entire plant *silky-haired.* Eastern side of Cascades–Sierra Nevada, and Great Basin. MAY–OCT.

SHORTLEAF CINQUEFOIL *Potentilla brevifolia*
Pinnate leaves have *1 pair* of rounded lateral leaflets and a terminal cluster of 3–5 leaflets, all deeply cut. Low alpine mat plant. Blue and Wallowa Mts. of Ore. JULY–AUG.

DRUMMOND'S CINQUEFOIL *Potentilla drummondii*
The basal pinnate leaves are *dark green* and have 2–5 pairs of leaflets. Each leaflet consists of 1–5 sharply and deeply cut subunits. 1–2 ft. Subalpine and alpine meadows. Sierra Nevada and north to B.C. JUNE–AUG.

STICKY CINQUEFOIL *Potentilla glandulosa*
5–9 strongly toothed leaflets are in pairs except for the terminal one. Flowers yellow to white. Sticky stems. 1–3 ft. Very common, many habitats. Pacific States. MAY–AUG.

FIVEFINGER CINQUEFOIL *Potentilla gracilis*
The *palmate, fanlike* leaves have 5–7 fingerlike leaflets. Many regional variations. Leaves may be bright green or silky-haired, and leaflet margins may be slightly to deeply lobed. Many habitats. Pacific States. JUNE–AUG.

BREWER'S CINQUEFOIL *Potentilla breweri*
Compare with Drummond's Cinquefoil to avoid confusion. The pinnate leaves are *grayish-white* with 4–6 pairs of rounded leaflets crowded together. Mid-mt. to alpine meadows. Sierra Nevada north to Ore. JUNE–AUG.

FANLEAF CINQUEFOIL *Potentilla flabellifoila*
Bright green palmate leaves have *3 broad leaflets.* The petals longer than the sepals. Low mat plant 4–12 in. High mt. meadows. Sierra Nevada north to B.C. JUNE–SEPT.

SILVERLEAF CINQUEFOIL *Potentilla argentea*
Silvery *starlike* palmate leaves have 5 deeply lobed leaflets. Sandy soil in pine forests. N.-cen. Wash. JUNE–JULY

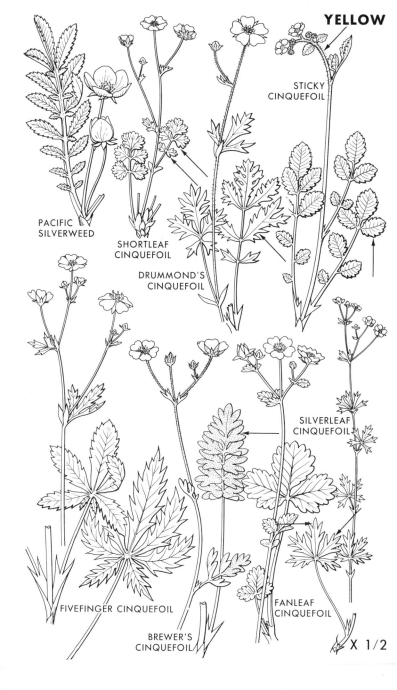

YELLOW

STICKY
CINQUEFOIL

PACIFIC
SILVERWEED

SHORTLEAF
CINQUEFOIL

DRUMMOND'S
CINQUEFOIL

SILVERLEAF
CINQUEFOIL

FIVEFINGER CINQUEFOIL

BREWER'S
CINQUEFOIL

FANLEAF
CINQUEFOIL

X 1/2

5 PETALS; MANY STAMENS;
PINNATE LEAVES WITH STIPULES AT BASE
IVESIA, GEUM

ROSE FAMILY (Rosaceae)
See also pp. W 92; Y 174; R 310; Br 404.

GORDON'S IVESIA *Ivesia gordonii*
The flower stem erect or prostrate and has a headlike cluster of flowers with *narrow linear* petals and 5 stamens. The basal rosette of bright green leaves has 10–25 pairs of leaflets. 2–8 in. Alpine and subalpine meadows. Mts. of Pacific States.
JUNE–AUG.

CLUB MOSS IVESIA *Ivesia lycopodioides*
Very similar to Gordon's Ivesia. Each flower has *oval to round* petals and 5 stamens. Alpine meadows. Sierra Nevada and White Mts. of Calif.
JULY–AUG.

MUIR'S IVESIA *Ivesia muirii*
The *silvery-gray, mousetail-like* leaves have 25–40 pairs of very tiny, almost indistinguishable leaflets. The pale yellow flowers are in congested clusters. Petals *linear,* 5 stamens. 1–7 in. Gravelly alpine slopes. Sierra Nevada.
JULY–AUG.

DWARF IVESIA *Ivesia pygmaea*
Above the leaves is a dense cyme with small yellow-petaled flowers that *each have 10 stamens.* The yellow-green pinnate leaves are in small basal rosettes. Each leaf has 10–20 pairs of tiny leaflets crowded together. 1–6 in. Rocky alpine slopes. Sierra Nevada.
JULY–AUG.

LARGE-LEAVED AVENS *Geum macrophyllum*
Note that each pinnate basal leaf has *a large rounded terminal* leaflet and smaller variable-sized pairs below. Leaves reduced upward on the stem. The few flowers nearly flat, becoming rounded seedheads. 1–3 ft. Moist meadows, woods. Pacific States.
APRIL–AUG.

PRAIRIE SMOKE *Geum ciliatum*
Flower buds are *distinct nodding bells* of *red* sepals which become small erect yellow flowers. Basal leaves pinnate with the leaflets narrowly cleft. Stem leaves few. $\frac{1}{2}$–2 ft. Rocky places 4000–8000 ft. Great Basin, and on east slope of Cascades–Sierra Nevada.
APRIL–AUG.

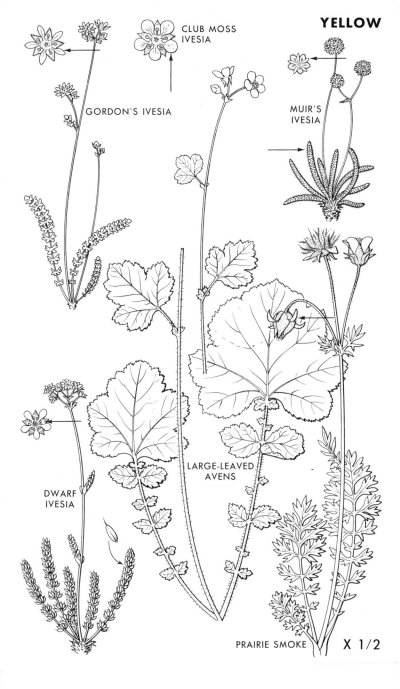

YELLOW

CLUB MOSS
IVESIA

GORDON'S IVESIA

MUIR'S
IVESIA

DWARF
IVESIA

LARGE-LEAVED
AVENS

PRAIRIE SMOKE   X 1/2

PEALIKE FLOWERS; COMPOUND LEAVES

PEA FAMILY (Leguminosae)
See also pp. W 94–96; Y 178–82;
O 224; R 318–26; B 376–80.

SHAMROCK Alien   *Trifolium dubium*
The 3 palmate leaflets have *blunt ends*. The leaf petiole base
has *triangular stipules*. The tiny pea flowers are in *tiny*
(⅛–¼ in.) *loose heads*. Stems often prostrate. 4–20 in. Many
habitats. Pacific States.   APRIL–SEPT.

HOP CLOVER Alien   *Trifolium agrarium*
Flowers are in a *beehive-like head*. Stems are erect and have
lancelike trifoliate leaves. 6–25 in. Common along roadsides in
Wash. and Ore., rarely in Calif.   JUNE–SEPT.

SPOTTED CLOVER Alien   *Medicago arabica*
Each leaflet has a *reddish spot*. Seedpods are spiny spirals.
6–24 in. Common. Pacific States.   ALL YEAR

BUR CLOVER Alien   *Medicago polymorpha*
Seedpods *round spiny spirals*. Leaf stipules at base of leaf
petiole are *strongly fringed* as linear teeth. The trifoliate leaflet
margins are strongly toothed. Stem prostrate. 6–18 in. Common in many habitats. Pacific States.   ALL YEAR

CALIFORNIA FALSE LUPINE *Thermopsis macrophylla*
The large yellow pea flowers are in a terminal raceme similar to
that of Lupines, but the broadly oval, somewhat gray leaflets
are in a *pinnately compound* leaf. Stems *silky-haired*. 1–3 ft.
Open places below 4000 ft. Coastal mts. from San Diego, Calif.,
to s. Ore.   MAY–JUNE

MOUNTAIN FALSE LUPINE   *Thermopsis montana*
(not shown)
Similar to California False Lupine. Leaves are *bright green*.
Stems *hairless*. 2–4 ft. Open places. Pacific States.
APRIL–JUNE

YELLOW SWEET CLOVER Alien   *Melilotus indica*
The tiny flowers are in *long spikes* with a long smooth stem
below. Trifoliate leaves on long petioles. A distinctive sweet
odor is emitted from the plant on hot days. 1–4 ft. Disturbed
places. Pacific States.   APRIL–OCT.

SULPHUR PEA   *Lathyrus sulphureus*
Note the vines climbing over shrubs and supporting themselves
by the *terminal tendril* of each pinnate leaf. The yellow to tan
flowers are tinted purple or orange. Vines to 10 ft. Calif. North
Coast Ranges to s. Ore., and west slope of Sierra Nevada.
APRIL–JULY

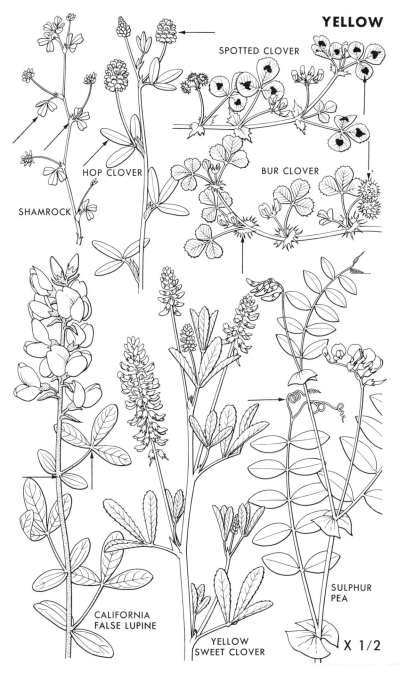

YELLOW

SHAMROCK

HOP CLOVER

SPOTTED CLOVER

BUR CLOVER

CALIFORNIA FALSE LUPINE

YELLOW SWEET CLOVER

SULPHUR PEA

X 1/2

PEALIKE FLOWERS;
PINNATE LEAVES; LOTUS

PEA FAMILY (Leguminosae)
See also pp. W 94–96; Y 178–82;
O 224; R 318–26; B 376–80.

BICOLORED LOTUS   *Lotus formosissimus*
Flowers *bicolored,* the banner petal yellow and the lower petals
pink to purple. Leaflets usually 5 per leaf. 1–2 ft. Moist open
places. West of Cascades and south through coast ranges to
Monterey, Calif., area.   MAY–JULY

GRAND LOTUS   *Lotus grandiflorus*
The *banner petal much larger* than the other petals. The 3 or
more flowers in each umbel tend to age reddish. *Dotlike* glandular stipules at the base of the leaf petiole. Each leaf has 7–9
oval and somewhat hairy leaflets. ½–2 ft. Dry slopes below
5000 ft. Mts. of Calif.   APRIL–JULY

MINIATURE LOTUS   *Lotus micranthus*
Each pinnate leaf of *3–5 oblong* leaflets. The pale yellow solitary flower tinted red and has a *1- to 3-leaflet bract* just below
it. Smooth, slender stems. 4–12 in. Open places. West of Cascades–Sierra Nevada.   APRIL–SEPT.

BIRDSFOOT LOTUS Alien   *Lotus corniculatus*
Note the *large pair* of almost *leaflike stipules* at the base of
each long leaf petiole. 3 oblong leaflets per leaf. Flowers yellow, the banner petal may be reddish. Prostrate stems. ½–2 ft.
Common. Pacific States.   MAY–SEPT.

TORREY'S LOTUS   *Lotus oblongifolius*
Each flower has a *yellow* banner petal and *white* lower petals.
1–3 leaflike bracts occur *immediately below* the flower umbel.
7–11 linear leaflets per leaf. Stem erect. ½–2 ft. Wet meadows.
Mts. of Calif. and s. Ore.   MAY–SEPT.

DESERT LOTUS   *Lotus tomentellus*
Plants prostrate, each succulent leaf has *5–6 blunt leaflets. 1–2
flowers* per peduncle. 2–10 in. Very common. Mojave,
Colorado Deserts.   FEB.–JUNE

SILVERLEAF LOTUS   *Lotus argophyllus*
Note the silvery-gray prostrate mat of wiry stems. Each leaf of
3–5 *clustered* leaflets. The 3- to 8-flowered umbel is attached
to the stem *without a peduncle.* Dry slopes below 5000 ft. Cen.
Calif. south to Baja.   APRIL–JULY

HILL LOTUS   *Lotus humistratus*
A *single flower* is above each leaf and *sessile* (without a
stem). Tiny yellow flower ages reddish. Stem and leaves
loosely gray-haired. Common. All of Calif.   MARCH–JULY

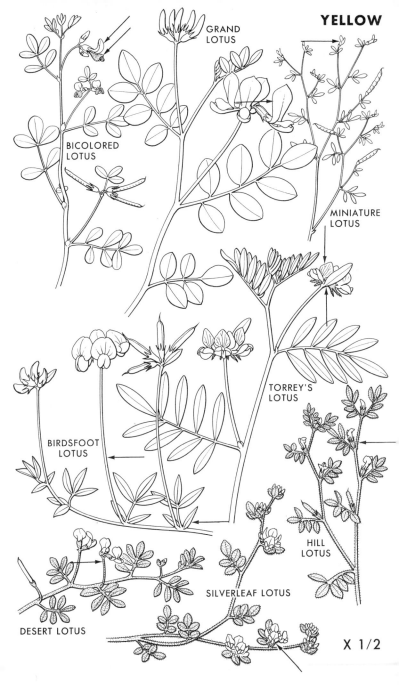

YELLOW

GRAND
LOTUS

BICOLORED
LOTUS

MINIATURE
LOTUS

TORREY'S
LOTUS

BIRDSFOOT
LOTUS

HILL
LOTUS

DESERT LOTUS

SILVERLEAF LOTUS

X 1/2

PEA FAMILY (Leguminosae)
See also pp. W 94–96; Y 178–82;
O 224; R 318–26; B 376–80.

LONGLEAF LOCOWEED   *Astragalus reventus*
Note the 13–41 slender *linear to lancelike* leaflets are in a long
pinnate leaf. Each yellow to tan flower has a purple-tinted keel
petal. Flowers in short terminal clusters. Pods slender with a
long, thin-beaked tip. Stem erect. 1–16 in. Flats, pine forests.
Great Basin.   APRIL–JUNE

SAN DIEGO LOCOWEED   *Astragalus oocarpus*
Each leaf has 19–35 oblong, round-tipped leaflets arranged in a
long tapering spray. The *erect* seedpod has a small abrupt
beak. 15–60 flowers per raceme. Stems erect, 2–4 ft. Mts. behind San Diego, Calif.   JUNE–AUG.

COILED LOCOWEED   *Astragalus curvicarpus*
The seedpod is semicircular or *coiled* into a complete ring. The
gray leaves have 7–9 loosely arranged oblong leaflets, with
blunt and notched tips. The yellow to tan or white flowers are
in 10- to 25-flowered racemes. Stems erect, ½–1½ ft. Sagebrush
areas. Great Basin.   MAY–JUNE

DIABLO LOCOWEED   *Astragalus oxyphysus*
The seedpod has a *one-sided bulge.* 17–27 leaflets per leaf.
2–4 ft. Common in grasslands. Calif. South Coast Ranges and
southern foothills of Sierra Nevada.   FEB.–JUNE

DOUGLAS'S LOCOWEED   *Astragalus douglasii*
The seedpod is a *short fat oval* with a *broad triangular tip.*
The gray pinnate leaves have 11–25 oblong leaflets, each with
blunt and notched tips. 10–35 yellow to tan flowers. Stems in
prostrate clumps. 1–3 ft. Fields, thickets below 7000 ft.
S. Calif. Mts. north to cen. Calif.   APRIL–AUG.

BUTTER LUPINE   *Lupinus luteolus*
Flowers are in *whorls* on a long raceme. The *bright green*
palmate leaves have broad leaflets. 1–3 ft. Dry slopes. Coast
Ranges of Ore. south to near Los Angeles.   MAY–AUG.

SULPHUR LUPINE   *Lupinus sulphureus*
The pale yellow flowers are irregularly arranged on each
raceme. The *silvery-gray* palmate leaves have narrow leaflets.
1–3 ft. Great Basin.   APRIL–JUNE

CALIFORNIA TEA   *Psoralea physodes*
Trifoliate leaflets *large and oval.* Flowers are in a *thick,
rounded cluster.* 1–3 ft. Open places. West of Cascades and
south along Coast Ranges to s. Calif.   APRIL–JUNE

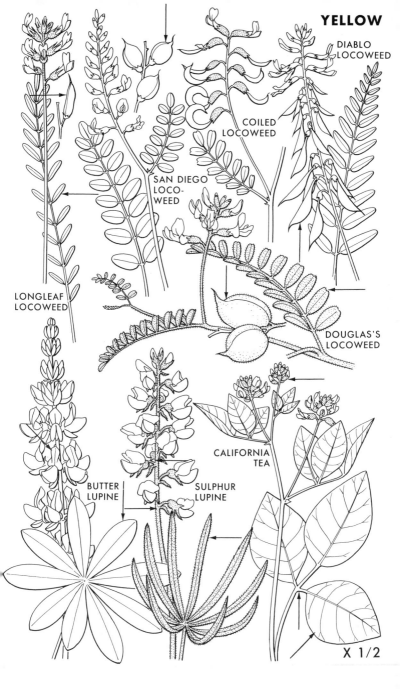

YELLOW

DIABLO
LOCOWEED

COILED
LOCOWEED

SAN DIEGO
LOCO-
WEED

LONGLEAF
LOCOWEED

DOUGLAS'S
LOCOWEED

CALIFORNIA
TEA

BUTTER
LUPINE

SULPHUR
LUPINE

X 1/2

LARGE SUNFLOWER HEADS; HUGE LEAVES

SUNFLOWER FAMILY (Compositae)
Sunflower Tribe: Heliantheae
See also pp. W 102–8; Y 184–220;
O 226; R 328–32; B 384; G 404.

BOLANDER'S WYETHIA   *Wyethia bolanderi*
Short (1–5 in.) oval leaves are *dark green and shiny*. Flower head has more than 20 ray flowers. ½–1 ft. Woodland openings. W. Sierra Nevada foothills.   MARCH–MAY

SOUTHERN WYETHIA   *Wyethia ovata*
The oval leaves have *both ends sharply* tapered and are silky-gray haired. 12–20 ray flowers per flower head. 4–12 in. Open hillsides below 6000 ft. Cen. and s. Calif.   MAY–AUG.

MOUNTAIN MULE EARS   *Wyethia mollis*
Leaves *oblong with rounded* tips and bases. Plant densely white-haired. 1–3 ft. Open slopes below 7000 ft. Calif. Coast Ranges and w. Sierra Nevada.   MARCH–JULY

GRAY MULE EARS   *Wyethia helenioides*
Flower head has *extra large oval* bracts. Gray-haired leaves are *elongated ovals*. 1–2 ft. Open woodlands. Calif. Coast Ranges and southern half of w. Sierra Nevada.   MARCH–JULY

GREEN MULE EARS   *Wyethia glabra*
The large oblong to oval *green leaves* have sharp *tapered tips and rounded basal* portions, slightly haired. ½–2 ft. Slopes below 3000 ft. Calif. Coast Ranges.   MARCH–MAY

NARROWLEAF MULE EARS   *Wyethia angustifolia*
The *long linear leaves* have a narrow tapering blade. ½–2 ft. Open slopes. Cen. Wash. to cen. Calif.   APRIL–JULY

ARROW-LEAVED BALSAMROOT
     Balsamorhiza sagittata
The velvety, silver gray-green, *arrowhead-like* leaves have *smooth* margins. Flower head bracts woolly-haired. ½–2 ft. Cascades–Sierra Nevada crest, Great Basin.   MAY–JULY

DELTOID BALSAMROOT   *Balsamorhiza deltoidea*
The green, nearly hairless *arrowhead-like* leaves have *partly toothed margins*. ½–3 ft. Below 7000 ft. West of Pacific States deserts.   MARCH–JULY

HOOKER'S BALSAMROOT   *Balsamorhiza hookeri*
Velvety gray, *ladderlike, pinnate* leaves. 4–12 in. N. Calif. and Great Basin.   APRIL–JUNE

CAREY'S BALSAMROOT   *Balsamorhiza careyana*
The *green triangular* leaves and flower head bracts slightly woolly-haired. 1–3 ft. Great Basin.   MARCH–JULY

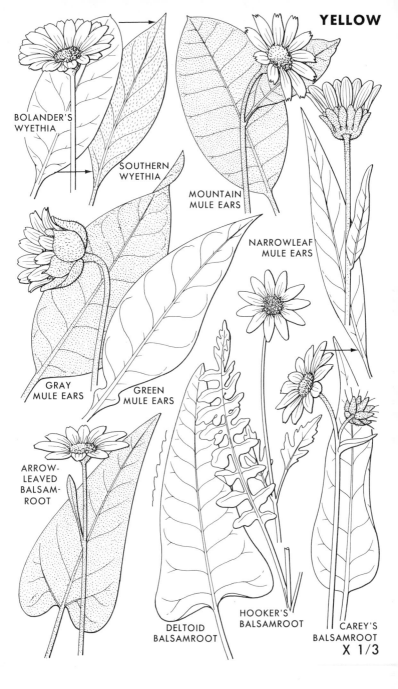

YELLOW

BOLANDER'S WYETHIA

SOUTHERN WYETHIA

MOUNTAIN MULE EARS

NARROWLEAF MULE EARS

GRAY MULE EARS

GREEN MULE EARS

ARROW-LEAVED BALSAM-ROOT

DELTOID BALSAMROOT

HOOKER'S BALSAMROOT

CAREY'S BALSAMROOT

X 1/3

TRUE SUNFLOWERS AND CONEFLOWERS

Sunflower Family (Compositae)
Sunflower Tribe: Heliantheae
See also pp. W 102–8; Y 184–220;
O 226; R 328–32; B 384; G 404.

PANAMINT SUNFLOWER　　　　*Enceliopsis argophylla*
Large *silvery* oval leaves are in basal clusters below the huge
sunflowers on *long naked* stems. 1–4 ft. Rocky western slope of
Panamint Mts., Death Valley Natl. Mon.　　　　April–June

NUTTALL'S SUNFLOWER　　　　*Helianthus nuttallii*
The shiny green *oval* leaves are scattered in pairs along an
elongated stem. 1–6 ft. Moist meadows. Great Basin and Los
Angeles Basin of s. Calif.　　　　July–Sept.

SLENDER SUNFLOWER　　　　*Helianthus gracilentus*
The long *broad lancelike* leaves have *serrated margins*. Slender, well-branched stems. Flower heads have yellow rays and a
red-purple to yellow center of disk flowers. 1–4 ft. Dry rocky
places. Calif. and sw. Ore.　　　　July–Nov.

DESERT SUNFLOWER　　　　*Geraea canescens*
The leaf blades are nearly *diamond-shaped* with a sharp *trian-
gular upper half*, occasional toothed margins. Covered by
dense velvety white hairs. Many golden flower heads. $\frac{1}{2}$–3 ft.
Very common on flats. Mojave, Colorado Deserts.
Feb.–May, Oct.–Nov.

CALIFORNIA CONE FLOWER　　　　*Rudbeckia californica*
Note the *large oblong cone* of greenish disk flowers above the
showy yellow ray flowers. Leaves broadly lancelike. 2–6 ft.
Mt. meadows. Calif. and s. Ore.　　　　July–Sept.

CALIFORNIA HELIANTHELLA　*Helianthella californica*
Note the dark green *lancelike leaf blade* has a tapering base
above the *long petiole*. Stems well-branched and often a dark
reddish color. $\frac{1}{2}$–2 ft. Very common. Open places below
7000 ft. Mts. of cen. and n. Calif.　　　　April–Sept.

CALIFORNIA SUNFLOWER　　　　*Helianthus californicus*
Note the very tall (to 15 ft.) single stout stem, well above all the
other adjacent plants. The narrow lancelike leaves have *no
petioles*. Flower head has *lancelike bracts*. Moist streambanks,
meadows at low elevations. Calif.　　　　June–Oct.

KANSAS SUNFLOWER　　　　*Helianthus annuus*
The *broad triangular* leaf blade has slightly toothed margins
and is a dull dark green. The flower head on a single stout stem
has numerous ray flowers and a reddish center of disk flowers.
State flower of Kansas. 1–10 ft. Very common. Pacific States.
Feb.–Oct.

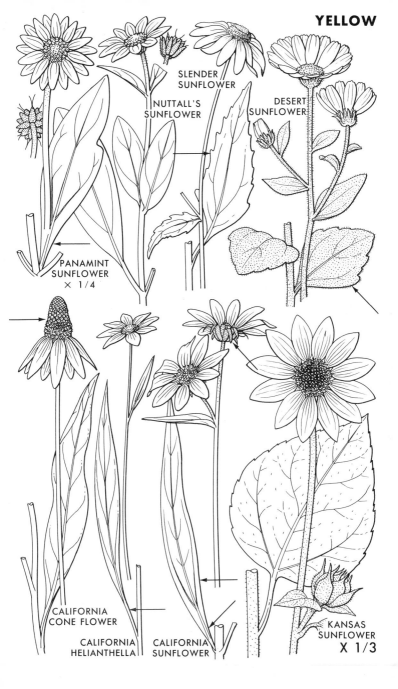

YELLOW

SLENDER
SUNFLOWER

NUTTALL'S
SUNFLOWER

DESERT
SUNFLOWER

PANAMINT
SUNFLOWER
× 1/4

CALIFORNIA
CONE FLOWER

CALIFORNIA
HELIANTHELLA

CALIFORNIA
SUNFLOWER

KANSAS
SUNFLOWER
X 1/3

COREOPSIS OR DAHLIALIKE FLOWERS

SUNFLOWER FAMILY (Compositae)
Sunflower Tribe: Heliantheae
See also pp. W 102–8; Y 184–220; O 226; R 328–32;
B 384; G 404.

All species on this page are in subtribe Coreopsidiae, which is easily distinguished by the *shiny green flower head bracts in 2 rows*. The outer of the 2 rows (few in number) bent downward. Inner row numerous and close-set.

DOUGLAS'S COREOPSIS *Coreopsis douglasii*
Leaves basal, nearly threadlike with 3 or more pinnate lobes. Outer row of flower head bracts *lancelike*. 2–10 in. Rocky places. Calif. South Coast Ranges at Jolon. MARCH–APRIL

STILLMAN'S COREOPSIS *Coreopsis stillmanii*
Outer row of flower head bracts *oblong*. Ray flowers are *broadly round-tipped*. Pinnate leaves divided 1–2 times into a few linear to spatula-shaped lobes with the terminal one broadest. 4–6 in. Grasslands. Central Valley of Calif.
MARCH–MAY

BIGELOW'S COREOPSIS *Coreopsis bigelovii*
Ray flowers are *square-tipped*. The outer row of flower head bracts *linear*. Leaves basal, linear with 2–5 or more *broad pairs* of lobes. ½–2 ft. Cen. and s. Calif. MARCH–MAY

LEAFYSTEM COREOPSIS *Coreopsis calliopsidea*
Flower head bracts oval to triangular. The mostly basal pinnate leaves have several linear lobes. ½–2 ft. Dry open slopes below 3000 ft. Cen. and s. Calif. MARCH–MAY

CALIFORNIA COREOPSIS *Coreopsis californica*
Outer flower head bracts are *long linear*. Leaves threadlike with one or few similar side branches. 2–10 in. Great masses on the Mojave Desert. MARCH–MAY

PLAINS TICKSEED *Coreopsis tinctoria*
The outer flower head bracts are *short and inconspicuous*. Each yellow ray flower has red-brown basal spots. Pinnate leaves are divided into 2–3 pairs of *long* linear lobes. 1–3 ft. Moist places. Occasional in Pacific States. JUNE–SEPT.

BUR MARIGOLD *Bidens cernua*
The *undivided lancelike* leaves have toothed margins and *no petioles*. The flower head has a few *long, leaflike* bracts in the outer row. Heads nodding in age. 2–7 ft. Wet lowland marshes. Pacific States. JULY–NOV.

GIANT SEA DAHLIA *Coreopsis gigantea*
Note the *thick,* woody, *few-branched trunk*. Threadlike pinnate leaves. Large dahlialike flowers. 1–6 ft. Sea cliffs and dunes. Calif. coast, San Luis Obispo south to Baja.
MARCH–MAY

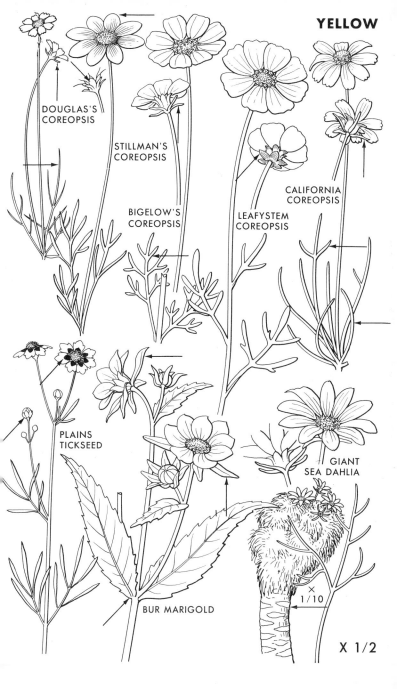

YELLOW

DOUGLAS'S
COREOPSIS

STILLMAN'S
COREOPSIS

BIGELOW'S
COREOPSIS

LEAFYSTEM
COREOPSIS

CALIFORNIA
COREOPSIS

PLAINS
TICKSEED

GIANT
SEA DAHLIA

BUR MARIGOLD

× 1/10

X 1/2

STICKY-HAIRED MADIAS

SUNFLOWER FAMILY (Compositae); Tarweed Tribe: Madiinae
See also pp. W 102–8; Y 184–220;
O 226; R 328–32; B 384; G 404.

PYGMY MADIA *Madia exigua*
Note the tiny circle of ray flowers which surround *only one disk flower*. The single-stemmed plants form large masses. Woodlands, plains. Pacific States. MAY–JULY

COAST MADIA Alien *Madia sativa*
The *rounded flower heads crowded* together at the top of a stout stem. Ray flowers dark yellow. Linear leaves crowded on stem. Strong resinous odor. 2–3 ft. Open places below 1000 ft. Coastal region of Pacific States. MAY–OCT.

WOODLAND MADIA *Madia madioides*
The flat flower head has its bracts in a *rounded bowl*. Stem *slender* with occasional *opposite pairs* of leaves that are long-haired and have tiny stubby lobes. 1–2 ft. Openings in woods. West of Cascades, south to Monterey. MAY–SEPT.

COMMON HARELEAF *Lagophylla ramosissima*
The small, pale yellow flower heads and stem have *rabbit-tail-like bracts* and leaves that are covered by long white hairs and yellow-stalked glands. Flower heads open in late afternoon and close the following midmorning. ½–4 ft. Common below 5000 ft. Calif., and Great Basin. MAY–OCT.

BLOW WIVES *Achyrachaena mollis*
Noted for the large round ball of *flat white* membranous pappus on maturing seedheads. Flower heads yellow *honey-comblike*. 4–15 in. Grasslands. Calif. and s. Ore.
APRIL–MAY

COMMON MADIA *Madia elegans*
Flower head bracts have an *urn-shaped outline* below the *large ray flowers*. The ray flowers are entirely yellow or have a red basal portion. Disk flower anthers black, except in 1 subspecies. Stems *well-branched*, linear leaves alternately arranged. ½–3 ft. All subspecies occur in colorful masses, the flowers opening in late afternoon and remaining so until the following midmorning. The 4 subspecies are: 1. ssp. *elegans* as above, 3000–8000 ft. in forest openings of Calif. mts. JUNE–AUG. 2. ssp. *vernalis* (not shown) same as ssp. *elegans*, but flowering much earlier and occurs in grasslands of valleys and foothills below 3000 ft. Calif. and Ore. FEB.–MAY. 3. ssp. *wheeleri* has *yellow* disk flower anthers. Conifer forests 5000–8000 ft. Calif. mts. 4. ssp. *densifolia* a late bloomer. Valleys and foothills west of mts. in Calif. and Ore. below 3000 ft.
AUG.–NOV.

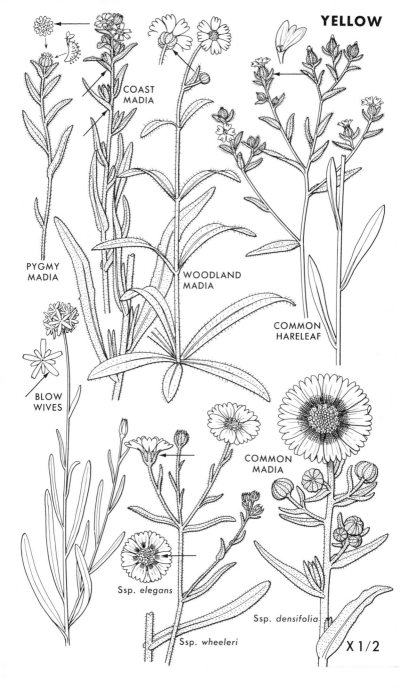

YELLOW

PYGMY MADIA

COAST MADIA

WOODLAND MADIA

COMMON HARELEAF

BLOW WIVES

COMMON MADIA

Ssp. elegans

Ssp. wheeleri

Ssp. densifolia

X 1/2

STICKY-HAIRED TARWEEDS

 Sunflower Family (Compositae); Tarweed Tribe: Madiinae
See also pp. W 102–8; Y 184–220; 0 226; R 328–32;
B 384; G 404.

KELLOGG'S TARWEED   *Hemizonia kelloggii*
Note the *5 oval ray flowers* and 6 disk flowers in each flower
head on the widely branching stem. The alternately arranged
linear leaves remotely toothed or lobed. Softly haired and
glandular throughout. ½–3 ft. Common. Open fields below
2000 ft. Cen. and s. Calif.   April–July

COAST TARWEED   *Hemizonia corymbosa*
The *basal leaves deeply lobed,* but linear above. Each flower
head has *18–35 ray flowers* and as many or more disk flowers.
Ray flower petals triangular in outline. Strong pleasant odor.
½–3 ft. Common on Calif. coast.   May–Oct.

FITCH'S SPIKEWEED   *Hemizonia fitchii*
The *narrowly linear, pinnate* leaves with spiny tips are
crowded along the stem. Each flower head has 10–20 short,
light yellow ray flowers. *Anthers black.* Stems stiffly branched,
leaves green, darkened by the glands. Strong pungent odor.
½–3 ft. Frequent. Open slopes below 3000 ft. Calif. and
s. Ore.   May–Nov.

FASCICLED TARWEED   *Hemizonia fasciculata*
Note the small *smooth* triangular to lancelike leaves which
clasp the stem. Flower head has 5 rounded ray flowers somewhat remote from each other. Seeds have a rumpled chunky
surface. ½–2 ft. Grasslands, woodlands. Cen. Calif. coast south
to Baja.   May–Sept.

COMMON SPIKEWEED   *Hemizonia pungens*
Note the *spiny dandelionlike* pinnate leaves. Numerous flower
heads are nestled among the spiny leaves. The anthers are
yellow. Stems stiffly branched. Pungent odor. ½–4 ft. Very
common in dry fields below 1000 ft. Calif. and occasionally
north to Wash.   April–Oct.

SAN DIEGO TARWEED   *Hemizonia paniculata*
The linear leaves have *sharp teeth.* Each flower head has 8 ray
and 8–13 disk flowers. Ray petals are as broad as long. Fragrant scented. ½–3 ft. Dry slopes at low elevations. Calif.
South Coast Ranges to Baja.   May–Nov.

STICKY TARWEED   *Holocarpha virgata*
Note the numerous conspicuous stalked glands on the short
pinecone-like branches that cover the entire plant. Disagreeable resinous odor. 1–4 ft. Common in grasslands below
3000 ft. Cen. to s. Calif.   June–Nov.

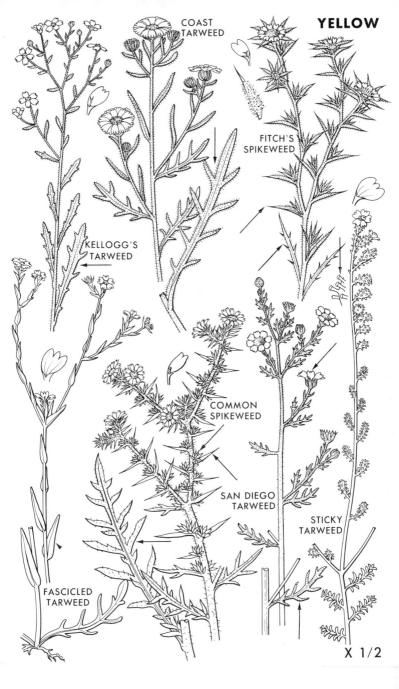

YELLOW

COAST TARWEED

FITCH'S SPIKEWEED

KELLOGG'S TARWEED

COMMON SPIKEWEED

SAN DIEGO TARWEED

STICKY TARWEED

FASCICLED TARWEED

X 1/2

STICKY-HAIRED TIDY TIPS (LAYIAS)

 SUNFLOWER FAMILY (Compositae): Tarweed Tribe: Madiinae
See also pp. W 102–8; Y 184–220; O 226;
R 328–32; B 384; G 404.

COASTAL TIDY TIPS *Layia platyglossa*
Ray flowers are white-tipped (compare with other 2 species).
The linear flower head bracts have *many short straight* hairs
covering the entire surface. Leaves linear, margins smooth or
with very short lobes. Disk flowers *without* subtending bracts.
4–12 inches. Grassy flats. Calif. Coast Ranges to Baja; western
side of Central Valley of Calif. MARCH–JUNE

FREMONT'S TIDY TIPS *Layia fremontii*
Ray flowers are white-tipped (compare with other 2 species).
Flower head bracts are linear with slightly *enlarged roundness*
at ends, nearly smooth without hairs. Pinnate ladderlike leaves
have numerous thin lobes. Disk flowers *have* subtending
bracts. 2–12 in. Grasslands. Central Valley of Calif. and
w. Sierra Nevada foothills. MARCH–MAY

SMOOTH LAYIA *Layia chrysanthemoides*
Ray flowers are white-tipped (compare with other 2 species).
Flower head bracts are *linear with hooked thornlike* hairs along
the margins. Leaves straplike with rounded projecting lobes
that often give the appearance of a can opener. Disk flowers
have subtending bracts. 4–15 in. Common, grasslands, woodlands. Calif. Coast Ranges. MARCH–MAY

SIERRA LAYIA *Layia pentachaeta*
Ray flowers completely golden. Strongly *comblike* leaves are
on the *upper stem.* Disk flowers have yellow anthers. 1–2 ft.
Grasslands, woodlands. W. Sierra Nevada foothills and southern end of Central Valley of Calif. MARCH–MAY

SLENDER LAYIA *Layia paniculata*
Note the completely golden, *tiny 3-lobed* ray flowers surrounding the many disk flowers of the buttonlike flowerheads. Plants
well-branched. 1–3 ft. Woodlands, chaparral. Calif. South
Coast Ranges. APRIL–MAY

WOODLAND LAYIA *Layia gaillardioides*
Ray flowers completely golden. Leaves straplike with *torn
margins.* Disk flowers *pepperlike* from black anthers. ½–2 ft.
Woodlands. Calif. Coast Ranges. APRIL–JUNE

GOLDEN LAYIA *Layia glandulosa ssp. lutea*
Ray flowers completely golden. The linear leaves are *smooth-
edged* on the upper stem. Disk flowers have yellow anthers.
4–12 in. Woodlands. Calif. South Coast Ranges.
APRIL–MAY

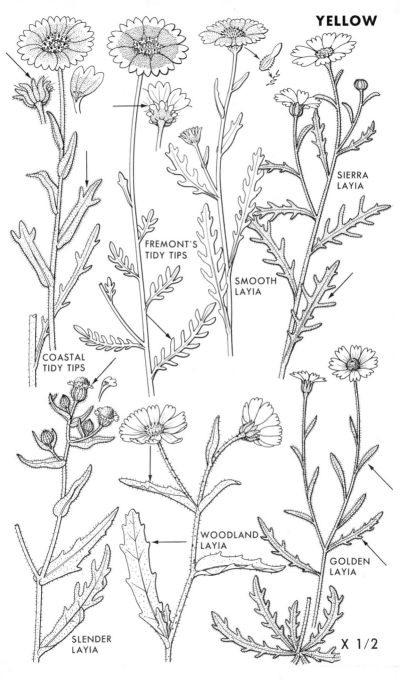

YELLOW

COASTAL TIDY TIPS

FREMONT'S TIDY TIPS

SMOOTH LAYIA

SIERRA LAYIA

SLENDER LAYIA

WOODLAND LAYIA

GOLDEN LAYIA

X 1/2

WOOLLY SUNFLOWERS

SUNFLOWER FAMILY (Compositae); Woolly
Sunflower Tribe: Helenieae
See also pp. W 102–8; Y 184–220; O 226;
R 328–32; B 384; G 404.

CUPPED MONOLOPIA　　　　　*Monolopia major*
The gray *cuplike base* of the flower head has *triangular flaps*
around the cup rim. Gray linear leaves have slightly sawtoothed margins. 4–25 in. Grasslands. Central Valley of Calif.;
San Francisco area south to Monterey.　　　MARCH–MAY

FLESHY JAUMEA　　　　　　*Jaumea carnosa*
Note the *smooth fleshy* linear leaves. The thick flower heads
have 6–10 narrow ray flowers. Stem nearly prostrate. 4–12 in.
Salt marshes, tidal flats along Pacific Coast.　　MAY–OCT.

WOOLLY MARIGOLD　　　　　*Baileya pleniradiata*
Note the *20–40 golden* to pale yellow ray flowers in each flower
head. Plant parts soft white woolly-haired. Leaves narrow
linear lobed, withering rather early. ½–2 ft. Common. Mojave,
Colorado Deserts.　　　　　MARCH–JUNE, OCT.–NOV.

DESERT MARIGOLD　　　　　*Baileya multiradiata*
Similar to Woolly Marigold. Basal leaves *broadly* pinnate
lobed and not withering early. ½–2 ft. Sandy and rocky
slopes. Eastern Mojave Desert.　　APRIL–JULY, OCT.–NOV.

DROOPING MARIGOLD　　　　*Baileya pauciradiata*
Note the *5–7 drooping* pale lemon-yellow ray flowers in each
flower head. Well-branched, soft woolly-haired stems. Pinnate
leaves with linear teeth. ½–2 ft. Common. Sand dunes.
Eastern Mojave and Colorado Deserts.　　FEB.–JUNE, OCT.

WHITNEYA　　　　　　　*Whitneya dealbata*
The broad oval leaves are light *blue-gray* and in *opposite* pairs.
Usually 1 or 2 erect unbranched stems with 1 or few large
golden flower heads. ½–1½ ft. Forest openings at mid-elevations. Sierra Nevada to Siskiyous.　　　　JUNE–OCT.

BLANKET FLOWER　　　　　*Gaillardia aristata*
Note the large yellow ray flowers around a *red dome* of disk
flowers. Leaves linear with short pairs of projecting lobes.
Often in great masses. 1–2 ft. Open prairies. B.C. south to Ore;
e. Great Basin.　　　　　　　MAY–SEPT.

VENEGASIA　　　　　　*Venegasia carpesioides*
Note the dark green *triangular leaves* arranged alternately
along the coarse, well-branched stem. The outer flower head
bracts rounded. 13–21 long narrow ray flowers in each flower
head. 3–8 ft. Shaded cliffs and streambanks. Along coast from
Monterey, Calif., south to Baja.　　　　FEB.–SEPT.

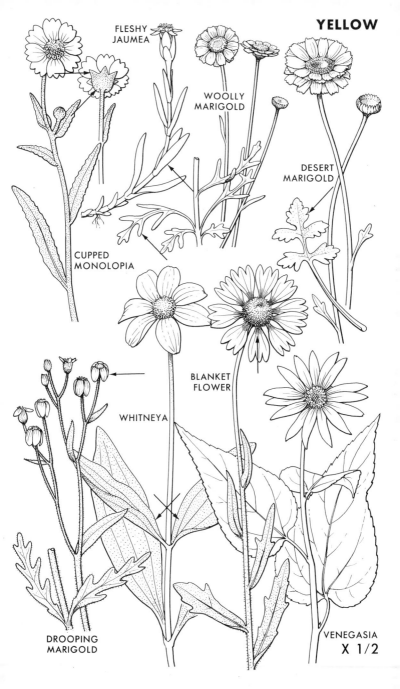

YELLOW

FLESHY
JAUMEA

WOOLLY
MARIGOLD

DESERT
MARIGOLD

CUPPED
MONOLOPIA

BLANKET
FLOWER

WHITNEYA

DROOPING
MARIGOLD

VENEGASIA
X 1/2

WOOLLY SUNFLOWERS; SNEEZEWEEDS

<small>Sunflower Family (Compositae); Woolly
Sunflower Tribe: Helenieae
See also pp. W 102–8; Y 184–220; O 226; R 328–32;
B 384; G 404.</small>

DWARF HULSEA *Hulsea nana*
The spatula-shaped leaves have *rounded linear lobes* along the margin, lightly gray-haired to green. The thick flower head has 15–25 linear ray flowers. 1–6 in. Volcanic soil at higher elevations. N. Calif. to Wash. July–Aug.

ALPINE HULSEA *Hulsea algida*
The long, linear, *troughlike leaves* have short teeth along the margins. Stems somewhat leafy. Large thick flower heads have 25–50 linear ray flowers. Clumplike plants. 4–16 in. Rocky alpine slopes. High mts., Pacific States. July–Sept.

PUMICE HULSEA *Hulsea vestita*
The woolly white-haired, *spatula-shaped* leaves are in a rosette below the leafless flower stems. Thick flower heads have many linear yellow rays, tinted red or purple. 3–12 in. Sandy pumice flats 6000–12,000 ft. S. Sierra Nevada south to San Jacinto Mts. of s. Calif. June–Aug.

ALPINE GOLDFLOWER *Hymenoxys grandiflora*
The leaves are divided into 3–5 threadlike divisions. Flat yellow *open pinwheel* flower heads. 1–2½ ft. Dry rocky slopes 4000–12,000 ft. Desert mts. of Calif. July–Oct.

ROSILLA *Helenium puberulum*
Note the 5–10 *tiny* ray flowers *nearly hidden* by the large round purple-brown disk flower head. Leaves lancelike and extending down the stem. 1–5 ft. Damp meadows, marshes below 3000 ft. Calif. and Ore. June–Oct.

BIGELOW'S SNEEZEWEED *Helenium bigelovii*
Solitary *globelike* flower heads, disk portion often yellow. Leaf base *extending above* stem. Leaves oval, smooth margined. 1–3 ft. Wet mt. meadows. Calif. to s. Ore. June–Aug.

WESTERN SNEEZEWEED *Helenium autumnale*
The round purple-brown flower head has 10–20 yellow ray flowers reflexed downward. Leaves oval, mostly *sawtooth-margined.* The leaf base *extends down* the stem. ½–2½ ft. Damp meadows in low mts. N. Calif. to Wash. July–Sept.

MOUNTAIN HELENIUM *Helenium hoopesii*
The *large flat* flower heads have 13–21 yellow-orange ray flowers. Leaves long and narrow with a base that *does not* extend along the stem. 1–3 ft. Common, mt. meadows. Sierra Nevada to se. Ore.; Great Basin. July–Sept.

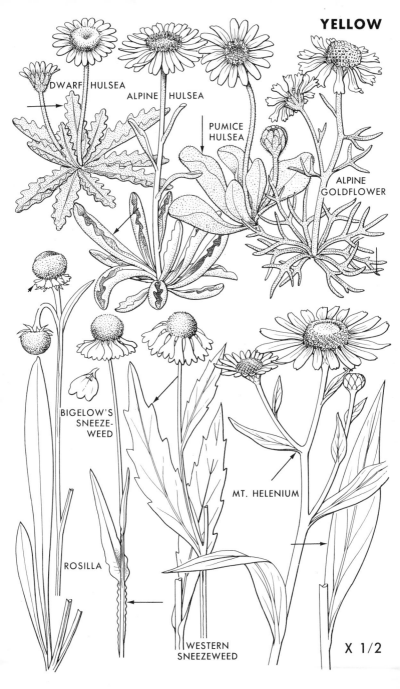

YELLOW

DWARF HULSEA

ALPINE HULSEA

PUMICE HULSEA

ALPINE GOLDFLOWER

BIGELOW'S SNEEZE-WEED

MT. HELENIUM

ROSILLA

WESTERN SNEEZEWEED

X 1/2

WOOLLY SUNFLOWERS AND GOLDFIELDS

SUNFLOWER FAMILY (Compositae); Woolly
Sunflower Tribe: Helenieae
See also pp. W 102-8; Y 184-220; O 226; R 328-32;
B 384; G 404.

FREMONT'S LASTHENIA   *Lasthenia fremontii*
All of the pinnate leaves have threadlike *linear segments*. Each flower head has 8-13 ray flowers. Each seed has *both* 4 slender and 4-8 minute toothlike bristles on top. 4-12 in. Drying pool depressions. Valleys of cen. Calif.   APRIL–MAY

GOLDFIELDS   *Lasthenia chrysotoma*
Flower head ray petal tips a lighter yellow, bottom half a yellow-orange. Flower head *bracts free* from each other. Stem slender, usually unbranched with opposite pairs of linear, sparsely haired leaves. Each seed has 4 linear bristles on top. In early spring this species forms *vast carpets of gold* in grasslands and woodlands below 4000 ft. Calif. and sw. Ore.

MARCH–MAY

SMOOTH LASTHENIA   *Lasthenia glabrata*
Flower head *bracts united* into a cup for ⅔ of their length. Each seed topped by 8-10 brown, spine-tipped teeth. Stems somewhat limp with *linear* leaves in opposite pairs, smooth throughout. 4-15 in. Wet fields below 1000 ft. West of Cascades and south to cen. Calif.   APRIL–JULY

WOOLLY LASTHENIA   *Lasthenia minor*
The basal pinnate leaves have a *wide central* portion with narrow linear lobes. Each flower head has 8-11 yellow ray flowers with a paler tip portion. Each seed has *both* 2-4 long, linear and 4-6 short, toothlike bristles on its top. Stem laxly branched, woolly-haired. 4-15 in. Damp stream bottoms, slopes below 3000 ft. Calif.   MARCH–MAY

WOOLLY SUNFLOWER   *Eriophyllum lanatum*
The *numerous,* single large yellow flower heads have 8-13 ray flowers on *long leafless peduncles*. Stems well-branched clumps. The leaves and stem are covered with a *loosely clumping* gray woolly hair. Leaves linear above, thin and pinnate below. ½-3 ft. Very common in many dry open places below 10,000 ft. Pacific States.   MAY–AUG.

WALLACE'S WOOLLY DAISY   *Antheropeas wallacei*
A miniature plant in a well-branched tuft. Leaves spatula-shaped and densely white woolly. Flower heads on short leafless peduncles. Tufted. 1-4 in. Sandy flats. Mojave, Colorado Deserts.   MARCH–MAY

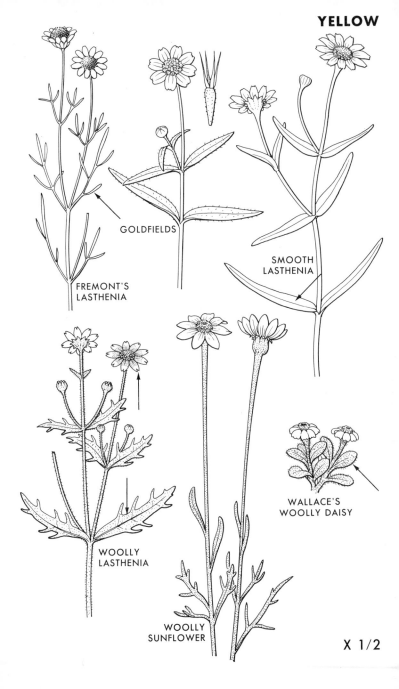

YELLOW

FREMONT'S
LASTHENIA

GOLDFIELDS

SMOOTH
LASTHENIA

WOOLLY
LASTHENIA

WOOLLY
SUNFLOWER

WALLACE'S
WOOLLY DAISY

X 1/2

WOOLLY SUNFLOWERS AND PINCUSHION HEADS

Sunflower Family (Compositae)
Woolly Sunflower Tribe: Helenieae
See also pp. W 102–8; Y 184–220; O 226;
R 328–32; B 384; G 404.

COMMON BLENNOSPERMA   *Blennosperma nanum*
Note the *succulent,* well-branched stem and linear, 2–3 lobed, pinnate leaves. The oval flower head bracts are *purple-tipped.* Each bract tip point has a *tuft of hairs.* One of first spring wildflowers. 2–8 in. Common as masses in low wet flats below 1500 ft. Central Valley of Calif. and s. Calif.   Feb.–April

CHINCH WEED   *Pectis papposa*
Flower head has distinct long, *linear, riblike* bracts. The narrowly linear, oppositely paired leaves have 2–5 pairs of marginal bristles near the base. Stem slender and widely branched. Heavy odor. 4–12 in. Sandy flats. Mojave, Colorado Deserts.   June, Sept.–Nov.

YELLOW HEAD   *Trichoptilium incisum*
Elongated leaves with *spiny teeth* and woolly hairs are on the low, well-branched stem. Pincushion flower heads solitary and well above the leaves. Broad mats 2–8 in. Sandy, rocky places. S. Mojave, Colorado Deserts.   Feb.–May, Oct.–Nov.

PRINGLE'S WOOLLY LEAF   *Eriophyllum pringlei*
Low tufted plant. Leaves linear, each has *3 terminal lobes,* densely white woolly. Pincushion flower heads are entirely of disk flowers. 1–2 in. Sandy flats. Western side of Mojave, Colorado Deserts.   April–June

PEBBLE PINCUSHION   *Chaenactis glabriuscula*
Large showy pincushion flower heads of disk flowers only. Leaves pinnate, divided broadly 1–3 times into thin linear segments. $\frac{1}{4}$–$1\frac{1}{4}$ ft. Common. Hot desert pavements. Mojave, Colorado Deserts and eastern side of Calif. South Coast Ranges.   March–May

COOPER'S PAPERFLOWER   *Psilostrophe cooperi*
Note the large, somewhat squat ray flowers and the linear leaves. Low, mounded plant. $\frac{1}{2}$–2 ft. Rocky slopes. E. Mojave Desert; Great Basin.   April–June, Oct.–Dec.

YELLOW

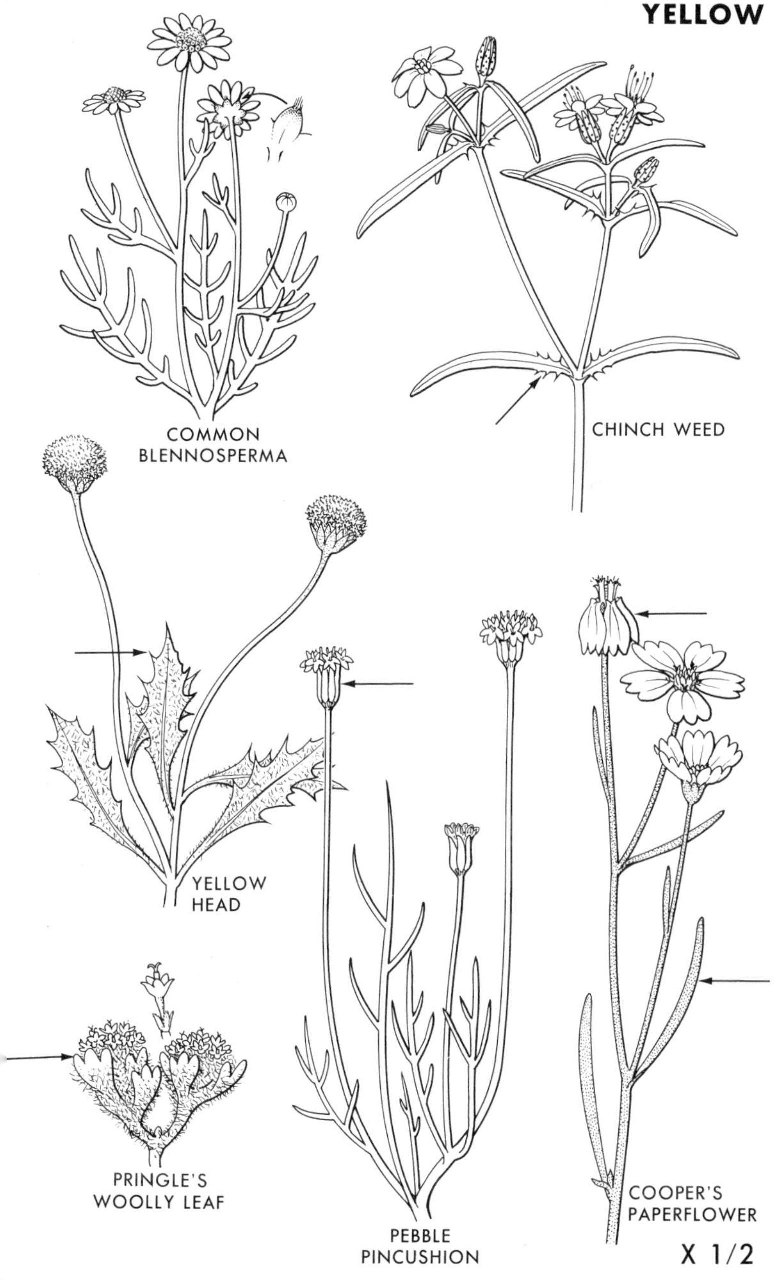
COMMON BLENNOSPERMA
CHINCH WEED
YELLOW HEAD
PRINGLE'S WOOLLY LEAF
PEBBLE PINCUSHION
COOPER'S PAPERFLOWER

X 1/2

GOLDEN MOUNTAIN ARNICAS

Sunflower Family (Compositae)
Senecio Tribe: Senecioneae
See also pp. W 102–8; Y 184–220; O 226;
R 328–32; B 384; G 404.

Flower head has a single row of linear bracts typical of the Senecio Tribe. *Arnica* bract surfaces have scattered hairs.

SOFT ARNICA   *Arnica mollis*
Note the 2–4 pairs of lancelike to narrowly oval or oblong leaves *without petioles*. Each leaf is 3–10 times longer than broad and the edges are smooth. Each broad flower head has 12–18 ray flowers. Bristles above the seed are gray-brown. ½–2 ft. Moist places. Mts. of Pacific States.   June–Sept.

SERPENTINE ARNICA   *Arnica cernua*
Note the small, dark green, spatula-like leaf blades with narrow petioles. Grows on greenish-blue serpentine rock. 4–12 in. Mid-mt. levels. Sw. Ore., nw. Calif.   April–July

MEADOW ARNICA   *Arnica chamissonis*
Note the solitary erect stem has *5–12 pairs of broad lancelike* leaves. The flower heads have somewhat round, pointed bracts, each with a *tuft of long hair* just inside the tip. 1–3 ft. Moist mt. meadows. Mts. of Pacific States.   June–Aug.

SEEP SPRING ARNICA   *Arnica longifolia*
Similar to Meadow Arnica. Flower head bracts sharply pointed and each *without* a tuft of hairs. The 5–12 pairs of leaves long linear, petiole with *some leaf surface*. Stems in *dense tufts*. 1–2 ft. Wet places. Mts. of Pacific States.   July–Sept.

HEARTLEAF ARNICA   *Arnica cordifolia*
Note the 2–3 pairs of *heart-shaped* leaves. Flower head of 9–14 ray flowers. Ray flower *tips pointed*. ½–2 ft. Open to shaded woods. Common. Mts. of Pacific States.   May–Aug.

SIERRA ARNICA   *Arnica nevadensis*
Leaf blade nearly oblong. The leaf blade extends along the petiole. Stem leaves 1–2 times larger than broad. 4–12 in. Open rocky streambanks. Mts. of Sierra Nevada to Wash.

July–Aug.

MOUNTAIN ARNICA   *Arnica latifolia*
Note the 2–4 pairs of the nearly *triangular leaves* with *toothed margins*. Lowermost leaf pair has distinct petioles. Flower heads have 8–12 ray flowers. ½–2 ft. Moist places. Mts. of n. Calif. to B.C.   June–Aug.

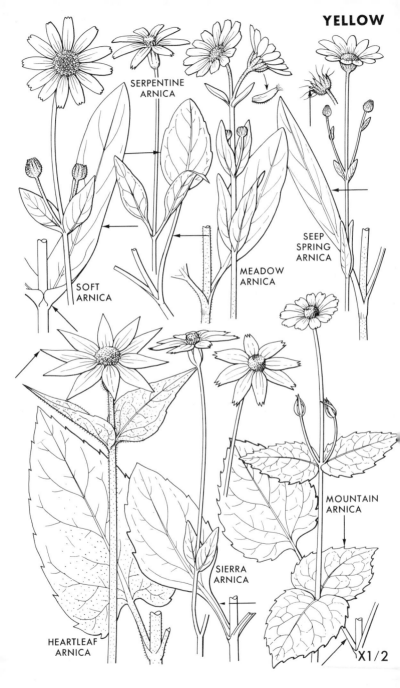

YELLOW

SERPENTINE ARNICA

SOFT ARNICA

MEADOW ARNICA

SEEP SPRING ARNICA

HEARTLEAF ARNICA

SIERRA ARNICA

MOUNTAIN ARNICA

X1/2

BUTTERWEEDS;
RAY FLOWERED SENECIOS

Sunflower Family (Compositae)
Senecio Tribe: Senecioneae
See also pp. W 102–8; Y 184–220; O 226;
R 328–32; B 384; G 404.

Senecio species flower head bracts are long linear and usually in a single row, often shiny green and black-tipped.

ROCKY MOUNTAIN BUTTERWEED
Senecio cymbalarioides
Note the flat-topped, toothed, *butter-fork–like* leaves are in a basal rosette. Many habitats. Pacific States.   May–Aug.

ARROWHEAD BUTTERWEED   *Senecio triangularis*
Note the lush and numerous *arrowhead-shaped* leaves along the entire stem. 1–4 ft. Wet meadows, mt. streams. Pacific States.   June–Sept.

FREMONT'S BUTTERWEED   *Senecio fremontii*
Spatula-like leaves are along the entire dwarf stem. 4–6 in. Alpine rock slides. Mts. of Pacific States.   July–Sept.

TOWER BUTTERWEED   *Senecio integerrimus*
The stout single *towerlike stem* has many *spoonlike* leaves at its base and a few small lancelike ones on the upper stem. Numerous flower heads are in a *congested cluster*. 1–3 ft. Dry open woods in mt. areas. Pacific States.   May–Aug.

BOLANDER'S BUTTERWEED   *Senecio bolanderi*
Leaves pinnate with a rounded terminal lobe and *paired lobes* below. ½–2 ft. Near coast. Pacific Coast.   May–July

WOOLLY BUTTERWEED   *Senecio canus*
Tufted, strongly white woolly, lancelike leaves on long petioles. Erect flower stem. ½–1½ ft. Open rocky places in mts. Pacific States.   May–Aug.

STREAMBANK BUTTERWEED   *Senecio pauciflorus*
The many *heart-shaped* leaves have long thin petioles and are in a basal rosette, becoming smaller on the upper stem. ½–2 ft. Moist alpine and subalpine meadows. Mts. of Pacific States.   June–Aug.

ALPINE BUTTERWEED   *Senecio werneriaefolius*
Spoonlike leaves with *long narrow handles* in basal clusters, well below the large dark golden-yellow flowers with domelike centers. 2–10 in. Rocky alpine slopes. Sierra Nevada and Great Basin Mts.   June–Aug.

TANSY BUTTERWEED Alien   *Senecio jacobaea*
Note the *finely cut, tansy-like* leaves distributed evenly along solitary or a few erect stems. 1–4 ft. West of Cascades-Sierra Nevada.   July–Sept.

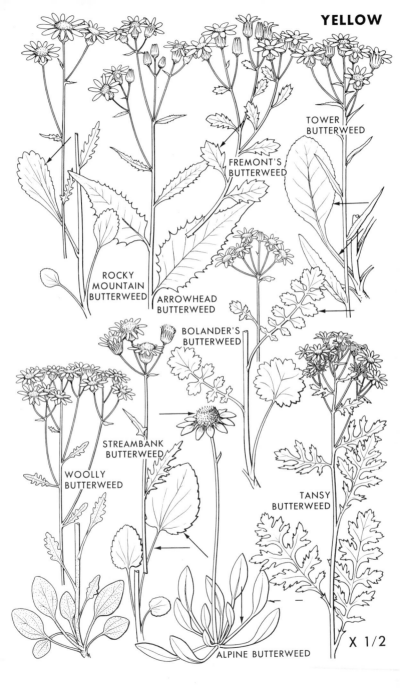

YELLOW

TOWER BUTTERWEED

FREMONT'S BUTTERWEED

ROCKY MOUNTAIN BUTTERWEED

ARROWHEAD BUTTERWEED

BOLANDER'S BUTTERWEED

STREAMBANK BUTTERWEED

WOOLLY BUTTERWEED

TANSY BUTTERWEED

ALPINE BUTTERWEED

X 1/2

SENECIO TRIBE; USUALLY NO RAY FLOWERS

SUNFLOWER FAMILY (Compositae)
Senecio Tribe: Senecioneae
See also pp. W 102–8; Y 184–220; O 226;
R 328–32; B 384; G 404.

Each flower head usually has 1 row of long linear bracts.

SPRING GOLD *Crocidium multicaule*
Flower head has 8–13 ray flowers. The stem has alternately arranged linear leaves with scattered tufts of woolly hair. 4–8 in. Grasslands. Cen. Calif. to Wash. MARCH–MAY

GREEN-LEAVED RAILLARDELLA *Raillardella scaposa*
Tufted clusters of *green linear leaves*. Pincushion flower heads. 1–6 in. Alpine ridges. Sierra Nevada to cen. Ore.
JULY–AUG.

SILKY RAILLARDELLA *Raillardella argentea*
Similar to preceding. Leaves *silky-haired*. 1–4 in. Alpine rocky ridges. Mts. of Calif., rarely in Ore. JULY–SEPT.

DESERT TURTLEBACK *Psathyrotes ramosissima*
White velvety-haired leaves are round to kidney-shaped in compact *turtlelike mounds*. The yellow pincushion flower head turns purple with age. Strong turpentine odor. 1–5 in. Common on sandy flats. Mojave, Colorado Deserts. MARCH–JUNE

TONGUE-LEAVED LUINA *Luina stricta*
Note the elongated *spikes* of pincushion flower heads above the *bright green tonguelike* leaves. 1–3 ft. Moist subalpine slopes. Mt. Rainier, Wash. JULY–AUG.

GERMAN IVY Alien *Senecio mikanioides*
The *climbing vines* have yellow-green heart-shaped leaves with 5–7 sharp angled points. Pincushion flower heads in clusters. Canyons near coast. Cen. Calif. DEC.–MARCH

COMMON BUTTERWEED Alien *Senecio vulgaris*
Pinnate leaves up entire stem. Pincushion flower heads in clusters. Flower head bracts black-tipped. Milky sap. 4–20 in. Common. Pacific States. ALL YEAR

CALIFORNIA BUTTERWEED *Senecio aronicoides*
Leaves oval bladed with petioles, all in a basal circle below the single stout, nearly leafless stem. Pincushion flower heads. Milky sap. 1–4 ft. Open woods. Sierra Nevada, Calif. North Coast Ranges to s. Ore. APRIL–JULY

CUTLEAF LUINA *Luina nardosmia*
Large rounded leaves have fingerlike lobes cut into the margins. Pincushion flower heads in branching sprays. 2–5 ft. Woods. Calif. North Coast Ranges, Cascades. MAY–AUG.

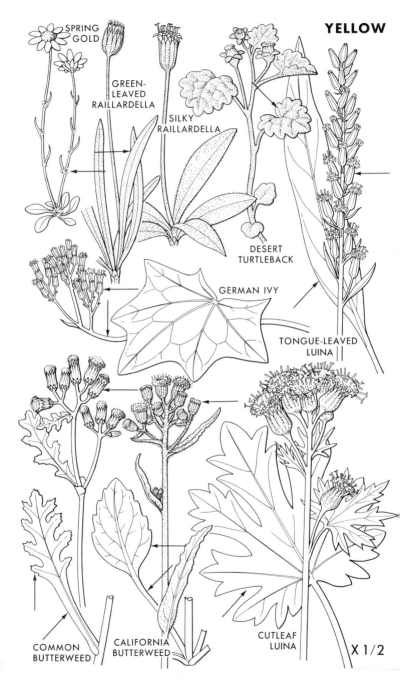

YELLOW

SPRING GOLD

GREEN-LEAVED RAILLARDELLA

SILKY RAILLARDELLA

DESERT TURTLEBACK

GERMAN IVY

TONGUE-LEAVED LUINA

COMMON BUTTERWEED

CALIFORNIA BUTTERWEED

CUTLEAF LUINA

X 1/2

EVERLASTINGS, THISTLES, SMELLY MAYWEEDS

SUNFLOWER FAMILY (Compositae)
See also pp. W 102–8; Y 184–220; O 226;
R 328–32; B 384; G 404.

Everlasting Tribe: Inuleae
PEARLY EVERLASTING   *Anaphalis margaritacea*
Note the terminal cluster of numerous oval flower heads consisting mostly of broad *white papery bracts* around a few yellow disk flowers. Leaves linear and alternately arranged. ½–3 ft. Common in open woods below 9000 ft. Pacific States.
JUNE–SEPT.

Thistle Tribe: Cynareae
YELLOW STAR THISTLE Alien   *Centaurea solstitialis*
Note the *long yellow spines* extending from the yellow flower heads. Leaves linear and extending down the stem. Stem leaves cottony-haired. Well branched. 1–5 ft. Disturbed places. Pacific States.   MAY–JAN.

Mayweed Tribe: Anthemidae
COMMON TANSY Alien   *Tanacetum vulgare*
Note the coarsely dissected pinnate leaves and the numerous dark yellow flower heads in flat clusters, *short ray flowers inconspicuous or absent.* Strong disagreeable odor. 2–3 ft. Disturbed places. Pacific Coast.   AUG.–OCT.

BRASS BUTTONS Alien   *Cotula coronopifolia*
Note the flat yellow buttonlike flower heads on a sprawling fleshy stem. Leaves linear to lancelike with linear teeth. Strong odored. 8–16 in. Muddy banks and salt marshes along Pacific Coast.   ALL YEAR

CAMPHOR DUNE TANSY   *Tanacetum camphoratum*
Similar to Douglas's Dune Tansy below. Each leaflet has small side branches of 2–5 *rounded lobes.* 1–3 ft. Rare in sand dunes within the city of San Francisco and a few nearby places in the Bay Area. Calif.   JUNE–SEPT.

DOUGLAS'S DUNE TANSY   *Tanacetum douglasii*
Note that each leaflet has small side branches of 2–5 *pointed lobes.* The broad flat flower heads have *tiny ray flowers* around the edge. ½–3 ft. Sand dunes along coast. Calif. to B.C.
MAY–AUG.

PINEAPPLE WEED Alien   *Matricaria matricarioides*
Note the yellow-green *pineapple-shaped flower cones* above the lacy pinnate leaves. Strong odored. 2–12 in. Common. Disturbed places. Pacific States.   ALL YEAR

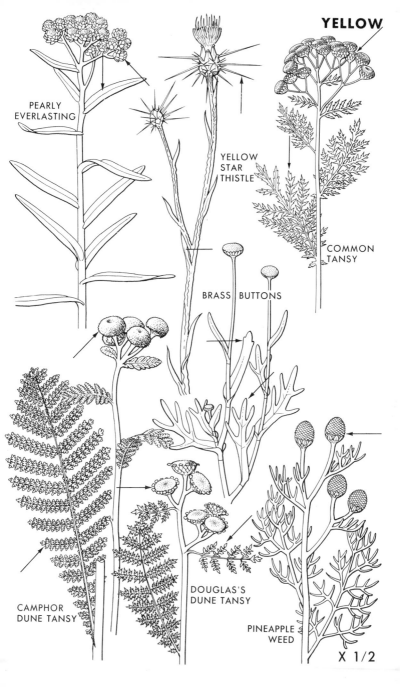

YELLOW

PEARLY
EVERLASTING

YELLOW
STAR
THISTLE

BRASS BUTTONS

COMMON
TANSY

CAMPHOR
DUNE TANSY

DOUGLAS'S
DUNE TANSY

PINEAPPLE
WEED

X 1/2

ASTERLIKE FLOWERS: GUMPLANTS

SUNFLOWER FAMILY (Compositae)
Aster Tribe: Astereae
See also pp. W 102–8; Y 184–220; O 226;
R 328–32; B 384; G 404.

GREAT VALLEY GUMPLANT   *Grindelia camporum*
The large *rounded* flower heads have half-curved, hooked bract
tips with a distinct white gummy liquid between them. The
erect stems have short linear leaves with sawtooth margins.
1–4 ft. Dry fields. Central Valley of Calif. and foothills
above.   MAY–OCT.

PUGET SOUND GUMPLANT   *Grindelia integrifolia*
Note the thick *spoonlike* leaves have sawtooth edges. A paired
species with *G. latifolia,* replacing it north along the coast.
½–3 ft. San Francisco north to B.C.   JUNE–OCT.

COASTAL GUMPLANT   *Grindelia latifolia*
The 2–3 large *flattened* flower heads have a white gum between
the hooked bracts. The smooth succulent stems prostrate or
partially erect. Leaves *tonguelike* (broadly oblong), the bases
clasping the stem, margins slightly sawtoothed. 1–2 ft. Sand
dunes, salt marshes. Calif. coast from San Francisco south to
Santa Barbara.   MAY–SEPT.

IDAHO RESIN WEED   *Grindelia nana*
The *rounded* flower heads have *completely looped* and hooked
bract tips with a distinct white gummy liquid between them.
The stem has long, linear, sawtooth-margined leaves mostly
near base. ½–3 ft. Dry open fields. Ne. Calif. and Great
Basin.   JUNE–OCT.

ALPINE GOLD DAISY   *Erigeron aureus*
Note the *pink to red fuzz* on the flower head bracts just below
the numerous bright yellow ray flowers. The leaf blade oblong
above a slender petiole. 3–6 in. Alpine rocky ridges. Cascades
from Wash. to B.C.   JULY–AUG.

RAYLESS DAISY   *Erigeron aphanactis*
The canary yellow pincushion flower head has only disk
flowers, which age to a red-brown. Elongated soft gray-haired
leaves. 4–12 in. Hot dry slopes. Great Basin, Mojave Desert.
                                                       MAY–SEPT.

ALPINE FLAMES   *Haplopappus apargioides*
The large solitary sub-hemispheric flower heads are above the
rosette of linear leaves, which have elongated sawtooth margins.
1–6 in. Rocky alpine fields. Sierra Nevada, White Mts. of
Calif.   JULY–SEPT.

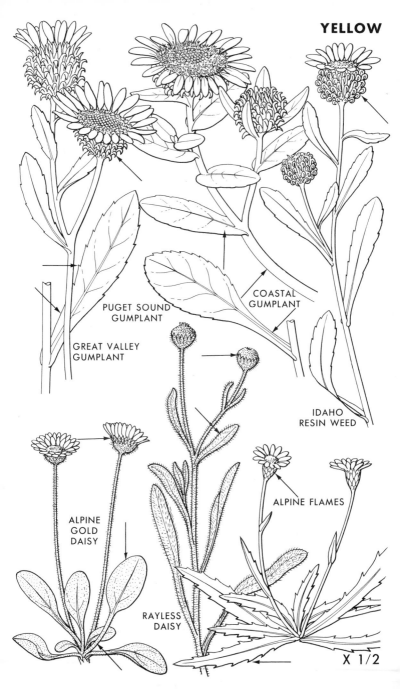

YELLOW

PUGET SOUND
GUMPLANT

GREAT VALLEY
GUMPLANT

COASTAL
GUMPLANT

IDAHO
RESIN WEED

ALPINE
GOLD DAISY

RAYLESS
DAISY

ALPINE FLAMES

X 1/2

ASTERLIKE FLOWERS: GOLDENRODS

SUNFLOWER FAMILY (Compositae)
Aster Tribe: Astereae
See also pp. W 102–8; Y 184–220; O 226; R 328–32;
B 384; G 404.

TELEGRAPH WEED   *Heterotheca grandiflora*
Note the many large rounded flower heads have linear yellow rays. All flower heads in a dense cluster near the top of the usually single erect telegraph pole–like stem. The thick leaves covered with dense and very short white hairs. Has a strong creosote-like odor. 1–7 ft. Open places at low elevations. Cen. and s. Calif. Flowering mostly in autumn.   ALL YEAR

HAIRY GOLDEN ASTER   *Heterotheca villosa*
Erect stems are in bushy clumps with *many oblong gray-green* leaves which are somewhat glandular. Flower heads have 10–16 ray flowers, narrowed near bases. 2–20 in. Open places. Great Basin.   JUNE–SEPT.

MEADOW GOLDENROD   *Solidago canadensis*
Note the large flower inflorescence forms a *wide diamond-shaped outline.* Stem densely leafy and thinly haired for entire length. Leaves lancelike and 3-nerved, the outer margins *sharply toothed.* Flower head bracts have a thin papery margin along entire length. About 13 short ray flowers per head, nearly the same length as the disk flowers. 1–3 ft. Meadows and open places. Flowering mostly in late autumn. Pacific States.
MAY–NOV.

ALPINE GOLDENROD   *Solidago multiradiata*
Stem erect, basal leaves *spatula-shaped,* becoming oval near the top of stem. Stems hairy, leaf *petiole fringed with hairs.* Flower head bracts lancelike with thick glandular area. Ray flowers 13 and longer than the disk flowers. 2–15 in. Subalpine and alpine rocky places. Sierra Nevada, White Mts., and Cascades of Wash. and B.C. (absent in Ore.).   JUNE–SEPT.

CALIFORNIA GOLDENROD   *Solidago californica*
Note the thick but short spikelike cluster of numerous flower heads. Often growing in clumps. Leaves dark green in dry mountain areas, but a felt gray in coastal regions. 1–4 ft. Common. Open places. Pine forests to sea level. West of mts. in Calif. and sw. Ore.   JULY–OCT.

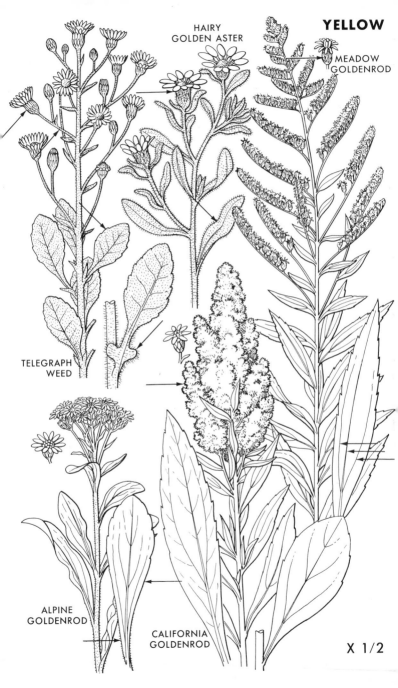

YELLOW

HAIRY
GOLDEN ASTER

MEADOW
GOLDENROD

TELEGRAPH
WEED

ALPINE
GOLDENROD

CALIFORNIA
GOLDENROD

X 1/2

Sunflower Family (Compositae)
Chicory Tribe: Cichorieae
See also pp. W 102–8; Y 184–220; O 226;
R 328–32; B 384; G 404.

SPEAR-LEAVED AGOSERIS *Agoseris retrorsa*
The basal rosette of linear leaves have long, *reverse-pointed, pinnate lobes.* Flower heads oblong, white feathery-tipped and not opening up. Each seed beaked. $\frac{1}{2}$–2 ft. Semiopen places. Mts. of Calif., rarely to Wash. MAY–AUG.

WOODLAND AGOSERIS *Agoseris heterophylla*
Flat rosettes of linear leaves. White feathery-tipped flower heads, not opening up. Seeds with a thin beak portion. 2–15 in. Flats below 7000 ft. Pacific States. APRIL–JULY

SEASIDE DANDELION *Agoseris apargioides*
Flat rosettes of thick gray straplike leaves with large terminal portions and paired lobes. Large dandelionlike flower heads. 2–8 in. Along coast. MARCH–AUG.

SCALEBUD *Anisocoma acaulis*
The cylindrical pale yellow flower heads are covered by *broad oblong* bracts both *dotted and edged with red.* Leaves basal. 2–8 in. Sandy washes. Mojave, Colorado Deserts.
APRIL–JUNE

DESERT DANDELION *Malacothrix glabrata*
Dandelionlike flower heads a *clear yellow, the center red* until the petals expand. The hairless, linear, pinnate-lobed leaves are in basal rosettes. *M. californica* very closely related but leaves woolly-haired. 4–16 in. Common in masses. Sandy flats. All of s. Calif. MARCH–JUNE

YELLOW TACKSTEM *Calycoseris parryi*
Stems covered with numerous tiny yellow *tack-shaped glands.* The linear, pinnate-lobed leaves are in basal rosettes. 4–12 in. Desert flats. Mojave, Colorado Deserts. APRIL–MAY

NODDING MICROSERIS *Microseris nutans*
Narrow straplike leaves have 2–4 pairs of sharp teeth near the center. Flat flower heads. Flat brown bristles on seed. 4–16 in. Moist mt. forests. Pacific States. APRIL–AUG.

DOUGLAS'S MICROSERIS *Microseris douglasii*
Spearlike central leaf blade has pinnate lobes pointing to the side or leaf tip. Flat brown bristles on seed. 2–18 in. Common, lowland grasslands. Calif., s. Ore. MARCH–MAY

CUTLEAF MICROSERIS *Microseris laciniata*
Smooth straplike leaf has pairs of linear *torn-looking* lobes. 1–3 ft. Moist meadows. Cen. Calif. to Wash. MAY–JULY

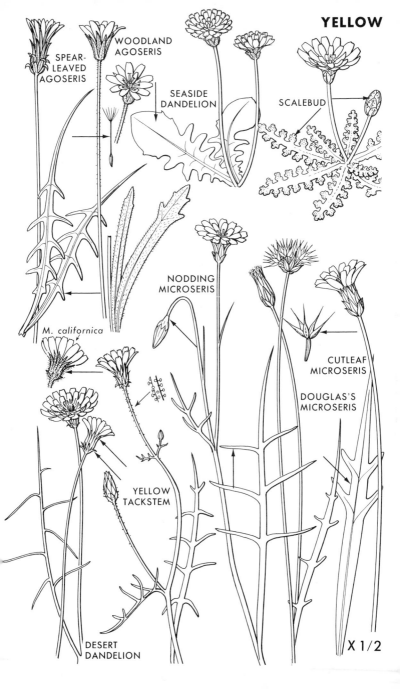

YELLOW

SPEAR-
LEAVED
AGOSERIS

WOODLAND
AGOSERIS

SEASIDE
DANDELION

SCALEBUD

M. californica

NODDING
MICROSERIS

CUTLEAF
MICROSERIS

DOUGLAS'S
MICROSERIS

YELLOW
TACKSTEM

DESERT
DANDELION

X 1/2

DANDELIONLIKE FLOWERS; MILKY SAP

SUNFLOWER FAMILY (Compositae)
Chicory Tribe: Cichorieae
See also pp. W 102-8; Y 184-220; O 226;
R 328-32; B 384; G 404.

YELLOW SALSIFY Alien   *Tragopogon dubius*
The *pointed beaklike* flower buds open into a lemon-yellow
flower head during morning hours. Later becoming a round
ball of brown parachuted seeds. Long linear grasslike leaves.
2-4 ft. Common. Pacific States.   MAY–JULY

FALSE DANDELION Alien   *Hypochoeris radicata*
Note the *long, slender, smooth* flower stems well above the
nearly flattened rosette of shallow-lobed leaves. 1-4 in. Disturbed places. Pacific States.   MARCH–JUNE

BRISTLY OX TONGUE Alien   *Picris echioides*
Note the *prickly bumps* on the broadly linear dark green
leaves. The stems are coarsely branched and have terminal
flower head clusters. 1-3 ft. Common. Calif.   JUNE–DEC.

COMMON SOW THISTLE Alien   *Sonchus oleraceus*
The smooth stems are well branched. The lobed spatula-
shaped leaves have prickly margins and clasp the stem. Flower
heads small. Seeds sharp-beaked. 1-6 ft. Common. Pacific
States.   ALL YEAR

WILLOW LETTUCE Alien   *Lactuca saligna*
The pinnate leaves are *narrowly linear and without* prickles on
the underside. Flowers open morning hours. Disturbed places.
Cen. Calif.; rarely elsewhere.   AUG.–NOV.

WALL LETTUCE Alien   *Lactuca muralis*
Note the thin highly divided leaf has strongly angular portions.
The dark yellow flower heads flower during morning hours and
the soft parachuted seeds become prominent during the afternoon. Seeds beaked. 2-4 ft. Frequent along roads and recently
logged areas. West of Cascades, B.C. to Ore.   JULY–SEPT.

WESTERN LETTUCE Alien   *Lactuca ludoviciana*
Note the broad, bright green, straplike leaves have *triangular
lobes* and earlike projections that clasp the stem. 2-7 ft.
Scattered localities. Pacific States.   JULY–SEPT.

PRICKLY LETTUCE Alien   *Lactuca serriola*
The single tall, white, erect stem has *broad,* dark gray-green,
pinnate lobed leaves. Yellow prickles cover *both sides* of each
leaf. The small flower heads are open during morning hours.
Fluffy parachuted seedheads. 2-5 ft. Disturbed places. Pacific
States.   MAY–SEPT.

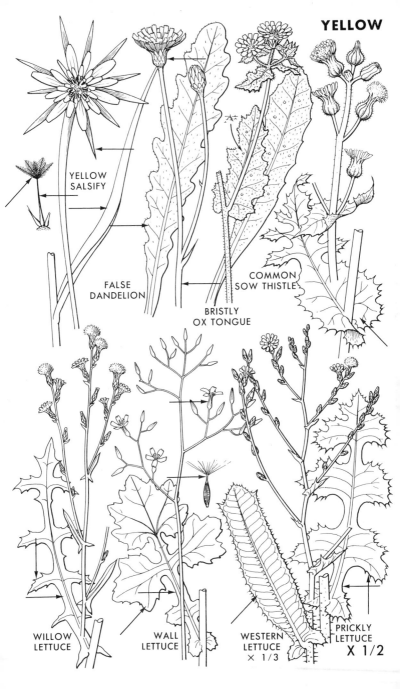

YELLOW

YELLOW
SALSIFY

FALSE
DANDELION

BRISTLY
OX TONGUE

COMMON
SOW THISTLE

WILLOW
LETTUCE

WALL
LETTUCE

WESTERN
LETTUCE
× 1/3

PRICKLY
LETTUCE

X 1/2

DANDELIONLIKE FLOWERS; MILKY SAP

SUNFLOWER FAMILY (Compositae)
Chicory Tribe: Cichorieae
See also pp. W 102–8; Y 184–220; O 226;
R 328–32; B 384; G 404.

SHAGGY HAWKWEED   *Hieracium horridum*
All plant parts covered by long, dense, shaggy white to brown hairs. Oblong leaves along the stem. 11–12 bright yellow ray flowers per head. 4–15 in. Common. Dry rocky places. 5000–12,000 ft. Mts. of Calif.   JULY–AUG.

BOLANDER'S HAWKWEED   *Hieracium bolanderi*
Leaves are in a basal rosette covered with scattered long hairs. Flower heads pale yellow, open mornings. 4–12 in. Woodlands. Calif. North Coast Ranges to sw. Ore.   JUNE–AUG.

HOUNDS-TONGUE HAWKWEED
     Hieracium cynoglossoides
Flower heads and upper stem bracts have clusters of long hair. Leaves elongate and *mostly clustered near stem base,* moderately covered with soft hairs. 1–4 ft. Dry open mt. forests. Mts. of Pacific States.   JUNE–AUG.

SCOULER'S HAWKWEED   *Hieracium scouleri*
The well spaced, elongated leaves *occur up the entire* stem length. Upper stem and flower heads are *nearly hairless.* 1–3 ft. Dry open woods. Cascades–Sierra Nevada. JUNE–AUG.

ROCKY MOUNTAIN DANDELION
     Taraxacum eriophorum
The straplike leaves and flower stem are *thickened.* Gray flower head bracts are *broadly rectangular.* 2–10 in. Alpine meadows. Mts. of B.C. and Wash. to Rocky Mts.

     MAY–SEPT.

SLENDER HAWKSBEARD   *Crepis atribarba*
Note the long stringy pinnate leaf lobes. Numerous bright yellow flower heads. 1–3 ft. Open places. B.C. and south on east side of Cascades; Great Basin.   MAY–JULY

TURKISH HAWKSBEARD Alien   *Crepis nicaeenis*
The tall erect stems have narrow dandelionlike leaves, softly haired. 1–2 ft. Woods. Coast of Wash., Ore.   JUNE–JULY

WESTERN HAWKSBEARD   *Crepis occidentalis*
Dandelionlike leaves broad. All plant parts covered with short *feltlike* hair. Erect stems have 10–30 flower heads in candelbra-like clusters. 5–12 in. Rocky places at mid-mt. elevations. Pacific States.   JUNE–JULY

COMMON DANDELION Alien   *Taraxacum officinale*
Bright green leaves have sharply cut and reversed lobes. Bright yellow flower heads. Soft fluffy pappus on long beaked seeds. 2–12 in. Common. Pacific States.   ALL YEAR

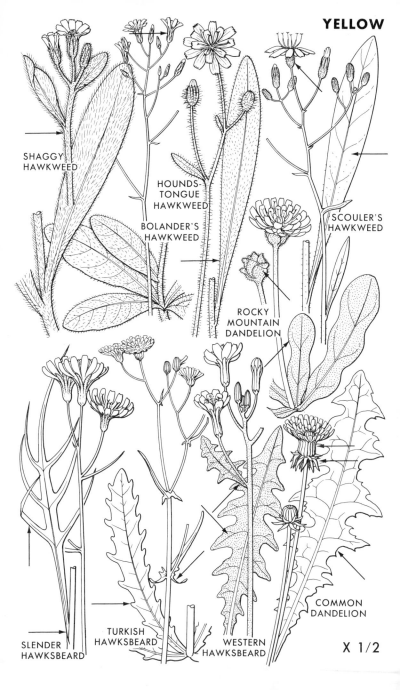

YELLOW

SHAGGY
HAWKWEED

HOUNDS-
TONGUE
HAWKWEED

BOLANDER'S
HAWKWEED

ROCKY
MOUNTAIN
DANDELION

SCOULER'S
HAWKWEED

SLENDER
HAWKSBEARD

TURKISH
HAWKSBEARD

WESTERN
HAWKSBEARD

COMMON
DANDELION

X 1/2

Orange
Flowers

Flowers that are truly orange or salmon are relatively few and are covered almost entirely by the next four color plates. Some flowers merge toward red — if in doubt look here and also under Pink to Red or Red-Purple Flowers, p. 233. When possible, the group characteristics given in the text page titles are repeated in each color section, and in the same order. Where the flowers on a page look nearly the same but your sample does not fit, you can also use the cross reference given for other colors.

4 PETALS OR FLOWERS PEALIKE

POPPY FAMILY (Papaveraceae)
See also p. W 22.

CALIFORNIA POPPY   *Eschscholzia californica*
Note the *flangelike double-rimmed* flower peduncle. Shiny *golden-orange bowl-shaped* flowers also vary to yellow, cream, or red. The lacy leaves are bluish. State flower of California. ½–2 ft. Fields. Calif. and Ore.   FEB.–NOV.

PYGMY POPPY   *Eschscholzia minutiflora*
Flowers *tiny* (¼ in.) yellow-orange. Flower stem leafy throughout. A single rim below ovary. 4–18 in. Sandy places. Mojave, Colorado Deserts.   MARCH–MAY

LOBB'S POPPY   *Eschscholzia lobbii*
Flowers (¾ in.) pale orange to yellow on a leafless stem. A single rim below ovary. 4–12 in. Open grassy places. Calif. Coast Ranges, w. Sierra Nevada.   MARCH–MAY

WIND POPPY   *Stylomecon heterophylla*
The orange-red petals have a *purple spot* above the green base. Style above ovary *elongated*. 1–3 ft. Grassy slopes. W. Sierra Nevada foothills, Calif. Coast Ranges to Baja.   APRIL–MAY

FIRE POPPY   *Papaver californicum*
Similar to Wind Poppy. Petals a brick red with only a basal green spot. Style *flush* with top of ovary. 1–2 ft. Requires fire to grow. Appearing mainly the first year after a chaparral fire. Calif. Coast Ranges, San Francisco area south to San Diego.   APRIL–MAY

MUSTARD FAMILY (Cruciferae)
See also pp. W 24–30; Y 140–48; R 266–68.

DOUGLAS'S WALLFLOWER   *Erysimum capitatum*
4-petaled *maltese cross* flowers. Flowers orange to bright yellow. ½–3 ft. Rocky places. Calif.   MARCH–JULY

PEA FAMILY (Leguminosae)
See also pp. W 94–96; Y 178–82; R 318–26;
B 376–80.

COLORADO RIVER HEMP   *Sesbania exaltata*
Long feathery pinnate leaves have pale green leaflets. The orange-yellow flowers have purple-spotted banner petals. The seedpod pencil-like. ½–10 ft. Flood plains, crop fields. Imperial Valley and Colorado River in Calif.   APRIL–OCT.

HOG POTATO   *Hoffmannseggia densiflora*
Note the glandular dotted and oblong *bipinnate* leaflets. Opened-up pealike flowers. Short sausagelike seedpods. Underground potatolike tubers. 4–16 in. Common. Mojave, Colorado Deserts.   APRIL–JUNE

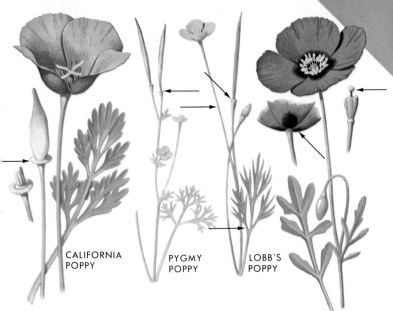

CALIFORNIA
POPPY

PYGMY
POPPY

LOBB'S
POPPY

WIND POPPY

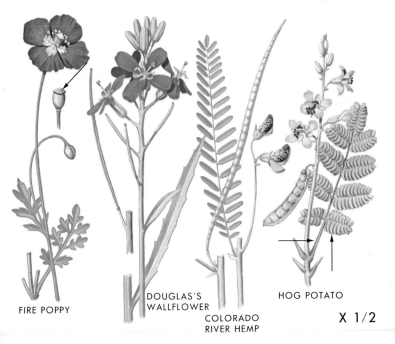

FIRE POPPY

DOUGLAS'S
WALLFLOWER

COLORADO
RIVER HEMP

HOG POTATO

X 1/2

5 TO MANY PETALS;
VARIOUS FLOWER SHAPES

SALTY DODDER *Cuscuta salina*
DODDER FAMILY (Cuscutaceae)
Note the *mat of wiry orange* stems. Tiny white tubular flowers. Salt or alkali marshes. Pacific States. Many other similar species not shown. MAY–SEPT.

BUTTERCUP FAMILY (Ranunculaceae)
See also pp. W 40–42; Y 154–58; R 280–82;
B 354–56, 382; G 404.

CAÑON DELPHINIUM *Delphinium nudicaule*
Note the orange-red flowers, *straight spurred,* above the semi-pinnate leaves. 1–2 ft. Semishaded woods. Calif. cen. Coast Ranges to sw. Ore., W. Sierra Nevada foothills. Compare with Scarlet Delphinium on p. 280. MARCH–JUNE

SUNFLOWER FAMILY (Compositae)
See also pp. W 102–8 Y 184–220; R 328–32;
B 384; G 404.

ORANGE AGOSERIS *Agoseris aurantiaca*
Numerous *burnt orange ray flowers* are in a flower head on a leafless stem. Basal leaves lancelike. Milky sap. $\frac{1}{2}$–2 ft. Dry mt. meadows. Pacific States. JUNE–AUG.

FLAME BUTTERWEED *Senecio greenei*
8–15 orange straplike ray flowers in each flower head. Leaf blades of basal leaves rounded. 4–12 in. Chaparral areas on serpentine rock. Calif. North Coast Ranges. MAY–JUNE

FORGET-ME-NOT FAMILY (Boraginaceae)
See also pp. W 78; Y 172; R 308; B 340–42.

FIDDLE NECK *Amsinckia intermedia*
Many small trumpet flowers are along the upper edge of a *coiled shepherd's crook.* 4 brown nutlets. $\frac{1}{2}$–3 ft. Common. Pacific States. MARCH–JUNE

PHLOX FAMILY (Polemoniaceae)
See also pp. W 72; Y 172; R 248–50, 306; B 360–64.

GRAND COLLOMIA *Collomia grandiflora*
Single erect stems are topped by a *headlike cluster* of long trumpet-like salmon flowers. $\frac{1}{2}$–3 ft. Open and lightly wooded slopes. Mts. of Pacific States. APRIL–AUG.

PURSLANE FAMILY (Portulacaceae)
See also pp. R 292–94.

TWEEDY'S LEWISIA *Lewisia tweedyi*
Large salmon flowers with 8–12 petals cascade from a broad (1–2 ft.) central rosette of spoonlike leaves. 6–8 in. Talus slopes. Wenatchee Mts. Wash. MAY–JULY

NASTURTIUM Alien *Tropaeolum majus*
TROPAEOLUM FAMILY (Tropaeolaceae)
Note the *large umbrellalike* leaves and the *spurred* flowers. 6–12 in. Frequent along Calif. Coast. ALL YEAR

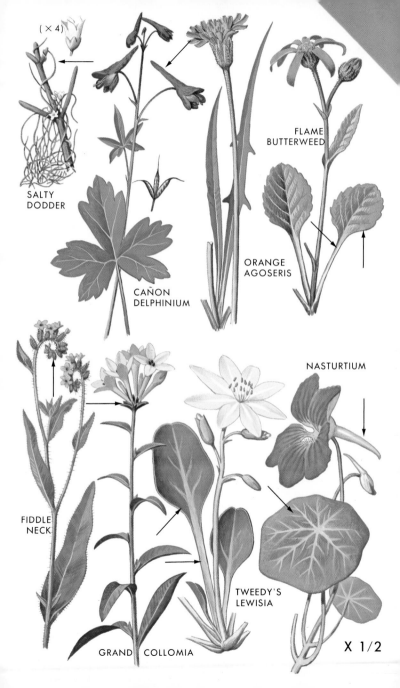

(× 4)

SALTY
DODDER

CAÑON
DELPHINIUM

FLAME
BUTTERWEED

ORANGE
AGOSERIS

NASTURTIUM

FIDDLE
NECK

TWEEDY'S
LEWISIA

GRAND COLLOMIA

X 1/2

3 OR 6 PETALS: LILIES

LILY FAMILY (Liliaceae)
See also pp. W 4–16; Y 122–24; O 230; R 252–56;
B 352; G 388–90.

HUMBOLDT'S TIGER LILY *Lilium humboldtii*
Tall single stems have 4–8 whorls of 10–20 lancelike leaves.
Numerous very large (3 in.) *nodding* orange flowers are purple
dotted. Stamens *spreading outward* at right angle. A *dry
habitat* species. 3–10 ft. Open forests. Mts. of Calif.
JUNE–JULY

COLUMBIA LILY *Lilium columbianum*
Similar to preceding. Lower stem leaves are in whorls of 5–9
leaves, the *upper scattered.* Small (1–2 in.) flowers, lemon-
yellow to deep red with a yellow center, maroon spotted.
Stamens *all parallel,* or barely spreading. 1–4 ft. Nw. Calif. to
B.C. and Great Basin. JUNE–JULY

COAST LILY *Lilium maritimum*
The 1–6 dark red-orange, maroon spotted, *bell-shaped* flowers
are *nodding.* Leaves *scattered* along the stem. 1–3 ft. Wet
coastal prairies and thickets. N. Calif. coast. JUNE–JULY

SIERRA TIGER LILY *Lilium parvum*
The *bell-shaped* flowers *erect or ascending.* Leaves mostly
scattered, a few in partial whorls. 2–5 ft. Wet thickets. 6000–
9000 ft. Sierra Nevada. JUNE–JULY

KELLY'S TIGER LILY *Lilium kelleyanum*
Flower completely orange to yellow with maroon dots. Petals
curved entire length. Anthers *short* (4–6 mm.). Lower stem
leaves *alternate,* the upper in whorls. Fragrant. 2–6 ft. Wet
banks in high mts. Sierra Nevada, Siskiyous. JULY–AUG.

LEOPARD LILY *Lilium pardalinum*
The nooding flowers orange with *some red to dark red,* many
maroon spots. Each petal curved from the *middle* outward.
Anthers *long* (7–15 mm.), stamens reflexed outward. Leaves in
whorls. Flowers usually not fragrant. 3–8 ft. *Wet ground*
below 6000 ft. Mts. of Calif. MAY–JULY

VOLLMER'S TIGER LILY *Lilium vollmeri*
Erect leaves clothe the stem. Outer half of petals *dark red,* the
inner half yellow-orange with maroon spots. 3 ft. Hillside
bogs. Nw. Calif., sw. Ore. JUNE–JULY

WESTERN TIGER LILY *Lilium occidentale*
Outer half of petals orange with maroon spots, inner base
green. Leaves narrowly linear in whorls. 2–3 ft. Swampy
thickets. Along nw. Calif.–sw. Ore. coast. JUNE–JULY

228

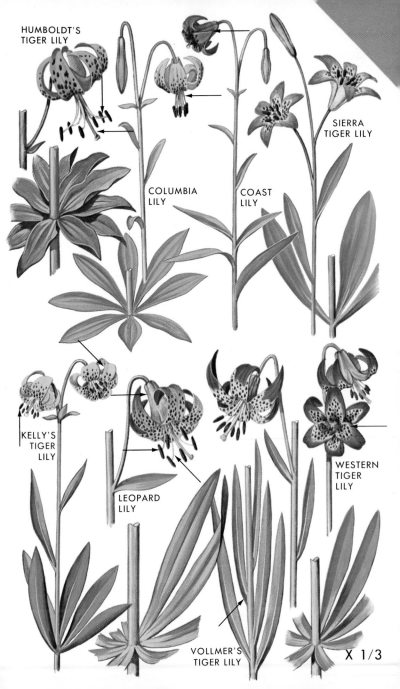

HUMBOLDT'S TIGER LILY

SIERRA TIGER LILY

COLUMBIA LILY

COAST LILY

KELLY'S TIGER LILY

LEOPARD LILY

WESTERN TIGER LILY

VOLLMER'S TIGER LILY

X 1/3

3 OR 6 PETALS: LILIES AND ORCHIDS

LILY FAMILY (Liliaceae)
See also pp. W 4–16; Y 122–24; O 228;
R 252–56; B 352; G 388–90.

SCARLET FRITILLARY *Fritillaria recurva*
Note the 1–5 widely separated, *nodding bells* are orange-red
with yellow spotting and a yellow interior. The 8–10 linear
leaves are in 2–3 whorls near the stem center. 1–3 ft. Dry open
woods. Sw. Ore., Calif. North Coast Ranges, Sierra Nevada.
MARCH–JULY

KENNEDY'S MARIPOSA TULIP *Calochortus kennedyi*
The 1–6 upright flower cups are orange to vermilion. Brown-
purple spots may be at the petal base. 4–8 in. Dry open slopes.
Mojave Desert, Calif. South Coast Ranges. APRIL–JUNE

ORCHID FAMILY (Orchidaceae)
See also pp. W 20; BG 390–92.

STRIPED CORALROOT *Corallorhiza striata*
Yellow and red *striped* flowers easily distinguish this species. It
often grows with the other coralroots, but flowers 2–3 weeks
earlier. ½–2 ft. Shady conifer forests. Most of Pacific States.
APRIL–AUG.

SPOTTED CORALROOT *Corallorhiza maculata*
Flowers are orange, reddish, or yellow except for the white
3-lobed lip which is crimson-spotted. The orange-yellow stems
arise from an underground coral-like mass. ½–2½ ft. Shady
conifer forests. Pacific States. MAY–AUG.

MERTENS' CORALROOT *Corallorhiza mertensiana*
Similar to Spotted Coralroot. Note the *prominent projection*
on the underside of the ovary immediately *behind* the petals.
Lip petal has *red lines.* ½–2 ft. Shady conifer forests. Calif.
Siskiyous north to B.C. and east. JUNE–AUG.

STREAM ORCHID *Epipactis gigantea*
Flowers yellow-green. The orange heart-shaped lip strongly
marked with red lines. Leaves strongly parallel-veined and
clasping the stem. 1–3 ft. Margins of springs, streams, and
lakes. Pacific States. APRIL–AUG.

CALYPSO ORCHID *Calypso bulbosa*
Each plant has a *single* bright pink flower on a leafless stem
above a *single oval* leaf. The slipperlike lip petal *tipped with 2
horns,* mottled with orange, yellow, and white (highly variable). 3–10 in. Rich humus of shady conifer forests. Most of
Pacific States, except in Calif. only from San Francisco north in
Coast Ranges. MARCH–JULY

230

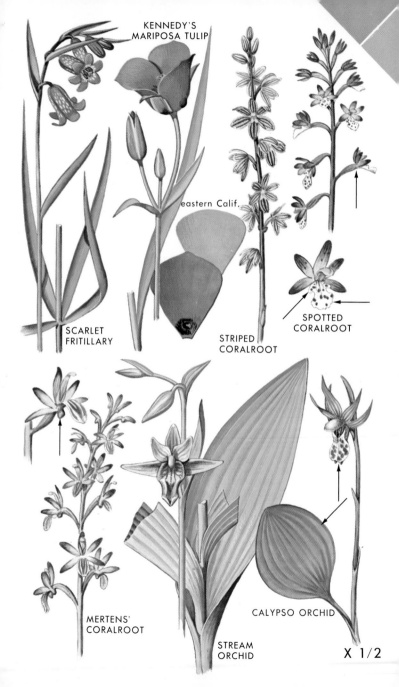

KENNEDY'S
MARIPOSA TULIP

eastern Calif.

SCARLET
FRITILLARY

STRIPED
CORALROOT

SPOTTED
CORALROOT

MERTENS'
CORALROOT

STREAM
ORCHID

CALYPSO ORCHID

X 1/2

Pink to Red
or Red-Purple
Flowers

In this category are not only the unmistakably pink or red flowers but also the variable lavender, lilac, and purple shades that lean toward the red side. True purple is a 50-50 mixture of red and blue, and it is sometimes difficult to decide on which side of the line a color is. Often a fresh red-purple flower will age a blue-purple. A majority of the purple flowers are in the red-purple category; if in doubt check Violet to Blue or Blue-Purple Flowers, p. 335. The Peas, Asters, and Daisies are particularly tricky. When possible, the group characteristics given in the text page titles are repeated in each color section, and in the same order. Where the flowers on a page look nearly the same but your sample does not fit, you can also use the cross reference given for other colors.

5-PETALED, 2-LIPPED TUBULAR FLOWERS

SNAPDRAGON FAMILY (Scrophulariaceae)
See also pp. Y 112–18; R 234–44, 310;
B 336–38, 372.

PURPLE CHINESE HOUSES   *Collinsia heterophylla*
Note the *pagoda-like slanted whorls* of numerous purple
flowers with *white* upper lips. Leaves narrowly triangular.
½–2 ft. Shady places at lower elevations. Calif.
MARCH–JULY

LEWIS'S MONKEY FLOWER   *Mimulus lewisii*
Note the large wine-red flowers (pale pink in Calif.) with darker
lines running down into the throat. Pedicels longer than the
calyx. The opposite oval leaves sticky-haired and with toothed
margins. 1–3 ft. Springy ground, streambanks in mts. Higher
mts. of Pacific States.   JUNE–SEPT.

SCARLET MONKEY FLOWER   *Mimulus cardinalis*
The large scarlet flower has the upper petal lobes *projecting
forward* of the lower. All petal tips are strongly *swept backward*. Leaves oval, coarsely toothed, sticky-haired. 1–3 ft.
Spring margins. Calif. to s. Ore.   APRIL–OCT.

TRICOLOR MONKEY FLOWER   *Mimulus tricolor*
The pink-purple flower has a long slender tube, but *not more
than twice* the length of the calyx. A *triangular spot* is on each
petal. The upper corolla throat is dark purple and the lower
white with a yellow patch which is also purple-dotted. Leaves
oval. 1–6 in. Edges of drying vernal pools. W. Sierra Nevada
foothills, Central Valley of Calif., and Calif. Coast Ranges to
Ore.   APRIL–JUNE

PANSY MONKEY FLOWER   *Mimulus angustatus*
Similar to preceding. Corolla tube is *more than 3–6 times* the
length of the calyx. Each petal has a *round* dark spot. Leaves
linear. Margins of shallow depressions. Foothills of Sierra
Nevada; Calif. North Coast Ranges.   APRIL–JUNE

KELLOGG'S MONKEY FLOWER   *Mimulus kelloggii*
The lower petal lobes *shorter* than the upper. The rose-purple
flowers have a *very long slender tube* and the throat is yellow
with red dots. Leaves lancelike. 2–12 in. Moist grassy places.
W. Sierra Nevada foothills, Calif. North Coast Ranges.
MARCH–JUNE

BOLANDER'S MONKEY FLOWER   *Mimulus bolanderi*
The red-purple flowers with white lines and purple spotting are
nearly hidden by the leaves. Petal lobes unequal, the upper
shorter. Lower lobe of stigma lancelike. Leaves very sticky.
½–2 ft. Dry places below 6000 ft. W. Sierra Nevada foothills,
Calif. Coast Ranges.   MAY–JULY

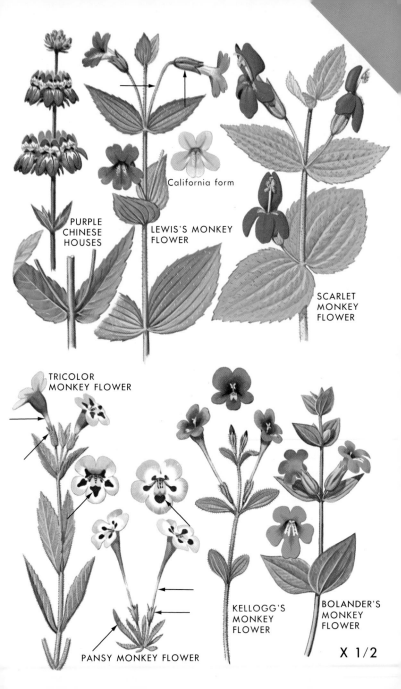

PURPLE
CHINESE
HOUSES

LEWIS'S MONKEY
FLOWER

California form

SCARLET
MONKEY
FLOWER

TRICOLOR
MONKEY FLOWER

KELLOGG'S
MONKEY
FLOWER

BOLANDER'S
MONKEY
FLOWER

PANSY MONKEY FLOWER

X 1/2

5-PETALED, 2-LIPPED TUBULAR FLOWERS

SNAPDRAGON FAMILY (Scrophulariaceae)
See also pp. Y 112–18; R 234–44, 310; B 336–8, 372.

BREWER'S MONKEY FLOWER   *Mimulus breweri*
Note the tiny ($\frac{1}{4}$ in.) pale pink to purple *rounded* flowers have nearly *equal lengthed* bilobed petals. 2–8 in. Moist forest floors, in masses. Mts. of Pacific States.   JUNE–AUG.

PYGMY MONKEY FLOWER   *Mimulus rubellus*
The tiny flowers ($\frac{1}{4}$ in.) somewhat *rectangular* with a *long lower bilobed* petal. Calyx lobes broadly rounded and fringed. 1–6 in. Washes. Mojave, Colorado Deserts.   APRIL–JUNE

SIERRA MONKEY FLOWER   *Mimulus leptaleus*
The tiny ($\frac{1}{4}$ in.) flower has distinctly *squared, undivided* petal lobes. The upper 2 petals pink and the lower 3 nearly white, all with a *central dark red line*. 1–4 in. Forest floors 7000 ft. and above. Sierra Nevada.   JUNE–AUG.

FREMONT'S MONKEY FLOWER   *Mimulus fremontii*
Round *equally lobed* rose-purple flowers are yellow or white ridged within. Pedicels *shorter* than the calyx. Stigma hidden. 2–8 in. Calif. South Coast Ranges to Baja.   APRIL–JUNE

DWARF MONKEY FLOWER   *Mimulus nanus*
Note the *protruding stigma and stamens.* Flower throat has dots, lines, and 2 yellow-haired ridges. 1–8 in. Sandy places. Cascades–Sierra Nevada; Great Basin.   MAY–AUG.

BIGELOW'S MONKEY FLOWER   *Mimulus bigelovii*
Stigma *hidden* inside corolla throat. Nearly equal-lobed pink to red-purple flowers. Two *round eyes* (may be pale) are on opposite sides of a pale yellow throat with purple dots. 2–12 in. Mojave, Colorado Deserts.   MAY–JUNE, OCT.

TORREY'S MONKEY FLOWER   *Mimulus torreyi*
Red-purple flowers have within the throat 2 yellow ridges margined by red and white zones. Leaves *petioled.* 2–16 in. Below 8000 ft. on western slope of Sierra Nevada.   MAY–AUG.

LAYNE'S MONKEY FLOWER   *Mimulus layneae*
The dark rose flower has a *white* throat with *rose dots* and a *dark blotch* in the crease of the lowermost *projecting* petal. 4–12 in. Calif. North Coast Ranges, w. Sierra Nevada.
    MAY–AUG.

CALICO MONKEY FLOWER   *Mimulus pictus*
Rounded white petal lobes have *dark red spiderweb-like* lines. 4–12 in. Cleared zone around shrubs. Southernmost Sierra Nevada foothills, Tehachapi Mts.   APRIL–MAY

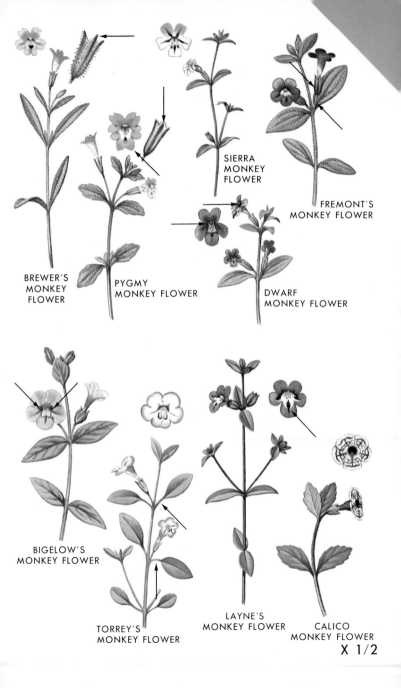

BREWER'S
MONKEY
FLOWER

PYGMY
MONKEY FLOWER

SIERRA
MONKEY
FLOWER

DWARF
MONKEY FLOWER

FREMONT'S
MONKEY FLOWER

BIGELOW'S
MONKEY FLOWER

TORREY'S
MONKEY FLOWER

LAYNE'S
MONKEY FLOWER

CALICO
MONKEY FLOWER

X 1/2

5-PETALED, 2-LIPPED TUBULAR FLOWERS

SNAPDRAGON FAMILY (Scrophulariaceae)
See also pp. Y 112–18; R 234–44, 310;
B 336–38, 372.

PALMER'S PENSTEMON *Penstemon palmeri*
Note the *short, broad, light pink* flower tube. Gray-green leaves a waxy blue, the upper pairs are *joined together to surround* the stem. 1½–4 ft. Rocky places. Mts. of Mojave Desert and Great Basin. MAY–JUNE

GRINNELL'S PENSTEMON *Penstemon grinnellii*
Underside of each flower has a *bulge,* dark pink to whitish. Upper leaf pairs *free* from each other. ½–2 ft. Dry slopes. Calif. South Coast Ranges; s. Sierra Nevada; mts. of s. Calif. APRIL–AUG.

RICHARDSON'S PENSTEMON *Penstemon richardsonii*
The broad lancelike leaves *strongly sawtoothed.* The bright pink flower tube *constricted for* ⅓ *length.* 1–3 ft. Rocky cliffs. Columbia River Gorge in Ore. and Wash. MAY–AUG.

ROYAL PENSTEMON *Penstemon spectablis*
The large bright rose-red flowers have a long tube, the *outer half abruptly enlarged.* Upper stem leaves *triangular and bright green,* each pair fused together. 2–3 ft. Dry slopes. Mts. around Los Angeles s. to Baja. APRIL–JUNE

MOUNTAIN PRIDE *Penstemon newberryi*
The bright rose-pink flowers have *woolly-haired anthers* and a bearded throat. Leathery, coarsely toothed, egg-shaped leaves. ½–1 ft. Low stems in mats over boulders. High Sierra Nevada, Calif. North Coast Ranges to sw. Ore. JUNE–AUG.

BRIDGES' PENSTEMON *Penstemon bridgesii*
The scarlet tubular flowers have 2 distinct lips with the lower sharply reflexed backward and the *upper protruding* forward. Gray-green linear leaves. 1–3 ft. Southern half of Sierra Nevada south to Baja; Great Basin. JUNE–AUG.

SCARLET BUGLER *Penstemon centranthifolius*
The scarlet tubular flowers have *open spreading* petal lobes. Stem and leaves *waxy blue,* upper leaf pairs clasp the stem. 1–4 ft. Dry places. Calif. Coast Ranges to Baja. APRIL–JULY

EATON'S FIRECRACKER *Penstemon eatonii*
Similar to Scarlet Bugler. The triangular leaves *green without* waxy blue coating. Petal lobes *not spreading.* 1–3 ft. Rocky slopes. San Bernardino Mts., east in mts. of Mojave Desert and s. Great Basin. MARCH–JULY

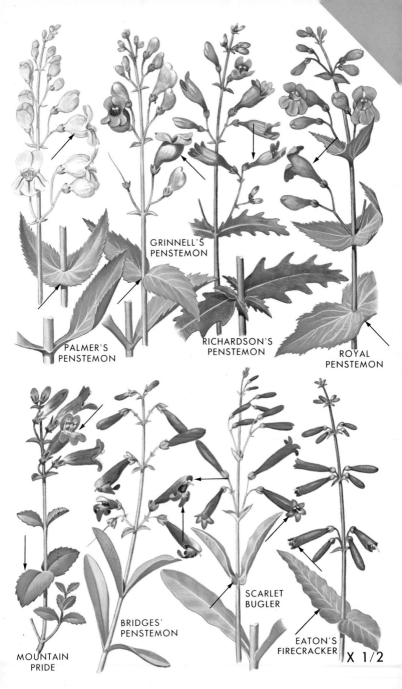

GRINNELL'S
PENSTEMON

PALMER'S
PENSTEMON

RICHARDSON'S
PENSTEMON

ROYAL
PENSTEMON

MOUNTAIN
PRIDE

BRIDGES'
PENSTEMON

SCARLET
BUGLER

EATON'S
FIRECRACKER

X 1/2

5-PETALED, 2-LIPPED SPOUTLIKE FLOWERS

SNAPDRAGON FAMILY (Scrophulariaceae)
See also pp. Y 112–18; R 234–44, 310;
B 336–38, 372.

INDIAN WARRIOR *Pedicularis densiflora*
Note the dark wine-red, flat, tubular flowers have a *stout straight upper beak* and a lower lip of 3 small lobes halfway back on the tube. Leaves pinnate. ½–2 ft. Frequent in shade of shrubs. Foothills of Calif. JAN.–JUNE

BABY ELEPHANTS HEAD *Pedicularis attollens*
Note the *short-snouted* elephant head produced by the *short* twisted upper petals and the ears by the *longer* lower petal lobes, light pink with purple markings. ½–1½ ft. Wet mt. meadows. Mts. of cen. Calif. to Ore. JUNE–SEPT.

BULL ELEPHANTS HEAD *Pedicularis groenlandica*
The red-purple, *long-snouted* elephant head produced by *long* twisted upper petals (snout) and the *shorter* lower petals (ears). 1–3 ft. Wet mt. meadows. Pacific States. JUNE–AUG.

PARROTS BEAK *Pedicularis racemosa*
The pale pink flowers consist of a curved sickle-like *parrot beak* and the lower 3 petals flattened behind it. The bright green leaves *lancelike and entire.* 1–2 ft. Dry woods of mid-mt. elevations. Most of Pacific States. JUNE–SEPT.

BIRDS BEAK LOUSEWORT *Pedicularis ornithorhyncha*
The dark red-purple flowers have a *birdlike beak* and are clustered on top of a *nearly leafless stem.* 4–12 in. Rocky alpine meadows. Mt. Rainier, Wash. to B.C. JULY–SEPT.

RED OWL CLOVER *Orthocarpus purpurascens*
The flowers and flower leaf bracts are *both dark red-purple.* The corolla has a *hooked beak* and 3 lower yellow or white sacs. Leaves threadlike. 4–16 in. Calif. MARCH–MAY

PAINTBRUSH OWL CLOVER *Orthocarpus castillejoides*
The *straight beaked* flowers subtended by white-tipped flower bracts. Lower leaves broad ribbons. 4–12 in. Salty marshes along coast. Monterey, Calif. north to B.C. MAY–AUG.

COPELAND'S OWL CLOVER *Orthocarpus copelandii*
Thick terminal spike of *broad, rounded, dark red-purple* flower leaf bracts. Corolla reddish. Stem leaves *lancelike.* 4–16 in. Mt. meadows. Cen. and n. Calif. to Ore. JUNE–AUG.

GOLDTONGUE *Orthocarpus tenuifolius*
A gold corolla (tongue) peeks above the *broad pink-tipped bracts.* Threadlike leaves. 4–12 in. Great Basin. MAY–AUG.

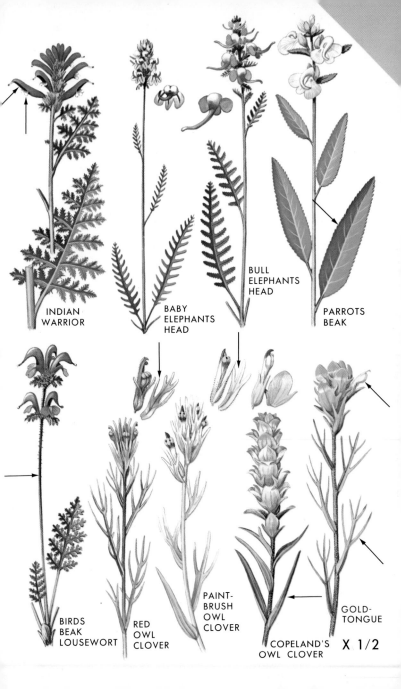

INDIAN WARRIOR

BABY ELEPHANTS HEAD

BULL ELEPHANTS HEAD

PARROTS BEAK

BIRDS BEAK LOUSEWORT

RED OWL CLOVER

PAINT-BRUSH OWL CLOVER

COPELAND'S OWL CLOVER

GOLD-TONGUE

X 1/2

5-PETALED, 2-LIPPED SPOUTLIKE FLOWERS

SNAPDRAGON FAMILY (Scrophulariaceae)
See also pp. Y 112–18; R 234–44, 310;
B 336–38, 372.

APPLEGATE'S PAINTBRUSH *Castilleja applegatei*
Flower leaf bracts 5-lobed (3 in lower flowers), calyx tips
narrow sharp points. Leaves *wavy-margined,* 3-lobed *or* one.
Stems sticky. ½–2 ft. Cen. Calif. to Ore. APRIL–AUG.

MARTIN'S PAINTBRUSH *Castilleja martinii*
Leaves linear, wavy-margined. The nearly erect, sharp pointed
corollas are *well exserted* above the 3-lobed *red and green*
flower leaf bracts. Short round-lobed calyx with red, yellow,
green, and brown zones. 1–2 ft. Dry slopes. Calif. Coast
Ranges to Baja; s. Sierra Nevada. MAY–SEPT.

FROSTY PAINTBRUSH *Castilleja pruinosa*
Flowers nearly hidden among the *tricolored flower leaf bracts*
which have red tips, a narrow yellow zone, and green base.
Calyx lobes sharp-pointed. Lower linear leaves and stem a
frosty gray due to *branched hairs.* 1–2 ft. Sierra Nevada
foothills north to nw. Calif. and sw. Ore. APRIL–AUG.

DESERT PAINTBRUSH *Castilleja chromosa*
Flower leaf bracts (dark red-brown) are relatively narrow with
5 long narrow lobes. Stem leaves have 3 or 5 narrow lobes.
Fluorescent pink to red flowers. ½–2 ft. Occurring with sagebrush. Mojave Desert, Great Basin. APRIL–AUG.

MONTEREY PAINTBRUSH *Castilleja latifolia*
Flower leaf bracts *broad and barely 3-lobed.* Stem leaves short
and broad. Rarely trilobed on upper stem. 1–2 ft. Sandy
places along coast of central Calif. FEB.–SEPT.

GIANT RED PAINTBRUSH *Castilleja miniata*
Colored flower leaf bracts and calyx have 3 or more narrow
sharp points. Leaves *flat, lancelike.* 1–3 ft. *Wet* meadows.
Mts. of Pacific States. MAY–SEPT.

COAST PAINTBRUSH *Castilleja affinis*
The colored flower leaf bracts of 4 or 6 *long narrow lobes.* Red
calyx lobes are also narrow linear. Leaves variable, narrow with
2 to 6 short lobes or simply linear. 1–2 ft. Dry woods. Coast
Ranges of Calif. south to Baja. MARCH–MAY

BRISTLY PAINTBRUSH *Castilleja hispida*
Flower leaf bracts *broad* and have 7 (*sometimes 5*) *short lobes.*
Calyx lobes short and rounded. Lowermost leaves linear, but
soon grading into 5 red-tipped lobes below flower portion.
1–2 ft. Forest openings. B.C. to northern ⅓ of Ore.
APRIL–AUG.

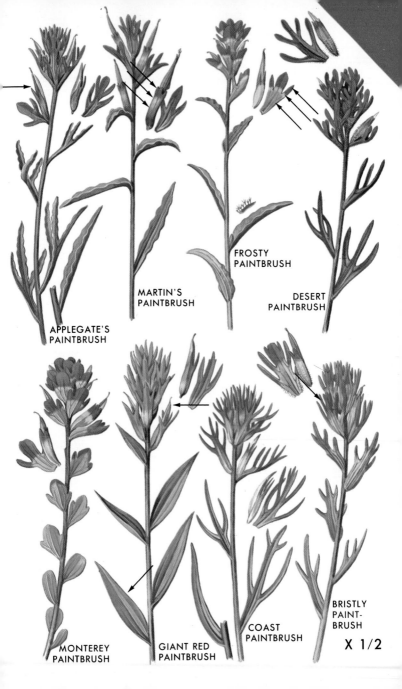

APPLEGATE'S
PAINTBRUSH

MARTIN'S
PAINTBRUSH

FROSTY
PAINTBRUSH

DESERT
PAINTBRUSH

MONTEREY
PAINTBRUSH

GIANT RED
PAINTBRUSH

COAST
PAINTBRUSH

BRISTLY
PAINT-
BRUSH

X 1/2

5-PETALED, 2-LIPPED SPOUTLIKE FLOWERS

Snapdragon Family (Scrophulariaceae)
See also pp. Y 112–18; R 234–44, 310; B 336–38, 372.

LEMMON'S PAINTBRUSH *Castilleja lemmonii*
Flower spike *bright magenta.* Calyx bracts broadly rounded.
Flower leaf bracts trilobed. Lower leaves lancelike. 4–12 in.
Wet alpine meadows. Sierra Nevada. June–Aug.

ALPINE PAINTBRUSH *Castilleja nana*
The purple and white flowers have a *black eye* (tip of spoutlike
corolla). Stem leaves 5- to 7-lobed. 1–6 in. Dry alpine meadows. Sierra Nevada and White Mts. June–Sept.

SHORTLOBE PAINTBRUSH *Castilleja brevilobata*
Both leaves and flower bracts *broad* with *3 very short round*
lobes, densely clustered. 4–8 in. Open stony places. Siskiyous
of nw. Calif. and sw. Ore. May–July

FELT PAINTBRUSH *Castilleja foliolosa*
Leaves and stem densely *white woolly.* Flower leaf bracts have
3 (or 5) lobes. Calyx tips *flat.* Stem leaves *linear* (or 3-lobed at
upper levels). 1–2 ft. Dry places. Calif. Coast Ranges south to
Baja; rarely in w. Sierra Nevada. March–June

CALIFORNIA THREADTORCH *Castilleja stenantha*
Long *threadlike* flower bract leaves red to orange–tipped.
Leaves linear. 1–5 ft. Moist places. Calif. May–Sept.

GREAT BASIN THREADTORCH *Castilleja exilis*
(not shown)
Similar to preceding. Great Basin region. June–Sept.

SUKSDORF'S PAINTBRUSH *Castilleja suksdorfii*
The flower bracts and calyx have *narrow sharp-pointed* lobes
and are a *bright red and yellow.* Leaves similar, but lowermost
linear. 1–2 ft. Wet subalpine meadows. Cascades: Mt. Adams,
Wash., south to Crater Lake, Ore. June–Sept.

WYOMING PAINTBRUSH *Castilleja linariaefolia*
The *widely spaced and long* (2 in.) flowers project at right
angles from the stem with 3-lobed leaf bracts at base. Linear
leaves yellow-green. 2–5 ft. Wyoming State Flower. Dry
woods, sagebrush flats. Great Basin. May–Sept.

FRANCISCAN PAINTBRUSH *Castilleja franciscana*
The red to orange flowers *project* at right angles from the stem,
with *linear* leaf bracts. Gray-green linear leaves. 1–3 ft.
Coastal region north and south of San Francisco. Also in
w. Sierra Nevada foothills. March–June

LEMMON'S PAINTBRUSH

ALPINE PAINTBRUSH

SHORT-LOBE PAINTBRUSH

FELT PAINTBRUSH

CALIFORNIA THREAD TORCH

SUKSDORF'S PAINTBRUSH

FRANCISCAN PAINTBRUSH

WYOMING PAINTBRUSH

X 1/2

4 OR 5 PETALS: SHOOTING STARS, PINKS

PRIMROSE FAMILY (Primulaceae)
See also pp. W 100; R 304; B 342.

ALPINE SHOOTING STAR *Dodecatheon alpinum*
Leaves *narrowly* linear. Always 4-petaled and has an *enlarged* stigma tip. 2–6 in. Wet alpine meadows. High mts. of Pacific States. MAY–AUG.

JEFFREY'S SHOOTING STAR *Dodecatheon jeffreyi*
Stigma tip *enlarged*. Leaves broad. 5 (or 4) petals. ½–2 ft. Wet mt. meadows. Pacific States. MAY–AUG.

HENDERSON'S SHOOTING STAR
Dodecatheon hendersonii
The *broadly oval* leaves have *abruptly tapering* petioles. Stigma tip *pointed*. The 5 (4 in San Francisco area) petals deep lavender or white with a band of yellow between the free lobes and the anther tube which is *always all dark*. 1–2 ft. Foothills west of Cascades–Sierra Nevada. FEB.–MAY

PADRES SHOOTING STAR *Dodecatheon clevelandii*
The 5 petals are pink with both white and yellow bands just above the dark maroon anther tubes with *yellow spots* at the tip. 1–2 ft. Calif. Coast Ranges to Baja. JAN.–FEB.

WESTERN SHOOTING STAR *Dodecatheon pulchellum*
The 5 petals magenta to lavender with a yellow or white band. Base of anther tube yellow, smooth or wrinkled, but not in definite lines. 2–24 in. Great Basin. APRIL–MAY

BONNEVILLE SHOOTING STAR
(not shown) *Dodecatheon conjugens*
Very similar to Western Shooting Star. Anther tube has wrinkles with definite lines. Great Basin. APRIL–JUNE

PINK FAMILY (Caryophyllaceae)
See also pp. W 54–60; R 282.

CALIFORNIA INDIAN PINK *Silene californica*
Each scarlet petal is divided into 4 *short* broad lobes with *rounded* tips. ½–1½ ft. Open woods. Calif. to s. Ore.
MARCH–AUG.

MEXICAN PINK *Silene laciniata*
Each scarlet petal is divided into 4 *narrowly linear* lobes with *sharp tips*. 1–2 ft. Wooded slopes. Calif. South Coast Ranges to Baja; desert mts. (outer lobes short). APRIL–JULY

MOSS CATCHFLY *Silene acaulis*
Each pink to lavender petal *tip is nearly rectangular* with 2 short round lobes and 2 small base appendages. 1–2 in. Forming mats on alpine slopes. Ore. and Wash. JUNE–AUG.

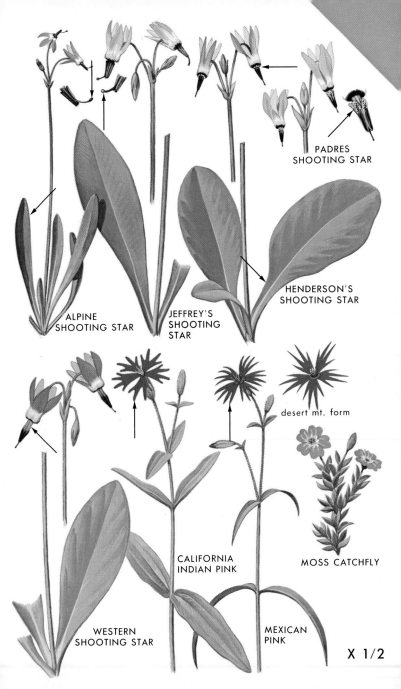

PADRES
SHOOTING STAR

ALPINE
SHOOTING STAR

JEFFREY'S
SHOOTING
STAR

HENDERSON'S
SHOOTING STAR

desert mt. form

CALIFORNIA
INDIAN PINK

MOSS CATCHFLY

WESTERN
SHOOTING STAR

MEXICAN
PINK

X 1/2

5 PETALS; UPRIGHT TRUMPETS

PHLOX FAMILY (Polemoniaceae)
See also pp. W 72; Y 172; O 226;
R 250, 306; B 360–64.

WHISKER BRUSH *Linanthus ciliatus*
The short (½ in.) slender-tubed flowers are pink with a *yellow and white throat* and a *round red dot* on each petal lobe. Flower bract and leaf *margins fringed* with whiskery hairs. Leaves 5- to 11-cleft. 1–4 in. Very common. Open places below 10,000 ft. Calif. to s. Ore. APRIL–AUG.

MUSTANG LINANTHUS *Linanthus montanus*
The showiest of the *Linanthus*. The long (to 2 in.) tubular flowers pink or white with a *triangular* purple spot on each petal lobe. Tube throat yellow. ½–2 ft. Steep dry banks below 5000 ft. Western slope Sierra Nevada. MAY–AUG.

FALSE BABY STARS *Linanthus androsaceus*
Corolla tube 1 to 3 *times longer* than the petal lobes. Upper corolla tube *broadly funnel-like* and yellow or white with the petal lobes pink (or white, or yellow). Leaves 5- to 9-cleft. 2–12 in. Fields. Calif. Coast Ranges to Baja. APRIL–JUNE

TRUE BABY STARS *Linanthus bicolor*
Corolla tube *threadlike, 5 to 10 times longer* than the short petal lobes. Petal lobes stiffly at right angles to the *non-flaring* tube. Petals bright red-pink above a distinct *yellow collar.* Leaves 3- to 7-cleft. 1–6 in. Open places. West of Cascades–Sierra Nevada. MARCH–JUNE

GROUND PINK *Linanthus dianthiflorus*
Few flowers per stem, *broad* (1 in.) *shallow pink bowls* with a dark center. Petal edges *sawtoothed.* 2–5 in. Common in sandy places. S. Calif. to Baja. FEB.–APRIL

GABRIEL'S TRUMPET *Gilia leptantha*
The *short, fat* (1 in.) trumpetlike flower bright pink with a yellow throat. Fernlike pinnate leaves cobwebby-haired, lobes rounded. ½–2 ft. S. Calif. Mts. APRIL–JULY

BANDED GILIA *Gilia cana*
Note the *yellow band* in the upper corolla tube between the pink to blue petal lobes and the dark purple base. Ladderlike pinnate leaves with *sharp tips* in basal rosettes. 4–24 in. Sandy flats. Mojave Desert, mts. to west. APRIL–AUG.

DESERT TRUMPET *Ipomopsis aggregata*
The fluorescent red to pink, trumpetlike flowers with *pointed petals* are in *clusters.* Sticky stems. Pinnate leaves. 1–3 ft. Great Basin and adjacent mts. to west. JUNE–SEPT.

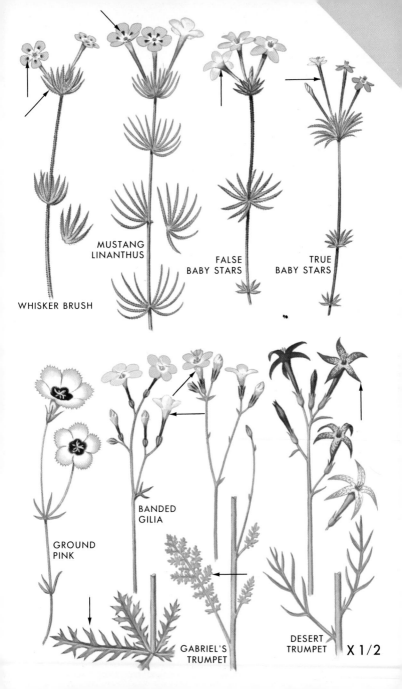

WHISKER BRUSH

MUSTANG
LINANTHUS

FALSE
BABY STARS

TRUE
BABY STARS

GROUND
PINK

BANDED
GILIA

GABRIEL'S
TRUMPET

DESERT
TRUMPET

X 1/2

5 PETALS; SHORT PHLOXLIKE TRUMPETS

Phlox Family (Polemoniaceae)
See also pp. W 72; Y 172; O 226; R 248-50, 306; B 360-64.

STANSBURY'S PHLOX *Phlox stansburyi*
The very long corolla tube is *2–4 times longer* than sepals. The pink, salmon, whitish petal lobes *narrow with small notched* tips. Leaves linear and flat. 4–8 in. Sagebrush deserts, Juniper woodlands. S. Great Basin mts. APRIL–JUNE

SHOWY PHLOX *Phlox speciosa*
The bright pink flowers have broad *deeply bilobed* petals and the corolla tubes are *1 length* longer than sepals. Flowers in loose clusters above the long lancelike leaves. ½–2 ft. Forests and sagebrush flats. Cen. Calif. mts., Great Basin.
APRIL–JUNE

LONG-LEAVED PHLOX *Phlox longifolia*
The *long* (½–1 in.) corolla tube and sepals are of *equal length*. Flowers broad-petaled. *Long* (¾ to 2 in.) *linear leaves*. 4–16 in. Open flats. Great Basin. APRIL–JULY

WOODLAND PHLOX *Phlox adsurgens*
Note the *broad oval* pairs of leaves along the creeping or erect stems. Pink flowers few in number. 4–12 in. Forest openings below 7000 ft. Nw. Calif. and w. Ore. MAY–AUG.

SPREADING PHLOX *Phlox diffusa*
The pink or white flowers are *broad-petaled*. Often seen as *showy mats*. Low shrubby stems with *sharp needlelike* yellow-green leaves. *Hairy* clusters between the sepals and at leaf bases. 4–12 in. Very common. Open places. 3000–14,000 ft. Mts. of Pacific States. MAY–AUG.

DESERT MOUNTAIN PHLOX *Phlox austromontana*
Similar to Spreading Phlox. Petal lobes *narrow*. Calyx and leaf bases *hairless*. The gray-green, sharp, needlelike leaves pungent-odored. 1–6 in. Dry rocky slopes. S. Calif. Mts.
MAY–JULY

CARPET PHLOX *Phlox caespitosa*
Very dense thin cushiony carpets (1–2 in. thick) made up of tiny linear leaves. The small, solitary, pale pink flowers appearing to *dot* the carpet. The tiny linear leaves have a *flat upper surface,* sticky-haired. High mts. Sierra Nevada, S. Calif. Mts., Great Basin. JUNE–AUG.

COVILLE'S PHLOX *Phlox covillei*
(not shown)
Very similar to Spreading Phlox. Leaves grooved on underside. Sierra Nevada and Great Basin. JUNE–AUG.

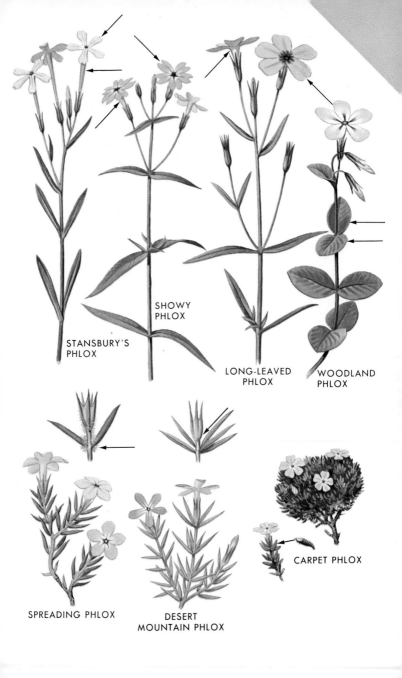

STANSBURY'S PHLOX

SHOWY PHLOX

LONG-LEAVED PHLOX

WOODLAND PHLOX

SPREADING PHLOX

DESERT MOUNTAIN PHLOX

CARPET PHLOX

3 PETALS: MARIPOSA TULIPS

LILY FAMILY (Liliaceae)
See also pp. W 4–16; Y 122–24; O 228–30;
R 252–56; B 352; G 388–90.

SQUARE MARIPOSA TULIP   *Calochortus venustus*
Note the *rectangular* yellow spot at the petal base. An upper
dark red spot has a yellowish border. Basic petal color rosy red
varying to the more normal white form (p. 16). 4–12 in. Red
form is found in cen. Sierra Nevada.   MAY–JULY

ROSY FAIRY LANTERN   *Calochortus amoenus*
Note the *lanternlike* rosy-red flowers hanging upside down.
Petal base has a fringed maroon gland. ½–2 ft. Semi-shaded
woods. W. Sierra Nevada foothills.   APRIL–JUNE

PINK STAR TULIP   *Calochortus uniflorus*
The fan-shaped petals are entirely pale baby pink. A bare
oblong gland at the petal base has a few long yellow hairs above
it as a fringe. Stem barely above the ground. Wet depressions.
West of Cascades–Sierra Nevada.   MARCH–MAY

PLUMMER'S MARIPOSA TULIP
     Calochortus plummerae
Each large pink petal has a central region of *numerous·long
yellow* hairs, each of which arises from a tiny *dark red spot.*
Petal base is strongly depressed with a long slender horn of
thick hairs. 1–2 ft. S. Calif. Mts.   MAY–JULY

SAGEBRUSH MARIPOSA TULIP
     Calochortus macrocarpus
The lavender *or* white flowers have long narrow *sepals exceed-
ing* the petals. A green stripe on the outside of each petal. The
petal base has a triangular gland in a zone of yellow hairs and a
curving *chevron band of dark maroon* above it. ½–2 ft. Dry
slopes. Great Basin.   JULY–AUG.

SPLENDID MARIPOSA TULIP   *Calochortus splendens*
Large bright pink petals have a small basal area of maroon with
a *round* gland and long loosely scattered yellow hairs above it.
½–2 ft. Dry openings, often on serpentine rock. Cen. and
s. Calif.   MAY–JUNE

STRIPED MARIPOSA TULIP   *Calochortus striatus*
The pink petals have numerous dark *red-striped* veins.
4–15 in. Alkali meadows. Mojave Desert.   APRIL–JUNE

SHY MARIPOSA TULIP   *Calochortus invenustus*
A large arched zone of dark maroon at the petal base has 2
small clusters of yellow hairs on *opposite sides* of the round
gland area. Pale pink to lavender petals have an outer green
strip and a raised basal bump. ½–1½ ft. Granitic sand. Mts. of
cen. and s. Calif.   MAY–AUG.

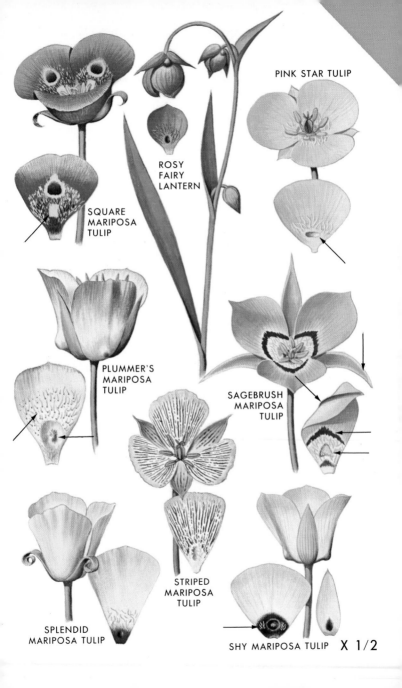

PINK STAR TULIP

ROSY
FAIRY
LANTERN

SQUARE
MARIPOSA
TULIP

PLUMMER'S
MARIPOSA
TULIP

SAGEBRUSH
MARIPOSA
TULIP

STRIPED
MARIPOSA
TULIP

SPLENDID
MARIPOSA TULIP

SHY MARIPOSA TULIP   X 1/2

3 OR 6 PETALS; LILY- OR IRIS-LIKE

LILY FAMILY (Liliaceae)
See also pp. W 4–16; Y 122–24; O 228–30;
R 252–56; B 352; G 388–90.

BOLANDER'S LILY *Lilium bolanderi*
The *nodding bell-like* flowers are dark wine-red. 1–4 ft. Dry
red clay soils. Sw. Ore. and adjacent Calif. JUNE–JULY

KELLOGG'S TIGER LILY *Lilium kelloggii*
Pink to red petals have *central parallel* white and yellow
bands, red dotted. 3–5 ft. *Dry* forests. Nw. Calif. JUNE

HENDERSON'S FAWN LILY *Erythronium hendersonii*
Red-purple petals lancelike with a *dark purple base*. Stigma
tip of 3 *blunt lobes*. Nodding starlike flowers are above a pair of
large fawn-spotted leaves. 4–12 in. Semi-shaded Oak woods.
Sw. Ore., barely into Calif. APRIL–JULY

COAST FAWN LILY *Erythronium revolutum*
Bright rose-pink petals have a *yellow base*. Stigma tip of 3
linear lobes. Nodding starlike flowers are above the large
fawn-spotted leaves. 4–12 in. Shady conifer woods along coast.
Nw. Calif. to B.C. MARCH–JUNE

ADOBE LILY *Fritillaria pluriflora*
Note the large pink *bell-shaped* flowers above the *broad* lance-
like leaves. Rare. ½–2 ft. Adobe soil. Foothills of nw. Sierra
Nevada and Calif. North Coast Ranges. FEB.–APRIL

ANDREWS' CLINTONIA *Clintonia andrewsiana*
The *tubular* deep rose-purple flowers are in terminal clusters.
5–6 broadly oval leaves. ½–2 ft. Redwood forests. Coast of
Calif. and sw. Ore. MAY–JULY

AMARYLLIS FAMILY (Amaryllidaceae)
See also pp. W 18; Y 124; R 256–62; B 352.

TWINING SNAKE LILY *Dichelostemma volublie*
Note the long (2–5 ft.) *pink twining* stem with an umbel of
numerous *short urn-shaped* pink flowers. Thickets. Lower
foothills of Sierra Nevada; Calif. Coast Ranges. APRIL–JUNE

FIRECRACKER FLOWER *Dichelostemma ida-maia*
Note the *bright red* firecracker-like flowers with *green* petal
lobes. 3 stamens. Open grassy slopes. Calif. North Coast
Ranges to s. Ore. MAY–JULY

IRIS FAMILY (Iridaceae)
See also pp. Y 126; B 350.

**DOUGLAS'S YELLOW-EYED GRASS,
GRASS WIDOWS** *Sisyrinchium douglasii*
Note the 6 *broad red-pink* petals and a *yellow eye* of stamens
whose column base is inflated (or not in some areas). Flowers
can vary to blue or white. A variable species complex with
S. inflatum and others sometimes named separately. Irislike
leaves. ½–1 ft. Moist woods. Great Basin and west of Cascades
south to n. Calif. MARCH–JUNE

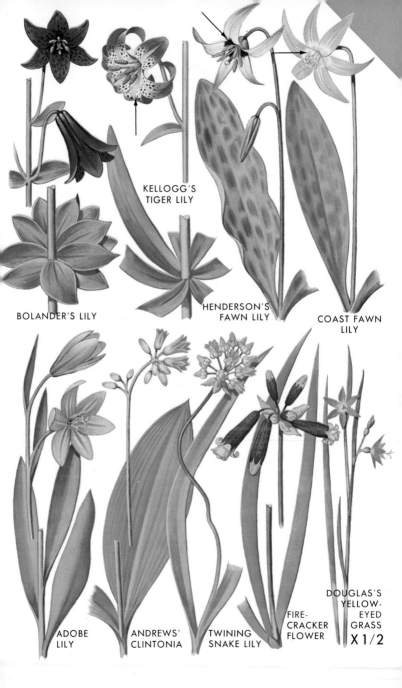

BOLANDER'S LILY

KELLOGG'S TIGER LILY

HENDERSON'S FAWN LILY

COAST FAWN LILY

ADOBE LILY

ANDREWS' CLINTONIA

TWINING SNAKE LILY

FIRE-CRACKER FLOWER

DOUGLAS'S YELLOW-EYED GRASS

X 1/2

3 OR 6 PETALS; SINGLE ERECT FLOWER, OR MANY IN AN UMBEL ON A LEAFLESS STEM

LILY FAMILY (Liliaceae)
See also pp. W 4–16; Y 122–24; O 228–30; R 252–56;
B 352; G 388–90.

GIANT TRILLIUM   *Trillium chloropetalum*
Note the *erect* dark purple to green-yellow petals immediately above the 3 large, broadly oval, *purple-mottled* leaves. ½–2 ft. Shady woods and thickets. West of Cascades–Sierra Nevada.
FEB.–MAY

WESTERN TRILLIUM   *Trillium ovatum*
The open white to pink flowers have *short oval* petals and are *on a long pedicel* above 3 oval, sharp-pointed, green leaves. ½–2 ft. Moist shady woods. Monterey, Calif. and north along coast to B.C.
MARCH–JUNE

ROUNDLEAF TRILLIUM   *Trillium petiolatum*
The 3 broad bright yellow-green leaves are *nearly round* on *long narrow petioles.* The 3-petaled flower is dark red-brown and nearly hidden among the leaves. 2–8 in. Moist meadows and woods. Eastern side of Cascades and east in Wash. and Ore.
APRIL–JUNE

AMARYLLIS FAMILY (Amaryllidaceae)
See also pp. W 18; Y 124; R 254–62; B 352.

PINK FUNNEL LILY   *Androstephium breviflorum*
Note that the 6 stamen filaments are *fused into a long protruding funnel.* Flowers light pink to purple. 2–8 in. Shifting sand dunes or firm sandy ground. Mojave Desert.
MARCH

EARTH BRODIAEA   *Brodiaea terrestris*
The red-purple to blue flowers *nestled on the ground.* The 3 white or pale blue bilobed staminodia above the petals are *square-topped* and *lean inward,* margins inrolled. The flower tube has a triangular outline. 0.1–3 in. above the ground. Open fields along immediate coast. Sw. Ore. to Lompoc, Calif. Ssp. *kernensis* has a similar flower, but has a stem 3–18 in. high. It occurs away from the coast. Calif. South Coast Ranges and southernmost Sierra Nevada foothills to mts. of s. Calif.
APRIL–JUNE

JOLON BRODIAEA   *Brodiaea jolonensis*
The rose-violet flower tube is *urn-shaped.* The 3 white staminodia are *erect* with bilobed, square-topped tips and inrolled margins. Ovary purple. 2–6 in. Open fields. Calif. South Coast Ranges to Baja.
APRIL–MAY

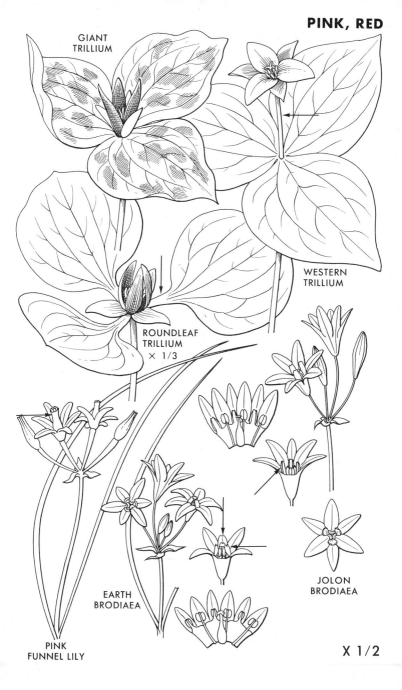

PINK, RED

GIANT
TRILLIUM

WESTERN
TRILLIUM

ROUNDLEAF
TRILLIUM
× 1/3

PINK
FUNNEL LILY

EARTH
BRODIAEA

JOLON
BRODIAEA

X 1/2

6 PETALS; UMBEL ON LEAFLESS STEM

AMARYLLIS FAMILY (Amaryllidaceae)
See also pp. W '18; Y 124; R 254–62; B 352.

ELEGANT BRODIAEA *Brodiaea elegans*
The funnel-like red-purple to purple flowers have 3 slightly *concave or flat* white staminodia *well away* from the 3 long lancelike anthers. ¼–2 ft. Very common species. Open fields. Cen. Calif. to w. Ore. MAY–JULY

HARVEST BRODIAEA *Brodiaea coronaria*
The rose to violet flowers have *3 hornlike* white staminodia with tightly inrolled margins. They are also *closely pressed* to the anthers. Flower tube base oblong. 2–10 in. Open fields. Cen. Calif. to B.C. APRIL–JUNE

VERNAL POOL BRODIAEA *Brodiaea minor*
The rose-pink flowers have a *constricted* flower tube and 3 white, short, nearly *square-tipped* staminodia. Petals *broad.* 1–4 in. Shallow pool depressions in foothills just below the treeline of w. Sierra Nevada. MARCH–APRIL

PURDY'S BRODIAEA *Brodiaea purdyi*
The rose-pink flower has a *constricted* flower tube and 3 *long narrow* white staminodia spreading *above* the petals. Petals *narrow.* 3–12 in. Open woodlands. Often on the blue-green serpentine rock. Sierra Nevada foothills. APRIL–JUNE

CALIFORNIA BRODIAEA *Brodiaea californica*
The light red-pink flowers have 3 *long white slender* staminodia with margins slightly enrolled. Anthers and petals *long lancelike.* Flower tube *short.* ½–3 ft. Grasslands, woodlands. Sierra Nevada foothills to Mt. Shasta. MAY–JULY

APPENDAGED BRODIAEA *Brodiaea appendiculata*
Similar to Calif. Brodiaea. Note the *forked linear appendages* on the back of each anther. Petals broader and shorter. ½–2 ft. Grasslands and lower Oak Woodlands. Western edge of Sierra Nevada foothills. APRIL–MAY

THREADLEAF BRODIAEA *Brodiaea filifolia*
The 3 white staminodia at top of the flower tube are *tiny and narrowly triangular.* The red-purple to blue flower tube is *short urnlike* with the petals at right angles. ½–1 ft. Shallow depressions. Perris to Vista, s. Calif. APRIL–MAY

ORCUTT'S BRODIAEA *Brodiaea orcuttii*
Similar to Threadleaf Brodiaea. The red-purple to blue flowers have 3 stamens and *no staminodia.* 2–10 in. Pool depressions on mesas at San Diego, Calif. MAY

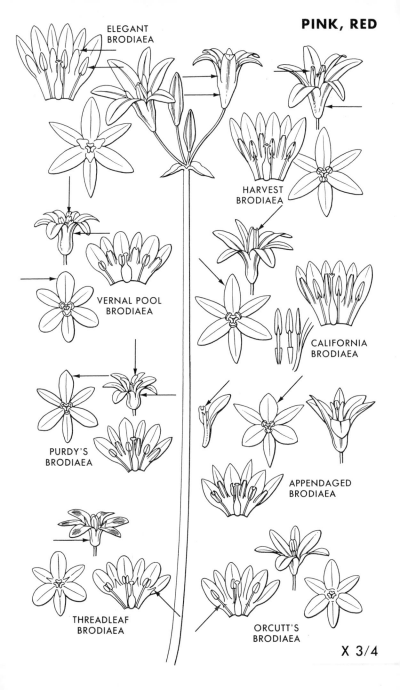

PINK, RED

ELEGANT BRODIAEA

HARVEST BRODIAEA

VERNAL POOL BRODIAEA

CALIFORNIA BRODIAEA

PURDY'S BRODIAEA

APPENDAGED BRODIAEA

THREADLEAF BRODIAEA

ORCUTT'S BRODIAEA

X 3/4

6 PETALS; UMBEL ON LEAFLESS STEM
DISTINCT ONION ODOR: WILD ONIONS

AMARYLLIS FAMILY (Amaryllidaceae)
See also pp. W 18; Y 124; R 254–62; B 352.

SWAMP ONION *Allium validum*
Each dark rose-purple flower has *long and narrow lancelike* petals. Stamens *extended* $\frac{1}{3}$ or more *above* petals. The dense, flat flower umbel is on a tall stem well above the numerous long *strap-shaped* leaves. 1–3 ft. Common. Wet mt. meadows. Pacific States. JUNE–SEPT.

HOOKER'S ONION *Allium acuminatum*
Note the 3 small, inner, triangular, bright rose to dark red petals have *minutely sawtoothed inrolled* margins. Small urnlike flowers. The umbel well above the 2–3 narrow leaves. 4–12 in. Semiopen to open slopes. Cen. Calif. to B.C.; also very common in Great Basin. MAY–JULY

NODDING ONION *Allium cernuum*
Note the *nodding umbel* of pink to white *bell-like* flowers. Petals nearly round. Linear leaves well below the flower umbel. 4–20 in. Moist mt. soils. B.C. to Ore. JUNE–JULY

GEYER'S ONION *Allium geyeri*
Flowers pink or white with a distinct *constriction* immediately below the reflexed *tiny and sharply triangular* petals. A thick rib on each petal back. In some areas the flowers are replaced by small bulblets. $\frac{1}{2}$–3 ft. Damp mt. meadows. Eastern side of Cascades; Great Basin. MAY–JUNE

COAST FLATSTEM ONION *Allium falcifolium*
The umbel of *short urnlike*, dark rose-red flowers are on a *flat ribbonlike* stem. Leaves flat and broad. Petal edges minutely undulate. 1–6 in. Open rocky slopes. S. Ore. and south in Calif. Coast Ranges to Monterey, Calif. MARCH–JULY

PINK STAR ONION *Allium platycaule*
The *narrow, sharp pointed,* bright pink petals form a distinct *constriction* above the ovary. Flowers are in a dense ball-like umbel nestled among the leaves. Both stem and leaves broad flattened ribbons. 1–6 in. Open mt. slopes. N. Sierra Nevada to s. Ore. MAY–AUG.

DWARF ONION *Allium parvum*
The 8 to 100 plus urnlike flowers pale pink to white and are in an umbel barely above ground. Petals *smooth-edged.* Flower stem and leaves flattened. 1–2 in. Very common. Stony flats. Great Basin. APRIL–JULY

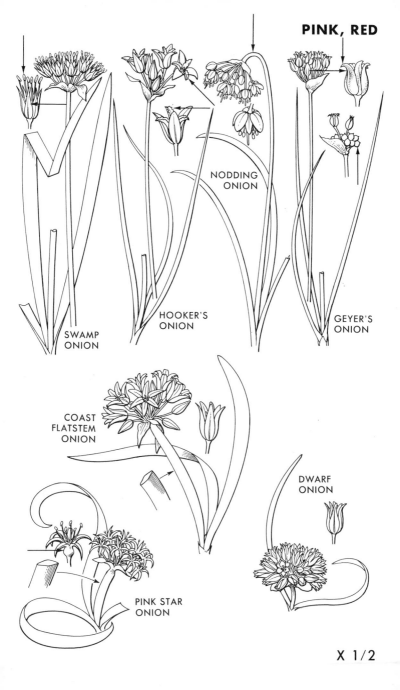

PINK, RED

SWAMP ONION

HOOKER'S ONION

NODDING ONION

GEYER'S ONION

COAST FLATSTEM ONION

PINK STAR ONION

DWARF ONION

X 1/2

6 PETALS; UMBEL ON LEAFLESS STEM
DISTINCT ONION ODOR: WILD ONIONS

AMARYLLIS FAMILY (Amaryllidaceae)
See also pp. W 18; Y 124; R 254–62; B 352.

SIERRA ONION *Allium campanulatum*
Note the loose ball-like umbel of the 15–40 *flat* rose-purple *star-shaped* flowers. 6 low triangular crests are on the ovary lobes. The 2–3 flat leaves drying up by flowering time. 2–12 in. Dry semiopen forests, thickets. Mts. of Calif. and sw. Ore.
MAY–JULY

GLASSY ONION *Allium hyalinum*
The flat flowers have nearly *round petals with a glassy* shine. 6–15 light pink to white flowers are in a very loose open umbel. Fleshy leaves. 1/2–1 ft. Moist grassy slopes along foothills of w. Sierra Nevada.
MARCH–JUNE

FRINGED ONION *Allium fimbriatum*
Each flower a *broad open bell.* Six long *craggy crests* are on top of the 3 ovary lobes. 8–40 pale pink to rose flowers with darker midribs. A single leaf twice as long as the flower stem. 1–4 in. Lower mts. of Calif.
MARCH–JULY

POM-PON ONION *Allium serratum*
Each flower a short tube with very *short reflexed petal tips.* Large round balls of numerous dark rose-pink flowers are on tall *round stems.* 8–16 in. Open grassy fields, serpentine soils. Inland portion Calif. Coast Ranges.
MARCH–MAY

OLYMPIC ONION *Allium crenulatum*
The pale pink petals are *broad-based and toothlike* with a dark pink midvein. The flat leaves and flower stem edges are minutely *sawtoothed.* 3–8 in. Rocky alpine meadows. Olympic Mts., rarely elsewhere B.C. to Ore.
APRIL–AUG.

ASPEN ONION *Allium bisceptrum*
Pairs of *triangular, sawtoothed* appendages occur on top of the ovary lobes. The pale to dark pink petals narrowly lancelike. Numerous open flowers are on an erect round stem. 1/2–1 ft. Common within aspen groves. Great Basin, and along east side of Cascades–Sierra Nevada.
MAY–JULY

BLUE MOUNTAIN ONION *Allium fibrillum*
Broad bell-like flowers have a central green midrib on each pink (or white) petal. Pairs of *low curving smooth-edged* appendages occur on top of each ovary lobe. 2–10 in. Moist places. Blue and Wallowa mts. of Ore.
MAY–JULY

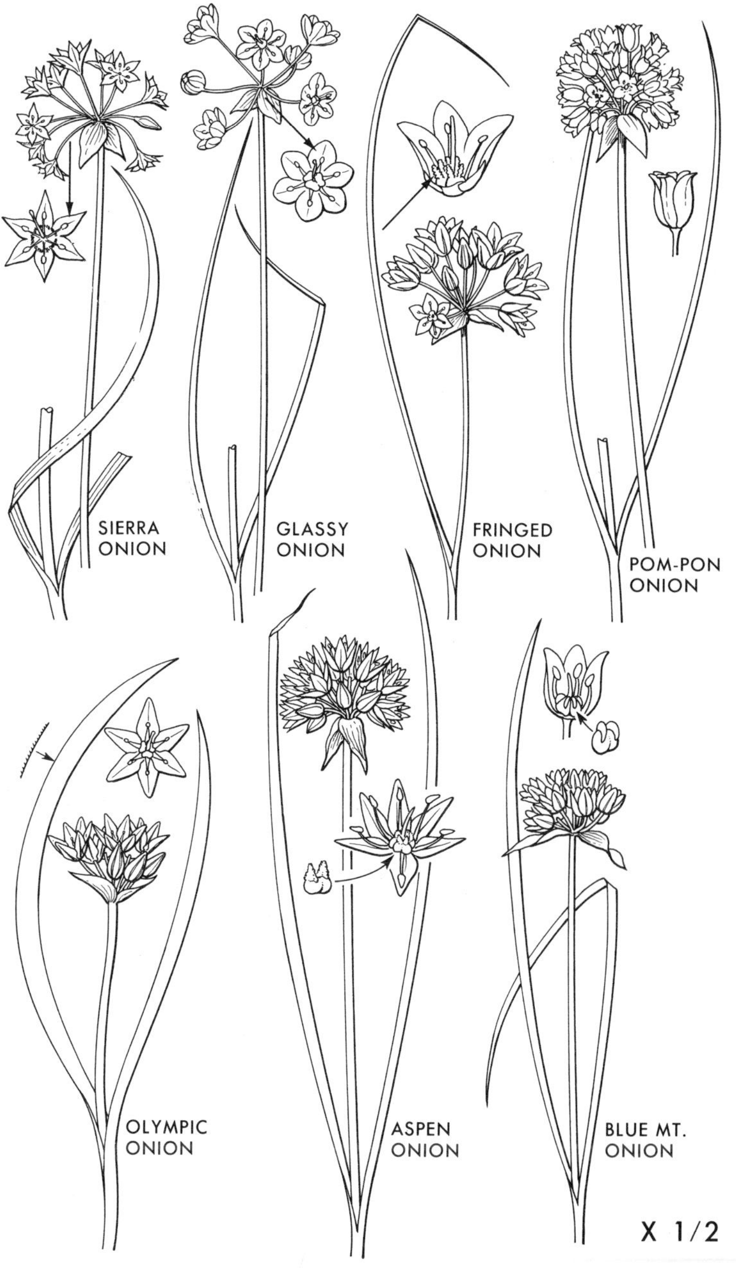

SIERRA
ONION

GLASSY
ONION

FRINGED
ONION

POM-PON
ONION

OLYMPIC
ONION

ASPEN
ONION

BLUE MT.
ONION

X 1/2

MANY PETALS: CACTUS

BEAVERTAIL CACTUS   *Opuntia basilaris*
The *blue beavertail-like* pads have small *eyespots* ringed by tiny spines, otherwise spineless. Flowers red-purple. 4–12 in. Common. Mojave, Colorado Deserts.   MARCH–JUNE

CLARET-CUP CACTUS   *Echinocerus triglochidiatus*
Short yellow-green oblong stems are in low spreading mounds. Flowers *scarlet-orange.* Long curly spines with white feltlike hairs at the base of the larger spines. 2–4 in. Dry mt. slopes. Mojave Desert, Great Basin.   APRIL–JUNE

ENGELMANN'S HEDGEHOGS   *Echinocerus engelmannii*
Elongated cylinderlike stems are in mounded clumps. Flowers red-purple. Each brown to gray spine cluster has 2–6 central flat spines and 6–12 shorter radial ones. 4–12 in. Rocky slopes. Mojave Desert to Baja and to Great Basin.   APRIL–MAY

BEEHIVE NIPPLE CACTUS   *Coryphantha vivipara*
The globular stem has nipplelike bumps, each with a terminal cluster of 3–5 central spines and 10–20 smaller ones around them. Flowers pink to red, or yellow. 1–5 in. Deserts. Ore. and Calif.   MAY–JUNE

FOXTAIL CACTUS   *Coryphantha alversonii*
Stem an oblong cylinder. Each cluster of 12–16 *stout spines* and 25–35 *slender ones* are of the *same length* around the former. Spines white with brown tips. Flowers bright red-purple with a deep red central vein. 4–8 in. Rocky slopes. Mts. of and near Joshua Tree Natl. Mon.   MAY–JUNE

YAQUI CACTUS   *Mammillaria tetrancistra*
Stem an elongated cylinder. Each spine cluster has a *flat ring* of straight white spines and one or more protruding *black hooked* spines. Flowers rose-pink to purple. 4–10 in. Rocky slopes. Mojave, Colorado Deserts. Great Basin.   APRIL

DEVILS-CLAW CACTUS   *Sclerocactus polyancistrus*
The short rounded solitary stem has numerous long spines. 9–11 spines per cluster, the lower all *hooked and red,* while the erect central ones are straight and white. Flowers red-purple. 3–6 in. Rocky slopes. Mojave Desert.   APRIL–MAY

COASTAL CHOLLA   *Opuntia prolifera*
Cylindrical stem sections *short and fat.* 6–12 long red-brown spines per cluster, with age becoming gray with yellow tips. Flowers red-purple. Treelike, 2–7 ft. Strictly along coast. Ventura Co., Calif., south to Baja.   APRIL–JUNE

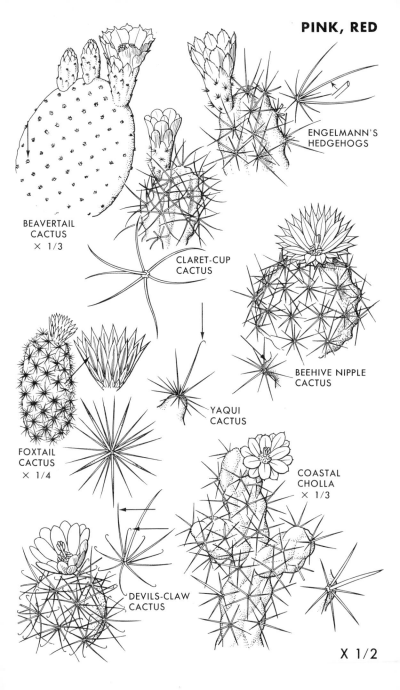

PINK, RED

BEAVERTAIL
CACTUS
× 1/3

ENGELMANN'S
HEDGEHOGS

CLARET-CUP
CACTUS

BEEHIVE NIPPLE
CACTUS

FOXTAIL
CACTUS
× 1/4

YAQUI
CACTUS

COASTAL
CHOLLA
× 1/3

DEVILS-CLAW
CACTUS

X 1/2

4-PETALED MALTESE CROSS

Mustard Family (Cruciferae)
See also pp. W 24–30; Y 140–48; O 224; R 268.

WILD RADISH Alien   *Raphanus sativus*
Seedpod a fat *cylinder with constrictions* between each seed.
Flowers pink or other colors, all at same location. Broad
pinnate leaves. 1–4 ft. Common. Pacific States. Feb.–July

OVAL SEAROCKET Alien   *Cakile edentula*
The flattened, pointed-oval seedpods have a *rounded base.*
Fleshy straplike leaves have short round-tipped lobes. Pink to
purple flowers. Stems are covered by a blue wax. 1–3 ft. Ocean
beaches. Pacific Coast.   Feb.–Nov.

HORNED SEAROCKET Alien   *Cakile maritima*
Similar to Oval Searocket. Seedpods have *2 hornlike pro-
truberances* near the base. Leaves deeply pinnate. Prostrate
stem. Ocean beaches. Cen. Calif. coast.   Feb.–Nov.

PURPLE-CROSS FLOWER Alien   *Chorispora tenella*
Seedpods *curving upward and sharp-pointed.* Elongated nar-
row-based petals. Stem and calyx have distinct scattered
glandular hairs. ½–1½ ft. Great Basin.   April–June

HEART-LEAVED JEWEL FLOWER
                              Streptanthus cordatus
The pointed sepals have a terminal *tuft of hairs.* The urn-
shaped flowers have red-purple or yellow petals with white tips.
Seedpods erect. Heart-shaped yellow-green leaves clasp the
upper stem, while the basal ones have a toothed spatula shape.
1–3 ft. Calif. desert mts. and north along Sierra
Nevada to s. Ore.   May–July

MOUNTAIN JEWEL FLOWER   *Streptanthus tortuosus*
Similar to preceding. The pointed red-purple *sepal tips are
bent downward* and are completely hairless. ½–3 ft. Common.
Hot rocky slopes. W. Sierra Nevada and Calif. Coast Ranges.
                                         April–Aug.

BRISTLY JEWEL FLOWER   *Streptanthus glandulosus*
Stems, leaves, and seedpods have scattered *bristlelike* hairs.
Linear pinnate lobed leaves, lancelike on upper stem. The
urn-shaped flowers have purple to white petals with purple
veins. Sepals oval. Seedpod horizontal or deflexed. 1–2 ft.
Rocky places. Calif. Coast Ranges.   April–June

DAGGER POD   *Phoenicaulis cheiranthoides*
The *broad twisted daggerlike* seedpods are in a loose brushlike
cluster. Gray lancelike leaves are in a basal rosette. 2–8 in.
Very common. East slopes of both Cascades and Sierra
Nevada, and all of Great Basin.   April–June

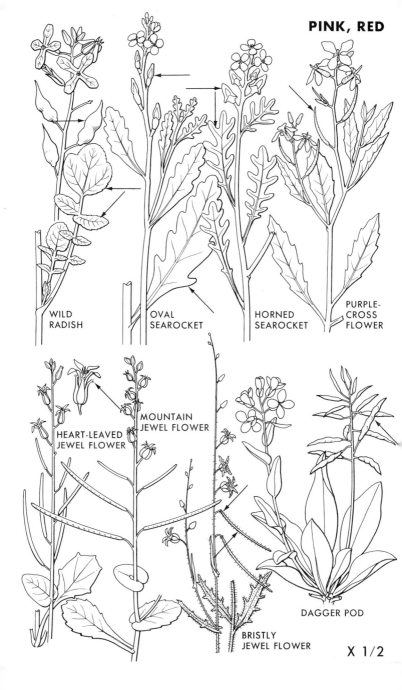

PINK, RED

WILD RADISH

OVAL SEAROCKET

HORNED SEAROCKET

PURPLE-CROSS FLOWER

HEART-LEAVED JEWEL FLOWER

MOUNTAIN JEWEL FLOWER

BRISTLY JEWEL FLOWER

DAGGER POD

X 1/2

4-PETALED MALTESE CROSS;
ROCK CRESSES

MUSTARD FAMILY (Cruciferae)
See also pp. W 24–30; Y 140–48; O 224; R 266.

ROSE ROCK CRESS   *Arabis blepharophylla*
Broad spatula-like leaves in a basal cluster have *long distinct
individual* hairs along the margins. Giant dark rose-purple
flowers. Seedpods erect. 2–8 in. Rocky slopes near coast.
Central coast of Calif.   FEB.–APRIL

SPREADING ROCK CRESS   *Arabis divaricarpa*
The *straight seedpods* are in a spreading *nearly erect* arrangement. The lower basal leaves are lancelike and slightly hairy,
becoming narrow arrowheads on the upper stem. 1–3 ft. Dry
mt. slopes. Pacific States.   JUNE–AUG.

LEMMON'S ROCK CRESS   *Arabis lemmoni*
Seedpods are *straight* or slightly curved and held by the *curved*
pedicels at a *right angle* or nearly so. The gray leaves are in a
basal rosette. 2–8 in. Rocky alpine slopes. High mts. of Pacific
States.   JUNE–AUG.

SICKLEPOD ROCK CRESS   *Arabis sparsiflora*
The *arching sicklelike* seedpods are held horizontally from the
stem. Basal leaves lancelike with shallowly toothed margins.
Clasping arrowheadlike leaves are on the upper stem. Scattered
long hairs. Flowers pink to purple. 1–3 ft. Dry mid-altitude
slopes. Pacific States.   FEB.–JULY

HOLBOELL'S ROCK CRESS   *Arabis holboellii*
The nearly straight to curving seedpods are *strongly reflexed
downward.* Gray spatula-shaped leaves with a few teeth are in
a basal rosette. The stout stem has narrow clasping arrowhead-like leaves. Flowers pink to white. ½–3 ft. Dry rocks.
Pacific States.   MAY–AUG.

YOSEMITE ROCK CRESS   *Arabis repanda*
The gray *broadly lancelike* leaves are toothed and mostly
basal. Flowers pink to white. Pedicels strongly erect with
upward curving seedpods. ½–3 ft. Semishaded dry slopes.
Sierra Nevada south to San Jacinto Mts.   JUNE–AUG.

PIONEER ROCK CRESS   *Arabis platysperma*
Note the few *broad erect* seedpods. Mostly linear gray basal
leaves. Flowers pink to white. 4–20 in. Rocky slopes at higher
elevations. Mts. of Pacific States.   JUNE–AUG.

MESA ROCK CRESS   *Arabis glaucovalvula*
Note the numerous *broad pendulous* seedpods. Flowers pink to
white. 6–18 in. Rocky mesas. Mojave Desert.   MARCH–MAY

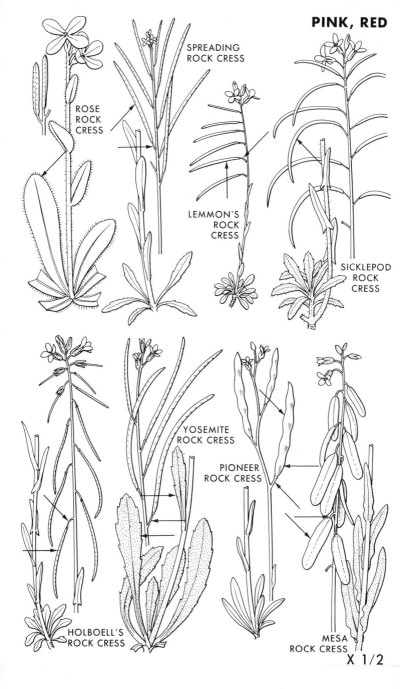

PINK, RED

ROSE ROCK CRESS

SPREADING ROCK CRESS

LEMMON'S ROCK CRESS

SICKLEPOD ROCK CRESS

HOLBOELL'S ROCK CRESS

YOSEMITE ROCK CRESS

PIONEER ROCK CRESS

MESA ROCK CRESS

X 1/2

4 SHOWY PETALS ON TOP OF OVARY

Evening Primrose Family (Onagraceae)
See also pp. W 32; Y 150–52; R 270–74.

HERALD-OF-SUMMER *Clarkia amoena*
Large pink to dark lavender petals usually have a *blotch of red* in the centers. Flower buds erect. 1–3 ft. Coastal fields. West of Cascades and s. to cen. Calif. June–Aug.

REDSPOT CLARKIA *Clarkia speciosa*
The large cream (or variously red) petals have a *bright red spot* near the white center. Buds erect. ½–2 ft. Calif. South Coast Ranges and s. Sierra Nevada foothills. May–July

WILLIAMSON'S CLARKIA *Clarkia williamsonii*
The large lavender wedge-shaped petals have a *purple spot* in the *upper half.* Buds erect. Ovary *8-ribbed.* 1–3 ft. Open fields. W. Sierra Nevada foothills. May–Aug.

RUBY CHALICE CLARKIA *Clarkia rubicunda*
The large bright rose-pink flowers have a *distinct bright red basal zone.* Ovary 4-ribbed. Buds erect. Dry open places. 1–3 ft. Point Reyes Natl. Seashore area and south along coast to San Luis Obispo, Calif. May–July

SLENDER CLARKIA *Clarkia gracilis*
The *small* (¾ in.) *vaselike* flowers completely pink to lavender. Flower buds and axis pendulous before flowering. Ovary 4-ribbed. 1–3 ft. Cen. Calif. to Wash. April–July

PUNCHBOWL CLARKIA *Clarkia deflexa*
The small *shallow punchbowl-like* flowers are on a *strictly erect stem* with *only* the buds pendulous. Ovary 4-ribbed. 1–3 ft. Calif. South Coast Ranges to Los Angeles. April–June

WINECUP CLARKIA *Clarkia purpurea*
Small cuplike flowers, each petal *fan-shaped,* solid purple or with a darker central spot. Flower buds erect. ½–2 ft. Open places. Cen. Ore., all of Calif. April–July

SPECKLED CLARKIA *Clarkia cylindrica*
The large petals are lavender-tipped, shading to a central zone with *pink flecks.* Petal bases a bright red-purple. Flower buds pendulous. Ovary 4-ribbed. ½–2 ft. Cen. Sierra Nevada foothills south to Los Angeles. April–July

DUDLEY'S CLARKIA *Clarkia dudleyana*
The oblong petals lavender-pink with *streaks of white* (½–1 in.). Ovary 8-ribbed. Pendulous flower buds. 1–2½ ft. Foothills of Sierra Nevada and south to s. Calif. May–July

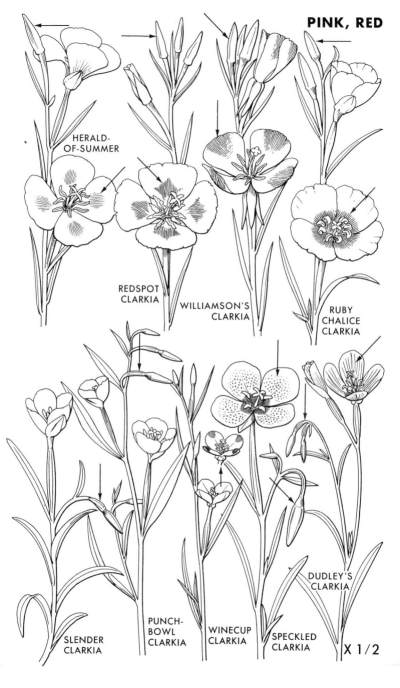

PINK, RED

HERALD-
OF-SUMMER

REDSPOT
CLARKIA

WILLIAMSON'S
CLARKIA

RUBY
CHALICE
CLARKIA

SLENDER
CLARKIA

PUNCH-
BOWL
CLARKIA

WINECUP
CLARKIA

SPECKLED
CLARKIA

DUDLEY'S
CLARKIA

X 1/2

4 SHOWY PETALS ON TOP OF OVARY

Evening Primrose Family (Onagraceae)
See also pp. W 32; Y 150–52; R 270–74.

ELEGANT CLARKIA *Clarkia unguiculata*
The pink *outer* petal lobe (with a darker red spot) *rectangular to round* on a *threadlike* base. 8 anthers. 1–3 ft. Common. Foothills of cen. and s. Calif. May–June

TONGUE CLARKIA *Clarkia rhomboidea*
The pink petal diamond-shaped with *2 rounded projections* near the red petal base. Compare with Diamond Clarkia. ½–4 ft. Open to semishaded slopes. Calif., Ore., and east of Cascades in Wash. May–July

DIAMOND CLARKIA *Clarkia modesta*
Small bright pink *diamond-shaped* petals (½ in.). Buds pendulous. 1–2½ ft. Dry slopes. Calif. Coast Ranges. Sierra Nevada foothills. April–May

BILOBED CLARKIA *Clarkia biloba*
Each pink petal tip divided into *two equal lobes*. 8 stamens. Stem erect. 1–3 ft. Dry open slopes. Foothills of w. Sierra Nevada. May–July

GUNSIGHT CLARKIA *Clarkia xantiana*
Each pink petal bilobed with a *central spinelike tooth*. A few petals in each flower purple-spotted. 8 stamens. ½–3 ft. Dry slopes. S. Sierra Nevada foothills and s. Calif. May–June

LOVELY CLARKIA *Clarkia concinna*
The bright pink petals have *3 equal lobes,* variously streaked. 4 stamens. Leaves broadly oval. 2–12 in. Open places. Calif. North Coast Ranges, n. Sierra Nevada foothills. May–July

BREWER'S CLARKIA *Clarkia breweri*
Each dark lavender 3-lobed petal has a *fingerlike central* lobe between 2 broad outer lobes. Delicious spicy fragrance. 2–8 in. Calif. South Coast Ranges. April–May

DEERHORN CLARKIA *Clarkia pulchella*
The lavender to rose-purple 3-lobed petal tip has a *broad central lobe* and 2 narrow outer ones. An opposite pair of slender sharp teeth are on the lower petal base. Leaves linear. ½–2 ft. Great Basin. May–June

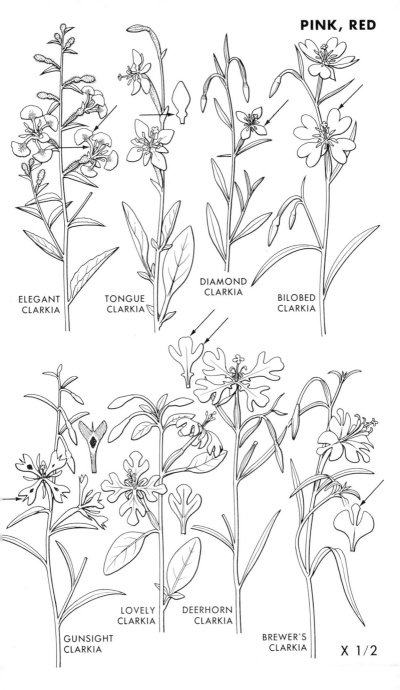

PINK, RED

ELEGANT
CLARKIA

TONGUE
CLARKIA

DIAMOND
CLARKIA

BILOBED
CLARKIA

GUNSIGHT
CLARKIA

LOVELY
CLARKIA

DEERHORN
CLARKIA

BREWER'S
CLARKIA

X 1/2

4 OR 6 PETALS ON TOP OF OVARY

EVENING PRIMROSE FAMILY (Onagraceae)
See also pp. W 32; Y 150–52; R 270–74.

RED FIREWEED   *Epilobium angustifolium*
Large bright red-purple petals have *1 round tip.* Numerous
flowers are in a long terminal spike. Alternate-leaved. 2–9 ft.
Common. Moist places. Pacific States.   JUNE–SEPT.

ROCK FRINGE   *Epilobium obcordatum*
Large red-purple petals have *bilobed tips.* Oval oppositely
arranged leaves. *Mats around* boulder bases. Alpine. Sierra
Nevada north to cen. Cascades and Blue Mts.   JULY–SEPT.

SMOOTHSTEM FIREWEED   *Epilobium glaberrimum*
Opposite paired leaves are a light *waxy blue.* Stems smooth.
1–3 ft. Wet places in mts. Pacific States.   JUNE–AUG.

PARCHED FIREWEED   *Epilobium paniculatum*
Linear leaves alternately arranged. Stem has peeling bark.
½–6 ft. Common, *dry* places. Pacific States.   JUNE–SEPT.

THREADSTEM FIREWEED   *Epilobium minutum*
Similar to preceding. Leaves *oppositely paired.* A tiny well-
branched plant in *dry places.* 1–4 in. Common. Pacific States.
                                                APRIL–AUG.

STICKY FIREWEED   *Epilobium glandulosum*
Stem minutely sticky-haired, leaves opposite. Tiny bulblike
swellings at base of stem. Tiny bilobed petals. 1–3 ft. Moist
places. Sierra Nevada to Wash.   JUNE–AUG.

WATSON'S FIREWEED   *Epilobium watsonii*
(not shown)
Similar to preceding. Stem base *without* the bulbs. 4–36 in.
Very common. Pacific States.   JUNE–SEPT.

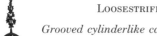

LOOSESTRIFE FAMILY (Lythraceae)

Grooved cylinderlike calyx appears like an inferior ovary.

CALIFORNIA LOOSESTRIFE   *Lythrum californicum*
Small 6-petaled (4–7) red-purple flowers are *pediceled.* Leaves
alternate. 2–6 ft. Marshes. Calif.   APRIL–OCT.

HYSSOP LOOSESTRIFE   *Lythrum hyssopifolia*
(not shown)
Similar to preceding. Small flowers *without pedicels.* Leaves
alternate. ½–2 ft. Pacific States.   APRIL–OCT.

PURPLE LOOSESTRIFE Alien   *Lythrum salicaria*
The *6 large* red-purple petals have a *wrinkled appearance.*
Leaves *opposite.* 1–6 ft. Marshes. Wash.   AUG.–SEPT.

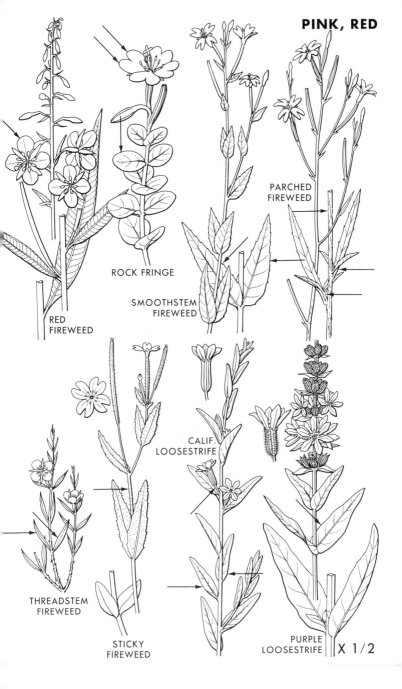

ROCK FRINGE

RED
FIREWEED

PARCHED
FIREWEED

SMOOTHSTEM
FIREWEED

CALIF.
LOOSESTRIFE

THREADSTEM
FIREWEED

STICKY
FIREWEED

PURPLE
LOOSESTRIFE

X 1/2

4 OR 6 PETALS; TINY TUBULAR
FLOWERS IN CLUSTERS

BUCKWHEAT FAMILY (Polygonaceae)
See also pp. W 34–38; Y 134–38; R 276–78.

MOUNTAIN SORREL *Oxyria digyna*
Note the bright green *kidney-shaped* leaves, mostly basal.
Many small red to yellow-green flowers in a spike. 2–10 in.
Common. Rocky alpine slopes. Pacific States. JULY–SEPT.

SHEEP SORREL Alien *Rumex acetosella*
Note the *slim arrowhead-like* dark green fleshy leaves which
are mostly near the stem base. Tiny red-yellow flowers are in
a loose terminal raceme. 4–16 in. Very common. Disturbed
places. Pacific States. MARCH–AUG.

DESERT RHUBARB *Rumex hymenosepalus*
Note the *very large* oblong leaves (4–12 in.). Stems are in dense
clumps. Tiny pink flowers are in terminal racemes. Each of the
heartlike red-brown seeds has flat finlike membranes around
the seed. 2–4 ft. Common. Sandy places; most common on
deserts. All s. Calif. JAN.–MAY

CURLY DOCK Alien *Rumex crispus*
The lower leaves lancelike with *curly margins.* Tiny red flowers
in dense clusters. The tiny red-brown seeds heart-shaped.
2–4 ft. Common. Pacific States. ALL YEAR

WATER SMARTWEED *Polygonum coccineum*
Large *oval* leaves (2–6 in. long). Smooth-edged papery sheaths
are at each stem joint. Stem erect to floating. A dense terminal
cluster of pink flowers are on a leafless stem. *P. amphibium* is
now included in this species. 1–2 ft. Ponds or nearly dry
ground. Pacific States. JUNE–SEPT.

WHORLED DOCK Alien *Rumex conglomeratus*
Note the *whorls* of tiny red flowers which soon become red-
brown seeds. Lower leaves oblong. 1–2 ft. Disturbed places.
Common. Pacific States. MAY–SEPT.

YARD KNOTWEED Alien *Polygonum aviculare*
The small sprawling *wiry* stems have numerous *tiny blue-green*
lancelike leaves with silvery bracts at their bases. Tiny pink,
green, or white flowers. 1–2 ft. Very common. Pacific States.
ALL YEAR

LADYS THUMB Alien *Polygonum persicaria*
The papery stem bracts *fringed.* The erect stems have lancelike
leaves and dense *pink thumblike* flower clusters. 1–5 ft. Common. Moist places. Pacific States. MARCH–NOV.

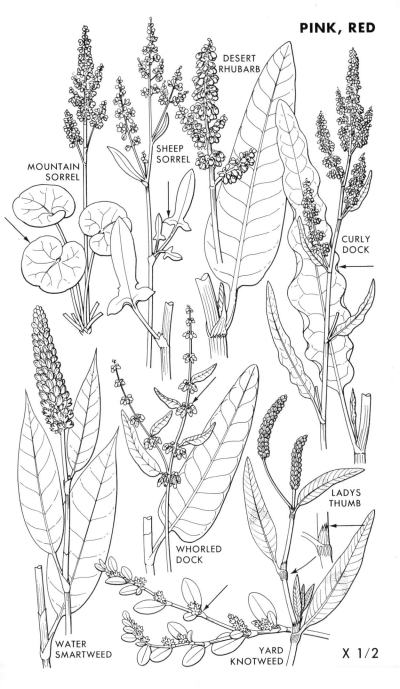

PINK, RED

MOUNTAIN
SORREL

SHEEP
SORREL

DESERT
RHUBARB

CURLY
DOCK

WATER
SMARTWEED

WHORLED
DOCK

LADYS
THUMB

YARD
KNOTWEED

X 1/2

4 OR 6 PETALS; TINY TUBULAR FLOWERS IN CLUSTERS

BUCKWHEAT FAMILY (Polygonaceae)
See also pp. W 34–38; Y 134–38; R 276–78.

ANGLESTEM ERIOGONUM   *Eriogonum angulosum*
The erect *angled stem* white-haired. Basal leaves broadly *lancelike with wavy* margins. Flower clusters are in a broad bowl of *rounded* bracts. Each flower rose and white. 4–12 in. Sandy soils. Calif. and Great Basin.   JUNE–JULY

OVAL-LEAVED ERIOGONUM   *Eriogonum ovalifolium*
A dense *basal mat* of tiny, white-woolly, egg-shaped leaves. Flower stems protruding above in round heads of pink, white, or yellow flowers. 4–8 in. Desert slopes to alpine. Mts. of Pacific States.   MAY–JULY

NAKED ERIOGONUM   *Eriogonum nudum*
Tall *naked* stems. A flat basal cluster of dark green oval leaves with clumps of woolly hair on long petioles. Flower cluster bracts oblong. Flowers pink (or white, yellow). ½–3 ft. Very common. Pacific States.   MAY–NOV.

FLAT-CROWNED ERIOGONUM   *Eriogonum deflexum*
Flower clusters *hang upside down.* The felt-haired basal leaves kidney-shaped to round. ½–2½ ft. Common. Rocky slopes. Deserts from se. Ore. to Baja.   MAY–OCT.

PARISH'S THREADSTEM ERIOGONUM
          Eriogonum parishii
A mound of numerous *minute* pink flowers on *long threadlike* pedicels. Leaves round gray-haired blades on long petioles. S. Sierra Nevada through mts. to Baja.   JULY–SEPT.

WICKER-STEMMED ERIOGONUM   *Eriogonum vimineum*
Erect red wicker-like stems have *hugging elongated cylinders* with clusters of pink (or white, yellow) flowers. Rounded basal leaves. Great Basin. All Calif.   APRIL–OCT.

THURBER'S ERIOGONUM   *Eriogonum thurberi*
A tiny wad of cotton is at the base of each squared petal. Oblong leaves are in a basal cluster, upper surface green, underside white, feltlike. 4–12 in. S. Calif.   APRIL–JULY

CLUSTERED SPINEFLOWER *Chorizanthe membranacea*
Each flower *umbrellalike* with 6 long hooked spines. 4–16 in. Rocky places. Cen. Calif.   APRIL–JULY

FRINGED SPINEFLOWER   *Chorizanthe fimbriata*
Each of the 6 red-pink flower lobes *fringed with bristles.* Tiny treelike plant. S. Calif. foothills.   APRIL–JUNE

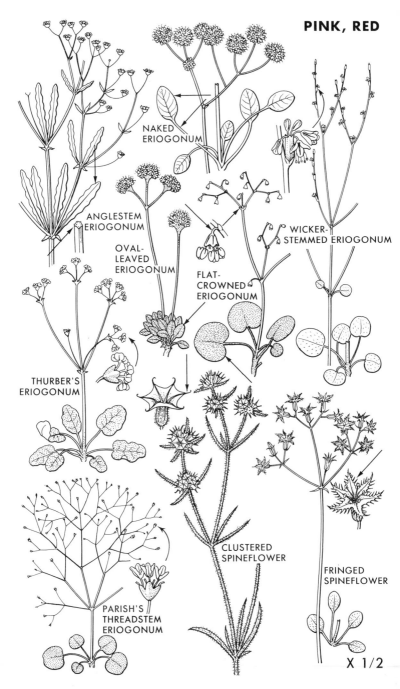

PINK, RED

NAKED
ERIOGONUM

ANGLESTEM
ERIOGONUM

WICKER-
STEMMED ERIOGONUM

OVAL-
LEAVED
ERIOGONUM

FLAT-
CROWNED
ERIOGONUM

THURBER'S
ERIOGONUM

PARISH'S
THREADSTEM
ERIOGONUM

CLUSTERED
SPINEFLOWER

FRINGED
SPINEFLOWER

X 1/2

4 OR 5 PETALS;
SPURS OR FLAT FLOWERS

Buttercup Family (Ranunculaceae)
See also pp. W 40–42; Y 154–58; O 226;
R 280–82; B 354–56, 382; G 404.

SCARLET DELPHINIUM *Delphinium cardinale*
Each leaf is divided into 5 *narrowly twisted* divisions. The *single spurred* flowers are scarlet with 2 upper yellow petals. Compare with Cañon Delphinium (p. 226) to avoid confusion. Calif. South Coast Ranges to Baja. May–July

CRIMSON COLUMBINE *Aquilegia formosa*
Note the *5-spurred nodding* red flowers with some yellow well above the 3-lobed pinnate leaves. 1–4 ft. Moist shady woods and streamsides. Pacific States. April–Aug.

Bleeding Heart Family (Fumariaceae)
See also pp. W 42; Y 158.

BLEEDING HEARTS *Dicentra formosa*
The flattened *heart-shaped* rose-pink flowers are in nodding clusters above lacy pinnate leaves. Occasional white flowered plants are to be expected. West of Cascades–Sierra Nevada crest. March–July

LONGHORN STEERSHEAD *Dicentra uniflora*
Note the flattened steershead-like petals and the *2 long* reflexed sepals which give the flower a Texas Longhorn appearance. A single pinnate leaf with 1–3 sections divided into broad lobes. 1–3 in. Very common, gravelly forest floors; mts. Sierra Nevada to Wash. and Great Basin. Feb.–June

SHORTHORN STEERSHEAD *Dicentra pauciflora*
The flattened steershead flower has *2 short* reflexed sepals, resembling a shorthorn steer. A single pinnate leaf with numerous narrow lobes. 1–3 in. Gravelly forest floors from mid-mt. elevations to alpine. Siskiyous south through Sierra Nevada. June–July

SCOULER'S CORYDALIS *Corydalis scouleri*
The 15–35 single-spurred pink flowers have the pedicel attached in the center. The waxy blue pinnate leaves have *long lancelike* leaflets. 2–4 ft. Moist shady woods. West of Cascades in Ore. April–July

SIERRA CORYDALIS *Corydalis caseana*
The waxy blue pinnate leaves have *numerous short oval* lobes. The 50 or more single-spurred pink to white flowers have purple tips and the spur is ⅔ longer than front portion from point of pedicel attachment. 2–3 ft. Shady moist places. N. Sierra Nevada to ne. Ore. June–Aug.

280

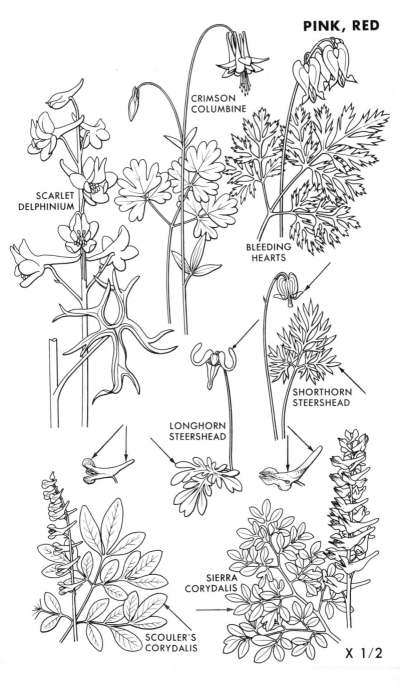

PINK, RED

CRIMSON COLUMBINE

SCARLET DELPHINIUM

BLEEDING HEARTS

SHORTHORN STEERSHEAD

LONGHORN STEERSHEAD

SCOULER'S CORYDALIS

SIERRA CORYDALIS

X 1/2

5 TO MANY PETALS VARIOUSLY ARRANGED

PINK FAMILY (Caryophyllaceae)
See also pp. W 54–60; R 246.

STICKY SAND SPURRY *Spergularia macrotheca*
The *leaves, stems, and sepals* covered by numerous long gray *glandular hairs.* Stems sprawling. 4–20 in. Common in salt marshes and alkali sinks. Pacific States. ALL YEAR

MARSH SAND SPURRY Alien *Spergularia media*
All plant parts *smooth* or rarely with very tiny, non-sticky, thornlike hairs. Seed capsules *hang downward.* Bright yellow-green fleshy linear leaves are usually in pairs. 2–12 in. Frequent along coast. Pacific States. ALL YEAR

RUBY SAND SPURRY Alien *Spergularia rubra*
The tiny linear leaves ($\frac{1}{2}$ in.) are in *dense whorls* with *large* papery bracts. *Only the sepals* glandular. 6–12 in. Very common in gardens, etc. Pacific States. ALL YEAR

WILD CARNATION Alien *Tunica prolifera*
The erect *wiry grasslike stem* has 2–3 pairs of papery bracts below the terminal clusters of red-pink *carnationlike* flowers. Usually in great masses. 1–2 ft. Woodlands. N. Sierra Nevada foothills. MAY–JUNE

REDWOOD SORREL *Oxalis oregana*
WOOD SORREL FAMILY See also p. Y 164. (Oxalidaceae)
Note the *3 cloverlike* leaves and the solitary pink upright funnel-like flowers. 2–12 in. Moist redwood and douglas fir forests along coast. Cen. Calif. to Wash. FEB.–SEPT.

SEATHRIFT *Armeria maritima*
LEADWORT FAMILY (Plumbaginaceae)
Note the dense *onionlike* umbel of pink flowers on a long leafless stem. Linear grasslike leaves. 2–20 in. Coastal beaches and bluffs. Pacific Coast. MARCH–AUG.

BUTTERCUP FAMILY (Ranunculaceae)
See also pp. W 40–42; Y 154–58; O 226; R 280–82;
B 354–56, 382; G 404.
The *Paeonias* are placed in the family Paeoniaceae by some botanists.

WESTERN PEONY *Paeonia brownii*
Note the hanging dark maroon flowers below the fleshy waxy-blue pinnate leaves. $\frac{1}{2}$–$1\frac{1}{2}$ ft. Mt. slopes. Cascades–Sierra Nevada and east in Great Basin. APRIL–JULY

CALIFORNIA PEONY (not shown) *Paeonia californica*
Similar to preceding. Calif. South Coast Ranges.
JAN.–MARCH

DESERT ANEMONE *Anemone tuberosa*
Cylinderlike seedheads. Light pink upright flowers. Leaves pinnate. 4–12 in. Frequent on Calif. deserts. MARCH–MAY

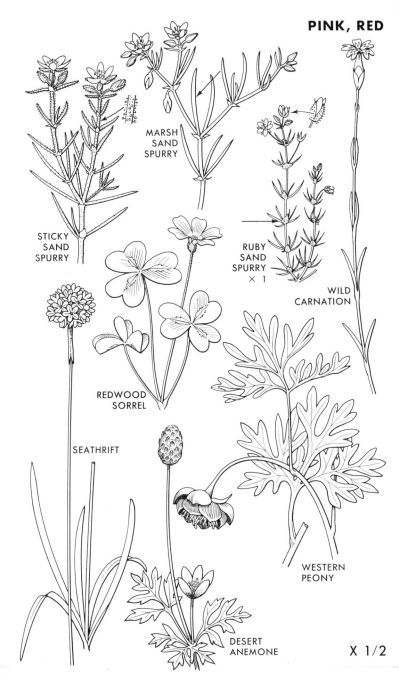

PINK, RED

STICKY SAND SPURRY

MARSH SAND SPURRY

RUBY SAND SPURRY × 1

WILD CARNATION

REDWOOD SORREL

SEATHRIFT

WESTERN PEONY

DESERT ANEMONE

X 1/2

5 DELICATE PETALS; LONG BEAKLIKE OVARY; GERANIUMS

GERANIUM FAMILY (Geraniaceae)
See also p. R 286.

CAROLINA GERANIUM *Geranium carolinianum*
Beaklike style *tips yellow-green* ending in a *short* tapering neck. The tiny flowers are on short pedicels and are in compact clusters. Sepals awn-tipped, petals notched. Leaves deeply 5-cleft and round-tipped. 8–16 in. Common. Pacific States.
MOST OF YEAR

CUT-LEAVED GERANIUM Alien *Geranium dissectum*
Similar to Carolina Geranium. Beaklike style *tips purple,* ending in a slender elongated constricted beak, densely haired. Leaves narrowly lobed and *sharp pointed.* Flower cluster loose. 1–2 ft. Common. Pacific States.
ALL YEAR

DOVES-FOOT GERANIUM Alien *Geranium molle*
A low, nearly prostrate, tiny-flowered species. Sepals *awnless,* petals notched. Leaves relatively *rounded* with only short blunt lobes. Seedpod stems *reflexed.* 3–8 in. Waste places, lawns. Common. Pacific States.
APRIL–SEPT.

OREGON GERANIUM *Geranium oreganum*
The large *rounded* petal lobes are *hairless on the inner* surface except for a very few at base. Upper stem leaves have 5–7 segments in a semicircle, lowermost leaves very narrowly lobed and in a complete circle. 1½–2 ½ ft. Meadows, woods. West of Cascades and south to ne. Calif.
MAY–AUG.

CALIFORNIA GERANIUM *Geranium californicum*
Stem hairs tipped with *yellow glands.* The large rounded petals (½ in.) are pale pink with dark red-purple veins and hairy on lower ½ of inner surface. Leaves 3- to 7-parted, compact, broad lobes. ½–2 ft. Moist mt. woods, meadows. Sierra Nevada from Yosemite south to San Diego Co.
JUNE–JULY

RICHARDSON'S GERANIUM *Geranium richardsonii*
Stem hairs tipped with *red glands.* The large rounded petals (¾ in.) are pale pink with purple veins. Leaves have 5–7 narrow segments with pointed lobes. 1–3 ft. Moist mt. meadows. East side of Cascades–Sierra Nevada.
JUNE–AUG.

STICKY GERANIUM *Geranium viscosissimum*
The large rounded petals have dark veins and a *downy nest* of hairs on lower ¼ of inner surface. The stout stems have very conspicuous *downy*-haired leaves with 5–7 broad, deeply parted segments in a complete circle. 1–2½ ft. Woods, meadows. East side of Cascades, Wash. to n. Calif.
MAY–AUG.

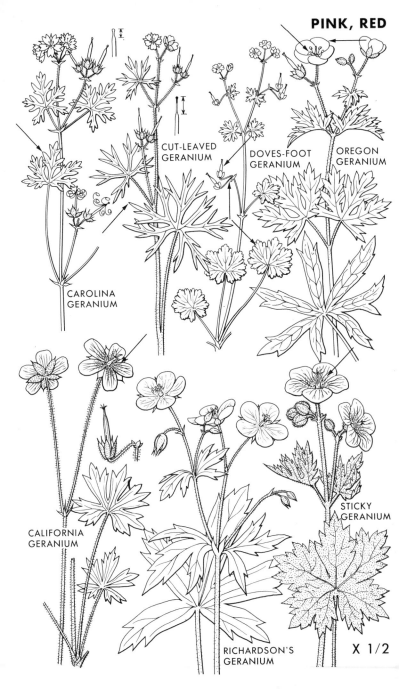

PINK, RED

CUT-LEAVED
GERANIUM

DOVES-FOOT
GERANIUM

OREGON
GERANIUM

CAROLINA
GERANIUM

CALIFORNIA
GERANIUM

STICKY
GERANIUM

RICHARDSON'S
GERANIUM

X 1/2

5 DELICATE PETALS; LONG BEAKLIKE OVARY OR CENTRAL COLUMN OF STAMENS

GERANIUM FAMILY (Geraniaceae)
See also p. R 284.

REDSTEM STORKSBILL Alien   *Erodium cicutarium*
Leaves *twice pinnate* into narrow sharp-pointed lobes. The long beaked seeds (¾–2 in.) coil when dry. Red stems are in prostrate rosettes. Small delicate rose petals. Pastures, disturbed places. Very common. Pacific States.   FEB.–MAY

WHITESTEM STORKSBILL Alien   *Erodium moschatum*
The pinnate leaves have *individual* oval leaflets in slightly unequal pairs. Seedpods relatively short. Calif.   FEB.–MAY

LONG-BEAKED STORKSBILL Alien   *Erodium botrys*
The elongated leaves have the lobes joined into a *central leaf blade area.* Seedbeak to 4 in. Calif.   MARCH–MAY

TEXAS STORKSBILL   *Erodium texanum*
Leaves *trilobed* with a *longer middle lobe.* Very large flowers (½–1 in.). Dry sandy places. ½–2 ft. Mojave, Colorado Deserts.   FEB.–MAY

ROUNDLEAF STORKSBILL   *Erodium macrophyllum*
Leaves *rounded.* Tiny flowers rose-pink to white with short beaks. 4–12 in. Calif. Coast Ranges and Central Valley of Calif.   MARCH–MAY

MALLOW FAMILY (Malvaceae)
See also pp. W 44; R 286–90.

DESERT HOLLYHOCK   *Sphaeralcea ambigua*
Note the *gray maplelike* leaves which are about *as wide as long.* Each globelike, red-orange to deep pink flower has the stamens formed into a central column. 2–5 ft. Common. Dry slopes, washes. Mojave, Colorado Deserts.   MARCH–JUNE

EMORY'S GLOBEMALLOW   *Sphaeralcea emoryi*
Similar to Desert Hollyhock. The *gray* leaves somewhat *arrowheadlike, longer* than wide. 1–3 ft. Mojave, Colorado Deserts.   MARCH–JUNE

MUNROE'S GLOBEMALLOW   *Sphaeralcea munroana*
Similar to Desert Hollyhock. Leaves *bright green,* slightly longer than wide and 5-cornered. 2–3 ft. Great Basin.   MAY–JULY

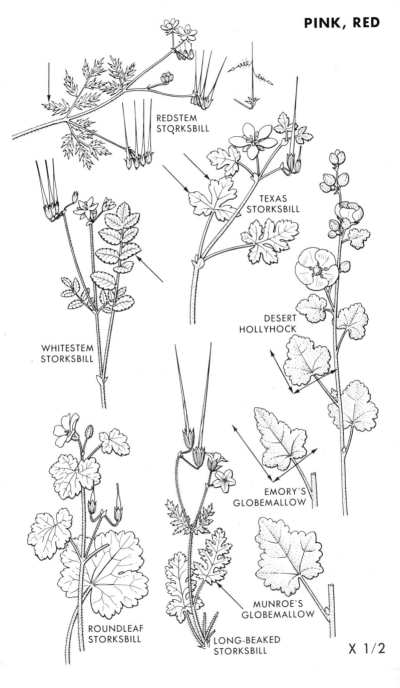

PINK, RED

REDSTEM STORKSBILL

TEXAS STORKSBILL

WHITESTEM STORKSBILL

DESERT HOLLYHOCK

EMORY'S GLOBEMALLOW

ROUNDLEAF STORKSBILL

MUNROE'S GLOBEMALLOW

LONG-BEAKED STORKSBILL

X 1/2

5 HOLLYHOCK-LIKE PETALS AND LONG CENTRAL COLUMN OF NUMEROUS STAMENS

MALLOW FAMILY (Malvaceae)
See also pp. W 44; R 286–90.

DESERT FIVESPOT *Malvastrum rotundifolium*
Note the large (1 in.) globe-shaped rose-pink flowers have a large *dark red spot* at the base of each petal. Leaves rounded. Stems erect. Stigma tips round-headed. 4–20 in. Common, flats. Mojave, Colorado Deserts. MARCH–MAY

PARRY'S MALLOW *Malvastrum parryi*
Open bowl-like pink flowers on *long pedicels*. Leaves cleft. Stigma tips round. 4–18 in. S. Central Valley of Calif.
MARCH–MAY

TRAILING MALLOW *Malvastrum exile*
Small (¼ in.) pale pink or white flowers along a *trailing* stem. Leaves trilobed. Stigma tips round headed. 4–18 in. Sandy flats. Mojave, Colorado Deserts. MARCH–MAY

WHEEL MALLOW Alien *Modiola caroliniana*
A *single,* nearly flat, *wheel-like* dull red flower (¼ in.) is above each maplelike leaf. Prostrate stems. Stigma tips round-headed. 1–2 ft. Waste places. Calif. APRIL–SEPT.

MOUNTAIN GLOBEMALLOW *Iliamna rivularis*
Note the *large maplelike* leaves. Flowers lavender to pink, in clusters. Stigma tips round-headed. 3–6 ft. East side of Cascades, B.C. to Ore. and Great Basin. JUNE–AUG.

UMBRELLA MALLOW Alien *Malva neglecta*
The small (½ in.) pale pink flowers have petals *longer than the sepals*. Dark green umbrellalike leaves. Stigma tips linear. ½–2 ft. Common. Pacific States. MAY–OCT.

CHEESE WEED Alien *Malva parviflora*
The tiny (¼ in.) pink to white flowers have very short petals which are the *same length as the sepals*. Leaves have 5 broad rounded lobes. Stigma tips linear. 1–3 ft. Common. Pacific States. ALL YEAR

HIGH MALLOW Alien *Malva sylvestris*
Large (1 in.) dark-veined rose-purple flowers. Leaves have 5–7 sharply pointed triangular lobes. Stem erect. Stigma tips linear. 1–4 ft. Mostly west of Cascades. MAY–SEPT.

MUSK MALLOW Alien *Malva moschata*
The very large (2 in.) flowers pink. Leaves deeply *divided into intricate* linear lobes. 1–2 ft. Roadsides, fairly common. West of Cascades, Ore. to Wash. MAY–JULY

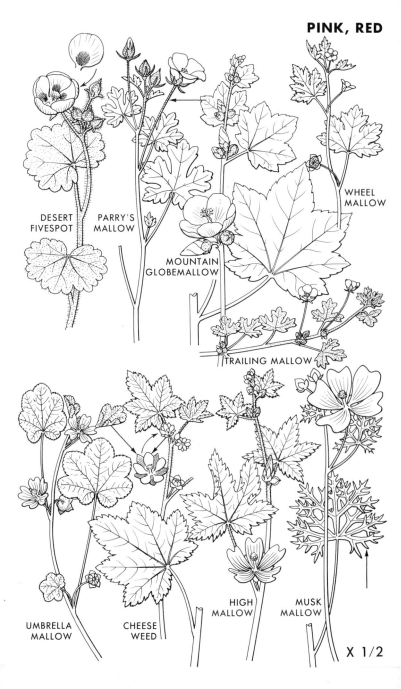

DESERT
FIVESPOT

PARRY'S
MALLOW

MOUNTAIN
GLOBEMALLOW

WHEEL
MALLOW

TRAILING MALLOW

UMBRELLA
MALLOW

CHEESE
WEED

HIGH
MALLOW

MUSK
MALLOW

X 1/2

5 HOLLYHOCK-LIKE PETALS AND LONG CENTRAL COLUMN OF NUMEROUS STAMENS

Mallow Family (Malvaceae)
See also pp. W 44; R 286–90.

FRINGED SIDALCEA *Sidalcea diploscypha*
The bract below each leaf or stem branch divided into long *linear fringes*. The pink flowers have dark red petal bases (rarely without). ½–2 ft. Dry open fields. W. Sierra Nevada foothills and Calif. Coast Ranges. APRIL–JUNE

HARTWEG'S SIDALCEA *Sidalcea hartwegii*
The flower bract is *undivided and very short*. The single slender grasslike stems have the leaves completely divided into a few linear lobes, lower leaves with lobed tips. ½–1 ft. Common as masses in open fields. Calif. Coast Ranges and w. Sierra Nevada foothills. MARCH–JUNE

CHECKER-BLOOM *Sidalcea malvaeflora*
Leaves *rounded* with 7–9 *very shallow lobes*. The *prominently white veined* petals of the pink to red-purple flower are in an elongated raceme. Stems sprawling. ½–2 ft. Common. Grassy slopes at low elevations. Calif. Coast Ranges and rarely in Sierra Nevada foothills. MARCH–JUNE

WAXY SIDALCEA *Sidalcea glaucescens*
Similar to Checker Bloom. Leaves waxy and deeply divided into 5 linear round-tipped lobes. Petals white-veined. 1–3 ft. 3000–11,000 ft. altitudes. Sierra Nevada and n. Calif. MAY–JULY

NEW MEXICO SIDALCEA *Sidalcea neomexicana*
The upper leaves have 5–9 linear lobes, while the basal ones are rounded with shallow lobes. The rose-colored flowers are on pedicels *as long as or longer than* the calyx. ½–3 ft. Moist mt. meadows. Great Basin. APRIL–JUNE

MEADOW SIDALCEA Alien *Sidalcea campestris*
The dark green leaves have *narrow sharp-pointed* segments. 2–6 ft. Damp fields. Willamette Valley, Ore. MAY–JULY

NELSON'S SIDALCEA *Sidalcea nelsoniana*
Flowers small (½ in.). Uppermost stem leaf *pitchfork-like*. Lowermost leaves semicircles. 1–3 ft. Well drained banks. Willamette Valley, Ore. MAY–JULY

OREGON SIDALCEA *Sidalcea oregana*
Note the *dense spikelike cluster* of pale to deep pink flowers and the shallowly 5- to 7-lobed basal leaves. The upper leaves are usually deeply lobed. ½–5 ft. Common in dry places. Calif. North Coast Ranges, all Ore. and Wash. JUNE–AUG.

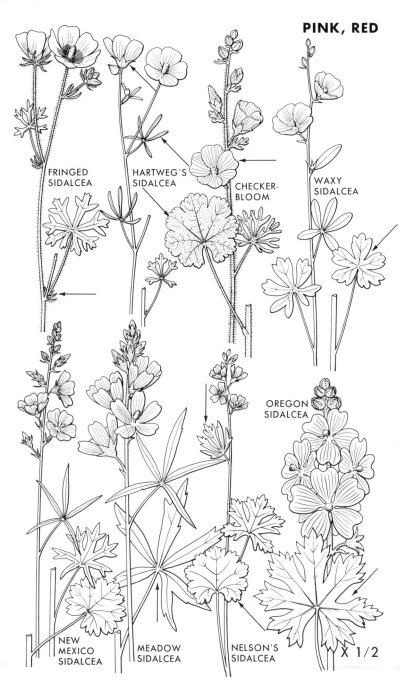

PINK, RED

FRINGED SIDALCEA

HARTWEG'S SIDALCEA

CHECKER-BLOOM

WAXY SIDALCEA

OREGON SIDALCEA

NEW MEXICO SIDALCEA

MEADOW SIDALCEA

NELSON'S SIDALCEA

X 1/2

5 TO MANY PETALS AND 2 SEPALS
LEAVES OFTEN FLESHY AND SMOOTH

PURSLANE FAMILY (Portulacaceae)
See also pp. O 226; R 294.

CANTELOW'S LEWISIA   *Lewisia cantelowii*
The tonguelike leaves with *toothed margins* are in a basal
rosette below the much branched and leafless flower stem.
Many small (¼ in.) pink flowers with deep pink veins.
½–1½ ft. Rocky cliffs in the deep western river canyons of the
n. Sierra Nevada.   MAY–JUNE

COLUMBIA LEWISIA   *Lewisia columbiana*
The *smooth-edged linear* leaves are in a flat basal rosette.
Flowers 6- to 9-petaled, pink with dark red lines. Rocky ledges.
Cascades, coast mts. of B.C. to n. Calif.; ne. Ore. MAY–AUG.

SOUTHWESTERN LEWISIA   *Lewisia brachycalyx*
The large, pale pink flowers with red lines are *nestled* in the flat
rosette of smooth, broadly linear leaves. 1–3 in. Rocky
meadows above 4500 ft. S. Calif. Mts.   MAY–JUNE

THREE-LEAF LEWISIA   *Lewisia triphylla*
Note the *3 long linear leaves* immediately below the small
flowers; otherwise leafless. 1–4 in. Often in masses, damp sandy
soils of semiopen conifer forests. Sierra Nevada north to all mt.
ranges of Ore. and Wash.   MAY–AUG.

BITTERROOT   *Lewisia rediviva*
Note the *very large* (2–3 in.) pink (or white) flowers have
numerous petals which nearly hide the linear, tufted, fleshy
leaves. State flower of Montana. 1–4 in. Open rocky flats.
W. cen. Calif., Great Basin.   MARCH–JULY

DWARF LEWISIA   *Lewisia pygmaea*
Many round linear leaves are in a tuft with the tiny pink to
white flowers in amongst the leaves. 1–3 in. Damp sand in
alpine zone. High mts. of Pacific States.   MAY–SEPT.

LEE'S LEWISIA   *Lewisia leana*
Round *linear* leaves are in a basal cluster. 6–8 pale red petals
with red veins. Rocky cliffs 6000–10,000 ft. Siskiyous; Fresno
Co. in Sierra Nevada.   JULY–AUG.

SISKIYOU LEWISIA   *Lewisia cotyledon*
The large (1 in.) *striking red-striped* petals (8–10) are white or
pink. *Spoon-shaped* leaves are in a basal tuft below the much
branched and leafless flower stems. 4–12 in. Rocky ledges
3000–9000 ft. Siskiyous.   APRIL–JULY

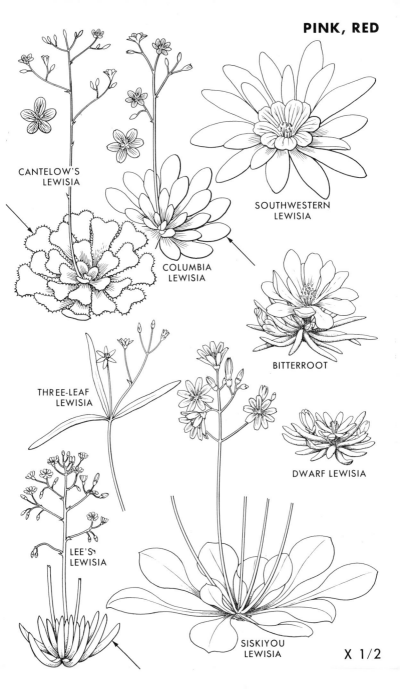

CANTELOW'S
LEWISIA

COLUMBIA
LEWISIA

SOUTHWESTERN
LEWISIA

BITTERROOT

THREE-LEAF
LEWISIA

LEE'S
LEWISIA

DWARF LEWISIA

SISKIYOU
LEWISIA

X 1/2

5 TO MANY PETALS AND 2 SEPALS
LEAVES OFTEN FLESHY AND SMOOTH

PURSLANE FAMILY (Portulacaceae)
See also pp. O 226; R 292.

WESTERN SPRING BEAUTY   *Claytonia lanceolata*
One opposite pair of dark green *lancelike leaves without peti-oles*. Flower light pink. Petal tips notched. 2–6 in. Moist woods and openings. Pacific States.   APRIL–JULY

SIERRA SPRING BEAUTY   *Claytonia nevadensis*
The fleshy dark green *oval to round* leaves are *long-petioled*. The pale pink petals round-tipped. 1–4 in. Wet alpine slopes. Cen. Sierra Nevada.   JULY–AUG.

CHAMISSO'S MONTIA   *Montia chamissoi*
Stems have *several opposite pairs* of fleshy lancelike leaves, and runner branches that bear bulblets. Flowers pink to white. 2–6 in. Wet places. Pacific States mts.   MAY–AUG.

MINER'S LETTUCE   *Montia perfoliata*
Fleshy green *umbrellalike* leaves have clusters of pale pink flowers appearing to rise from the top. 4–12 in. Very common. Shaded moist places. Pacific States.   JAN.–JULY

LINEAR MONTIA   *Montia spathulata*
The tufted erect stem has an opposite pair of fleshy *linear* to spatula-like leaves. Pale pink *bilobed* petal tips. 1–2 in. Open dry slopes. Foothills. Pacific States.   FEB.–JULY

SIBERIAN CANDYFLOWER   *Montia sibirica*
Broad oval opposite-paired stem leaves are without petioles. Lower leaves broad spoons. ½–2 ft. Moist woods. Mts. of cen. Calif. to B.C. and Great Basin.   MARCH–SEPT.

LITTLELEAF MONTIA   *Montia parvifolia*
Leaves *alternately* arranged. Numerous *side-branching* flower stems rise from *small rosettes of tiny* fleshy spoon-shaped leaves. Plants connected by runners. ½–1 ft. Wet rocks. Mts. of cen. Calif. to B.C., and Great Basin.   MAY–AUG.

RED MAIDS Alien   *Calandrinia ciliata*
Petals *bright red and round*-tipped. Sepal edges *hairy-margined*. 2–24 in. Very common. Pacific States.

FEB.–MAY

PUSSY PAWS   *Calyptridium umbellatum*
The *flat clusters* of dark green spatula-like leaves have many prostrate red stems *radiating* beyond with dense rose-pink or white *pussy paw–like* terminal clusters. 2–10 in. Common. Open mt. flats. Calif. to B.C.   MAY–AUG.

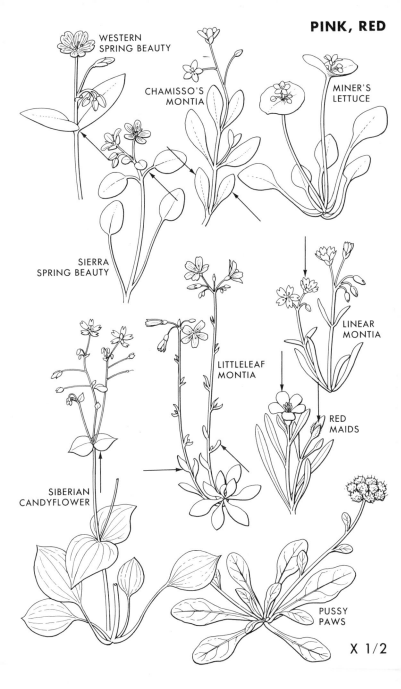

PINK, RED

WESTERN
SPRING BEAUTY

CHAMISSO'S
MONTIA

MINER'S
LETTUCE

SIERRA
SPRING BEAUTY

LINEAR
MONTIA

LITTLELEAF
MONTIA

RED
MAIDS

SIBERIAN
CANDYFLOWER

PUSSY
PAWS

X 1/2

5-PETALED WAXY NODDING FLOWERS, URNLIKE OR CROWNLIKE

WINTERGREEN FAMILY (Pyrolaceae)
See also pp. W 46–48.

SUGARSTICK *Allotropa virgata*
The single erect stem has *red and white stripes* that resemble a candystick. The urnlike white flowers have red stamens. A saprophyte, this plant obtains its nutrition from decaying humus. ½–2 ft. Shady conifer woods with deep humus. Cen. Calif. to B.C. MAY–AUG.

PINE-DROPS *Pterospora andromedea*
The red to white, urnlike flowers are pendulous and loosely scattered on single completely red stems. 1–3 ft. Frequent in dry shady conifer woods. A saprophyte. Pacific States.
JUNE–AUG.

SNOW PLANT *Sarcodes sanguinea*
The bright red urn-shaped flowers are in a fleshy *Christmas tree–like spike*. The plant is a saprophyte. Flowers immediately as snow clears from the forest floor. Uncommon — do not pick. 4–12 in. Shady conifer forests with deep humus. Mts. Calif. to s. Ore., and Nevada. MAY–JULY

BOG WINTERGREEN *Pyrola asarifolia*
The large *rounded* leathery leaves are in a basal cluster. The pale pink to dark red flowers have the style off to one side. Flowers nodding along an elongated raceme. ½–1½ ft. Moist woods. Mts. of Pacific States. JUNE–SEPT.

WESTERN PRINCES PINE *Chimaphila umbellata*
The *lancelike* dark green leathery leaves have a spiny toothed margin and are arranged in *whorls* below the nodding *crownlike* pink to red flowers. 10 stamens. 4–12 in. Frequent, dry conifer woods. Pacific States. JUNE–AUG.

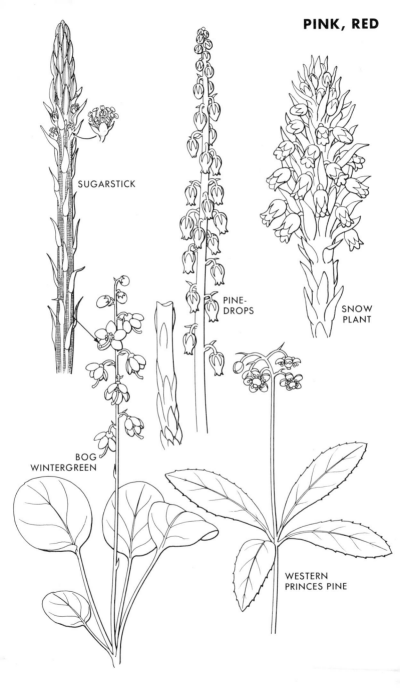

SUGARSTICK

PINE-
DROPS

SNOW
PLANT

BOG
WINTERGREEN

WESTERN
PRINCES PINE

5 PETALS; FLOWERS IN UMBEL CLUSTER OR CYME; THICK MILKY SAP

DOGBANE FAMILY (Apocynaceae)
See also p. B 382.

CYCLADENIA *Cycladenia humilis*
The sprawling stem has 2–3 pairs of *thick oval* leaves and 1–5 rose-purple funnel-shaped flowers. 4–8 in. Volcanic soils. Calif. Coast Ranges, n. Sierra Nevada. MAY–JULY

INDIAN HEMP *Apocynum cannabinum*
The erect stem has *ascending* pairs of long broad lancelike leaves. The small bell-like flowers are in scattered cymes along the stem, pink to white. Damp flats below 5000 ft. Pacific States. JUNE–SEPT.

SPREADING DOGBANE *Apocynum androsaemifolium*
Note the *drooping* pairs of oval leaves and the terminal cymes of small, pink to white, bell-shaped flowers. ½–2 ft. Frequent, mt. slopes. Pacific States. JUNE–SEPT.

MILKWEED FAMILY (Asclepiadaceae)
See also p. W 62.

CALIFORNIA MILKWEED *Asclepias californica*
Large opposite pairs of white *velvety-haired* oval leaves. Flowers *dark maroon*. Rounded saclike hoods. ½–3 ft. Dry slopes. S. Sierra Nevada foothills and Calif. South Coast Ranges to Baja. APRIL–JULY

PURPLE MILKWEED *Asclepias cordifolia*
The stem *and* loose umbel of flowers are *both red-purple*. The smooth stem and leaves are a *waxy blue*. 1–3 ft. Frequent on dry semiopen forest slopes. Cen. Calif. to s. Ore. MAY–JULY

SHOWY MILKWEED *Asclepias speciosa*
Note the long *curving toothlike hoods*, pink or creamy. A curved horn is exserted toward the central column from the cupped hood. White velvety leaves are oval to oblong in opposite pairs. 1–4 ft. Calif. and Great Basin. MAY–AUG.

SOLANOA MILKWEED *Asclepias solanoana*
Note the *round balls* of red-purple flowers on a *trailing* stem that hugs the ground. The opposite-paired, feltlike leaves are broadly heart-shaped. 1–2 ft. Open blue-green serpentine soils. Calif. North Coast Ranges. JUNE

FRINGED MILKVINE *Sarcostemma cynanchoides*
The purple petal edges *hairy*. The slim arrowhead-shaped leaves are in opposite pairs along a climbing vine. Common. Dry places in valleys of s. Calif. and deserts. APRIL–JULY

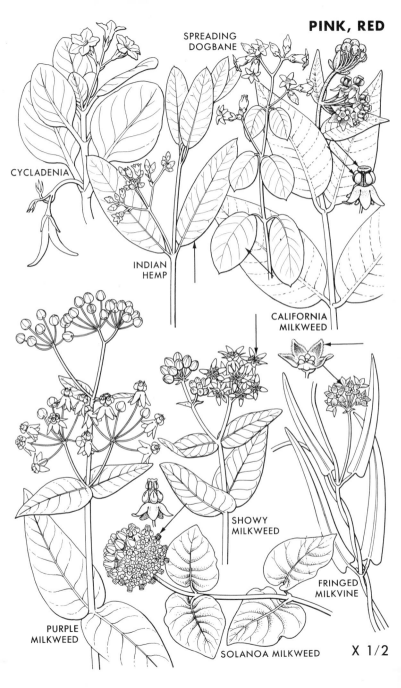

PINK, RED

SPREADING DOGBANE

CYCLADENIA

INDIAN HEMP

CALIFORNIA MILKWEED

SHOWY MILKWEED

FRINGED MILKVINE

PURPLE MILKWEED

SOLANOA MILKWEED

X 1/2

3–5 LOBED, TUBULAR FLOWERS IN UMBELS WITH LARGE BRACTS

FOUR O'CLOCK FAMILY (Nyctaginaceae)
See also pp. W 100; Y 120.

COAST FOUR-O'CLOCK   *Mirabilis laevis*
The small (½–1 in.) leaves oval. A single rose-purple flower for each calyx-like bract. Many flowers are clustered at each branch tip, but with individual calyxlike bracts. ½–3 ft. Common. Rocky slopes below 3000 ft. Cen. to s. Calif. west of deserts.   DEC.–JUNE

DESERT FOUR-O'CLOCK   *Mirabilis multiflora*
The *huge* (2–6 in.) leaves broadly triangular to oval. The several rose-red tubular flowers are within a *large cup* of calyx-like bracts. 1–3 ft. Dry rocky places. Calif. deserts; southern end of Central Valley of Calif. and Great Basin.   APRIL–AUG.

DESERT SAND VERBENA   *Abronia villosa*
The tubular rose flowers with white centers are in umbels. Flowers, bracts, and stems all have long sticky whiskery hairs. Leaves broadly oval on long trailing stems. Flower umbels have lancelike bracts. 4–20 in. Sandy places. S. Great Basin, Mojave Desert south to Baja; also Los Angeles area south to Baja.   FEB.–AUG.

BEACH PANCAKE   *Abronia maritima*
The *thick and fleshy pancake-like* leaves are oval to round. The short exposed stem erect. The dark red flowers are in umbels. ½–2 ft. Coastal sand dunes. S. cen. and s. Calif. coast.   FEB.–OCT.

BEACH SAND VERBENA   *Abronia umbellata*
The *thin* elongated oval leaves are on long trailing stems. The rose to white flowers are in umbels with lancelike bracts. *Coastal sand dunes.* B.C. to Baja.   MOST OF YEAR

TRAILING WINDMILLS   *Allionia incarnata*
The rose to cream windmill-like flowers are usually in 3's (often appearing as one flower). Trailing stem has gray oval leaves with undulate margins. Stem and leaves sticky-haired. Flowers open morning hours. Dry rocky slopes. Mojave, Colorado Deserts; Great Basin.   APRIL–SEPT.

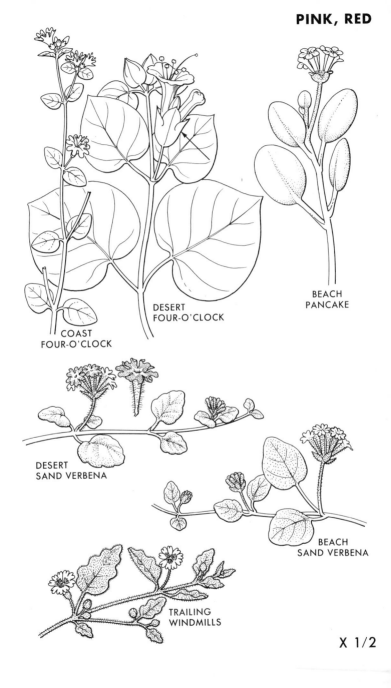

COAST
FOUR-O'CLOCK

DESERT
FOUR-O'CLOCK

BEACH
PANCAKE

DESERT
SAND VERBENA

BEACH
SAND VERBENA

TRAILING
WINDMILLS

X 1/2

5 TINY PETALS; FLOWERS IN UMBELS

CARROT FAMILY (Umbelliferae)
See also pp. W 64–68; Y 168–70; G 404.

MOJAVE LOMATIUM *Lomatium mohavense*
The low flat pinnate leaves have gray *hoarfrost-like* hairs. The tiny red-purple flowers are in small rounded umbels. Leaves divided 3–4 times into small pinnate lobes. Seeds have wing margins as wide as the narrow seed body. 4–12 in. Common on flats. Mojave, Colorado Deserts; s. end of Central Valley of Calif. APRIL–MAY

GIANT-SEEDED LOMATIUM *Lomatium macrocarpum*
Low pinnate leaves are divided 2–3 times into sharp-pointed linear segments. Tiny red-purple, yellow, or white flowers. Long ($\frac{1}{2}$–1 in.) *flattened* seeds have an outer wing narrower than the seed body. $\frac{1}{2}$–2 ft. Dry rocky places. Cen. Calif. to B.C. MARCH–JUNE

FERN-LEAVED LOMATIUM *Lomatium dissectum*
Stems *erect* and well branched, the leaves mostly basal. Leaves broadly divided 2–4 times into linear oblong segments with rounded tips. Flowers purple or yellow. Short oval seeds ($\frac{1}{2}$–$\frac{3}{4}$ in.) with narrow margin wings. 3–5 ft. Rocky places. Pacific States. APRIL–JUNE

PURPLE SANICLE *Sanicula bipinnatifida*
Leaf petiole *conspicuously broad* with a *spiny margin.* Flowers are in purple (or yellow) *balls* that have *long feathery stamens.* Rounded spiny seeds. $\frac{1}{2}$–2 ft. Common at low elevations. Yellow form most common on western slope of Sierra Nevada; otherwise, west of Cascades–Sierra Nevada from B.C. to Baja. MARCH–MAY

MOJAVE
LOMATIUM

GIANT-SEEDED
LOMATIUM

FERN-LEAVED
LOMATIUM

PURPLE
SANICLE

X 1/2

5-PETALED FLAT STARS OR PINWHEEL FLOWERS WITH A SHORT TUBE BELOW

GENTIAN FAMILY (Gentianaceae)
See also pp. W 100; B 342–44; G 394.

EUROPEAN CENTAURY Alien   *Centaurium umbellatum*
The bright red-pink flowers are in *dense umbel-like* clusters.
Each individual flower without a pedicel. Basal leaves forming
a distinct rosette. ½–1½ ft. Open fields. West of Cascades and
south to n. Calif. Less common east to Idaho.   JULY–AUG.

MONTEREY CENTAURY   *Centaurium muhlenbergii*
Similar to European Centaury. Basal leaves *loosely arranged
in pairs.* The bright pink flowers are *without pedicels* and each
flower is without a bract. 4–12 in. Moist open places. Calif.
Coast Ranges to Ore.; Great Basin.   JUNE–AUG.

CHARMING CENTAURY   *Centaurium venustum*
The few *long-pediceled* flowers rose-colored with white throats
and red dots. Petal lobes more than half as long as the flower
tube. Anthers linear. 4–12 in. Dry slopes below 6000 ft. Cen.
and s. Calif.   MAY–AUG.

PRIMROSE FAMILY (Primulaceae)
See also pp. W 100; R 246; B 342.

SCARLET PIMPERNEL Alien   *Anagallis arvensis*
The numerous flat scarlet flowers have the petals barely joined
into a tube. A sprawling well-branched stem. Blue-flowered
plants of this species are mixed in at some localities. 4–12 in.
Very common. Pacific States.   MARCH–SEPT.

SIERRA PRIMROSE   *Primula suffrutescens*
Tubular bright *carmine-red pinwheel-like* flowers are on a
leafless stem above the basal tuft of spatula-shaped leaves with
the tips toothed. ½–1 ft. Under alpine rocky cliffs. Sierra
Nevada and Siskiyous of Calif.   JULY–AUG.

CLIFF DOUGLASIA   *Douglasia laevigata*
The deep rose pinwheel flowers are in umbels on erect leafless
stems. Basal clusters of *tiny strap-shaped* leaves. Growing in
mats. Rocky alpine slopes to coastal bluffs. West of Cascades
in Wash. and south to nw. Ore.   MARCH–AUG.

PACIFIC STARFLOWER   *Trientalis latifolia*
Note the flat *umbrellalike* cluster of oval leaves at the top of a
leafless stem. The small flat pink star-shaped flowers are on
long *threadlike* pedicels. Also see Arctic Starflower under White,
p. 100, to avoid confusion. 2–8 in. Frequent in shady woods.
West of Cascades–Sierra Nevada crest.   APRIL–JULY

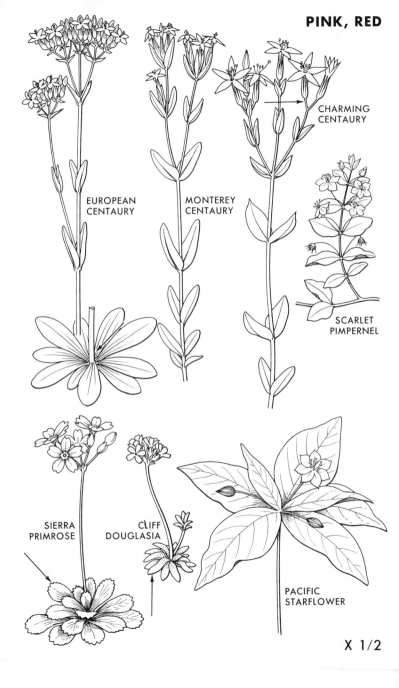

PINK, RED

CHARMING
CENTAURY

EUROPEAN
CENTAURY

MONTEREY
CENTAURY

SCARLET
PIMPERNEL

SIERRA
PRIMROSE

CLIFF
DOUGLASIA

PACIFIC
STARFLOWER

X 1/2

5 PETALS; SMALL UPRIGHT TRUMPETS

PHLOX FAMILY (Polemoniaceae)
See also pp. W 72; Y 172; O 226;
R 248–50; B 360–64.

SLENDER PHLOX *Microsteris gracilis*
Petal tips *notched.* The tiny (½ in. or less) rose to lavender, phlox-like flowers have long slender yellow-throated tubes and are in *terminal clusters.* Calyx tips narrow and short. Sticky-haired lancelike leaves. 2–8 in. Very common, open grassy places. Pacific States. MARCH–AUG.

STAINING COLLOMIA *Collomia tinctoria*
Similar to Slender Phlox. Petal tips *rounded.* Adjacent to the flower cluster are long *linear needlelike* leaves which extend well beyond the clusters of tiny pink flowers with red-violet tubes. The calyx tips broadly triangular at the base and narrowing to a slender tip. Crushed leaves result in a yellow stain. Sticky-haired. 2–8 in. Common, dry open hillsides. Great Basin, Calif. JUNE–AUG.

TINY TRUMPET *Collomia linearis*
The *long narrow* trumpetlike pink to purple flowers (½–¾ in.) are in dense headlike clusters. Single erect stems have many long broad lancelike leaves. 4–24 in. Open places. Common. Pacific States. MAY–OCT.

VARI-LEAF COLLOMIA *Collomia heterophylla*
The variably broad leaves have *sharply cleft margins* and are widely spaced along the stem. Leaves do not conceal the clusters of trumpetlike, rose to white flowers. Sticky-haired. 2–8 in. West of Cascades–Sierra Nevada. APRIL–AUG.

PINK FALSE GILIA *Allophyllum divaricatum*
Leaves have *keylike pinnate lobes.* Sticky-haired. The *long trumpetlike* flowers have pink petal lobes and red-purple tubes, in headlike clusters. Skunky odor. 4–24 in. Open places below 6000 ft. Common. Calif. APRIL–JUNE

BROADLEAF GILIA *Gilia latifolia*
The basal cluster of *broad leaves* have coarse ragged margins with spiny teeth, sticky-haired. The short funnel-shaped flowers red-pink. Bad odor if handled. 4–12 in. Common on flats. Mojave, Colorado Deserts. MARCH–MAY

ROCK GILIA *Gilia scopulorum*
The rose-lavender funnel-shaped flowers have a long tube which is a paler lavender, or yellow. Stem erect and *well-branched.* Most of the broad keylike pinnate leaves are sticky-haired and in a basal rosette. 4–12 in. Dry streambeds, slopes. Mojave Desert. APRIL–MAY

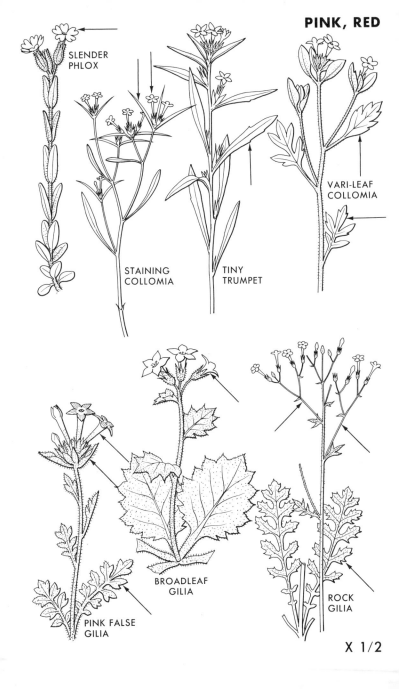

PINK, RED

SLENDER
PHLOX

STAINING
COLLOMIA

TINY
TRUMPET

VARI-LEAF
COLLOMIA

PINK FALSE
GILIA

BROADLEAF
GILIA

ROCK
GILIA

X 1/2

5 UNITED PETALS AS TRUMPETS, PINWHEELS; FLOWERS IN COILED CLUSTERS OR SINGLE

WATERLEAF FAMILY (Hydrophyllaceae)
See also pp. W 74–76; Y 172; B 366–70.

TRUMPET PHACELIA *Phacelia bicolor*
The small, pink-lobed, yellow-tubed trumpets are in coils. Each leaflet of the pinnate leaf is subdivided a second time. Entire stem leafy. 2–20 in. Sandy places. E. Ore. south to western side of Mojave Desert. MAY–AUG.

FREMONT'S PHACELIA *Phacelia fremontii*
The coils of *large* pale pink to bluish flowers have yellow throats and tubes. Calyx lobes spatula-shaped. The bright green pinnate leaves have simple rounded lobes, mostly at stem base. 2–18 in. Often in masses. Calif. deserts, Great Basin, southern end Central Valley of Calif. MARCH–MAY

PURPLE MAT *Nama demissum*
Flat mats of *solitary* dark red-purple trumpet-shaped flowers on short stems. Sticky linear leaves. 1–6 in. Sandy flats. Mojave, Colorado Deserts. MARCH–MAY

ROTHROCK'S NAMA *Nama rothrockii*
Note the terminal *headlike cluster* of lavender to red-purple tubular flowers. Erect stem has short lancelike leaves with a *toothlike margin.* Strongly sticky-haired. 6–12 in. Open sandy slopes of s. Sierra Nevada and San Bernardino Mts.
JULY–AUG.

LOBB'S NAMA *Nama lobbii*
The dark red-purple flowers are in clusters along *trailing stems.* Linear leaves and stem white felt-haired. 2–12 in. Dry open places. Mid-mt. areas. N. Sierra Nevada to Trinity Mts. and Siskiyous of nw. Calif. JUNE–AUG.

FORGET-ME-NOT FAMILY (Boraginaceae)
See also pp. W 78; Y 172; O 226; B 340–42.

PINK STICKSEED *Hackelia mundula*
The bright pink pinwheel flowers have *tiny pink teeth* in an inner row. Each flower produces 4 spiny nutlike seeds. Leaves linear. 1–3 ft. Shady openings in forests at higher elevations. Cen. and s. Sierra Nevada. JUNE–JULY

MORNING GLORY FAMILY (Convolvulaceae)
See also p. W 70.

BEACH MORNING GLORY *Calystegia soldanella*
The *large pink* Morning Glory–like flowers are scattered along a prostrate stem with large *kidney-shaped* leaves. Common on sand dunes. Entire Pacific Coast. APRIL–SEPT.

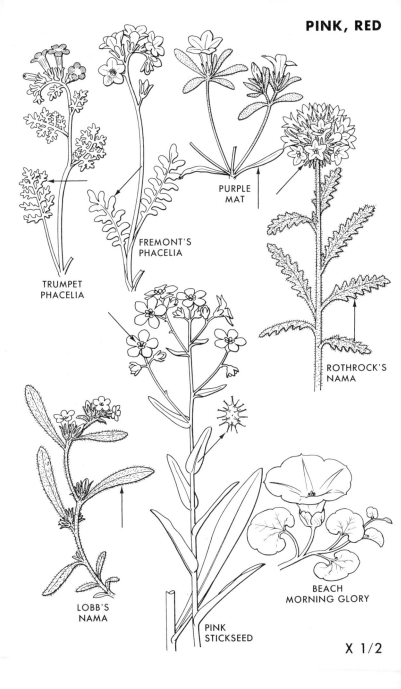

PINK, RED

TRUMPET
PHACELIA

FREMONT'S
PHACELIA

PURPLE
MAT

ROTHROCK'S
NAMA

LOBB'S
NAMA

PINK
STICKSEED

BEACH
MORNING GLORY

X 1/2

4 OR 5 PETALS; UPRIGHT STARS, URNS, NODDING BELLS, OR 2-LIPPED TUBES.

SEDUM FAMILY (Crassulaceae)
See also pp. Y 164–66.

KINGSCROWN *Sedum rosea*
Note the *terminal headlike* cluster of tiny 4-petaled dark wine-red flowers on *erect* fleshy stems. 4–10 in. Damp rocky places. Higher mts. of Pacific States. MAY–AUG.

ROSY SISKIYOU SEDUM *Sedum laxum*
Pink to rosy flowers are on stems that originate from the center of the basal cluster of *square-tipped* leaves. Upper leaves rounded. 2–12 in. Rocky slopes. Calif. North Coast Ranges to sw. Ore. JUNE–JULY

CHALK DUDLEYA *Dudleya pulverulenta*
Note the *huge chalk covered* basal cluster of pointed oval leaves. Flower stem originates from the side. Upper leaves heart-shaped. Dark red urnlike flowers. 1–2 ft. Rocky cliffs near coast. Cen. Calif. to Baja. MAY–JULY

LANCELEAF DUDLEYA *Dudleya lanceolata*
Flower stems originate from the side of the basal cluster of *lancelike leaves.* Flowers red to orange. 1–1½ ft. Rocky places. Santa Barbara, Calif. south to Baja. MAY–JULY

SNAPDRAGON FAMILY (Scrophulariaceae)
See also pp. Y 112–18; R 234–44; B 336–38, 372.

FOXGLOVE Alien *Digitalis purpurea*
Note the tall spike of *large, cascading,* pink to white, 2-lipped, tubular flowers. 2–6 ft. Frequent along coast. Occasional elsewhere in Pacific States. MAY–SEPT.

CALIFORNIA FIGWORT *Scrophularia californica*
Short red-brown tubular flowers have 2 *projecting* upper petals. Coarse stems and large *triangular* leaves. 3–6 ft. Moist thickets. Calif. and west of Cascades. FEB.–AUG.

BELLARDIA Alien *Bellardia trixago*
The tubular flowers have 2 prominent pink ridges along the lower white lip. Coarsely toothed lancelike leaves. ½–2 ft. Wet ditches. Cen. and s. Calif. APRIL–MAY

ROSE FAMILY (Rosaceae)
See also pp. W 92; Y 174–76; G 404.

PRAIRIE SMOKE *Geum ciliatum*
Flower buds are distinct *nodding bells* of red sepals which become small erect yellow flowers. Basal leaves pinnate. ½–2 ft. Rocky places 4000–8000 ft. Great Basin and on eastern slopes of Cascades–Sierra Nevada. APRIL–AUG.

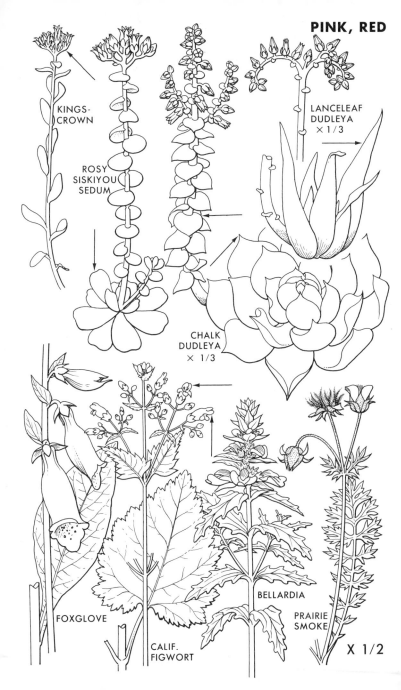

PINK, RED

KINGS-CROWN

ROSY SISKIYOU SEDUM

LANCELEAF DUDLEYA × 1/3

CHALK DUDLEYA × 1/3

FOXGLOVE

CALIF. FIGWORT

BELLARDIA

PRAIRIE SMOKE

X 1/2

5-PETALED, 2-LIPPED TUBULAR FLOWERS; SQUARE STEM AND 4 NUTLIKE SEEDS

Mint Family (Labiatae)
See also pp. W 82; R 314; B 374.

NETTLELEAF HORSEMINT   *Agastache urticifolia*
Note the large terminal *brushlike cluster* of tubular 2-lipped flowers. Coarsely toothed triangular leaves. Strong odor. 3–6 ft. Frequent in mts. Pacific States.   JUNE–SEPT.

CLASPING HENBIT Alien   *Lamium amplexicaule*
The *long, slender,* bright red-purple, tubular flowers are in whorls. The *rounded* upper leaves *clasp* the stem. 2–16 in. Disturbed places. Pacific States.   MARCH–AUG.

RED HENBIT Alien   *Lamium purpureum*
Note the *distinct petiole* below the small heart-shaped leaf blade. Upper stem a *4-sided pagoda* of numerous flowers hidden under the leaves. 2–12 in. Pacific States.
APRIL–SEPT.

RIGID HEDGE NETTLE   *Stachys rigida*
The lower flower lip *tonguelike,* with a distinct *line* of rose-purple dots around the entire margin. Lower flower lip tip slightly bilobed and squared. A sharp tiny sac is on lower side of the short flower tube. 4 stamens. Sepal tips spines. Stem erect with *oval* scallop-margined leaves. 2–4 ft. Damp bottomlands. All Calif. and Ore.   JULY–AUG.

WHITESTEM HEDGE NETTLE   *Stachys albens*
The small pale pink flowers have projecting *round scooplike* lower lips. The flower tube *hidden* within the calyx. Calyx lobes round-tipped. Soft *cobwebby white* woolly hair covers the stem and leaves. 4 stamens. 1–4 ft. Damp streambottoms below 8000 ft. Cen. and s. Calif.   MAY–OCT.

CALIFORNIA HEDGE NETTLE   *Stachys bullata*
Lower flower lip lobe rounded and *all pink.* Medium length flower tube. 4 stamens. Calyx lobes spine-tipped. 1–3 ft. Coastal slopes. San Francisco to s. Calif.   APRIL–SEPT.

CHAMISSO'S HEDGE NETTLE   *Stachys chamissonis*
Flowers *long-tubed* (1–2 in.) with a scooplike lower lip. 4 stamens. 2–3 ft. Thickets. Calif. Coast to B.C.   JUNE–OCT.

PITCHER SAGE   *Salvia spathacea*
The *large* (4–12 in.) dark green *triangular* leaves gray-haired beneath. The calyx lobes elongated above the flower tube into a *pitcherlike spout.* The lower flower lip of *2 round lobes.* 2 stamens. 1–3 ft. Open to shady slopes. Calif. South Coast Ranges south to Orange Co.   MARCH–MAY

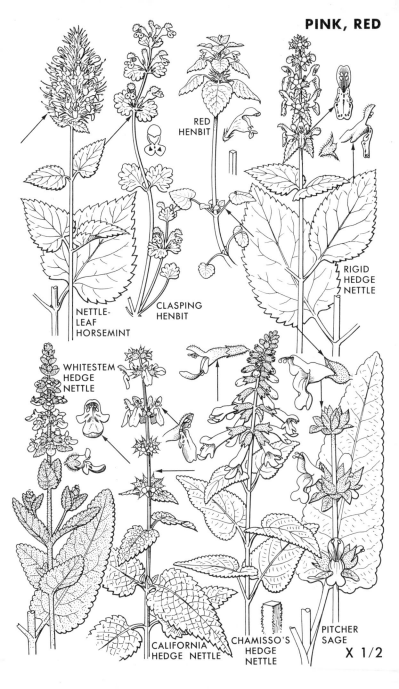

PINK, RED

NETTLE-LEAF HORSEMINT

CLASPING HENBIT

RED HENBIT

RIGID HEDGE NETTLE

WHITESTEM HEDGE NETTLE

CALIFORNIA HEDGE NETTLE

CHAMISSO'S HEDGE NETTLE

PITCHER SAGE

X 1/2

5-PETALED, 2-LIPPED TUBULAR FLOWERS
SQUARE STEM AND 4 NUTLIKE SEEDS

Mint Family (Labiatae)
See also pp. W 82; R 312; B 374.

COYOTE MINT *Monardella odoratissima*
Note the *flat head* of numerous slender, pale red-purple to dirty
white flowers. Note *fringe of hairs* at top of the calyx tube.
Stem leaves lancelike. ½–2 ft. A variable species found at
many elevations. Great Basin and most of Ore. and Calif.
JUNE–SEPT.

FIELD MINT Alien? *Mentha arvensis*
Note the dense *whorls* of pale pink flowers nearly *hidden by
long* leaves. Leaves bright green with sharp sawtooth margins.
½–3 ft. Moist places. Pacific States. JULY–OCT.

PENNYROYAL Alien *Mentha pulegium*
Similar to Field Mint. The dense *whorls* of pale pink flowers
are *well exposed* by the short gray leaves. 1–3 ft. Moist places.
Ore. and Calif. JUNE–SEPT.

SPEARMINT Alien *Mentha spicata*
Note whorls of pale lavender flowers *form a spike well above*
the crinkly lancelike leaves. The 2 flower lips not widely
separated. Plant nearly hairless. 1–4 ft. Moist disturbed
places. Pacific States. JUNE–OCT.

CREEPING CHARLIE *Glecoma hederacea*
Note the *round to kidney-shaped* leaves along a creeping stem.
Long slender pink to red-purple flowers are in whorls. 1–3 in.
Shady woods. N. Calif. to Wash. MARCH–JUNE

DOUGLAS'S POGOYNE *Pogogyne douglasii*
Flowers are in *long dense oblong* spikes. The red-purple to
violet 2-lipped flower has a *pale yellow spot* on the lower lip.
Leaves lancelike. 2–16 in. Dry bottoms of shallow winter
pools. Throughout cen. Calif. MAY–JULY

SACRAMENTO POGOYNE *Pogogyne zizyphoroides*
Flowers are in short dense spikes. The 2-lipped pink to red-
purple flower has an *all pale pink* lower lip. Leaves *oval to
oblong*. 2–12 in. Dry bottoms of shallow winter pools. Cen.
Calif. north to s. Ore. JULY–AUG.

DWARF SKULLCAP *Scutellaria nana*
The snapdragon-like flower has an upper red-purple *snout* and
a lower creamy yellow *skirt*. Also note the *hornlike lip* on the
upper side of the calyx. 2–4 in. Dry volcanic soils. Great
Basin. JUNE–AUG.

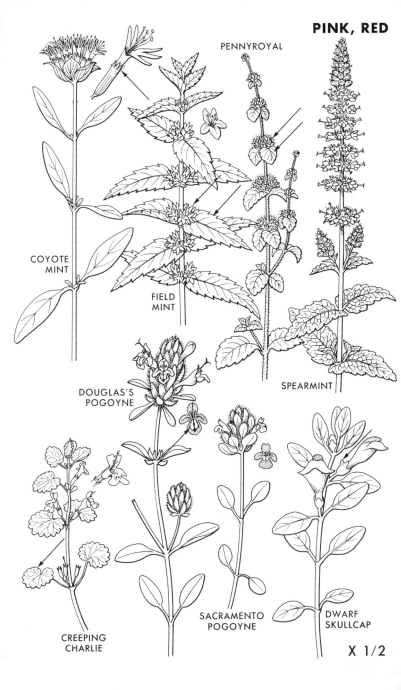

PINK, RED

PENNYROYAL

COYOTE
MINT

FIELD
MINT

SPEARMINT

DOUGLAS'S
POGOYNE

CREEPING
CHARLIE

SACRAMENTO
POGOYNE

DWARF
SKULLCAP

X 1/2

5 PETALS; MISCELLANEOUS TUBULAR
FLOWERS ABOVE AN INFERIOR OVARY

TWINFLOWER *Linnaea borealis*
Honeysuckle Family (Caprifoliaceae)
Note the *twin pair of nodding* pink tubular flowers on a leafless
stem. The stem trailing with shiny oval leaves. 2–6 in. Semishaded woods or thickets. N. Calif. to B.C. June–Sept.

Valerian Family (Valerianaceae)
See also p. W 100.

SHORT-SPURRED PLECTRITIS *Plectritis congesta*
The slender flower tube base *short with a short spur*. The
slender erect stems have a terminal headlike cluster of small
pink to rose flowers. Leaves in opposite pairs. ½–1½ ft. Open
grassy places. West of Cascades and south to nw. Calif.
April–June

ROTUND PLECTRITIS *Plectritis macrocera*
The *upper portion* of the corolla tube broad with a *fat rounded
spur*. The lower corolla tube longer than the spur. Leaves
broad. ½–2 ft. Moist open to semishaded places. Pacific
States. March–May

LONG-SPURRED PLECTRITIS *Plectritis ciliosa*
Note the *elongated slender spur* which extends well beyond the
ovary. Two red dots are present, one on each side of the middle
petal lobe. Leaves narrow. ½–1½ ft. Open moist grassy places.
Mostly west of Cascades–Sierra Nevada. March–May

Teasel Family (Dipsacaceae)

FULLER'S TEASEL Alien *Dipsacus fullonum*
Note the terminal elongated *cone of spiny bracts*. Below each
bract and nearly hidden are irregular rose-purple flowers. The
terminal cone subtended by several linear spiny leaves. Stem
and leaf midribs spiny. 1–6 ft. Disturbed places. Pacific
States. May–Sept.

Bluebell Family (Campanulaceae)
See also pp. B 346–48.

CARDINAL FLOWER *Lobelia cardinalis*
Note the *bright red 2-lipped* flowers in a terminal cluster. The
petal lobes narrow, flower tube often completely slit along one
side. Each flower twisted on the pedicel. Leaves lancelike to
linear. 1–3 ft. Marshy places. S. Calif. Aug.–Oct.

316

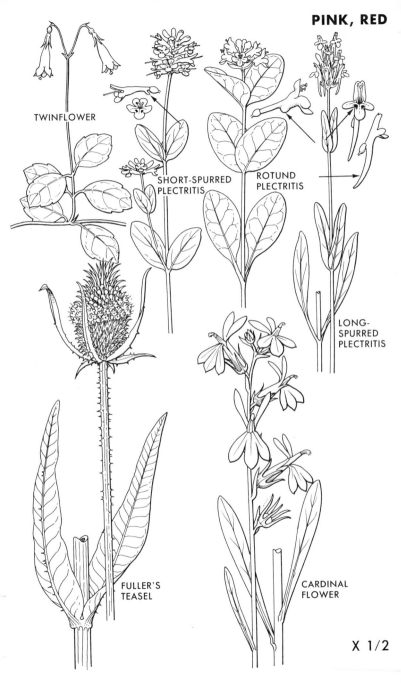

PINK, RED

TWINFLOWER

SHORT-SPURRED PLECTRITIS

ROTUND PLECTRITIS

LONG-SPURRED PLECTRITIS

FULLER'S TEASEL

CARDINAL FLOWER

X 1/2

PEALIKE FLOWERS; COMPOUND LEAVES

PEA FAMILY (Leguminosae)
See also pp. W 94–96; Y 178–82;
O 224; R 318–26; B 376–80.

SPANISH LOTUS *Lotus purshianus*
One *pale rose* flower with *1 leaflike bract* on a long pedicel above the trifoliate lancelike leaflets. Numerous long pale gray hairs. ½–3 ft. Pacific States. APRIL–OCT.

BUCK LOTUS *Lotus crassifolius*
The *waxy blue* leaflets elliptical, 7–19 per leaf. Stems *stout*. Leaf petiole stipules are *short and round*. A bract of 1–5 leaflets below each flower cluster. Flowers tipped with dull red-purple above a yellow basal region. 1–4 ft. Frequent below 8000 ft. Pacific States. MAY–AUG.

ROSY LOTUS *Lotus aboriginum*
The *bright green* leaflets oblong, 9–19 per leaf. Flowers in dense clusters, red-purple with white tips. A bract of 3–5 leaflets below each flower cluster. Erect *wiry* stems. Leaf petiole stipules sharply *triangular*. 1–2 ft. Banks in open forests. Coastal region Wash. south to Calif. MAY–JULY

WESTERN SWEETVETCH *Hedysarum occidentale*
Spike of 20–75 red-purple flowers *cascading downward*. Each pinnate leaf has 9–21 oval leaflets. Seedpods *beadlike*. 1–3 ft. High Olympics, Cascades of Wash. JUNE–SEPT.

STIVER'S LUPINE *Lupinus stiversii*
Flowers *3-colored;* the 2 outer wing petals pink, the upper banner petal yellow, and the lower keel petals white. Flowers in a terminal cluster. Each palmate leaf has 6–9 leaflets. 4–16 in. Below 6000 ft. W. Sierra Nevada foothills to San Bernardino Mts. and Santa Lucia Mts. APRIL–JULY

BALLOON CLOVER *Trifolium depauperatum*
The tiny flower head has *tiny inflated* flowers. Flower head bract smooth-lobed. Leaflets vary from narrow lancelike to square-tipped. 4–10 in. Fields at low elevations. West of deserts, Calif. to cen. Ore., rarely to B.C. MARCH–JUNE

BULL CLOVER *Trifolium fucatum*
The large wedge-shaped leaflets *white-spotted*. Pink flowers inflating into large sacs. Flower heads large (1–3 in. wide). ½–2 ft. Wet places. W. Calif. and Ore. APRIL–JUNE

GIANTS-HEAD CLOVER *Trifolium macrocephalum*
The pale pink flower heads *giant* (1–3 in. wide). Each *lupine-like leaf* of 5–9 wedge-shaped leaflets. 4–12 in. Open rocky meadows. Great Basin. APRIL–JULY

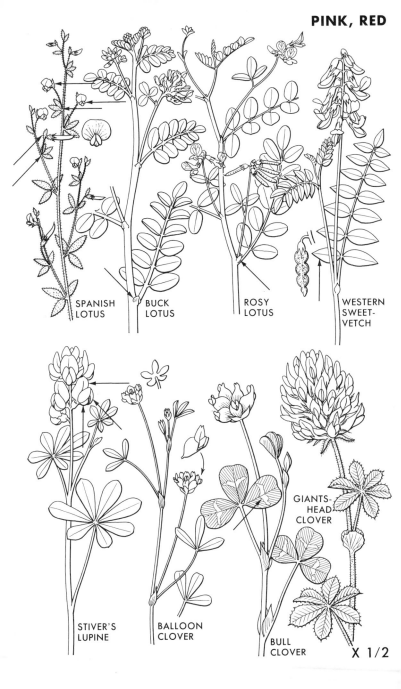

SPANISH
LOTUS

BUCK
LOTUS

ROSY LOTUS

WESTERN
SWEET-
VETCH

STIVER'S
LUPINE

BALLOON
CLOVER

BULL
CLOVER

GIANTS-
HEAD
CLOVER

X 1/2

PEALIKE FLOWERS;
3-LEAFLET CLOVERS

PEA FAMILY (Leguminosae)
See also pp. W 94–96; Y 178–82;
O 224; R 318–26; B 376–80.

RED CLOVER Alien   *Trifolium pratense*
Each oblong leaflet has a *central white chevron.* The *large*
(1 in.) oval red flower head is without a bract below it. Leaf
stipules tailed. ½–2 ft. Pacific States.   APRIL–OCT.

CRIMSON CLOVER Alien   *Trifolium incarnatum*
Note the *elongated cylinderlike* flower head of bright red
flowers without a bract below it. Leaflets wedge-shaped.
½–2 ft. Frequent, roadsides. N. Calif.   APRIL–AUG.

PLUMED CLOVER   *Trifolium plumosum*
Similar to Crimson Clover. Flower heads pale pink. Long
narrow silky plumelike leaflets and stipules. ½–1½ ft. Dry
meadows. Blue and Wallowa Mts. of ne. Ore.   MAY–AUG.

BOWL CLOVER   *Trifolium cyathiferum*
The calyx tips of individual flowers are of *branched spines.* A
bowl-shaped membrane surrounds each flower head. 4–12 in.
Moist places. Cen. Calif. to B.C.   MAY–AUG.

MAIDEN CLOVER   *Trifolium microcephalum*
Note the *tiny pale pink flower heads* (¼ in.) surrounded by a
shallow bowl-like bract that has broad spine-tipped lobes.
Leaflets have bilobed tips and serrated margins. Stipules triangular. ½–1½ ft. Pacific States.   APRIL–AUG.

COW CLOVER Alien   *Trifolium wormskjoldii*
A flat *spine-pointed* bract below the pale purple to white flower
heads. Calyx lobes *needlelike.* Oblong blunt-tipped leaflets.
4–12 in. Moist places. Pacific States.   MAY–OCT.

WHITE-TOPPED CLOVER   *Trifolium variegatum*
Leaflets *narrowly oblong,* margins coarsely sawtoothed. Leaf
stipules have ragged edges. Each red-purple flower white- or
pink-tipped. Calyx lobes broadly triangular with a single long
spine. 4–16 in. Common. Pacific States.   APRIL–JULY

TOMCAT CLOVER   *Trifolium tridentatum*
Leaflets *narrowly lancelike* and flowers *white-tipped.* Each
calyx lobe has 3 sharp points. ½–2 ft. Frequent. West of
Cascades–Sierra Nevada.   MARCH–JULY

BEARDED CLOVER   *Trifolium barbigerum*
Flowers dark red-purple with the upper half white in a *large
green punchbowl bract,* on long leafless peduncles. ½–1 ft.
Moist meadows. Calif. Coast Ranges.   APRIL–JUNE

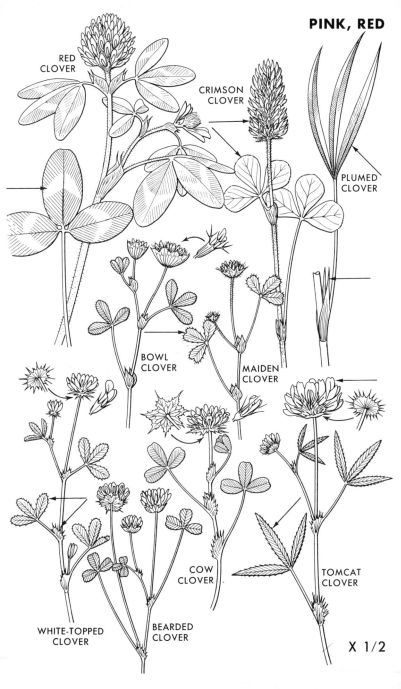

PINK, RED

RED CLOVER

CRIMSON CLOVER

PLUMED CLOVER

BOWL CLOVER

MAIDEN CLOVER

WHITE-TOPPED CLOVER

BEARDED CLOVER

COW CLOVER

TOMCAT CLOVER

X 1/2

PEALIKE FLOWERS; INFLATED SEEDPODS

PEA FAMILY (Leguminosae)
See also pp. W 94–96; Y 178–82;
O 224; R 318–26; B 376–80.

CRIMSON SHEEPPOD   *Astragalus coccineus*
Note the *bright crimson* flowers. 7–15 oval leaflets per leaf.
Short curved seedpods. Plant white woolly-haired. 1–2 ft.
Outwash fans. Mojave, Colorado Deserts.   MARCH–MAY

KING'S LOCOWEED   *Astragalus calycosus*
Wing petals narrow and the *tips bilobed.* 2–6 pink to dark red
flowers. Low silvery tufted stems. Short seedpods. 2–6 in.
Rocky slopes. Mojave Desert, Great Basin.   MAY–JUNE

PURSH'S SHEEPPOD   *Astragalus purshii*
Low tufted plants have large white woolly seedpods. 7–19
oblong leaflets per leaf. Deep red-purple to yellow flowers.
2–6 in. Mts. of cen. Calif.; Great Basin.   APRIL–AUG.

LAYNE'S LOCOWEED   *Astragalus layneae*
The purple mottled *sickle-shaped* seedpod has a distinct groove
on the underside. 13–21 leaflets per leaf. Yellow flowers have
the *wing petals purple-tipped.* 2–18 in. Common. Mojave,
Colorado Deserts.   MARCH–MAY

MOTTLED LOCOWEED   *Astragalus lentiginosus*
Seedpod a strongly *inflated sausage* with a *flattened triangular*
tip curved upward. 11–19 oval leaflets are nearly hairless.
Flowers vary from red-purple to pale yellow to white. A highly
variable and widespread species. 4–16 in. Pacific States.
                                                        MAY–AUG.

WHITNEY'S LOCOWEED   *Astragalus whitneyi*
Seedpods inflated sausages with purple mottling. Red-purple
flowers have white-tipped wing petals. 9–19 linear leaflets.
Stem prostrate. 2–10 in. Dry mt. slopes. Eastern side of
Cascades–Sierra Nevada; Great Basin.   MAY–SEPT.

ALPINE LOCOWEED   *Astragalus alpinus*
Note the long stems with a cluster of white flowers that have
red-purple petal tips. 13–23 *bright yellow-green* leaflets per
leaf. Plants completely hairless, but seedpods *black-haired.*
2–12 in. Subalpine forests. Mts. of B.C. to Wash., and Wallowa
Mts. of Ore.   JUNE–AUG.

GAMBELL'S DWARF LOCOWEED
                              Astragalus gambelianus
Tiny pink flowers with white wing petals are in tight heads.
Tiny square-tipped leaflets. Tiny seedpods. 2–12 in. Common
in thick masses. Coast Ranges, s. Ore. to Baja, and Sierra
Nevada foothills.   MARCH–JUNE

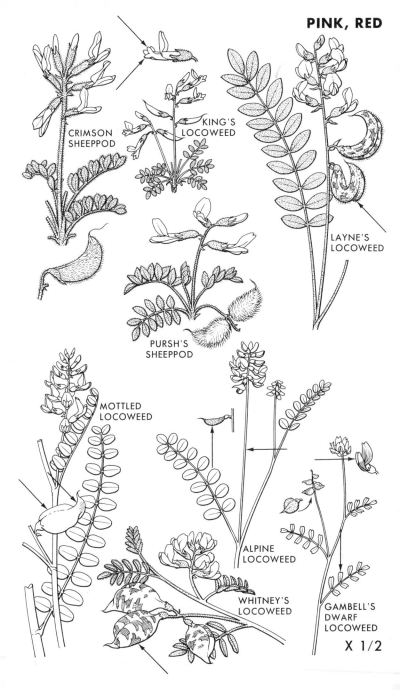

PINK, RED

CRIMSON SHEEPPOD

KING'S LOCOWEED

LAYNE'S LOCOWEED

PURSH'S SHEEPPOD

MOTTLED LOCOWEED

ALPINE LOCOWEED

WHITNEY'S LOCOWEED

GAMBELL'S DWARF LOCOWEED

X 1/2

PEA FLOWERS; TENDRIL-TIPPED LEAVES

Pea Family (Leguminosae)
See also pp. W 94–96; Y 178–82;
O 224; R 318–26; B 376–80.

SIERRA NEVADA PEA   *Lathyrus nevadensis*
4–8 *oval* leaflets per leaf, the terminal tendril slightly curled or
often reduced to a very short *single tail-like* appendage. 2–7
red-purple to blue flowers. Vines ½–2 ft. Foothills and mts.
Cen. Calif. to B.C.   APRIL–JULY

TORREY'S PEA   *Lathyrus torreyi*
Pinnate leaves *finely haired,* 10–16 oval to elliptical leaflets
with the terminal tendril a *short single bristle.* The *1–2 flowers*
pale lilac to blue. Vines 4–16 in. Semiopen woods. Coastal
region, Monterey, Calif., to Wash.   MAY–JUNE

OREGON PEA   *Lathyrus polyphyllus*
Note the *very large oval stipules* at base of leaf petioles. The
pinnate leaf has 10–16 oval, *well alternated* leaflets and a
terminal tendril. 5–13 red-purple to blue flowers in a 1-sided
raceme. Calyx teeth hairy-fringed. Vines 1–4 ft. Along coast.
Calif. North Coast Ranges to Wash.   MAY–JUNE

PACIFIC PEA   *Lathyrus vestitus*
Note the minutely gray-haired *lancelike* leaflets (usually 10) in
opposite pairs, and a terminal tendril. Leaf stipule large and
triangular with a wavy margin. 5–20 flowers have a red-purple
banner petal and *white* wing petals. Vines to 1½ ft. Mostly
Calif. and Ore. coast.   APRIL–JUNE

BEACH PEA   *Lathyrus japonicus*
Note the *large triangular stipules* at the base of the pinnate
leaves *and nearly as long* as the oval leaflets. Flowers 2–8,
banner petal completely dark purple while the wing and keel
petals are white. Vines 1–4 ft. Coastal beaches. N. Calif. to
B.C.   MAY–SEPT.

SOUTHERN CALIFORNIA PEA   *Lathyrus laetiflorus*
The pale pink (nearly white) 5–12 flowers have *pink lines* and
are on *very long peduncles.* Leaf stipules at base of each leaf
large and lancelike. 8–12 leaflets per leaf and usually alternately arranged. Vines 3–9 ft. S. Calif. Mts. south to Baja.

                                                 APRIL–JUNE

BRUSH PEA   *Lathyrus pauciflorus*
Note the *starlike stipules* at the base of each leaf petiole. The
pinnate leaf has 8–10 narrowly linear leaflets and a terminal
tendril. Mostly 4–7 pink to red-purple flowers that age a dark
blue. Vines 1–3 ft. Dry mt. slopes. All cen. Calif.; Great
Basin.   APRIL–JUNE

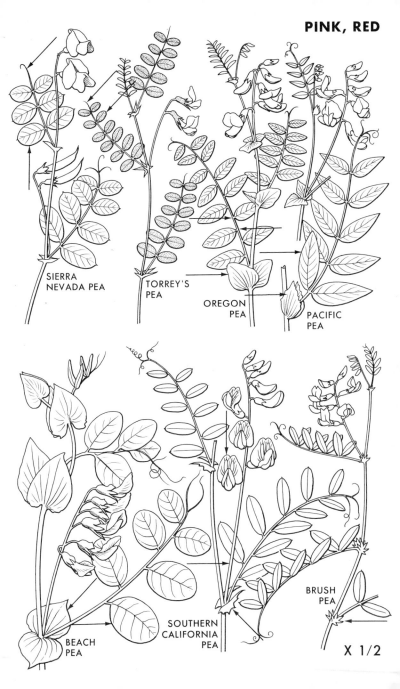

PINK, RED

SIERRA NEVADA PEA

TORREY'S PEA

OREGON PEA

PACIFIC PEA

BEACH PEA

SOUTHERN CALIFORNIA PEA

BRUSH PEA

X 1/2

PEA FLOWERS; TENDRIL-TIPPED LEAVES

PEA FAMILY (Leguminosae)
See also pp. W 94–96; Y 178–82;
O 224; R 318–26; B 376–80.

TANGIER PEA Alien   *Lathyrus tingitanus*
The *short* flower peduncles have *1–3 bright rose-red* flowers.
Flowers nestled amongst the leaves and tendrils. Each ten-
driled leaf has 2 rounded leaflets. Stem flattened. Vines 3–8 ft.
Bluffs along coast. Calif. and Ore.   MAY–JULY

EVERLASTING PEA Alien   *Lathyrus latifolius*
Flower peduncle *very long,* placing the 5–15 bright red-purple
flowers well above the stem and leaves. (Some plants are
white-flowered). Each leaf has 2 *lancelike* leaflets. Main stem
flattened. Vines 2–8 ft. Common about old settlements, etc.
Pacific States.   MAY–SEPT.

SILKY BEACH PEA   *Lathyrus littoralis*
Stem and leaves densely *silky-haired.* 4–8 oval leaflets per leaf
with the terminal tendril reduced to a leaflike bristle. 2–6 pink
or red-purple flowers per peduncle. $\frac{1}{2}$–2 ft. Coastal beaches.
Monterey, Calif., to B.C.   APRIL–JULY

PRIDE OF CALIFORNIA   *Lathyrus splendens*
Upper *banner petal elongated and reflexed* backward until
nearly parallel with rest of flower. 4–12 crimson or deep rich
red flowers per peduncle. 6–10 rounded leaflets per leaf. Vines
2–10 ft. Thickets. Mts. of San Diego Co., Calif., to Baja.
                    APRIL–JUNE

SPRING VETCH Alien   *Vicia sativa*
1–2 red-purple flowers are *near the base* of each leaf. The 4–8
pairs of narrow leaflets are blunt-tipped with *tiny bristles.*
1–3 ft. Pacific States.   APRIL–JULY

GIANT VETCH   *Vicia gigantea*
Note the *long pyramid-shaped* (in outline) leaf with 8–12 pairs
of linear leaflets. Numerous red-purple flowers per raceme (or
pale yellow in some areas). Stems smooth. Vines 2–6 ft. Shady
woods. Along Pacific Coast.   MARCH–JULY

WINTER VETCH Alien   *Vicia villosa*
10 to many flowers per raceme. 8–12 pairs of linear leaflets per
leaf. Stems lightly haired. Vines 2–5 ft. Pacific States.
                    MARCH–JULY

AMERICAN VETCH   *Vicia americana*
4–9 *dark red to blue-purple* flowers in each raceme. 4–8 pairs of
oval leaflets, spine-tipped. Slightly haired vines 2–4 ft. Open
fields. Pacific States.   APRIL–JULY

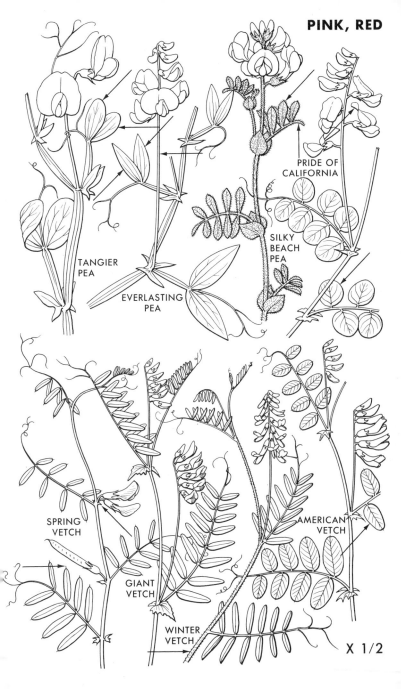

PINK, RED

TANGIER PEA

EVERLASTING PEA

PRIDE OF CALIFORNIA

SILKY BEACH PEA

SPRING VETCH

GIANT VETCH

WINTER VETCH

AMERICAN VETCH

X 1/2

SPINY THISTLES: CIRSIUM

Sunflower Family (Compositae)
Thistle Tribe: Cynareae
See also pp. W 102–8; Y 184–220;
O 226; R 328–32; B 384; G 404.

BULL THISTLE Alien   *Cirsium vulgare*
Note the spiny leaf blade *extends* from the petiole *down the stem.* Flower heads red-purple. 2–4 ft. Common. Disturbed places. Pacific States.   June–Sept.

COULTER'S THISTLE   *Cirsium coulteri*
The bright red flower heads are on *long leafless stems.* The bright green flower head bracts have considerable cobwebby hair. Leaves straplike with very short triangular lobes. 2–5 ft. Common, dry slopes. Many areas of Calif.   May–July

ANDERSON'S THISTLE   *Cirsium andersonii*
Long straplike leaves *immediately below* the single *bright rose-red* flower heads. Leaves and flower heads distant from each other on elongated stems. Lower stem leaves *highly divided* with each lobe often widest at the outer end. 2–4 ft. Dry mt. slopes. Sierra Nevada and nw. Calif.   June–Oct.

STEENS MT. THISTLE   *Cirsium peckii*
Single erect stem has flower heads *clustered at base of each leaf* along most of stem. 2–4 ft. Steen and Pueblo Mts. of cen. Ore.   June–Sept.

COBWEB THISTLE   *Cirsium occidentale*
Note the *very dense white cobwebby*-haired bracts of each red-purple flower head. Bracts of flower head *awl-like.* 2–4 ft. Common. Dry open places. Calif.   May–July

CALIFORNIA THISTLE   *Cirsium californicum*
Flowers pale pink. Flower head bracts shiny green with *small tufts* of cottony hair near each bract base. Stem gray with a few *very short leaves* (2–4 in.). 1–4 ft. Common. Dry open places. Cen. and s. Calif.   April–July

CANADA THISTLE Alien   *Cirsium arvense*
The pink to red-purple *marblelike* flower heads numerous and small ($\frac{1}{2}$ in.). Flower heads, stem, and leaves shiny and smooth as if varnished. The slender lancelike leaves have shallowly lobed spiny margins, green on both sides. 1–3 ft. Disturbed places. Pacific States.   June–Sept.

CLUSTER THISTLE   *Cirsium brevistylum*
Note the congested *terminal clusters of large round* bright pink to red-purple flower heads at the *end of each branch.* Flower head spines white woolly. 1–7 ft. Cascades, coast mts. from Olympics south to s. Calif.   April–Sept.

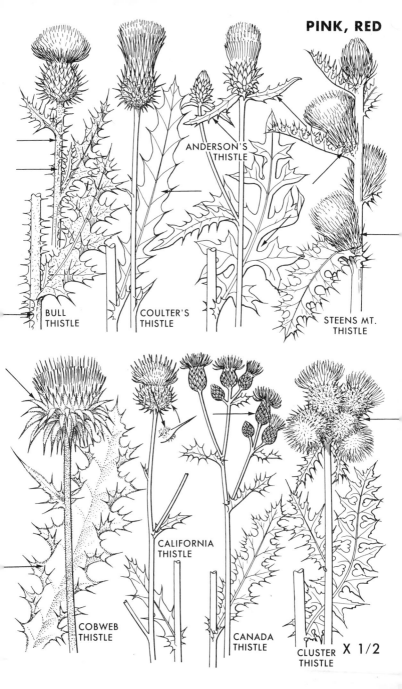

PINK, RED

ANDERSON'S THISTLE

BULL THISTLE

COULTER'S THISTLE

STEENS MT. THISTLE

COBWEB THISTLE

CALIFORNIA THISTLE

CANADA THISTLE

CLUSTER THISTLE

X 1/2

SPINY THISTLES; EVERLASTINGS; PINCUSHIONS; OR DANDELIONLIKE SUNFLOWERS

SUNFLOWER FAMILY Compositae)
See also pp. W 102–8; Y 184–220; O 226;
R 328–32; B 384; G 404.

Thistle Tribe: Cynareae

CARDOON Alien *Cynara cardunculus*
Note the giant spiny *artichoke-like* electric-purple flower heads. The stout stems have long (1–2 ft.) deeply pinnate leaves armed with *numerous long yellow spines.* 2–6 ft. Rolling hills on east side of San Francisco Bay area; hills of Orange Co., Calif. MAY–SEPT.

MILK THISTLE Alien *Silybum marianum*
Note the spiny *shiny green* leaves with *white veins and spots.* The stout erect stem has many red-purple flower heads. 3–7 ft. Very common. Calif. and Ore. MAY–JULY

RUSSIAN KNAPWEED Alien *Centaurea repens*
Slender erect stems, becoming well branched in upper portion with numerous *small, rounded,* dark red-purple flower heads. Linear leaves. Only spines on this thistle are at leaf tips and flower head bracts. 1–3 ft. Pacific States. MAY–SEPT.

Everlasting Tribe: Inuleae

ROSY EVERLASTING *Antennaria rosea*
The small *rosy papery-bracted cylinderlike* flower heads are around a tiny white center. Stem and leaves covered by a layer of soft feltlike hair. 2–24 in. Very common. Many different habitats. Pacific States. MOST OF YEAR

Woolly Sunflower Tribe: Helenieae

HOLE-IN-THE-SAND PLANT *Nicolletia occidentalis*
The elongated flower head has short *bright deep red* ray flowers. Each flower head bract has an *orange gland spot* near the tip. Narrow spine-tipped pinnate leaves. Plant parts waxy blue. Foul smelling if handled. $\frac{1}{2}$–2 ft. Sandy places. W. Mojave and Colorado Deserts. APRIL–JUNE

SPANISH NEEDLES *Palafoxia arida*
Leaves *linear.* On top of each seed are *needlelike* bristles with a central midrib. Pincushion flower heads. $\frac{1}{2}$–3 ft. Sandy washes. Mojave, Colorado Deserts. JAN.–SEPT.

Chicory Tribe: Cichorieae

TWIGGY WREATH PLANT *Stephanomeria virgata*
The all ray-flowered head has 4–15 red-backed florets. Highly branched leafless stems. Seeds smooth-sided. 2–7 ft. Common. Calif. to sw. Ore. JULY–SEPT.

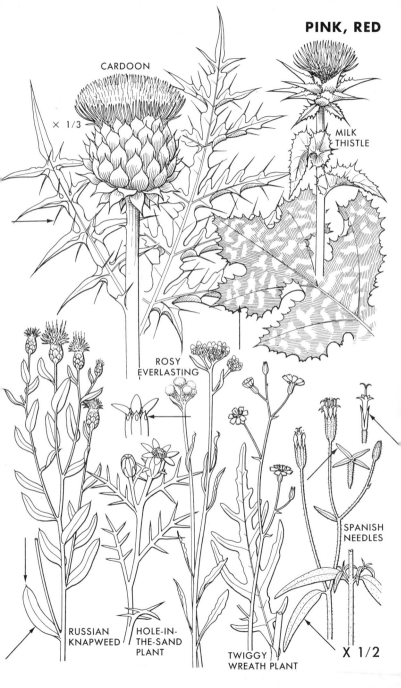

PINK, RED

CARDOON

× 1/3

MILK THISTLE

ROSY EVERLASTING

SPANISH NEEDLES

RUSSIAN KNAPWEED

HOLE-IN-THE-SAND PLANT

TWIGGY WREATH PLANT

X 1/2

ASTERS AND DAISIES

SUNFLOWER FAMILY (Compositae)
Aster Tribe: Astereae
See also pp. W 102–8; Y 184–220; O 226;
R 328–32; B 384; G 404.

DESERT ASTER *Xylorhiza tortifolia*
Note the *spiny-margined lancelike* leaves on the numerous
erect stems. Flower head of 40–60 red-purple to blue or white
ray flowers. 1–3 ft. Dry slopes and dry streambeds. Mojave,
Colorado Deserts. MARCH–MAY OCT.

WANDERING DAISY *Erigeron peregrinus*
The lower stem leaves are nearly *lancelike* and with only a few
scattered hairs. The stems erect. The pale pink to rose-purple
ray flowers (30–80 per head) are *each broad and flat.* Very
common. ½–2½ ft. Mt. meadows. Pacific States.
JULY–SEPT.

CUT-LEAVED DAISY *Erigeron compositus*
A low plant with *fan-shaped leaves,* each with cut lobes.
1–10 in. Rocky ridges. Mts. of Pacific States. MAY–AUG.

LEAFY DAISY *Erigeron foliosus*
The erect stems have many narrowly linear leaves which are
loosely covered with many short hairs. The pink to pale blue
daisylike flower heads have 20–60 ray flowers. ½–3 ft. Open
places. Pacific States. MAY–AUG.

ALPINE ASTER *Aster alpigenus*
Most of the long linear leaves are in basal clusters below the
thick erect leafless stems which have a *solitary* pink to purple
flower head. A few small bract-like leaves may be scattered
along upper stem. 2–16 in. Mt. meadows at mid to alpine zone.
Mts. of Pacific States. JUNE–SEPT.

CHILEAN ASTER *Aster chilensis*
Flower heads small with conspicuous outer bracts. Stem leaves
very short and linear, close to stem. A few large lancelike leaves
near stem base. Each individual ray flower broad. 1–4 ft. Dry
open places at lower elevations. Common. Pacific States.
JULY–NOV.

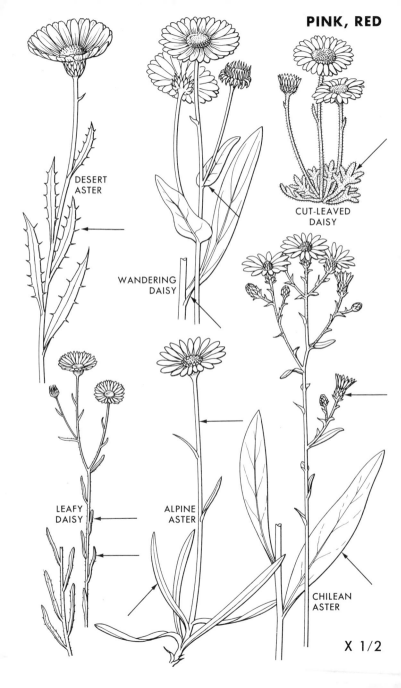

PINK, RED

DESERT ASTER

CUT-LEAVED DAISY

WANDERING DAISY

LEAFY DAISY

ALPINE ASTER

CHILEAN ASTER

X 1/2

Violet to Blue
or Blue-Purple
Flowers

The truly violet and blue flowers are in this category. The blue-purple flowers are also presented here but are difficult to separate from the red-purples. True purple is a 50-50 mixture of red and blue; thus it is sometimes difficult to decide on which side of the line a color is. Often a fresh red-purple flower will age a blue-purple. A majority of the purple flowers are in the red-purple category — if in doubt check Pink to Red or Red-Purple Flowers, p. 233. When possible, the group characteristics given in the text page titles are repeated in each color section, and in the same order. Where the flowers on a page look nearly the same but your sample does not fit, you can also use the cross references given for other colors.

5 PETALS; 2-LIPPED TUBULAR FLOWERS

SNAPDRAGON FAMILY (Scrophulariaceae)
See also pp. Y 112–18; R 234–44, 310;
B 336–38, 372.

PINCUSHION PENSTEMON *Penstemon procerus*
Tiny to small ($\frac{1}{4}$–$\frac{3}{4}$ in.) blue-purple flowers with a *white* throat are in a *declined position* within dense clusters. 1–12 in. Drier mt. meadows. Pacific States.　　　　　　　　JUNE–AUG.

MEADOW PENSTEMON *Penstemon rydbergii*
Dense clusters of tiny ($\frac{1}{2}$ in.) blue-purple flowers with *distinct white* throats are in an *ascending position*. $\frac{1}{2}$–2 ft. Moist mt. meadows. Sierra Nevada, Great Basin.　　　　　　MAY–AUG.

GLOBE PENSTEMON *Penstemon globosus*
Note the *large lantern-globe-like* cluster of dark blue to blue-purple flowers. Broad *bright green* lancelike leaves. Stem hairless. 1–2 ft. Meadows. Wallowa Mts.　　　　JUNE–AUG.

SISKIYOU PENSTEMON *Penstemon anguineus*
A *vertical column* of long brown hairs is at the corolla tube *mouth*. Short (1 in.) blue-purple flowers. Plant *sticky*-haired. 1–2$\frac{1}{2}$ ft. Forested slopes. Crater Lake, Ore., south to Calif. North Coast Ranges.　　　　　　　　　　JUNE–AUG.

WILCOX'S PENSTEMON *Penstemon wilcoxii*
Long *flattened* flowers have a linear ridge on top. Lower flower lip *projecting* beyond the upper. Plant glandular, with a cold wet feeling if handled. *Yellow-green triangular* leaves. 1–3 ft. Forest openings. Wallowa Mts.　　　　　　　　MAY–JULY

SHOWY PENSTEMON *Penstemon speciosus*
Low *spreading* stems of bright blue-purple flowers. Corolla tube *potbellied*. $\frac{1}{2}$–3 ft. Open mt. slopes. Cascades–Sierra Nevada crest, Great Basin.　　　　　　　　　MAY–JULY

GAY PENSTEMON *Penstemon laetus*
Stems erect and *distinctly sticky-haired*. Flowers blue-violet to red-purple ($\frac{3}{4}$–1$\frac{1}{2}$ in.) $\frac{1}{2}$–3 ft. Dry open mt. slopes. Cen. Calif. north to coastal Ore.　　　　　　　　　　MAY–JULY

FOOTHILL PENSTEMON *Penstemon heterophyllus*
Similar to Gay Penstemon, but the *stem smooth* to minutely haired (but not sticky). 1–3 ft. Sierra Nevada foothills and Calif. Coast Ranges south to San Diego.　　　APRIL–JULY

AZURE PENSTEMON *Penstemon azureus*
Similar to last 2 species. The *smooth,* waxy blue, *broadly oval* leaves clasp the stem. Flowers deep blue-purple. $\frac{1}{2}$–2 ft. Dry open slopes. Cen. Calif. to sw. Ore.　　　　　MAY–JULY

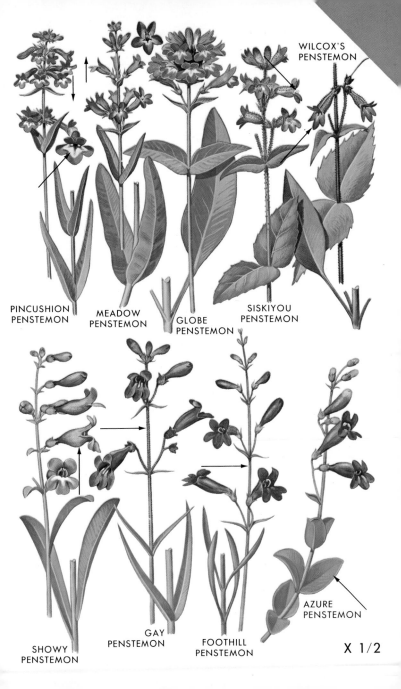

PINCUSHION PENSTEMON

MEADOW PENSTEMON

GLOBE PENSTEMON

SISKIYOU PENSTEMON

WILCOX'S PENSTEMON

SHOWY PENSTEMON

GAY PENSTEMON

FOOTHILL PENSTEMON

AZURE PENSTEMON

X 1/2

5 PETALS; 2-LIPPED TUBULAR FLOWERS

Snapdragon Family (Scrophulariaceae)
See also pp. Y 112–18; R 234–44, 310; B 336–38, 372.

LOWBUSH PENSTEMON   *Penstemon fruticosus*
Stems ascending, lancelike leaves *sawtoothed*. The long tubed bright blue-lavender flowers have a white-haired throat. 4–12 in. Cascades crest and east.   May–Aug.

CARDWELL'S PENSTEMON   *Penstemon cardwellii*
(not shown)
Very similar to preceding. *West* of Cascades.   May–Aug.

DAVIDSON'S PENSTEMON   *Penstemon davidsonii*
The *long* deep blue-purple flowers are somewhat flattened. Both the projecting lower lip and anthers *woolly-haired*. Mat-like stems. Alpine. Cascades–Sierra Nevada.   June–Aug.

WOODLAND PENSTEMON   *Penstemon nemorosus*
The thin *oval leaves* sharply toothed. The rose-purple to maroon flowers are short but broad. 1–3 ft. West of Cascades to nw. Calif.   June–Aug.

GAIRDNER'S PENSTEMON   *Penstemon gairdneri*
All 5 bright blue-purple petal lobes are *large, rounded*, and at *right angles* to short narrow tube. 4–16 in. Rocky walls. Se. Wash. and ne. Ore.   May–June

GIANT TONELLA   *Tonella floribunda*
Large purple marked *butterfly* flowers are in whorls. Leaves *3-parted linear* lobes. 4–18 in. Rocky canyon walls. Se. Wash. and ne. Ore.   April–June

Bladderwort Family (Lentibulariaceae)

COMMON BUTTERWORT   *Pinguicula vulgaris*
A *single, spurred violet* flower is above a rosette of sticky leaves. 2–8 in. Mossy places. Nw. Calif. to B.C.   May–Aug.

Broomrape Family (Orobanchaceae)
See also p. W 82.

CHAPARRAL BROOMRAPE   *Orobanche bulbosa*
The purple flowers are in a dense *Christmas tree cluster* of branching stems. Flower tube abruptly wider at edge of calyx. Bulblike stem base. 4–12 in. Calif.   April–July

DESERT BROOMRAPE   *Orobanche cooperi*
Erect *spikelike stems* have the long tubular purple flowers on *very short pedicels*. Flower tube tapering evenly. 4–12 in. Great Basin and deserts to Baja.   Jan.–Sept.

NAKED BROOMRAPE   *Orobanche uniflora*
Calyx lobes *longer* than the *calyx tube*. One purple flower on a *single* stem (others are nearby). A root parasite. 1–2 in. Pacific States.   April–Aug.

CLUSTERED BROOMRAPE   *Orobanche fasciculata*
Calyx lobes *shorter* than *calyx tube*. Numerous flowers are in a cluster of stems. 1–6 in. Pacific States.   May–July

LOWBUSH
PENSTEMON

DAVIDSON'S
PENSTEMON

WOODLAND
PENSTEMON

GAIRDNER'S
PENSTEMON

GIANT
TONELLA

COMMON
BUTTERWORT

CHAPARRAL
BROOMRAPE

DESERT
BROOMRAPE

NAKED
BROOMRAPE

CLUSTERED
BROOMRAPE

X 1/2

5-PETALED TRUMPETS IN COILED CLUSTER
4 NUTLIKE SEEDS

FORGET-ME-NOT FAMILY (Boraginaceae)
See also pp. W 78; Y 172; O 226; R 308; B 342.

GRAND HOUNDS-TONGUE *Cynoglossum grande*
Leaf blade *broadly oval* with a petioled base. The large
wheel-like bright blue flowers have an inner row of *white* teeth.
1–3 ft. Shady woods. Cen. Calif. to B.C. MAY–JULY

WESTERN HOUNDS-TONGUE *Cynoglossum occidentale*
Similar to preceding. Leaves *linear, petioleless.* 8–16 in.
Openings in woods. Cen. Calif. to s. Ore. MAY–JULY

BURGUNDY HOUNDS-TONGUE Alien
Cynoglossum officinale
Thick flowered sprays of small nodding red-purple wheel-like
flowers have an inner row of *similar* colored teeth. Numerous
linear leaves. 1–4 ft. Pacific States. MAY–JULY

BLUE WEED Alien *Echium vulgare*
Stout spikelike stems have many short curving sprays of dark
blue flowers. Stiff stem hairs *each* arise from a *distinct black
basal spot.* 1–3 ft. Pacific States. JUNE–AUG.

FORGET-ME-NOT Alien *Myosotis sylvatica*
The tiny (¼ in.) flat wheel-like flowers a pale blue, 5 white teeth
on the inner tube rim. Nutlets *smooth.* ½–2 ft. Moist shady
places. Pacific States. FEB.–AUG.

JESSICA'S STICKSEED *Hackelia micrantha*
Tiny (¼ in.) flowers pale blue with 5 inner white teeth. Each of
the 4 nutlets has ca. 10 thick stalks topped by tiny reverse
hooked spines in a *ring around* each seed. 1–2 ft. Frequent in
mt. meadows. Cen. Calif. to B.C. JUNE–AUG.

VELVETY STICKSEED *Hackelia velutina*
The *large* (¾ in.) flowers bright blue. The inner toothlike
appendages *broad and exserted.* Each seed *completely covered*
by tiny stalks with hooks. Sierra Nevada. JUNE–JULY

BUGLE LUNGWORT *Mertensia oblongifolia*
The short stem (6–14 in.) has *narrow lancelike* leaves. The
flower tube twice the length of the outer collarlike portion.
6–14 in. Open slopes. Great Basin. APRIL–MAY

TRUMPET LUNGWORT *Mertensia longiflora*
The short stem (ca. 8 in.) has *broad elliptical* leaves and *very
long* flower tubes (2–4 times that of the outer collarlike portion). 2–10 in. Great Basin. APRIL–JUNE

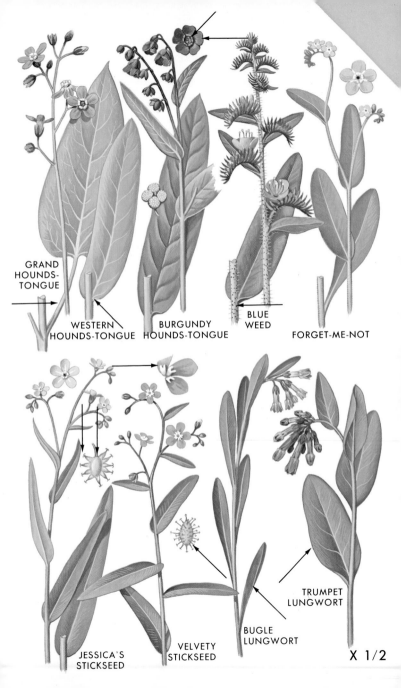

GRAND HOUNDS-TONGUE

WESTERN HOUNDS-TONGUE

BURGUNDY HOUNDS-TONGUE

BLUE WEED

FORGET-ME-NOT

JESSICA'S STICKSEED

VELVETY STICKSEED

BUGLE LUNGWORT

TRUMPET LUNGWORT

X 1/2

5-PETALED VASELIKE OR
PINWHEEL FLOWERS

FORGET-ME-NOT FAMILY (Boraginaceae)
See also pp. W 72; Y 172; O 226; R 308; B 340.

OREGON LUNGWORT   *Mertensia bella*
The bright blue *bell-like* flowers (½ in.) are in loose racemes.
Leaves oval. ½–2 ft. Moist meadows. Cen. Ore. to northern
edge of Calif.   MAY–JULY

FRINGED LUNGWORT   *Mertensia ciliata*
The dark blue flowers have a short rounded tube below a wider
funnel-like portion. Sepal margins *fringed* with hairs. Leaves
broadly lancelike and *without petioles*. 2–3 ft. Moist places in
mts. Pacific States.   MAY–AUG.

TALL LUNGWORT   *Mertensia paniculata*
Similar to Fringed Lungwort. Sepal *margins hairless*. Leaves
petioled. ½–5 ft. Wet meadows and cliffs. Olympics, Cascades,
and Great Basin.   MAY–AUG.

PRIMROSE FAMILY (Primulaceae)
See also pp. W 100; R 246, 304.

CUSICK'S PRIMROSE   *Primula cusickiana*
The *large blue pinwheel-like* flowers with yellow centers are on
a leafless stem above the basal tuft of spatula-shaped leaves.
Delightful violet-like odor. 1–4 in. Common on moist rocky
slopes immediately after snow melts. Wallowa and Blue Mts.
of Ore.; adjacent Idaho.   MARCH–JUNE

GENTIAN FAMILY (Gentianaceae)
See also pp. W 100; R 304; B 344; G 394.

ALKALI CHALICE   *Eustoma exaltatum*
The broad *punchbowl-like* blue-pink flowers have a white
central ring and basal *bilobed* purple spots. 1–2 ft. Along
alkali-crusted streams. S. Calif. and Baja.   ALL YEAR

STAR SWERTIA   *Swertia perennis*
The dull blue-purple to greenish *flat starlike* flowers have *2
round patches* of fringed hairs at the base of each petal.
4–12 in. Alpine meadows and mt. marshes. Sierra Nevada
north to B.C.; Great Basin.   JULY–SEPT.

NEWBERRY'S GENTIAN   *Gentiana newberryi*
The broad vaselike flower with dark purplish bands on the
outside has a faint electric blue tint on the white interior. A
completely blue-flowered form via hybrid crossing with
Gentiana calycosa (p. 344) occupies only the northernmost
range of this species. 3 torn-looking filaments between each of
the petal tips. 1–5 in. Alpine meadows. Sierra Nevada, White
Mts. of Calif. north to s. Ore.   JULY–SEPT.

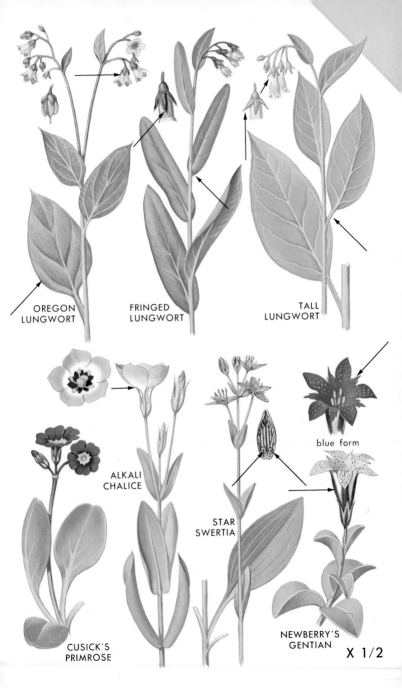

OREGON
LUNGWORT

FRINGED
LUNGWORT

TALL
LUNGWORT

CUSICK'S
PRIMROSE

ALKALI
CHALICE

STAR
SWERTIA

blue form

NEWBERRY'S
GENTIAN

X 1/2

4- OR 5-PETALED UPRIGHT
VASELIKE FLOWERS

GENTIAN FAMILY (Gentianaceae)
See also pp. W 100; R 304; B 342; G 394.

EXPLORERS GENTIAN   *Gentiana calycosa*
Note the broadly *forked filaments* between the rounded and
reflexed petal lobes of the deep blue broadly vaselike flower,
tiny yellow dots are often present. Calyx lobes highly variable
in size and shape. 6–24 in. Moist meadows, rocky hillsides.
Pacific States.   JULY–OCT.

MARSH GENTIAN   *Gentiana affinis*
The elongated flower tube is *narrowly vaselike*. The inner area
between petal lobes has a *single* short tooth. Flower blue-
purple and somewhat green-bronze on the petal backs. Marshy
open places to thickets. N. Calif. to B.C., and Great Basin.
                                           JULY–SEPT.

KINGS SCEPTER GENTIAN   *Gentiana sceptrum*
Note the flat, *smooth ledge* between the petal lobes. Flower
tube topped by 5 rounded but triangular petal lobes which
barely reflex to an open position (1–1½ in.). Flowers clustered
near the stem top on long bractless pedicels. ½–2 ft. Wet
meadows, marshes. West of Cascades and south to n. Calif.
coast.   JULY–SEPT.

MENDOCINO GENTIAN   *Gentiana setigera*
Note the *numerous long hairlike* bristles between the awn-
tipped petal lobes of the large blue bell-like flowers. Few
flowered. 8–12 in. Marshy places. Nw. Calif. and sw. Ore.
                                           JULY–SEPT.

NORTHERN GENTIAN   *Gentiana amarella*
Note the *fringe of hairs* (actually 2 sets of hairs) across the
inside of the 5 petal lobe bases. The tubular light purple to
pink flowers are clustered along the stem. 2–20 in. Common.
Moist meadows. Sierra Nevada north to B.C., and Great
Basin.   JUNE–SEPT.

HIKERS GENTIAN   *Gentianopsis simplex*
Note the single *windmill or maltese cross*–like blue flower
without any bracts, 4-petaled. 3–6 pairs of lancelike leaves
along stem. 2–8 in. Very wet mt. meadows. Cen. Calif. to cen.
Ore.   JULY–AUG.

TUFTED GENTIAN   *Gentianopsis holopetala*
Note the single blue narrowly tubular flowers with 4 *short
triangular* petal lobes that are partially reflexed. Sepals dark-
ribbed. Lower leaves in a basal cluster, spatula-shaped.
2–16 in. Wet mt. meadows. Sierra Nevada, San Bernardino Mts.
of Calif. and mts. of Great Basin.   JULY–SEPT.

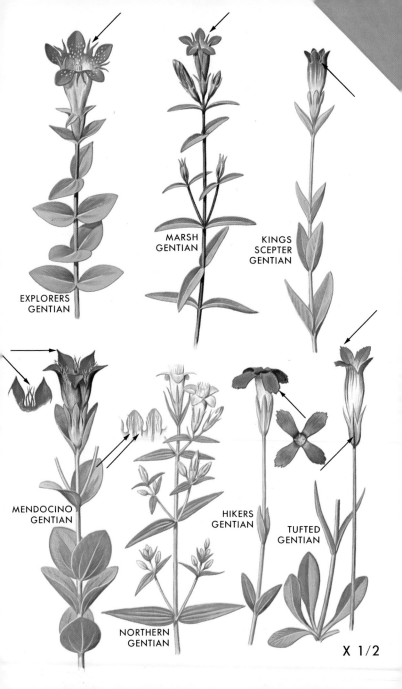

EXPLORERS
GENTIAN

MARSH
GENTIAN

KINGS
SCEPTER
GENTIAN

MENDOCINO
GENTIAN

NORTHERN
GENTIAN

HIKERS
GENTIAN

TUFTED
GENTIAN

X 1/2

5-PETALED BLUEBELL OR 2-LIPPED
FLOWERS WITH AN
INFERIOR OVARY BELOW

BLUEBELL FAMILY (Campanulaceae)
See also pp. R 316; B 348.

SCOTCH BLUEBELL *Campanula rotundifolia*
The petal lobes not reflexed on the *broad bell-like* flowers, sepal
lobes *linear and short.* Most leaves linear. Mt. meadows.
Common. N. Calif. and rest of Pacific States. JUNE–SEPT.

SCOULER'S BLUEBELL *Campanula scouleri*
The stem leaves are broad ovals with toothed margins and *have
a definite petiole.* The baseball bat–like *style well extended*
from the broad pale blue bell-like flowers with broad tapering
petal tips. ½–3 ft. Dry woods. N. Sierra Nevada and nw. Calif.
north along Cascades. JUNE–AUG.

CALIFORNIA BLUEBELL *Campanula prenanthoides*
The stem leaves, linear to lancelike with toothed margin, are
attached *without a petiole.* The baseball bat–like style well
extended beyond the bright blue bell-like flowers with narrow
petal tips. ½–3 ft. Dry semiopen woods. Cen. Calif. to s. Ore.
JUNE–SEPT.

OLYMPIC BLUEBELL *Campanula piperi*
Note the spatula-like leaves with *sharply toothed margins* and
the broad *open dishlike* blue flowers and deeply lobed petals.
2–4 in. Alpine rocky ledges. Olympic Mts. JULY–AUG.

ALASKA BLUEBELL *Campanula lasiocarpa*
Note the large *tapering funnel-like* flowers and the broad
lancelike sepal lobes with toothed margins. Calyx tube hairy.
Leaves are in a basal cluster, spatula-like and toothed. In low
mats. 2–6 in. Alpine ridges. Cascades of Cen. Wash. to B.C.
JULY–AUG.

CUPPED VENUS LOOKING GLASS
Triodanis perfoliata
The blue to lavender flowers are *nestled* above each round to
heart-shaped leaf, *which clasps the stem.* Calyx lobes as broad as
long. 4–12 in. Open places. Pacific States. MAY–AUG.

COMMON BLUE CUP *Githopsis specularioides*
Erect stems have tiny (¼ in.) *bright blue cuplike* flowers among
the long linear calyx lobes. 2–8 in. Most common the year after
a forest fire. Pacific States. MAY–JUNE

ROTHROCK'S LOBELIA *Lobelia dunnii*
2-lipped flowers all purple. *Sessile lancelike* leaves. 1–2 ft.
Damp streamsides. Cen. Calif. to Baja. JULY–SEPT.

346

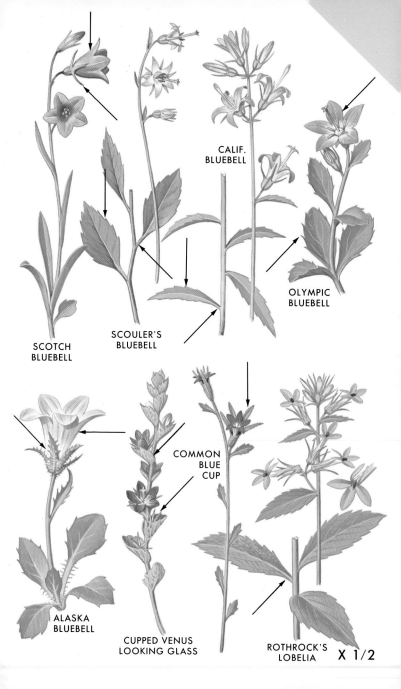

CALIF.
BLUEBELL

OLYMPIC
BLUEBELL

SCOULER'S
BLUEBELL

SCOTCH
BLUEBELL

ALASKA
BLUEBELL

COMMON
BLUE
CUP

CUPPED VENUS
LOOKING GLASS

ROTHROCK'S
LOBELIA

X 1/2

2-LIPPED FLOWER ON TOP OF LONG PEDICEL-LIKE INFERIOR OVARY

BLUEBELL FAMILY (Campanulaceae)
See also pp. R 316; B 346.

CUPPED DOWNINGIA *Downingia insignis*
Lip petal has dark purple to black lines across the top and *2 large yellow-green* spots within a white field. A long *hooked* anther column. 4–10 in. Bottoms of drying ditches. Central Valley of Calif., ne. Calif. MARCH–MAY

BACH'S DOWNINGIA *Downingia bacigalupii*
Lip petal has 2 large *orange-yellow* spots within a white field. A long *hooked* (blue-striped) anther column. 2–12 in. Blue masses in wet ditches. Great Basin. MAY–JULY

ELEGANT DOWNINGIA *Downingia elegans*
Similar to Bach's Downingia. Lip petal has a central white field *without* yellow spots. 4–16 in. Muddy vernal pools. N. Calif. to Wash.; Great Basin. JUNE–SEPT.

TWO-HORNED DOWNINGIA *Downingia bicornuta*
Note the *2 blue-purple nipplelike* projections on the lower lip. A pair of *bristles are twisted* together at the tip of the nearly *hidden* anthers. Lower lip has a large white center, 2 small yellow spots. 2–6 in. Wet ditches. Central Valley of Calif. north to s. Ore. APRIL–JULY

VALLEY DOWNINGIA *Downingia pulchella*
Note the 3 dark spots alternating with the 2 yellow spots in the large white central area of the lower lip. 2–6 in. Muddy flats, vernal pools. Cen. Calif. APRIL–JUNE

TOOTHED DOWNINGIA *Downingia cuspidata*
The lower flower lip has *3 nearly equal* lobes and the 2 upper ones are *narrowly diverging.* The flowers bright blue, the lower lip has a large central white area with a *large yellow spot* (or nearly divided into 2). 2–6 in. Muddy flats. Calif. MARCH–JUNE

FRINGED DOWNINGIA *Downingia concolor*
A *fringe of hairs* are along the margins of the 2 upper petals. A *single purple spot* within the large white area of the lower lip. 2–5 in. Muddy flats, vernal pools. Calif. Coast Ranges south to San Diego area. MAY–JULY

CASCADE DOWNINGIA *Downingia yina*
Dark purple flowers have a lower lip with a ring of white around a large central yellow area with 2 low ridges and a band of dark purple above. Anther column barely visible. Muddy meadows, marshes. Cen. Calif. to Wash. APRIL–AUG.

FOLDED DOWNINGIA *Downingia ornatissima*
The two top petal lobes *coiled and folded flat backward.* Central lip area white with yellow on 2 middle ridges and 3 purple spots in throat. 3–12 in. Wet pools and ditches. Central Valley of Calif. APRIL–MAY

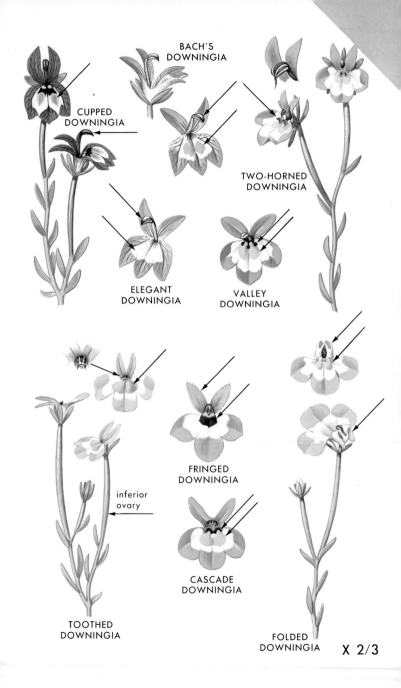

BACH'S
DOWNINGIA

CUPPED
DOWNINGIA

TWO-HORNED
DOWNINGIA

ELEGANT
DOWNINGIA

VALLEY
DOWNINGIA

inferior
ovary

FRINGED
DOWNINGIA

CASCADE
DOWNINGIA

TOOTHED
DOWNINGIA

FOLDED
DOWNINGIA

X 2/3

3 OR 6 PETALS; FLAT IRISLIKE LEAVES

Iris Family (Iridaceae)
See also pp. Y 126; R 254.

DOUGLAS'S IRIS *Iris douglasiana*
Top of ovary *nipplelike*. Both floral tube and pedicel are of nearly equal length (1–2 in.). Flowers blue-purple. ½–3 ft. Grassy slopes along Calif. and Ore. coast. Feb.–April

LONG-TUBED IRIS *Iris tenuissima*
Corolla tube above the ovary very long (2–4 in.), the top an enlarged cylinder. Pedicel below ovary very short. Numerous *blue-purple lines* on a *white petal*. 1–2 ft. Woodlands. N. Calif. April–June

BOWL-TUBED IRIS *Iris macrosiphon*
Corolla tube above ovary *very long and bowl-shaped* at the top. Pedicel below ovary *very short*. Flowers variable, blue to yellow or cream. ½–1½ ft. Shady woods. Calif. Coast Ranges, w. Sierra Nevada foothills. April–June

TOUGH-LEAF IRIS *Iris tenax*
Corolla tube *stout* and *short* (¼ in.) above the barrel-shaped ovary. Pedicel below ovary about 1 in. Petals dark blue-purple to creams and yellows. 1–2 ft. West of Cascades in Wash. to northernmost edge of Calif. April–June

HARTWEG'S IRIS *Iris hartwegii*
Corolla tube above ovary *short and stout*. Pedicel below ovary *very long*. *Narrow* blue petals. (Also see Yellow p. 126). 1–2 ft. Mts. of s. Calif. May–June

MUNZ'S IRIS *Iris munzii*
Corolla tube *stout* and *very short* above the barrel-like ovary. Pedicel below ovary *short* (1–2 in.). Petals powdery blue. 1–2 ft. Foothills s. Sierra Nevada. March–April

ROCKY MOUNTAIN IRIS *Iris missouriensis*
Flower tube above ovary a very short bowl-like enlargement. Pedicel below ovary very long (to 8 in.). Flowers dark blue or paler. Petals elongated with a central dark *yellow-orange stripe and diverging* dark blue lines on a *white* background. 1–3 ft. Great Basin. May–July

LONG-PETALED IRIS *Iris longipetala*
(not shown)
Similar to preceding. Cen. Calif. coast. April–May

CALIFORNIA BLUE-EYED GRASS *Sisyrinchium bellum*
Dark purple 6-petaled stars with a darker center. Stem has *2 or more branches* and flowers. 4–16 in. Open grassy places. Pacific States. Feb.–July

IDAHO BLUE-EYED GRASS *Sisyrinchium idahoense*
Light blue 6-petaled stars on *long unbranched* stems. 4–16 in. Mt. meadows. Pacific States. July–Aug.

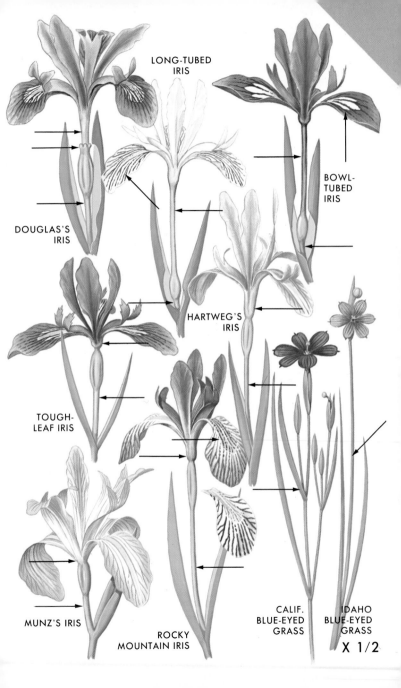

LONG-TUBED
IRIS

BOWL-
TUBED
IRIS

DOUGLAS'S
IRIS

HARTWEG'S
IRIS

TOUGH-
LEAF IRIS

MUNZ'S IRIS

ROCKY
MOUNTAIN IRIS

CALIF.
BLUE-EYED
GRASS

IDAHO
BLUE-EYED
GRASS

X 1/2

3 OR 6 PETALS; UMBELS OR RACEMES

AMARYLLIS FAMILY (Amaryllidaceae)
See also pp. W 18; Y 124; R 254–62.

BLUE DICKS *Dichelostemma pulchellum*
Flower tube a *short round inflated* ball. *6 hidden anthers* within a series of projections. Congested flower umbel. 6–18 in. Very common. Pacific States. JAN.–MAY

ROUNDTOOTH OOKOW *Dichelostemma multiflorum*
Flower tube is elongated with a *strong constriction* at top and 3 *toothlike* projections with the *tips rounded.* 3 hidden stamens. 1–3 ft. S. Ore. to cen. Calif. MAY–JUNE

FORKTOOTH OOKOW *Dichelostemma congestum*
Similar to preceding. Elongated flower tube only *slightly constricted* at top. 3 toothlike projections have the *tips strongly forked.* 1–3 ft. Cen. Calif. to Wash. APRIL–JUNE

DOUGLAS'S TRITELEIA *Triteleia douglasii*
Flower tube short and round-based. Petal lobe margins *wavy. Linear* anthers on *narrow linear or absent filaments.* 1–3 ft. Open grassy places. Ore. and Wash. APRIL–JULY

HOWELL'S TRITELEIA *Triteleia howellii*
Similar to preceding. Petal lobe margins usually smooth. Anthers *broad* on filaments *broader than the anther.* 1–3 ft. Mostly west of Cascades, but up Columbia R. APRIL–JUNE

WALLY BASKET *Triteleia laxa*
Petal lobes bent at a *low angle* from the *long funnel-like tube.* The ovary and style *hidden from view.* The 6 anther bases attached at *2 levels.* Blue flowers. 1–4 ft. Common, open grasslands. Cen. Calif. to s. Ore. APRIL–JUNE

BRIDGES' TRITELEIA *Triteleia bridgesii*
Petal lobes *erect,* crownlike, forming a distinct right-angle flare at the top of the funnel-like tube. A white zone at base of petals inside of corolla. The ovary and style *project above* the stamens. ½–2 ft. Blue-green serpentine rock soils. Cen. Calif. to s. Ore. APRIL–JUNE

LILY FAMILY (Liliaceae)
See also pp. W 4–16; Y 122–24; O 228–30;
R 252–56; B 352; G 388–90.

COMMON CAMAS *Camassia quamash*
Long linear purple to white petals, 1 lower petal *slightly larger.* 1–3 ft. Moist meadows. Pacific States. APRIL–JULY

PURPLE SOAP PLANT *Chlorogalum purpureum*
The purple flowers have a *short* basal tube. Linear leaves *wavy-margined.* Jolon area, Calif. South Coast Ranges.
MAY–JUNE

352

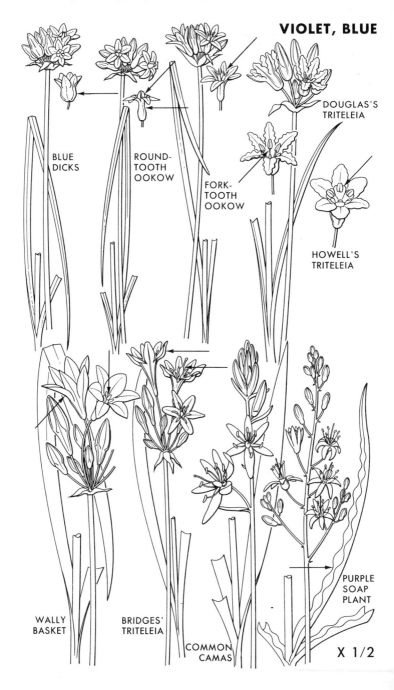

VIOLET, BLUE

DOUGLAS'S
TRITELEIA

BLUE
DICKS

ROUND-
TOOTH
OOKOW

FORK-
TOOTH
OOKOW

HOWELL'S
TRITELEIA

WALLY
BASKET

BRIDGES'
TRITELEIA

COMMON
CAMAS

PURPLE
SOAP
PLANT

X 1/2

5-PETALED, SPURRED DELPHINIUMS

BUTTERCUP FAMILY (Ranunculaceae)
See also pp. W 40–42; Y 154–58; O 226; R 280–82;
B 354–56, 382; G 404.

MONKS-HOOD   *Aconitum columbianum*
The upper sepal forms a *hood* much like a monk's (not spurred)
over a *round head* of purple segments. Leaves deeply 3- to 5-
cleft. 1–7 ft. Wet mt. meadows. Pacific States.   JUNE–AUG.

POISON DELPHINIUM   *Delphinium trolliifolium*
Royal blue sepals reflexed backward with the smaller petals
projected forward. The 2 lower petals bilobed and forming an
arching tunnel. Flowers in a large bottlebrush. 3–6 ft. Marshy
places. West of Cascades south to nw. Calif.   APRIL–JULY

MOUNTAIN MARSH DELPHINIUM
                                Delphinium polycladon
The *broad and rounded* purple sepals folded forward into a
funnel. The lower 2 petals *within* the funnel facing *forward,*
very hairy, and bilobed. Spur tip points downward. 2–3 ft.
Springy hillsides. High Sierra Nevada.   JULY–AUG.

CALIFORNIA COAST DELPHINIUM
                                Delphinium californicum
Similar to preceding. Flowers *dull blue to green.* Spur short
and stout, arched. The lower 2 petals barely bilobed, hairy.
Leaves broad, 5–7 divisions. 2–5 ft. Marshy seeps on slopes.
Cen. Calif. coast.   APRIL–JUNE

ROYAL DELPHINIUM   *Delphinium variegatum*
The *short stem* has very large, royal blue flowers. Leaves
divided into 3 *narrow ribbonlike* divisions which fork 3–5 times
at *regular* intervals. Leaf segments folded or collapsed together, densely long-haired. 1–2 ft. Fields. Calif. Coast
Ranges; Sierra Nevada foothills.   MARCH–MAY

PARRY'S DELPHINIUM   *Delphinium parryi*
Long spike of large bright blue flowers on tall stem, sepals
cupped forward. Leaves divided into *threadlike divisions* (1–2
times), hairless. Lower petals deeply bilobed, hairy. 1–3 ft.
Calif. South Coast Ranges to Baja.   APRIL–MAY

HANSEN'S DELPHINIUM   *Delphinium hanseni*
Dark purple to nearly white flowers in a *dense spike.* Lower
basal leaves *broad,* barely divided, the upper well divided and
twisted. 2–3 ft. Sierra Nevada foothills.   APRIL–JUNE

FOOTHILL DELPHINIUM   *Delphinium hesperium*
Leaves have *rust-colored veins* on underside. Leaves narrowly
divided into *shiny* green divisions. Dark or pale blue flowers in
spikes. The 2 lower petals in a rounded dome, heavily haired.
1–2 ft. Calif. Coast Ranges.   MAY–JULY

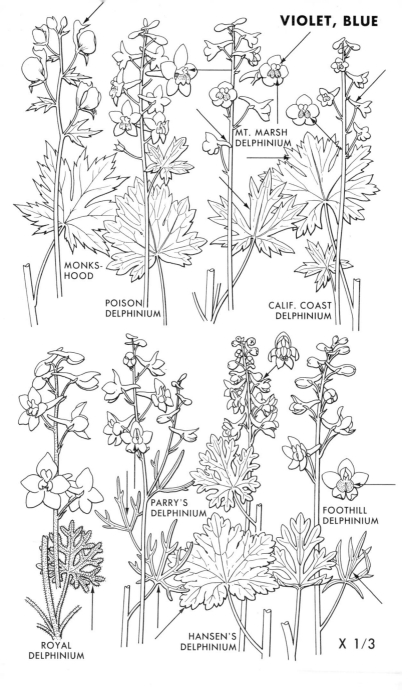

VIOLET, BLUE

MONKS-
HOOD

POISON
DELPHINIUM

MT. MARSH
DELPHINIUM

CALIF. COAST
DELPHINIUM

ROYAL
DELPHINIUM

PARRY'S
DELPHINIUM

HANSEN'S
DELPHINIUM

FOOTHILL
DELPHINIUM

X 1/3

5-PETALED, SPURRED DELPHINIUMS

BUTTERCUP FAMILY (Ranunculaceae)
See also pp. W 40–42; Y 154–58; O 226; R 280–82;
B 354–56, 382; G 404.

PARISH'S DESERT DELPHINIUM *Delphinium parishii*
Flowers *pale sky blue*. The large *sepals reflexed* backward.
Leaves have 3–5 oblong lobes. ½–2 ft. Mojave, Colorado
Deserts, and west to s. Central Valley of Calif. MARCH–JUNE

ANDERSON'S DELPHINIUM *Delphinium andersonii*
The dark purple flowers on smooth red stems. Spur tip often
flexed downward. The lower 2 petals dark purple, bilobed. The
smooth blue-green leaves *narrowly divided to base*. ½–2 ft.
Common, loose soils. Great Basin. APRIL–JUNE

BILOBED DELPHINIUM *Delphinium nuttallianum*
Stout hairy stems. Leaves few, divided into 3–5 narrow divisions, *tips sharp*. Flowers bright blue to pale purple. Upper 2
petals white, strongly *purple-veined*. Lower 2 petals *strongly
bilobed*. 4–12 in. Great Basin. MARCH–JULY

OLYMPIC DELPHINIUM *Delphinium glareosum*
Round leaves with *broad fanlike* divisions clustered at stem
base. ½–1 ft. Alpine ridges. Olympic Mts. JUNE–AUG.

COAST DELPHINIUM *Delphinium decorum*
Leaves have 3 main divisions, each with 2–3 round lobes. Stem
hairy. Sepals oblong, blue-purple with a *central line* of hairs.
Lower petals oval and strongly bilobed, hairy. 4–12 in. Calif.
coastal region to s. Ore. MARCH–JUNE

MENZIES' DELPHINIUM *Delphinium menziesii*
Stem, leaves, and flowers *hairy*. Leaves of 5 segments, each
deeply 3-lobed with blunt tips. Pedicels spreading from stem.
Sepals deep rich blue. The 2 upper petals each have a distinct
rounded tooth projecting over the 2 lower petals. ½–2 ft. West
of Cascades and south to n. Calif. APRIL–JULY

ZIGZAG DELPHINIUM *Delphinium patens*
Slender wiry zigzag stem. Each leaf of 3–5 *simple wedges*.
Sepals dark blue, spur pointing upward. Upper 2 petals white
with blue lines. A distinct rounded lobe projects over each of
the lower bilobed petals, often with a central tuft of hairs.
½–2 ft. Cen. and s. Calif. MARCH–JUNE

TOWER DELPHINIUM *Delphinium glaucum*
Sharp pointed purple sepals are in a shallow funnel. The 2
lower petals folded together, *not bilobed*. Bottlebrush flower
clusters. Dull green leaves with sharp lobes. 3–6 ft. High mt.
marshy thickets. Pacific States. JULY–SEPT.

356

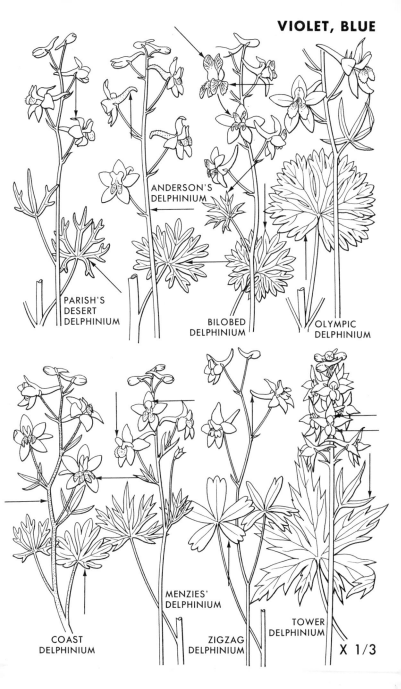

VIOLET, BLUE

PARISH'S DESERT DELPHINIUM

ANDERSON'S DELPHINIUM

BILOBED DELPHINIUM

OLYMPIC DELPHINIUM

COAST DELPHINIUM

MENZIES' DELPHINIUM

ZIGZAG DELPHINIUM

TOWER DELPHINIUM

X 1/3

5 PETALS; BILATERAL SYMMETRY: VIOLETS

Violet Family (Violaceae)
See also pp. W 52; Y 162–64.

BECKWITH'S VIOLET *Viola beckwithii*
A spectacularly beautiful violet. Flowers purple-violet to red-purple with large yellow center and purple whiskery lines. Leaves *divided* into 3 main parts, each with linear lobes. 1–2 in. Soggy early spring sagebrush flats. March–May

WESTERN DOG VIOLET *Viola adunca*
Note the *long erect stems* have rounded to heart-shaped leaves and *lancelike bracts* below the petiole base. Flowers deep to pale violet. 1–8 in. Moist openings in woods. Very common. Pacific States. March–Aug.

ENGLISH VIOLET Alien *Viola odorata*
Note the strong *pleasant odor,* even from a distance. The dark violet-purple flowers have 4 *narrow and twisted* petals and 1 flat lip petal. Thick rhizomes (cordlike stems) along the ground surface. Leaves rounded to heart-shaped and short-pediceled. 2–4 in. Common about old towns. Calif. Dec.–March

OLYMPIC VIOLET *Viola flettii*
The flowers purple-violet, the lower lip petal *long and narrow* with a large yellow basal spot. The lateral petal pair *yellow-bearded.* Leaves broadly *kidney-shaped.* 1–6 in. Alpine slopes. Olympic Mts. of Wash. June–Aug.

KIDNEY-LEAF VIOLET *Viola nephrophylla*
Stemless plant. Leaves broad kidney-shaped to heart-shaped. Flowers deep blue-violet with white basal hairs. The 3 lower petals veined and *well bearded.* 2–6 in. Moist cool shady places. Mts. of San Diego, Calif., area north on eastern slopes of Cascades–Sierra Nevada to B.C.; Great Basin. May–July

BLUE-RUNNER VIOLET *Viola palustris*
Plant stemless, but has *runners* to next plant. Leaves small, rounded to heart-shaped. Flowers lilac to nearly white. 3–6 in. Cool damp thickets and forest floors. N. Calif. to B.C.

May–July

VIOLET, BLUE

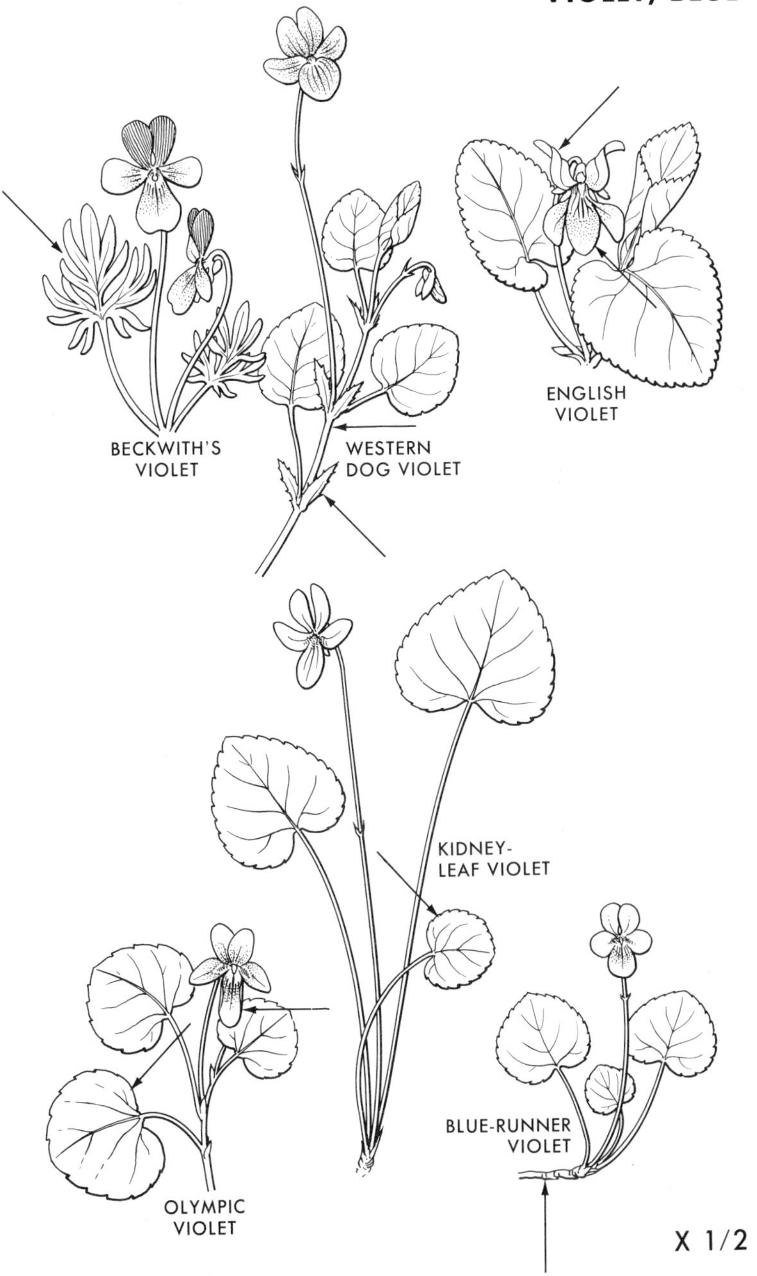

BECKWITH'S
VIOLET

WESTERN
DOG VIOLET

ENGLISH
VIOLET

KIDNEY-
LEAF VIOLET

OLYMPIC
VIOLET

BLUE-RUNNER
VIOLET

X 1/2

5 PETALS; SMALL UPRIGHT TRUMPETS

PHLOX FAMILY (Polemoniaceae)
See also pp. W 72; Y 172; O 226; R 248–50, 306;
B 362–64.

BIRDS-EYE GILIA *Gilia tricolor*
Note the short, broad, bowl-like, dark blue-violet flowers with the *tube* yellow to orange and having 5 pairs of tiny short purple lines. Narrow linear pinnate leaves. 4–6 in. Very common. Grasslands. Cen. Calif. MARCH–APRIL

BLUE-HEADED GILIA *Gilia capitata*
Note the *round balls* of dark or pale blue flowers on tall erect stems with linear-lobed pinnate leaves. ½–3 ft. Grassy hillsides. Most of Pacific States. APRIL–AUG.

CALIFORNIA GILIA *Gilia achilleaefolia*
Note the *dense fan-shaped* flower heads on a naked peduncle. Flowers blue-violet throughout. The pinnate leaves linear-lobed with final tips scythe-shaped. ½–2 ft. Open places at low elevations. Calif. Coast Ranges. MAY–JUNE

BLUE FALSE GILIA *Allophyllum gilioides*
The tiny dark violet-blue flowers are in loose heads (4–8 in.). Leaves linear with 2–5 pairs of simple linear lobes. 4–18 in. Foothills and mts. of Calif. APRIL–JUNE

MINIATURE GILIA *Gilia capillaris*
Tiny ¼-in., pale violet to pink (or white), funnel-shaped flowers often streaked with purple. Rarely the tube is yellow with purple spots. Leaves *linear* along entire stem. 1–12 in. Common in masses. Open sandy places. Mts. and foothills. Pacific States. JUNE–AUG.

BROAD GILIA *Gilia latiflora*
The pale or dark purple flower is a *long, wide-tubed* trumpet with white at the base of the petal lobes. Straplike pinnate leaves have small bilobed toothed divisions. 4–12 in. Western Mojave Desert, Calif. South Coast Ranges. MARCH–MAY

GREAT BASIN GILIA *Gilia leptomeria*
Leaves all in a basal rosette, *narrowly straplike* with small *triangular* lobes as if cut by pinking shears. Petal lobes frequently 3-toothed. 2–8 in. Juniper woodlands. Great Basin, Mojave Desert. APRIL–JUNE

STAR GILIA *Gilia stellata*
Similar to preceding. Basal rosette leaves have the leaflets *bilobed or trilobed*. Stems and leaflets covered with numerous *long glandular hairs*. Simple round-tipped petal lobes. 4–16 in. Sandy places. Mojave, Colorado Deserts. MARCH–MAY

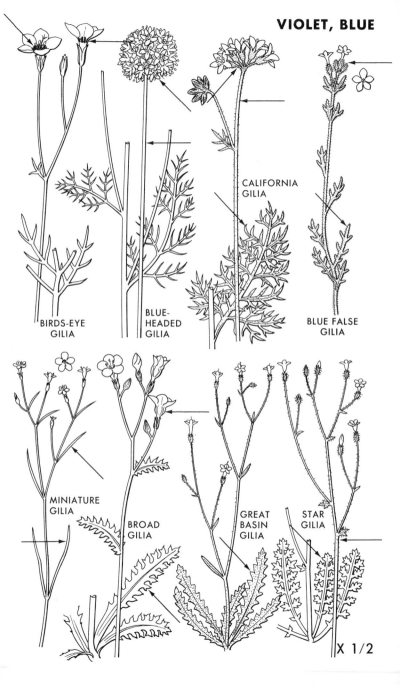

VIOLET, BLUE

BIRDS-EYE GILIA

BLUE-HEADED GILIA

CALIFORNIA GILIA

BLUE FALSE GILIA

MINIATURE GILIA

BROAD GILIA

GREAT BASIN GILIA

STAR GILIA

X 1/2

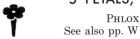

5 PETALS; SMALL UPRIGHT BOWLS

PHLOX FAMILY (Polemoniaceae)
See also pp. W 72; Y 172; O 226; R 248–50, 306;
B 360–64.

WESTERN POLEMONIUM   *Polemonium occidentale*
Flat blue pinwheel flowers. Petal lobes narrow and twice as long as the tubular portion. Each pale yellow-green pinnate leaf has a *long bare petiole* and 19–27 lancelike leaflets. $\frac{1}{2}$–3 ft. Marshy places. Pacific States.   JUNE–AUG.

ROYAL POLEMONIUM   *Polemonium carneum*
Flowers are broad shallow bowls of purple to light pink, with yellow throats. Petal lobes broadly oval. The pinnate leaves thick, dark green, and shiny. Leaflets *clothe petiole to its base.* 1–3 ft. Grassy openings. Along cen. Calif. coast north to and including Cascades.   APRIL–AUG.

SHOWY POLEMONIUM   *Polemonium pulcherrimum*
Short-stemmed. The small pale blue flowers shallowly bowl-like with a yellow tube. The 11–23 pale yellow-green leaflets *sticky-haired.* Bad odor if handled. 2–12 in. Higher mts. of Pacific States.   MAY–AUG.

SIERRA SKY PILOT   *Polemonium eximium*
Note the *large rounded head* of bright, dark blue-purple flowers on erect leafless stems above the basal cluster of pinnate leaves. Leaves have numerous *tiny 3- to 5-parted leaflets.* 4–12 in. Sandy alpine ridge lines. Sierra Nevada. JULY–AUG.

DESERT CALICO   *Langloisia matthewii*
Unequal bowl-shaped flowers have blue to red spots. Petal lobes *as long as* corolla tube. Leaves with spiny teeth. 1–6 in. Sandy flats. Mojave, Colorado Deserts.   APRIL–JUNE

SCHOTT'S CALICO   *Langloisia schottii*
Unequal bowl-shaped flowers blue, pink, or tan. Petal *lobes short,* $\frac{1}{3}$ to $\frac{1}{2}$ as long as corolla tube. Triangular toothed leaf lobes, each tipped with *1 spine.* Sandy places. Calif. South Coast Ranges; Mojave, Colorado Deserts.   MARCH–JUNE

SPOTTED LANGLOISIA   *Langloisia punctata*
Pale blue regular bowl-shaped flower with *numerous spots* and paired yellow dots on each petal. Leaves triangular, 3- to 5-lobed with spiny tips. 1–6 in. Rocky slopes. Mojave Desert and White Mts.   APRIL–JUNE

BRISTLY LANGLOISIA   *Langloisia setosissima*
Dark violet bowl-shaped flowers have a *few dark lines.* Leaves triangular-lobed, spines in pairs. 1–3 in. Open places. Great Basin to Mojave, Colorado Deserts.   APRIL–JULY

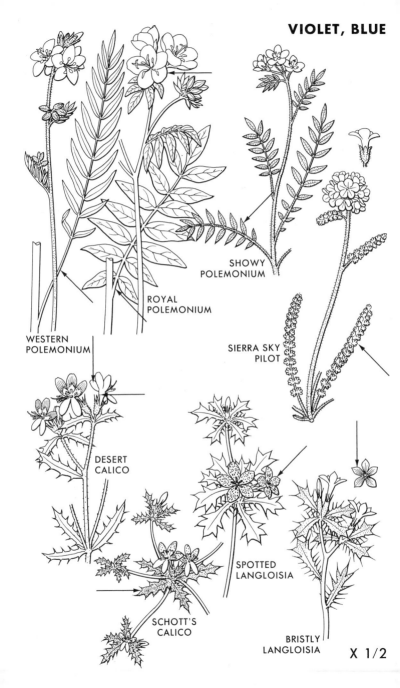

VIOLET, BLUE

SHOWY
POLEMONIUM

ROYAL
POLEMONIUM

WESTERN
POLEMONIUM

SIERRA SKY
PILOT

DESERT
CALICO

SPOTTED
LANGLOISIA

SCHOTT'S
CALICO

BRISTLY
LANGLOISIA

X 1/2

5 PETALS; SMALL TRUMPETS IN WOOLLY OR STICKY FLOWER HEADS; SPINY LEAVES

Phlox Family (Polemoniaceae)
See also pp. W 72; Y 172; O 226; R 248–50, 306;
B 360–62.

SAPPHIRE WOOL STAR   *Eriastrum sapphirinum*
Short (½ in.) funnel-shaped, *dark sapphire blue* flowers have petal lobes as long as the yellow tube below. Bract below the few flowered clusters 3-lobed, membrane margins smooth. Leaves linear to 3-lobed. 4–12 in. S. Calif. Mts. May–Sept.

TEHACHAPI WOOL STAR   *Eriastrum pluriflorum*
The *deep blue-violet* funnel-shaped flowers have the stamens attached *at and between* the petal lobes. Leaves with 3–9 *threadlike lobes.* 4–16 in. S.-cen. Calif.   May–July

DESERT WOOL STAR   *Eriastrum eremicum*
The long (¾-in.) *pale blue* trumpet-shaped flower has its petals *arranged unequally,* stamens of unequal lengths. 2 yellow spots in flower tube. Spiny leaves of 5–9 linear pinnate lobes. Leaves and calyx densely *cobwebby-haired.* 2–10 in. Sandy places. Mojave, Colorado Deserts.   April–June

GIANT WOOL STAR   *Eriastrum densifolium*
The long trumpetlike flowers are in a *dense headlike* cluster on long slender *woody* stems. ½–2 ft. Sandy slopes. Calif. South Coast Ranges, S. Calif. Mts.   May–Oct.

MINIATURE WOOL STAR   *Eriastrum diffusum*
The tiny (¼-in.), pale blue to white, short tubular flowers are in terminal clusters, each subtended with a 3- to 7-lobed and somewhat arching bract. Pinnate leaves *shiny green.* 2–6 in. Sandy places. Mojave, Colorado Deserts.   March–May

SKUNKWEED   *Navarretia squarrosa*
The blue to purple tubular flowers are in *shiny pincushion-like* clusters. Broad *shiny* pinnate leaves. Glandular hairs have a strong skunky odor. 2–20 in. Open fields. West of Cascades and south to cen. Calif.   June–Sept.

NEEDLE NAVARRETIA   *Navarretia intertexta*
Pale blue to white flowers are in dense clusters. Shaggy-haired leaves. Stem *brown* with crisped white hairs. 2–8 in. Dried pool depressions. Pacific States.   May–Aug.

DOWNY NAVARRETIA   *Navarretia pubescens*
The *erect miniature trees* have a terminal ball of *dark purple* flowers. Dark green, *finely divided,* sticky leaves. 4–12 in. Woodlands. Calif. Coast Ranges, Sierra Nevada.   May–July

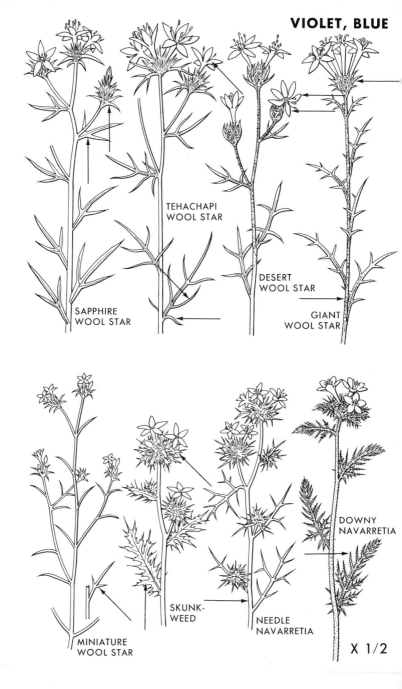

VIOLET, BLUE

TEHACHAPI
WOOL STAR

SAPPHIRE
WOOL STAR

DESERT
WOOL STAR

GIANT
WOOL STAR

MINIATURE
WOOL STAR

SKUNK-
WEED

NEEDLE
NAVARRETIA

DOWNY
NAVARRETIA

X 1/2

5 UNITED PETALS AS BELLS OR BOWLS; FLOWERS IN COILED CLUSTERS

WATERLEAF FAMILY (Hydrophyllaceae)
See also pp. W 74–76; Y 172; R 308; B 368–70.

BLUE FIESTA FLOWER *Pholistoma auritum*
Broad, dark blue, bowl-like flowers have a *nipplelike* tube below. Dandelionlike leaves. Stem has *reversed prickles.* 1–4 ft. Foothills cen. and s. Calif. MARCH–MAY

MEADOW NEMOPHILA *Nemophila pedunculata*
Leaves all opposite. Each flower on a pedicel *as long as* adjacent leaf. Tiny white bell-like flower has blue spots. Sepals lancelike. 4–12 in. Pacific States. APRIL–AUG.

FIVESPOT *Nemophila maculata*
A large *purple spot* on each petal tip of a large white bowl-like flower. Sierra Nevada foothills. APRIL–JULY

BABY BLUE-EYES *Nemophila menziesii*
Large, bright to pale blue flower bowls. Leaves pinnate lobed on sprawling succulent stems. Ssp. *atomaria* is similar except the flower is white with radiating lines of dots. 4–12 in. Moist fields. S. Ore., Calif. MARCH–MAY

VARI-LEAF NEMOPHILA *Nemophila heterophylla*
Lower stem leaves *oppositely* paired, but *alternately* arranged above. Flowers broadly bowl-shaped, blue to white. 4–12 in. Semishady places. Cen. Calif. to sw. Ore. MARCH–JULY

EASTWOOD'S NEMOPHILA *Nemophila pulchella*
Note the opposite completely pinnate leaves with opposite oval lobes and a *terminal 3-lobed* leaflet. The small ($\frac{1}{2}$ in.) broad dishlike flowers are deep blue with a white center. 4–16 in. Shady woods. Foothills Sierra Nevada, and inner Calif. South Coast Ranges. APRIL–JUNE

CALIFORNIA WATERLEAF *Hydrophyllum occidentale*
The large pinnate leaves have broad linear lobes, each with a few sharp teeth along the lower edge. Cluster of violet to white bowl-like flowers on *tall stems.* Petal tips *slightly bilobed.* $\frac{1}{2}$–2 ft. Shady woods. West of Cascades and south to cen. Calif. APRIL–JULY

DWARF WATERLEAF *Hydrophyllum capitatum*
A rounded cluster of flowers *low to ground,* i.e., nearly stemless. The pinnate leaves have slender leaflets. Flowers purple, lavender, or white. Petal tips *rounded.* 4–16 in. Moist places. Sierra Nevada, Great Basin. MARCH–JULY

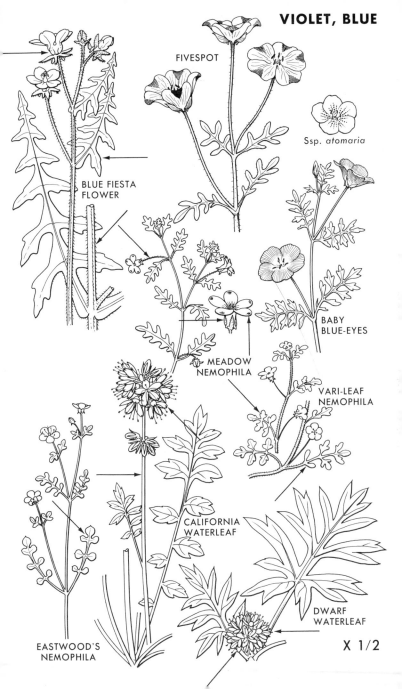

VIOLET, BLUE

FIVESPOT

Ssp. *atomaria*

BLUE FIESTA
FLOWER

BABY
BLUE-EYES

MEADOW
NEMOPHILA

VARI-LEAF
NEMOPHILA

CALIFORNIA
WATERLEAF

DWARF
WATERLEAF

EASTWOOD'S
NEMOPHILA

X 1/2

5-PETALED SMALL BELLS IN COILS

WATERLEAF FAMILY (Hydrophyllaceae)
See also pp. W 74–76; Y 172; R 308; B 366–70.

DRAPERIA *Draperia systyla*
Pale violet flowers have *long slender tubes.* The low slender stem has *oval* hairy leaves in pairs. 4–16 in. Dry shady woods. Sierra Nevada to Siskiyous. MAY–AUG.

COMMON PHACELIA *Phacelia distans*
Pinnate leaves usually oppositely arranged, coarsely toothed leaflets on erect stems. Flowers bright blue in tightly coiled cymes. ½–3 ft. Cen. and s. Calif. MARCH–JUNE

BRANCHING PHACELIA *Phacelia ramosissima*
Stems coarse, sprawling, or weakly erect. The pinnate leaflets *alternately arranged,* coarsely toothed. Flowers blue to dirty white in dense, tightly coiled cymes. 2–3 ft. Open places. Common. Calif., Great Basin. MAY–AUG.

TANSY PHACELIA *Phacelia tanacetifolia*
Long sprawling stems have *compound fernlike* leaves. Each primary leaflet subdivided 1–2 more times into tiny rounded lobes. Flowers pale blue. 1–3 ft. S. Calif. MARCH–MAY

CHINESE LANTERN PHACELIA *Phacelia ciliata*
Note the very large papery *lantern-like calyxes* on long curving sprays. Alternate pinnate leaflets subdivided into round lobes. 4–24 in. Frequent. W. Calif. MARCH–MAY

LONG-STALKED PHACELIA *Phacelia longipes*
Rounded wavy-margined leaves have *very long petioles.* Stems well branched. The shallowly lobed flowers blue or white in long loose coils. 4–16 in. Mid-mt. slopes. Calif. South Coast Ranges to San Gabriel Mts. in s. Calif. APRIL–JULY

EISEN'S PHACELIA *Phacelia eisenii*
(not shown)
Similar to preceding. Flowers in *very loose* uncoiled cymes. 1–6 in. Under conifer trees. Sierra Nevada. JUNE–AUG.

LINEARLEAF PHACELIA *Phacelia linearis*
Stems stiffly erect. Despite its name, most of the stem leaves have *3 linear lobes,* sometimes single. The broad flowers purple to nearly white in tightly coiled cymes. ½–2 ft. Dry open slopes. Common. Great Basin. APRIL–JUNE

LOW PHACELIA *Phacelia humilis*
Dark violet flowers in *distinct coils* are in low mounds. *Lance-like* leaf blades are *on long slender* petioles. 2–8 in. Colorful carpets on sagebrush flats. Great Basin. MAY–JULY

368

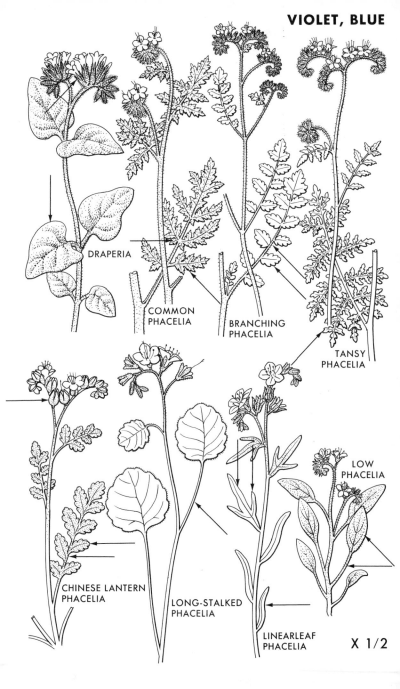

VIOLET, BLUE

DRAPERIA

COMMON
PHACELIA

BRANCHING
PHACELIA

TANSY
PHACELIA

CHINESE LANTERN
PHACELIA

LONG-STALKED
PHACELIA

LINEARLEAF
PHACELIA

LOW
PHACELIA

X 1/2

5-PETALED SMALL BELLS IN COILS

WATERLEAF FAMILY (Hydrophyllaceae)
See also pp. W 74–76; Y 172; R 308; B 366–68.

ALPINE PHACELIA *Phacelia sericea*
Note the tall *pokerlike* clusters of deep purple well above the *silvery*-haired leaves. Leaves pinnate with deeply cut linear lobes. 4–16 in. Rocky places in alpine area. N. Calif. north to B.C.; Great Basin. JUNE–AUG.

SCALLOP PHACELIA *Phacelia crenulata*
Note the many curving sprays of dark blue-purple flowers above the *shiny red* stems. The broad *elongated* leaves a dark shiny green, varying from a few lobes to many. ½–2 ft. Common. Sandy flats. Mojave, Colorado Deserts. MARCH–JUNE

CALIFORNIA BELLS *Phacelia minor*
Note the *large short bell-like* purple flowers have a *yellowish-white spot* on the inside of each petal. Leaves oval with toothed margins. ½–2 ft. Dry places. Mts. of s. Calif. and edge of deserts. MARCH–JUNE

STICKY PHACELIA *Phacelia viscida*
The large bright blue *dishlike* flowers have a *gingham* inner circle of purple dots on white. Stems erect. Leaves broadly oval, irregularly toothed margins. Large, black-headed glands on calyx and stem. ½–3 ft. Open places along coast. Monterey to San Diego, Calif. MARCH–JUNE

BALLHEAD PHACELIA *Phacelia hydrophylloides*
The purple to blue flowers are in *dense round balls*. Leaves broad triangular with rounded lobes. 4–12 in. Open dry woods. Sierra Nevada to s. Ore. JUNE–AUG.

BOLANDER'S PHACELIA *Phacelia bolanderi*
Stems sprawling to erect. Leaves have a terminal broad oblong blade with toothed margins, hairy. The broad flowers pale blue to lilac in loosely coiled cymes. 1–2 ft. Open slopes on immediate coast. San Francisco to s. Ore. MAY–JULY

CALIFORNIA COAST PHACELIA *Phacelia californica*
Note the *crinkled silvery gray* leaves with none to 3 pairs of side leaflets. Stems stout with large coils of blue flowers. 1–3 ft. Rocky slopes. Cen. Calif. coast. APRIL–AUG.

DESERT BELLS *Phacelia campanularia*
Large and *long tubular* dark blue flowers. Leaves heart-shaped. 1–4 ft. Sandy slopes, washes. Forms great masses in a good year. Mojave, Colorado Deserts. FEB.–MAY

370

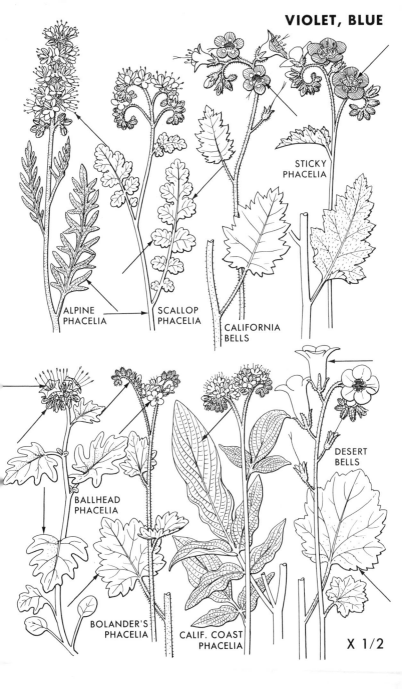

VIOLET, BLUE

ALPINE
PHACELIA

SCALLOP
PHACELIA

CALIFORNIA
BELLS

STICKY
PHACELIA

BALLHEAD
PHACELIA

BOLANDER'S
PHACELIA

CALIF. COAST
PHACELIA

DESERT
BELLS

X 1/2

4 OR 5 PETALS; 2-LIPPED TUBULAR FLOWERS

<small>SNAPDRAGON FAMILY (Scrophularaceae)</small>
See also pp. Y 112–18; R 234–44, 310; B 336–38.

GIANT BLUE-EYED MARY *Collinsia grandiflora*
The large (³/₄ in.) flowers attached at *right angles to the calyx.*
The pediceled blue-violet flowers with *white, squared* upper
petals are *in whorls.* Stems smooth. 4–16 in. Open places.
West of Cascades south to nw. Calif. APRIL–JULY

MAIDEN BLUE-EYED MARY *Collinsia parviflora*
Nearly *hidden* among long linear leaves, the tiny (¹/₄ in.) flowers
are attached to calyx at a *half right angle* (45 degrees). Corolla
tube strongly inflated at top of bend. Upper petal lobes
rounded. Stems smooth. 2–16 in. Moist shady places. Pacific
States. MARCH–JULY

SPINSTERS BLUE-EYED MARY *Collinsia sparsiflora*
The pediceled flowers purple or white (¹/₂ in.) with the corolla
tube bent in the calyx at about 45 degrees. Flowers are in
opposite pairs on long pedicels. Stems smooth. 2–12 in. Open
grassy fields. Cen. Calif. to Wash. MARCH–MAY

STICKY BLUE-EYED MARY *Collinsia rattanii*
Plant parts *sticky-haired.* The whorls of flowers are pale blue
with the upper lip white and with a yellow base, purple-dotted.
2–8 in. Common. Flats and slopes at many elevations. West of
Cascades south to Calif. MAY–AUG.

CUSICK'S SPEEDWELL *Veronica cusickii*
Single erect stems have *fleshy shiny green* oval leaves without
petioles. Terminal cluster of *large* blue-violet (¹/₂ in.) flowers.
Upper petal lobe very broad with lines of purple dots. Only 2
stamens. 2–8 in. Moist alpine meadows. Pacific States (rare in
Calif.). JULY–AUG.

ALPINE BROOKLIME *Veronica alpina*
Stems erect; leaves oval, thin, and hairy. Loose terminal
clusters of tiny (¹/₄ in.) flowers. 2 stamens. ¹/₂–3 ft. Wet places.
Pacific States. MAY–AUG.

AMERICAN BROOKLIME *Veronica americana*
The *large* leaves lancelike. Flowers in *long sprays.* ¹/₂–2 ft.
Marshy places. Common. Pacific States. MAY–SEPT.

SNOW QUEEN *Synthyris reniformis*
The pale blue flowers are short *flattened funnels* in terminal
clusters. The round to heart-shaped leaves have toothed
margins. 2–8 in. Moist shady woods. West of Cascades and
south to San Francisco area. FEB.–MAY

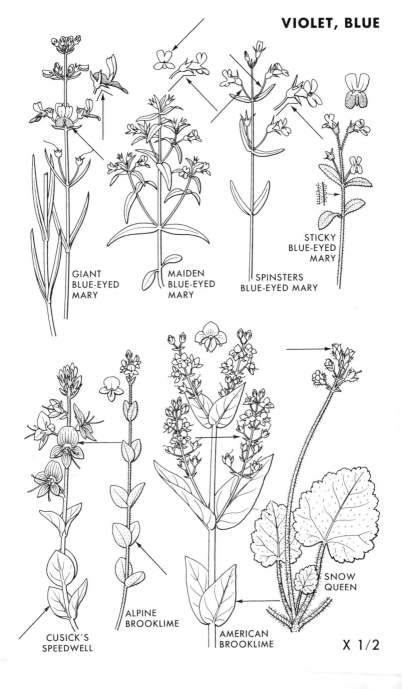

VIOLET, BLUE

GIANT
BLUE-EYED
MARY

MAIDEN
BLUE-EYED
MARY

SPINSTERS
BLUE-EYED MARY

STICKY
BLUE-EYED
MARY

CUSICK'S
SPEEDWELL

ALPINE
BROOKLIME

AMERICAN
BROOKLIME

SNOW
QUEEN

X 1/2

5-PETALED, 2-LIPPED TUBULAR FLOWERS
SQUARE STEM AND 4 NUTLIKE SEEDS

WESTERN VERBENA Alien   *Verbena lasiostachys*
VERVAIN FAMILY   (Verbenaceae)
Note the many *long slender spikes* of blue, pink, or white flowers on tall stems with *narrowly trilobed* leaves. 1–4 ft. Disturbed places. Pacific States.   JUNE–SEPT.

MINT FAMILY (Labiatae)
See also pp. W 82; R 312–14.

SELF-HEAL   *Prunella vulgaris*
Note the *thick oblong spike* of purple-brown bracts with blue flowers. Leaves oval. Calyx of 2 long and 3 shorter spur-tipped lobes. 4–20 in. Semishaded places. Pacific States.
     MAY–SEPT.

THISTLE SAGE   *Salvia carduacea*
Note the *dense woolly-haired* whorls of lavender 2-lipped flowers with 2 stamens. Bracts and leaves *spiny, thistle-like*. Strong sage odor. 4–20 in. Calif. South Coast Ranges through S. Calif. Mts. to Baja; s. Sierra Nevada.   MARCH–JUNE

CHIA   *Salvia columbariae*
Note the *headlike* clusters of *tiny* 2-lipped purple flowers. 2 stamens. Bracts spine-tipped. The dark green leaves semi-pinnate-lobed. 4–20 in. Common. Most of Calif.; Great Basin.
     MARCH–JUNE

CREEPING SAGE   *Salvia sonomensis*
The *basal clusters* of light gray *lancelike* leaves forming mats. Flowers blue-violet, the upper lip nearly absent. 2 stamens. 4–16 in. Common under shrubs. Foothills of Sierra Nevada and Calif. Coast Ranges to s. Calif.   MAY–JUNE

DANNY'S SKULLCAP   *Scutellaria tuberosa*
Leaves *broadly oval,* coarsely toothed margins. The blue corolla tube bent above the hairy calyx. Lower petal lip has a small *central* notch. 2–8 in. Cen. Calif. to sw. Ore.   MARCH–JULY

NARROWLEAF SKULLCAP   *Scutellaria angustifolia*
The *long tubular* purple corolla is *bent* above the calyx, which has a hornlike crest on the top side. Gray leaves *long linear,* 4–12 in. Lower elevations. Pacific States.   APRIL–JUNE

VINEGAR WEED   *Trichostema lanceolatum*
The *curved* tubular corolla tube is *twisted* so that the long curving stamens point toward the stem. 4–24 in. Strong sage odor. Very common. Ore. to Baja.   JUNE–OCT.

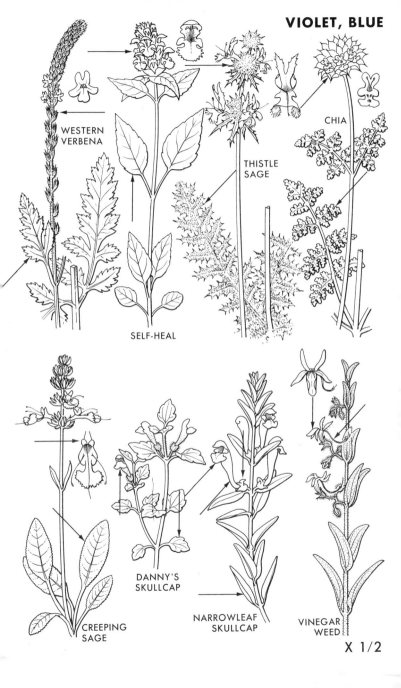

VIOLET, BLUE

WESTERN VERBENA

CHIA

THISTLE SAGE

SELF-HEAL

CREEPING SAGE

DANNY'S SKULLCAP

NARROWLEAF SKULLCAP

VINEGAR WEED

X 1/2

PEA FLOWERS; PALMATE LEAVES; LUPINES
FLOWERS IN DISTINCT WHORLS

PEA FAMILY (Leguminosae)
See also pp. W 94–96; Y 178–82; O 224;
R 318–26; B 378–80.

ELEGANT LUPINE   *Lupinus lepidus*
Flowers a *deep rich blue,* banner petal has a large *square* white
spot. Leaflets 5–9, lancelike, densely hairy on both sides.
Racemes densely flowered. 2–18 in. Alpine flats. Pacific
States. Also lowlands west of Cascades.   JUNE–SEPT.

VALLEY LUPINE   *Lupinus subvexus*
Leaflets *narrow,* 5–9. Flowers dark blue-violet. A vertical
white zone has black flecks and *turns rosy red* with age.
6–16 in. Valleys. Cen. Calif. to s. Ore.   APRIL–JUNE

DOUGLAS'S LUPINE   *Lupinus nanus*
Flowers (½ in.) a *rich blue.* Banner petal *low rounded,* with a
white spot (base yellow) and a few dark flecks. Pedicels *as long
as or longer* than the flower. Leaflets linear, both sides long-
haired. Grows with *L. bicolor.* 4–20 in. Calif. Coast Ranges,
Sierra Nevada foothills.   APRIL–MAY

MINIATURE LUPINE   *Lupinus bicolor*
Tiny (¼ in.) *deep blue* flowers. Banner petal *oblong with a
squared top* and a white spot with dark dots. Pedicel *shorter
than* the flower. 1–3 flower whorls. Linear leaflets hairy above.
6–16 in. Pacific States.   MARCH–JUNE

ARROYO LUPINE   *Lupinus succulentus*
Leaflets *broad, dark green* and hairless above, tips rounded.
The *deep purple* flowers have a *rusty red* vertical zone with a
small yellow spot below. Stems *stout, fleshy.* ½–2 ft. Grassy
slopes below 2000 ft. Cen. and s. Calif.   FEB.–MAY

BROADLEAF LUPINE   *Lupinus latifolius*
Leaflets 7–9, *broad* rounded tips. Flowers blue with a white
center, aging *brown.* Upper leaf surface *bright green* 1–4 ft.
Moist mt. woods. Pacific States.   APRIL–AUG.

SIERRA LUPINE   *Lupinus grayi*
Leaves *semisilvery to gray* haired. Banner petal has a *bright
yellow* spot, the sides *slightly* curved backward. ½–2 ft. Dry
woods. Western slope of Sierra Nevada.   MAY–JULY

GUARD LUPINE   *Lupinus excubitus*
Similar to preceding. Note the *silvery white* leaves and stems.
Banner petal has the sides *strongly* folded backward. 1–5 ft.
Rocky slopes. S. Calif. Mts., desert mts.   APRIL–JULY

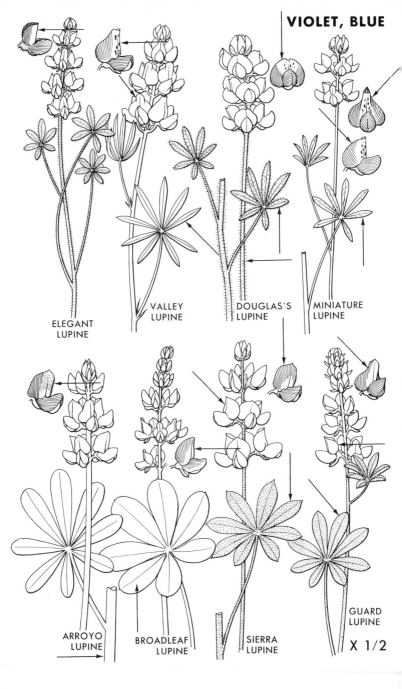

VIOLET, BLUE

ELEGANT
LUPINE

VALLEY
LUPINE

DOUGLAS'S
LUPINE

MINIATURE
LUPINE

ARROYO
LUPINE

BROADLEAF
LUPINE

SIERRA
LUPINE

GUARD
LUPINE

X 1/2

PEA FLOWERS; PALMATE LEAVES; LUPINES
LEAF TOPS HAIRY; FLOWERS NOT WHORLED

PEA FAMILY (Leguminosae)
See also pp. W 94–96; Y 178–82; O 224;
R 318–26; B 376–80.

STINGING LUPINE *Lupinus hirsutissimus*
Long *stiff yellow stinging* hairs on all plant parts. DO NOT TOUCH THIS PLANT — VERY PAINFUL! Red-violet to magenta flowers; banner petal often has a yellow blotch. ½–3 ft. Woods, thickets. Calif. South Coast Ranges to Baja.
MARCH–MAY

COULTER'S LUPINE *Lupinus sparsiflorus*
Tall plants. Leaflets *linear,* 5–9. Flowers light blue to lilac, banner petal has a *yellow spot.* In loosely arranged raceme. Keel petals short and broad, curved upward, hairy fringe on lower margins near base and often above as well. ½–16 in. Open slopes. S. Calif.
MARCH–MAY

BREWER'S LUPINE *Lupinus breweri*
Flowers *royal blue.* Banner petal has a bright *white* central zone. Flower cluster short, somewhat *pyramidlike to headlike.* Stems and leaves *shaggy-haired,* silvery to brown-yellow. Low prostrate to short erect stem. 2–12 in. Higher mt. forest to alpine flats. Calif. to Ore.
JUNE–AUG.

SPURRED LUPINE *Lupinus caudatus*
Leaflets *somewhat silvery-*haired. Flowers in *dense broad cylinders* of numerous flowers. Flowers deep blue with a white central area which may have pale yellow at the bottom. 1–2 ft. Open places. Great Basin.
MAY–SEPT.

KELLOGG'S LUPINE *Lupinus confertus*
Note the *long narrow spike* of tightly packed flowers. Flowers pale blue-pink with pale yellow spots. Upper portion of banner petal a flat semicircle as flower opens, reflexing backward with age and turning a *brown-red.* 1–2 ft. Meadows, woods. Eastern slope Sierra Nevada, S. Calif. Mts.
JUNE–AUG.

TAHOE LUPINE *Lupinus meionanthus*
Leaflets narrowly lancelike, short cottony-haired. Dense flower raceme. Flower *dull blue,* banner petal like a *nurse cap* resting on a boat (wing and keel petals). ½–3 ft. Eastern slope Sierra Nevada to ne. Calif.
JULY–AUG.

BAJADA LUPINE *Lupinus concinnus*
Low *prostrate* stems. Short flower clusters *nearly hidden* among the leaves. Plants densely haired. Petals lilac, *edged with red-purple.* Banner petal has a yellow center. 2–8 in. Dry desertlike places. Cen. and s. Calif.
MARCH–MAY

378

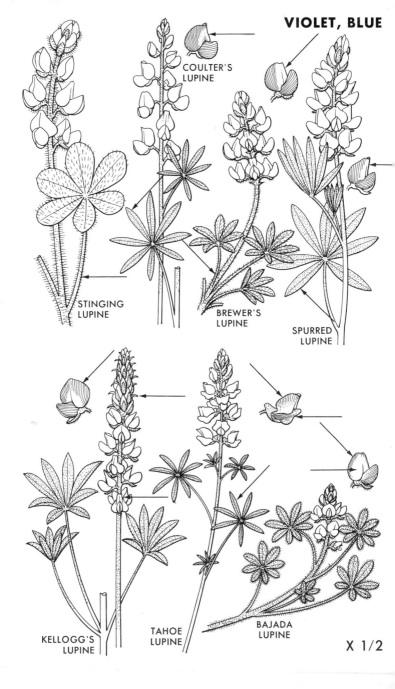

VIOLET, BLUE

STINGING LUPINE

COULTER'S LUPINE

BREWER'S LUPINE

SPURRED LUPINE

KELLOGG'S LUPINE

TAHOE LUPINE

BAJADA LUPINE

X 1/2

PEA FLOWERS; PALMATE LEAVES; LUPINES LEAF TOP HAIRLESS; FLOWERS NOT WHORLED

PEA FAMILY (Leguminosae)
See also pp. W 94–96; Y 178–82; O 224; R 318–26; B 376–80.

ALFALFA Alien   *Medicago sativa*
Leaves *trifoliate.* Small ($\frac{1}{4}$ in.) violet to purple flowers in a *dense raceme.* Stipules lancelike. Seedpod curled 2–3 times. 1–3 ft. Common. Pacific States.   ALL YEAR

BENTHAM'S LUPINE   *Lupinus benthamii*
The tall *spirelike stems have wheel-like* leaves of *extremely narrow linear* spiderlike leaflets (undersurface hairy). Stems and sepals have *conspicuous long hairs scattered* about. Flowers light to deep blue with a yellow center, drying red-violet. 1–4 ft. Grasslands, woodlands. Both sides of Central Valley of Calif. and south to Los Angeles area.
         MARCH–JUNE

SILVERY LUPINE   *Lupinus argenteus*
Stems *silver-haired.* Leaflets somewhat narrow, *troughlike,* hairless, but sometimes with scattered hairs. The flowers blue or lilac, *back* of banner petal hairy. Lower leaves drying up before flowering time. 1–2 ft. Dry slopes. Great Basin.
         MAY–OCT.

BLUE-POD LUPINE   *Lupinus polyphyllus*
The many (9–17) *very large and broad* leaflets have pointed tips. Flowers blue, purple, or red tinted. Banner petal broadly curved, back side hairless. Keel petals *strongly curved* with a narrow tip, margins completely hairless. 2–5 ft. Moist woods, meadows. Pacific States.   MAY–AUG.

COLLAR LUPINE   *Lupinus truncatus*
The nearly *square-tipped* leaflets are wedge-shaped. Leaf and branch bases have enlarged *collars.* Small flowers pale violet with a white center. 1–2$\frac{1}{2}$ ft. Open grassy places. Calif. South Coast Ranges to Baja.   MARCH–MAY

SWEET LUPINE   *Lupinus odoratus*
Note the strong pleasant *violet-like odor* of the rounded *royal blue* flowers with a large white center. $\frac{1}{2}$–1 ft. Common here and there on flats. Mojave Desert.   APRIL–MAY

ARIZONA LUPINE   *Lupinus arizonicus*
Note the fleshy stem and leaves. The leaflets *broad* and *bright green,* long hairs beneath. Flowers purple-pink with a yellow center. To avoid confusion, compare with *L. sparsiflorus,* p. 378, which also occurs with this species. 1–2 ft. Very common. Mojave, Colorado Deserts to Baja.   DEC.–MAY

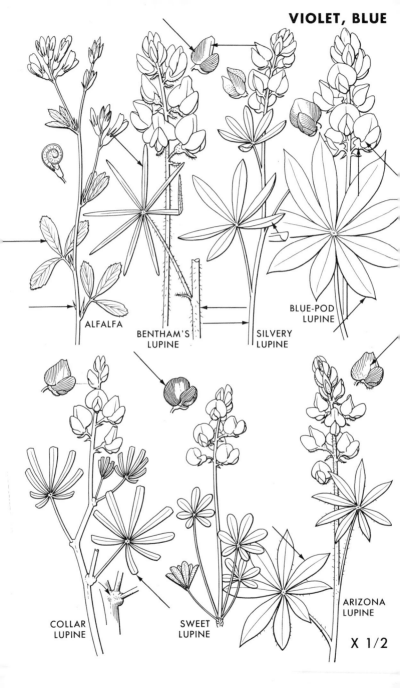

VIOLET, BLUE

ALFALFA

BENTHAM'S
LUPINE

SILVERY
LUPINE

BLUE-POD
LUPINE

COLLAR
LUPINE

SWEET
LUPINE

ARIZONA
LUPINE

X 1/2

5 OR 6 PETALS; MISCELLANEOUS BLUE FLOWERS

 BLUE ANEMONE *Anemone oregana*
BUTTERCUP FAMILY (Ranunculaceae)
See also pp. W 40–42; Y 154–58; O 226; R 280–82; B 354–56.
A *single* large blue flower above the *3 leaves* which each have
3–5 leaflets. 4–12 in. Wash. and Ore. mts. MARCH–JUNE

 WESTERN BLUE FLAX *Linum perenne*
FLAX FAMILY See also p. W 52. (Linaceae)
Large blue-petaled flowers on a tall slender stem. *Short linear*
leaves. ½–2 ft. Pacific States. MAY–SEPT.

 PERIWINKLE Alien *Vinca major*
DOGBANE FAMILY See also p. R 298. (Apocynaceae)
Note the dark blue *pinwheel-like* flowers on semi-vinelike stems
with short, oval, dark green leaves. Grows in masses. Milky
sap. 1–2 ft. West of Cascades–Sierra Nevada. ALL YEAR

 SHORT-LEAVED AMSONIA *Amsonia brevifolia*
DOGBANE FAMILY See also p. R 298. (Apocynaceae)
Note the *pale lead-blue* pinwheel-like flowers in terminal
clusters on long stems with *green* lancelike leaves. Milky sap.
1–2 ft. Mojave, Colorado Deserts. MARCH–MAY

 FELTLEAF AMSONIA (not shown) *Amsonia tomentosa*
DOGBANE FAMILY See also p. R 298. (Apocynaceae)
Similar to preceding. Leaves *felt gray.* Same area.
MARCH–MAY

 PURPLE NIGHTSHADE *Solanum xanthi*
NIGHTSHADE FAMILY See also pp. W 80; Y 172. (Solanaceae)
Note the flat, deep violet to lavender, *starlike* flowers on the
somewhat bushy stems. Leaves oval. Greenish berry. 1–3 ft.
Dry slopes. Cen. and s. Calif. FEB.–JULY

 LENNOA FAMILY (Lennoaceae)

DESERT CHRISTMAS TREE *Pholisma arenarium*
Note the dense *christmas tree* cluster of tubular purple flowers
with white borders. 4–8 in. Sandy places. Mojave, Colorado
Deserts. APRIL–JULY

SAND FOOD *Ammobroma sonorae*
A tan *half tennis ball–like* cluster of hairs and purple flowers.
1–2 in. Sand dunes. Colorado Desert. APRIL–MAY

 PICKEREL WEED FAMILY (Pontederiaceae)

WATER HYACINTH Alien *Eichhornia crassipes*
Note the *globelike petiole base* which acts as a buoy for this
floating plant. The large flowers pale purple, the uppermost
petal has a *large yellow spot* (6 petals total). 1–2 ft. Floating in
masses on waterways. Lower Central Valley and Santa Ana
River systems in Calif. JUNE–OCT.

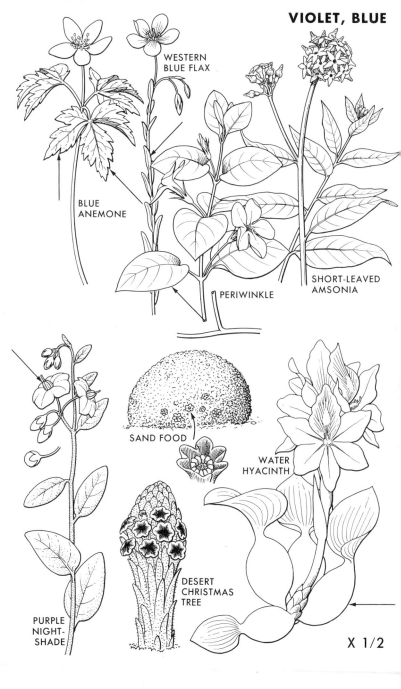

VIOLET, BLUE

WESTERN BLUE FLAX

BLUE ANEMONE

PERIWINKLE

SHORT-LEAVED AMSONIA

SAND FOOD

WATER HYACINTH

DESERT CHRISTMAS TREE

PURPLE NIGHT-SHADE

X 1/2

ASTERS & OTHER SUNFLOWERS

SUNFLOWER FAMILY (Compositae)
See also pp. W 102–8; Y 184–220; O 226;
R 328–32; G 404.

Aster Tribe: Astereae

SEASIDE DAISY   *Erigeron glaucus*
The *broad* violet to pale lavender flower heads have about 100
ray flowers. Spatula-shaped leaves have the blade extending
along the petioles. Flower head bracts *sticky-haired*. 4–16 in.
Coastal bluffs. Calif. and Ore. coasts.   APRIL–AUG.

DWARF ALPINE DAISY   *Erigeron pygmaeus*
Low, dwarf cushions of gray-haired lancelike leaves. Very large,
single, purple or lavender, daisylike flower heads. 1–3 in.
Alpine slopes. Sierra Nevada, White Mts.   JULY–AUG.

CASCADE ASTER   *Aster ledophyllus*
Stems have numerous broad sessile lancelike leaves on the
upper stems. But *nearly leafless* near stem base. Pale blue to
pink flower heads have 6–15 ray flowers. 1–2 ft. Semiopen
woods. Mts. of nw. Calif.; Cascades.   JULY–SEPT.

GIANT MOUNTAIN ASTER   *Aster modestus*
Each flower head has *numerous, narrow filament-like* purple
ray flowers and a large center of yellow disk flowers. Flower
head bracts also very narrow. Flower heads on leafless stems.
1½–3 ft. Mt. meadows. B.C. to Ore.   JULY–AUG.

LEAFY-HEADED ASTER   *Aster foliaceus*
Note the *many leafy bracts* immediately around the flower
head. Broad arrowheadlike leaves have clasping bases. Flower
heads blue, rose-purple, or violet with 15–50 ray flowers.
½–3 ft. Woods. Cen. Calif. to B.C.   JULY–SEPT.

Chicory Tribe: Cichorieae

BLUE SAILORS Alien   *Cichorium intybus*
Note the large, flat, *pale blue, windmill-like* flower heads on
well-branched *leafless* stems. Basal leaves dandelionlike.
1–4 ft. Pacific States.   JUNE–OCT.

SALSIFY Alien   *Tragopogon porrifolius*
Flower head has *only* purple ray flower. Milky sap. Waxy blue
linear leaves and stem. Flower heads becoming round brown
balls of parachuted seeds. Pacific States.   APRIL–AUG.

Thistle Tribe: Cynareae

BACHELORS BUTTON Alien   *Centaurea cyanus*
The erect stems slender with fluffy heads of blue, purple, pink,
or white disk flowers only. Leaves linear and light gray-haired.
1–3 ft. Occasional. Pacific States.   MAY–OCT.

384

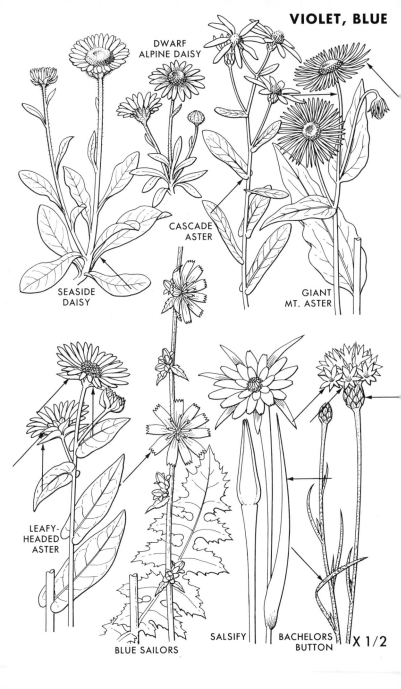

VIOLET, BLUE

DWARF
ALPINE DAISY

SEASIDE
DAISY

CASCADE
ASTER

GIANT
MT. ASTER

LEAFY-
HEADED
ASTER

BLUE SAILORS

SALSIFY

BACHELORS
BUTTON

X 1/2

Brown and Green Flowers

Brown, red-brown, and green flowers are included in this section. Some are 2-colored flowers; if in doubt also check the other color. When possible, the group characteristics given in the text page titles are repeated in each color section, and in the same order. Where the flowers on a page look nearly the same but your sample does not fit, you can also use the cross references given for other colors.

3 OR 6 PETALS; LILYLIKE FLOWERS

Lily Family (Liliaceae)
See also pp. W 4–16; Y 122–24; O 228–30;
R 252–56; B 352; G 390.

STINK BELLS   *Fritillaria agrestis*
The *5–12 linear* leaves are crowded on the *lower half* of the
waxy blue stem. The nodding 1–5 bell-like flowers are greenish-white outside and purple-brown inside. Strong bad odor.
1–2 ft. Grasslands. Central Valley of Calif.; Calif. Coast
Ranges.   March–April

SPOTTED MOUNTAIN BELLS *Fritillaria atropurpurea*
The 7–14 broadly linear leaves are in whorls or alternate on the
upper stem, lower stem *naked.* The 1–4 nodding bell-like
flowers are brown-purple with *thin windowlike spots* of white
and yellow. Petal tips tapered only at tip. 5–24 in. Mid-mts.
Sierra Nevada to s. Ore.; Great Basin.   April–July

BROWN BELLS   *Fritillaria micrantha*
The *light green* linear leaves are in whorls of 4–6 and are only
on the *upper half* of the stem. The small brown bell-like flowers
are *usually not mottled.* A narrow gland is present on the lower
petal. ½–3 ft. Forests below 6000 ft. Western slope of Sierra
Nevada.   April–June

CHOCOLATE LILY   *Fritillaria biflora*
The 3–7 linear leaves are crowded on the *lower stem in a rosette*
just above the ground. The 1–7 bell-like flowers are dark
brown. ½–1½ ft. Grassy slopes below 3000 ft. Calif. Coast
Ranges and south to San Diego area.   Feb.–June

KAMCHATKA FRITILLARY *Fritillaria camschatcensis*
The linear leaves are in *1–3 whorls of 5–9 each.* The 2–7 flowers
are *large* dark brown bells. Insides of petals have tiny raised
parallel ridges. Islands of Wash. and coast of B.C.
                                             May–July

MISSION BELLS   *Fritillaria lanceolata*
The nodding *bowl-shaped flowers* are brown-purple and *mottled* with greenish-yellow and purple spots. Petals tapered from
the middle. The narrow linear leaves are in several whorls of
3–5 on the upper stem, lower stem naked. 1–3 ft. Woods, grassy
places below 5000 ft. Very common. Calif. Coast Ranges north
to B.C.   Feb.–June

FETID ADDERS-TONGUE   *Scoliopus bigelovii*
The broadly oblong leaves are purple-mottled. The green
flowers with red veins are on long sprawling pedicels. Bad
smelling. 3–6 in. Moist coastal redwood forests. Monterey,
Calif., north to sw. Ore.   Jan.–March

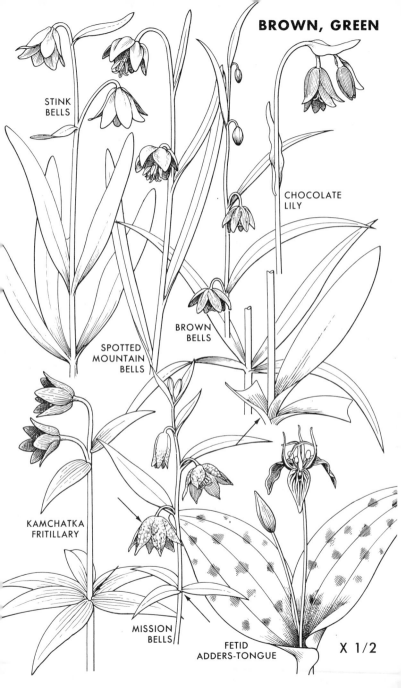

BROWN, GREEN

STINK
BELLS

CHOCOLATE
LILY

SPOTTED
MOUNTAIN
BELLS

BROWN
BELLS

KAMCHATKA
FRITILLARY

MISSION
BELLS

FETID
ADDERS-TONGUE

X 1/2

3 OR 6 PETALS; SPIKE STEMS
ARROWGRASS, LILIES, ORCHIDS

 SALTMARSH ARROWGRASS   *Triglochin maritimum*
ARROW GRASS FAMILY   (Juncaginaceae)
The tall *arrowlike stem* has numerous tiny flowers above the tuft of fleshy grasslike leaves. Poisonous to cattle. 1–2 ft. Salt and alkaline marshes. Pacific States.   APRIL–AUG.

LILY FAMILY (Liliaceae)
See also pp. W 4–16; Y 122–24; O 228–30;
R 252–56; B 352; G 388.

GREEN CORN LILY   *Veratrum viride*
The dull green flowers are in terminal *drooping branches* above the tall *cornlike* stalks and leaves. Each of the petals has a dark green V at its base. Wet meadows. Nw. Calif. north to B.C.; Great Basin.   JUNE–SEPT.

WESTERN STENANTHIUM   *Stenanthium occidentale*
The flowers are small bells with tints of purple and hang from a leafless stem. Linear grasslike leaves. 1–2 ft. Wet places. West of Cascades south to nw. Calif.   JUNE–AUG.

ORCHID FAMILY (Orchidaceae)
See also pp. W 20; O 230; BG 392.

GREEN REIN ORCHID   *Habenaria sparsiflora*
The spur slender and *as long as or longer than* the lip petal. The spike densely flowered. 1–2 ft. Wet boggy places. Common. Mts. of sw. Ore. and all of Calif.   JUNE–AUG.

NORTHERN HABENARIA   *Habenaria hyperborea*
The upper sepal and the 2 upper petals are close together forming a distinct hood above the lip petal. The linear curving spur *shorter than* the lip petal. Leaves lancelike. ½–2 ft. Boggy places in mts. Not common in Pacific States area.
    JUNE–AUG.

MALE HABENARIA   *Habenaria saccata*
The spur petal is a *broad sac and shorter* than the lip petal. The flowers are on a spike above lancelike leaves. Boggy places. N. Calif. to B.C. and Great Basin.   JUNE–SEPT.

ALASKA HABENARIA   *Habenaria unalascensis*
The single quite slender stem has tiny green flowers scattered along the spike. Spur petal shorter than the ovary. Leaves *dried up* by flowering time. 1–3 ft. *Dry* woods. Pacific States.
    APRIL–AUG.

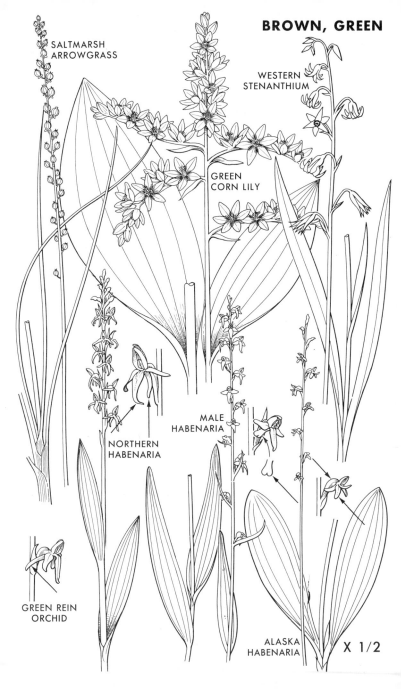

BROWN, GREEN

SALTMARSH ARROWGRASS

WESTERN STENANTHIUM

GREEN CORN LILY

NORTHERN HABENARIA

MALE HABENARIA

GREEN REIN ORCHID

ALASKA HABENARIA

X 1/2

3 PETALS; BILATERAL SYMMETRY, ORCHIDS

Orchid Family (Orchidaceae)
See also pp. W 20; O 230; BG 390.

CALIFORNIA LADYS-SLIPPER
Cypripedium californicum
Each of the 3–15 flowers has *short* brown-yellow sepals. The slipper petal is white, pale pink, or brown spotted. Leaves oval in an alternate arrangement. 1–4 ft. Wet rocky hillsides below 5000 ft. Coast Ranges of Calif. from San Francisco north to sw. Ore. May–June

BROWNIE LADYS-SLIPPER *Cypripedium fasciculatum*
This orchid has only *2 large oppositely* paired oval leaves close to the ground. The 1–8 flowers are in a *cluster* just above the leaves. All flower parts a greenish yellow with brown veins. 2–12 in. Conifer forests, often under dogwood understory. Calif. north Coast Ranges; n. Sierra Nevada to B.C. and Great Basin. April–July

YELLOW LADYS-SLIPPER *Cypripedium calceous*
The usually single flower has a *bright yellow slipper* petal, while the other petals are green to brown. Several alternate oval leaves. 1–1½ ft. Under aspen-conifer forest. Rare in our area. Ore. to B.C. and east. May–June

MOUNTAIN LADYS-SLIPPER *Cypripedium montanum*
The 1–3 flowers are *each above a leaf.* Flower parts are a dark brown except for the white slipper petal with purple veins. The 4–7 alternately arranged oval leaves each clasp the stem. 1–2 ft. Moist woods. Mts. from Monterey and Yosemite, Calif., north to B.C. May–Aug.

HEARTLEAF TWAYBLADE *Listera cordata*
The stem has a *single opposite pair* of broad, somewhat heart-shaped leaves at the center level of the stem. Above the leaves is a long loosely flowered spike. The long lower lip petal is narrow with a *forked tip.* 4–8 in. Dense shady woods. Nw. Calif. to B.C. and Great Basin. April–Aug.

BROAD-LIPPED TWAYBLADE *Listera convallarioides*
The lower lip petal is *broadly wedge-shaped and notched.* Leaves broadly oval in one opposite pair. 4–8 in. Margins of shaded mossy springs. Mts. of Pacific States. June–Aug.

NORTHWESTERN TWAYBLADE *Listera caurina*
The lower lip petal is broadly *wedge-shaped* with the tip *rounded or slightly pointed.* Leaves broadly oval in one opposite pair. 4–12 in. Damp woods 4000 ft. and higher. Nw. Calif. to B.C. June–Aug.

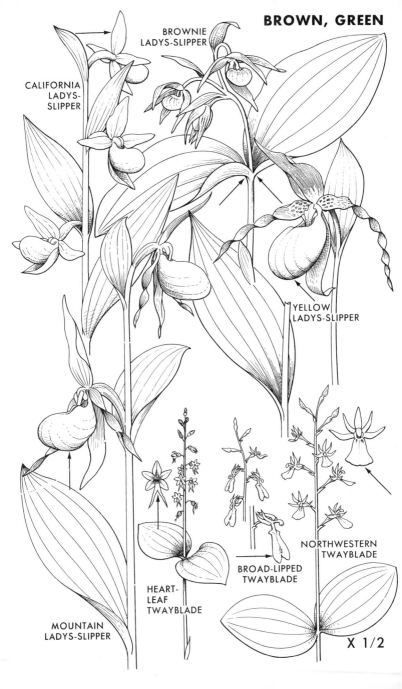

BROWN, GREEN

CALIFORNIA LADYS-SLIPPER

BROWNIE LADYS-SLIPPER

YELLOW LADYS-SLIPPER

MOUNTAIN LADYS-SLIPPER

HEART-LEAF TWAYBLADE

BROAD-LIPPED TWAYBLADE

NORTHWESTERN TWAYBLADE

X 1/2

4-PETALED, GREENISH-WHITE FLOWERS
WITH PURPLE AND BLACK DOTS

GENTIAN FAMILY (Gentianaceae)
See also pp. W 100; R 304; B 342–44.

MONUMENT PLANT   *Frasera speciosa*
Each petal has *twin* hairy gland spots. The single tall monu-
ment-like stem has linear *leaves in whorls.* Leaves not white-
margined. 3–6 ft. Open slopes in mts. Calif. North Coast
Ranges, Sierra Nevada north to B.C., and Great Basin.

JUNE–AUG.

PARRY'S FRASERA   *Frasera parryi*
The petals are black-dotted and each has a *single U-shaped*
hairy gland spot. The oppositely paired, triangular leaves are
white-margined and smooth. Single stout stem. 2–4 ft. Common. Dry places below 6000 ft. S. Calif. Mts. to Baja.

APRIL–JULY

DESERT FRASERA   *Frasera albomarginata*
Each petal has a *single oblong fringed* gland spot which is open
for ⅘ its length. The well-branched stem has white-margined
leaves in whorls of 3–4. Plant smooth. ½–2 ft. Rocky places in
Juniper forests. E. Mojave Desert Mts. and Great Basin.

MAY–JULY

INYO FRASERA   *Frasera puberulenta*
Each petal has a *single keyhole-like gland* area which is fringed
with hairs along the top portion. The oppositely paired,
white-margined leaves are covered with a frosty coating of
short hairs. Stout stems. 4–12 in. Dry slopes 8000–11,000 ft.
Eastern side of Sierra Nevada and White Mts. of Calif.

JUNE–AUG.

WHITESTEM FRASERA   *Frasera albicaulis*
Each lancelike petal has a single oblong *elongated teardrop*
gland area which is fringed around all of the margin. The
greenish-white flowers have a faint blue tint. The oppositely
paired, white-margined leaves are long, linear, and mostly near
the base of the stem. Stem and leaves thinly haired. 1–2 ft.
Open places on plains and lower mts. s. B.C. and south
throughout Great Basin. Also Calif. North Coast Ranges and
nw. Sierra Nevada foothills.   MAY–JULY

PINE FRASERA   *Frasera neglecta*
Each petal has a single *squarish gland spot* fringed only at the
top with hairs. The petals are greenish-white with *purple
veins.* Stem and leaves smooth. ½–1½ ft. Dry slopes, 4000–
8000 ft. S. Calif. Mts. and deserts.   MAY–JULY

394

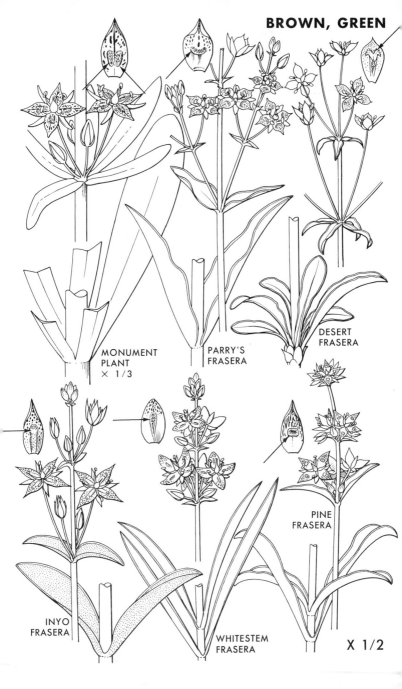

BROWN, GREEN

MONUMENT
PLANT
× 1/3

PARRY'S
FRASERA

DESERT
FRASERA

INYO
FRASERA

WHITESTEM
FRASERA

PINE
FRASERA

X 1/2

PLANTAINS; MISTLETOES; PICKLEWEEDS

Plantain Family (Plantaginaceae)

BROADLEAF PLANTAIN Alien   *Plantago major*
Note the *broadly oval leaves* in a basal cluster, smooth and somewhat fleshy. The tiny white flowers are soon replaced by the dense brown seed spikes. 2–16 in. Lawns, disturbed places. Common. Pacific States.   April–Sept.

PATAGONIA PLANTAIN Alien   *Plantago patagonica*
Note the dense *long silky hairs* on both the slender leaves and flower stem. 2–8 in. Plains. Great Basin.   May–June

ENGLISH PLANTAIN Alien   *Plantago lanceolata*
The *long lancelike* leaves are in a basal cluster below the dense brown flower spikes. ½–3 ft. A familiar plant in most home yards. Pacific States.   All Year

DWARF PLANTAIN   *Plantago erecta*
A diminutive plantain with softly haired linear leaves and a thick cylinderlike flower spike. 2–6 in. Very common in dry grassy places below 4000 ft. W. Calif. and Ore.
     March–June

DESERT PLANTAIN   *Plantago insularis*
(not shown)
Similar to preceding. Mojave, Colorado Deserts.   Jan.-May

Mistletoe Family (Loranthaceae)

GREENLEAF MISTLETOE   *Phoradendron tomentosa*
Note the thick *leathery green leaves* are in opposite pairs on woody twigs that hang from the host tree in large shrubby masses. Berries white or pink. 1–2 ft. Parasite on Oaks, Walnuts, etc. Calif. and Ore.   All Year

MESQUITE MISTLETOE   *Phoradendron californicum*
The *leafless twiggy stems* are in large clusters. Berries red. Common parasite on mesquite shrubs. 4–24 in. Mojave, Colorado Deserts and to Baja.   All Year

WESTERN DWARF MISTLETOE
     Arceuthobium campylopodum
The dwarf yellow-green stems are in small clusters. Leaves reduced to tiny bracts. The pink berries *explode* when touched and shoot the seed a considerable distance. 2–24 in. Conifer branches. Pacific States.   All Year

SLENDER PICKLEWEED   *Salicornia europaea*
Goosefoot Family See also p. BrG 398.   (Chenopodiaceae)
The succulent erect stem jointed and cylindrical. Leaves minute. Flowers minute and sunk into the joints. 1–2 ft. Alkaline and salt marshes. Pacific States.   July–Nov.

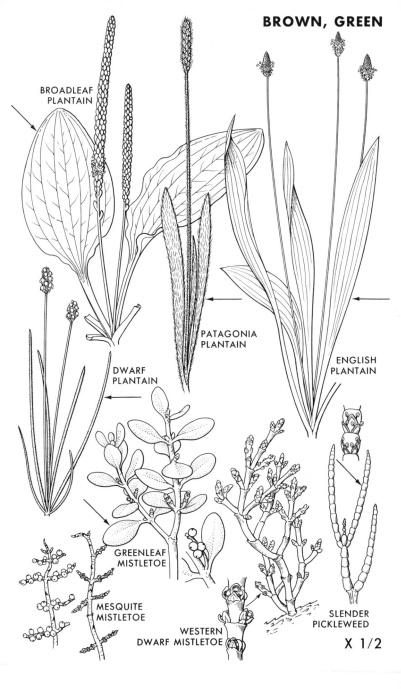

BROWN, GREEN

BROADLEAF PLANTAIN

PATAGONIA PLANTAIN

DWARF PLANTAIN

ENGLISH PLANTAIN

GREENLEAF MISTLETOE

MESQUITE MISTLETOE

WESTERN DWARF MISTLETOE

SLENDER PICKLEWEED

X 1/2

TINY INDISTINGUISHABLE GREEN FLOWERS

GOOSEFOOT FAMILY (Chenopodiaceae)
See also p. BG 396.

LAMBS QUARTER Alien *Chenopodium album*
The *triangular* leaves are covered by a white granular covering. Tiny flowers in thick spikes. 1–7 ft. Common. Pacific States. JUNE–OCT.

NETTLE FAMILY (Urticaceae)

STINGING NETTLE Alien *Urtica dioica*
Flowers are in *loose stringy* clusters above each pair of velvety leaves. Armed with painful stinging hairs. 3–7 ft. Moist thickets. Pacific States. JAN.–OCT.

RUSSIAN TUMBLEWEED Alien *Salsola kali*
Note the short bractlike leaves have spiny tips and the seed capsules appearing as if pink to orange flowers. The multiple branching stems forming a very large bushy ball, which when blown about is the familar tumbleweed. 1–4 ft. Pacific States. ALL YEAR

AMARANTH FAMILY (Amaranthaceae)

PROSTRATE AMARANTH *Amaranthus blitoides*
The nearly *prostrate* stem has *intermittent clusters* of small green flowers mixed with long bristles. Leaves pale green, oval. May become a tumbleweed. 1–5 ft. Disturbed places. Pacific States. JUNE–OCT.

GREEN AMARANTH Alien *Amaranthus retroflexus*
An *erect* plant with dense *terminal spikes* of chaffy green flowers mixed with long bristlelike bracts. The oval leaves gray-green. 1–5 ft. Common. Pacific States. JUNE–OCT.

SPURGE FAMILY (Euphorbiaceae)
See also p. W 100.

PETTY SPURGE Alien? *Euphorbia peplus*
The paired oval stem leaves are *short-petioled*. Flower gland has *2 slender horns*. Plants yellow-green throughout. Milky sap. 4–12 in. Common in yards. Pacific States. ALL YEAR

CHINESE CAPS *Euphorbia crenulata*
The smooth, paired stem leaves are spatula-shaped and *without petioles*. Flower glands *thickly horned* and look like an ancient chinese hat or a devil's head. Milky sap. 1–3 ft. Dry places. Calif. MARCH–AUG.

TURKEY MULLEIN *Eremocarpus setigerus*
Note the rosette of *gray-green oval* leaves with long petioles. Tiny flowers. 1–8 in. Very common. Dry open places. Calif. and Ore. MAY–OCT.

398

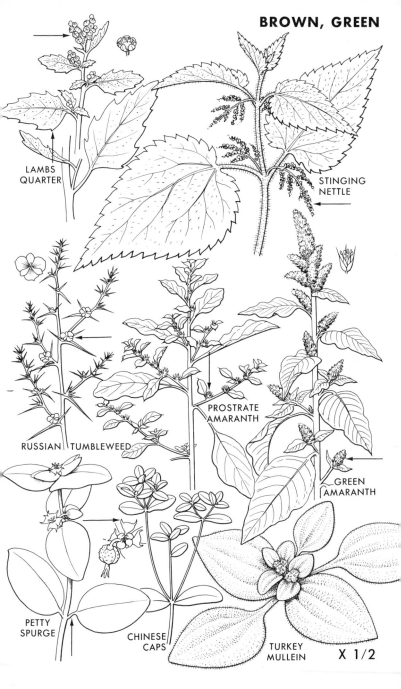

BROWN, GREEN

LAMBS QUARTER

STINGING NETTLE

RUSSIAN TUMBLEWEED

PROSTRATE AMARANTH

GREEN AMARANTH

PETTY SPURGE

CHINESE CAPS

TURKEY MULLEIN

X 1/2

WILD GINGERS; CATTAILS

Birthwort Family (Aristolochiaceae)
All of the *Asarums* have a strong ginger odor when handled.

LEMMON'S WILD GINGER *Asarum lemmoni*

Note the *short and reflexed* triangular-tipped petals (really
sepals) hugging the floral cup. Flowers a dark brown-red and
usually hidden below the large rounded heart- to kidney-
shaped leaves. 2–6 in. Wet shady woods at mid-elevations.
Sierra Nevada. May–June

HARTWEG'S WILD GINGER *Asarum hartwegii*

Note the short to *medium length triangular* petals (really
sepals) spreading at right angles to the floral cup. Flower a
dark brown-red and usually hidden below the large, dark green,
heart-shaped leaves. The toothlike appendage above each
anther is longer than the entire stamen. 2–6 in. Shady woods.
Sierra Nevada to sw. Ore. May–June

LONG-TAILED GINGER *Asarum caudatum*

Note the *long, slender-tailed* petals (really sepals). Leaves
heart-shaped. The toothlike appendage above the anther is
shorter than the entire stamen. 1–6 in. Shady woods. West of
Cascades and south in Coast Ranges to Monterey.
April–July

Cattail Family (Typhaceae)

BROADLEAF CATTAIL *Typha latifolia*

Above the thick sausagelike female flowers is a slender tail of
male flowers which *touch* (no space between) the female area.
Leaves broad (1–1½ in. wide). 3–8 ft. Freshwater marshes.
Pacific States. June–July

NARROWLEAF CATTAIL *Typha angustifolia*

Flower stems stiff with a thick brown *sausagelike cat* of
numerous female flowers and a *slender tail* of male flowers
above. Note the *bare interval* between the 2 flower areas.
Narrow (¼–½ in.) erect straplike leaves deep green and overtopping the flower spikes. Tall marsh plants growing in dense
clumps. Freshwater marshes at low elevations. Cen. Calif.
May–June

TULE CATTAIL *Typha domingensis*
(not shown)

Similar to preceding. Pale green leaves *broad* (½–1 in.) with
the tops equal only to top of female flowers (fat sausage
portion), rarely overtopping the entire flower spike. 6–9 ft.
Common. Freshwater and slightly subsaline (tidal) water.
Calif. and Ore. June–July

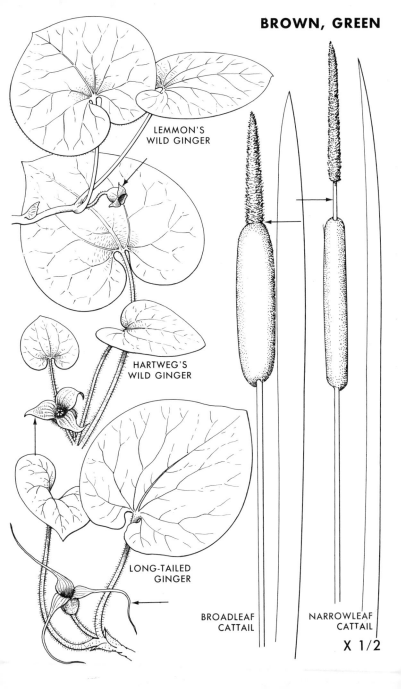

LEMMON'S
WILD GINGER

HARTWEG'S
WILD GINGER

LONG-TAILED
GINGER

BROADLEAF
CATTAIL

NARROWLEAF
CATTAIL

X 1/2

4–5 DAINTY PETALS; 2 HORNLIKE STYLES ROUNDED TO MAPLELIKE LEAVES

SAXIFRAGE FAMILY (Saxifragaceae)
See also pp. W 84–90, 100.

SIERRA BOLANDRA *Bolandra californica*
The *slender twisted petals* are green with purple tips. The flowers are in a loose panicle above the round to heart-shaped leaves which are palmately veined. 4–10 in. Wet rocks near waterfalls. Sierra Nevada. JUNE–JULY

BRISTLE FLOWER *Tolmiea menziesii*
The cylindrical flower tube is tipped by 4 petals and is surrounded by a calyx with 3 equal teeth and 2 short lateral ones. Greenish with some purple. Leaves maplelike. 2–8 in. Moist woods. Calif. North Coast Ranges to Cascades. MAY–AUG.

FRINGE CUPS *Tellima grandiflora*
The *cuplike* flowers have straplike petals whose *tips are fringed.* The petals white, but aging soon to a brown-red. The flowers are scattered along a spike above the maplelike leaves. Stems hairy. 1–3 ft. Common in moist woods, streambanks. Calif. Coast Ranges and n. Sierra Nevada north to B.C.
APRIL–JULY

BREWER'S BISHOPS CAP *Mitella breweri*
Each threadlike petal consisting of a central shaft and 6–10 side branches. Each petal *alternate* to stamens. Leaves rounded, *always shorter* than wide. ½–2 ft. Moist mt. banks. Sierra Nevada north to B.C. APRIL–AUG.

FIVE-POINT BISHOPS CAP *Mitella pentandra*
Similar to Brewer's Bishops Cap. Each petal *opposite* a stamen. Elongate maplelike leaves. ½–2 ft. Wet streambanks and shady woods. Sierra Nevada and ne. Calif. and north and east in mts. MAY–AUG.

SAUCER MITERWORT *Mitella ovalis*
The greenish-yellow flowers have petals consisting of a slender central shaft and 1 pair (or sometimes 2) of threadlike lateral lobes. Petals *alternate* to stamens. Flowers scattered on a spike above the elongated maplelike leaves. 4–12 in. Damp places. Shady forests along coast from San Francisco to B.C. and most of Cascades. APRIL–MAY

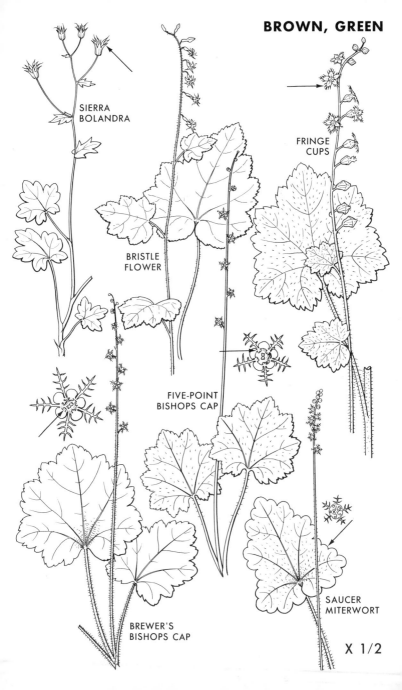

BROWN, GREEN

SIERRA BOLANDRA

BRISTLE FLOWER

FRINGE CUPS

FIVE-POINT BISHOPS CAP

BREWER'S BISHOPS CAP

SAUCER MITERWORT

X 1/2

MISCELLANEOUS GREEN AND BROWN FLOWERS

BUTTERCUP FAMILY (Ranunculaceae)
See also pp. W 40–42; Y 154–58; O 226;
R 280–82; B 354–56, 382.

FALSE BUGBANE *Trautvetteria caroliniensis*
Large palmately lobed leaves (4–8 in. wide) are below the green petalless flowers on a tall stem. 2–3 ft. Moist woods, swamps. N. Calif. to B.C; Great Basin. MAY–AUG.

ROSE FAMILY (Rosaceae)
See also pp. W 92; Y 174–76; R 310.

WESTERN GREAT BURNET *Sanguisorba annua*
The cylinderlike spike of red-brown flowers is on a long wiry stem above the *comblike* leaves. 3–18 in. Open places. Pacific States. MAY–JULY

MARSH BURNET *Sanguisorba officinalis*
Similar to Western Great Burnet. The pinnate leaflets *elliptical*. Marshes and bogs. 1–3 ft. Coastal region of B.C. south to nw. Calif. Also inland on Mt. Hood, Ore. JULY–AUG.

SUNFLOWER FAMILY (Compositae)
See also pp. W 102–8; Y 184–220; O 226;
R 328–32; B 384.

WOOLLY MARBLES *Psilocarphus brevissimus*
Note the *marble-sized white woolly balls* that are usually few to many per clump. Tiny linear leaves. Low flat clumps. 1–4 in. Extremely common on drying flats and in fields at lower elevations. Calif. and north to s. Wash. APRIL–JUNE

COCKLEBUR *Xanthium strumarium*
Note the large *oblong burs* have numerous stiff *hooked hairs*. Leaves broadly triangular. Flowers minute. Disturbed places. Pacific States. JULY–NOV.

CARROT FAMILY (Umbelliferae)
See also pp. W 64–68; Y 168–70; R 302.

MOUNTAIN SWEET CICELY *Osmorhiza chilensis*
Each branch of the few low pinnate leaves usually have 3 deeply cut leaflets. The erect leafless flower stem terminated by loose umbels of tiny flowers. These soon become sharp pointed seeds that are covered by *upward pointing barbs* and also have a *slender barbed tail*. Leaves hairy. 1–4 ft. Dry semiopen woods below 8000 ft. Mts. of Pacific States. APRIL–JULY

WESTERN SWEET CICELY *Osmorhiza occidentalis*
Similar to preceding. Pinnate leaf branches usually have 5 *sawtoothed leaflets*. Leaves hairless. The long sharp pointed seeds are *smooth*. 1–4 ft. Dry semiopen woods. Central Calif.; Great Basin north to B.C. APRIL–JULY

BROWN, GREEN

WESTERN
GREAT BURNET

MARSH
BURNET

WOOLLY
MARBLES

FALSE
BUGBANE

COCKLEBUR

MOUNTAIN
SWEET
CICELY

WESTERN
SWEET
CICELY

X 1/2

Index

An italicized number indicates that the species is not illustrated.

Smooth   Glandular   Haired   Starlike hairs   Mealy   Rasplike

SURFACE TRAITS OF STEMS, LEAVES, ETC.

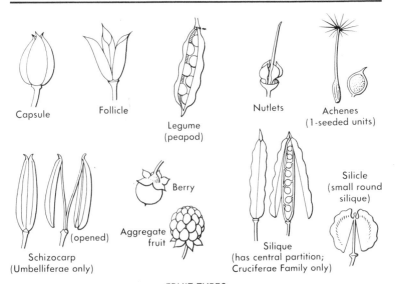

Capsule

Follicle

Legume (peapod)

Nutlets

Achenes (1-seeded units)

Schizocarp (Umbelliferae only)

Berry

Aggregate fruit

Silique (has central partition; Cruciferae Family only)

Silicle (small round silique)

FRUIT TYPES

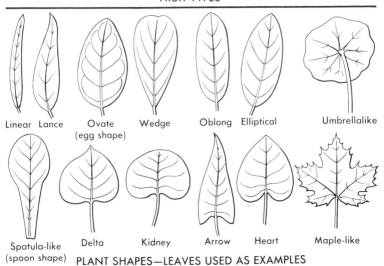

Linear   Lance   Ovate (egg shape)   Wedge   Oblong   Elliptical   Umbrellalike

Spatula-like (spoon shape)   Delta   Kidney   Arrow   Heart   Maple-like

PLANT SHAPES—LEAVES USED AS EXAMPLES

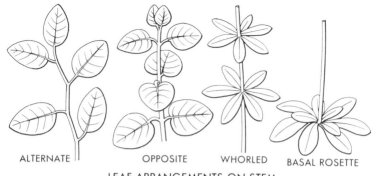

ALTERNATE   OPPOSITE   WHORLED   BASAL ROSETTE

LEAF ARRANGEMENTS ON STEM

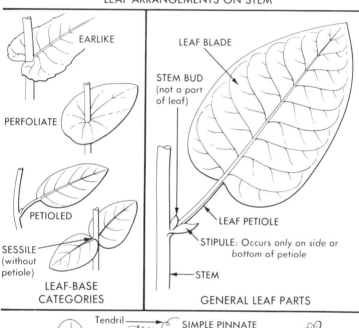

EARLIKE

PERFOLIATE

PETIOLED

SESSILE
(without
petiole)

**LEAF-BASE
CATEGORIES**

LEAF BLADE

STEM BUD
(not a part
of leaf)

LEAF PETIOLE

STIPULE: Occurs *only* on *side* or
bottom of petiole

STEM

GENERAL LEAF PARTS

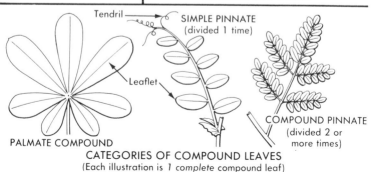

Tendril   SIMPLE PINNATE
(divided 1 time)

Leaflet

COMPOUND PINNATE
(divided 2 or
more times)

PALMATE COMPOUND

CATEGORIES OF COMPOUND LEAVES
(Each illustration is *1 complete* compound leaf)